D0409614

Against the Flow

Against the Flow
Reflections of an Individualist

Samuel Brittan

ATLANTIC BOOKS
LONDON

First published in Great Britain in 2005 by Atlantic Books, an imprint of
Grove Atlantic Ltd.

1 3 5 7 9 8 6 4 2

A CIP catalogue record for this book is available from the British Library.

1 84354 377 X

Typeset by FiSH Books, London
Printed in Great Britain by
Creative Print & Design (Wales) Ltd, Ebbw Vale

Atlantic Books
An imprint of Grove Atlantic Ltd
Ormond House
26–27 Boswell Street
London WCIN 3JZ

To Toby, Andrew, Louisa and Jaine
who have enabled me to
continue publishing in the electronic era.

But above all, individualism, if it can be purged of its defects and its abuses, is the best safeguard of personal liberty in the sense that, compared with any other system, it greatly widens the field for the exercise of personal choice. It is also the best safeguard for the variety of life, which emerges precisely from this extended field of personal choice, and the loss of which is the greatest of all the losses of the homogenous or totalitarian state. For this variety preserves the traditions which embody the most secure and successful choices of former generations; it colours the present with the diversification of its fancy; and being the handmaid of experience as well as of tradition and of fancy, it is the most powerful instrument to better the future.

J. M. Keynes, *The General Theory*

The only purpose for which power can be rightly exercised over any member of a civilized community, against his will, is to prevent harm to others. His own good, either physical or moral, is not a sufficient warrant.

John Stuart Mill, *On Liberty*

Contents

Preface

The origin of this book is my belief that some essays, lectures and short comments I have written over the last few years make more sense if read alongside each other – although not at a single sitting! In deciding which material to use and which to jettison, I have tried to keep in mind the inevitable lag between putting together a volume such as this and the time when the reader eventually sees it. For example, at the time of writing I have no idea who the President of the USA will be on publication day and am not even absolutely sure who will be the British Prime Minister.

The subtitle 'Reflections of an Individualist' may need a little explanation. I was looking for something less antiseptic than the label I had previously used to describe my outlook, namely redistributive market liberalism. This was, I discovered, invented by John Kay partly in order to dissociate himself from it. Unlike Kay, I stick to the basic idea, but I needed something with a broader and more personal flavour. The word 'individualism' was once associated with abrasive personalities proud to exhibit a craggy disregard for others. But it is beginning to lose such associations and indeed fall into disuse altogether. I therefore thought it worth rescuing and making the leitmotif of this volume. I thus had no hesitation in reprinting an essay specifically on individualism at the start of Part Six, as it provides the framework for that part and indeed the volume as a whole.

Keynes is often cited as saying 'When facts change, I change my mind.' There is no suggestion in Robert Skidelsky's authoritative three-volume biography that he ever said anything as banal as this. What he is more likely to have said is, 'When I change my mind, I say so. What do you do?'

There are two types of change of mind. One is the application of the same beliefs to a changing set of circumstances. The other is changes in the beliefs themselves. I do not have many fundamental changes of this second kind to report, but quite a few of the first.

Probably the biggest one is the forcible realization of something that most people have always known but kept too long at the very back of their minds. This is that the first duty of government is to look after the security of its citizens. That duty must come before everything else, including the provision of the public services on which today's political debate so obsessively focuses.

There is always a balance to be struck between protecting citizens from violence and their property from destruction, and the preservation of civil liberties. We have to be on our guard against those who have never put a high value on the latter and who have simply used terrorism as an excuse to promote clampdowns in which they have always believed. We must equally guard against those who use a professed concern for civil liberties as a shield for their own lack of commitment to the struggle against terrorism

External security is a more contestable notion. There is clearly a difference between the threat to individual citizens which might have resulted from the Kaiser triumphing over Lloyd George in the First World War and the genocidal results if Hitler had won the Second, or the threat to the whole western way of life from violent fundamentalists today.

The first international part of this book begins with my early reactions to the destruction of the Twin Towers in New York on September 11, 2001. This essay led to sharper critical comment than anything else I have written before or since. But I do not retract anything and do not believe that the invasion and mishandling of Iraq have invalidated it. Near the end of that same part I have tried my hand at a more theoretical essay on ethics and foreign policy. Some people may be dissatisfied that I have emerged only with maxims and presumptions rather than firm rules of conduct. The outcome doubtless reflects the deficiencies of the author, but also, I am afraid, the inherent difficulty of the subject matter. As will be all too obvious, I claim no special expertise on the details of foreign policy, but I have been reflecting on its logic since I was in short trousers and my interest in it dates back at least as far as my interest in economic policy, for which I am more widely known.

A word on the essay on arms exports which opens Part Two on political economy. It follows on naturally from the international chapters. But in order to make my case I have had to discuss issues such as the balance of payments, employment and related matters which are called in aid by the arms lobby. Indeed the first part of that essay can be regarded as my attempt to state some of the principles of macroeconomics, not quite on the back of a postcard, but at least in a very few pages. It may therefore be of interest even to those who do not want to get involved in the arms controversy.

Part Three starts with an impressionistic, and some might say arrogant, sketch of British government economic policy over half a century. This whole part is highly selective. The essays in it concentrate on topics where I have had something to say and therefore do not cover anything like the full range of topics discussed in the British public debate.

Part Four discusses some of the principles of what, for want of a better term, I have called economic management. I have deliberately minimized the amount of material on the economic conjuncture, whether British or international, as this is liable to date extremely quickly. This part, and some of the chapters in the following Part Five dealing with European Union issues may be more difficult to approach for readers who have not been immersed in these matters than the rest of the book.

By family origin and personal leaning I have always been a European and could never be anything else. But that is a very different matter from cheer-leading for the European Union which, despite its welcome enlargement, is faltering badly; and here my reservations are unfortunately unlikely to date.

Some biographical essays are collected in Part Seven. They cover a diverse collection of personalities, none of whose teachings can be followed hook, line and sinker, but all of whom are worth attention. The essays in this section also differ considerably in nature. The one on Keynes was written for a collection of studies on the great man and thus deals with only some selected topics. Those on Hayek and Norman Angell were commissioned by major reference books and are therefore more comprehensive in nature. I wrote the essay on Ayn Rand to satisfy my own curiosity about an unusual woman who attracted great attention in North America but is hardly known on the eastern side of the Atlantic. Milton Friedman is the only one of these luminaries with whom I have had some modest personal acquaintance and the chapter on him is more of a pen portrait. The essay on Bertrand Russell obviously deals with only a few aspects of that philosopher's thought; but it provides a suitable note on which to end this part.

The final part, Part Eight, contains some thoughts on economics as a subject. Economics is and has to be what economists do. The subject has now acquired such a huge body of technique and so many branches that commentators can only be outsiders looking in. This need not stop them making either sympathetic or pointed remarks. But I see my role more like that of a science correspondent writing about what scientists are doing rather than as a participant myself. The best case I can make for economics is to reflect on the greater nonsense that most non-economists utter.

One shift of emphasis which some readers might notice is that I no longer feel it necessary to be tactful when talking about socialism. In the past I tried hard to find elements of value in it. This is partly because there were people I respected who called themselves socialists, and also because some socialist movements had come to embody some radical and iconoclastic elements which one was unlikely to find in conservative parties. But the collapse of 'real existing socialism' in the Soviet Union and its former satellites in 1989 should have taken away the need for any such tactfulness. The time has long arrived to recognize that all forms of collectivism, of which socialism is one, were a twentieth-century false turning for radicals and progressives.

I am sometimes asked if any censorship is applied to my press articles. The answer is 'Only self-censorship – to get them into the available space'. Like some other authors of collected essays I have worked hard to elimate duplication where avoidable. But this cannot always be done without absurdity. For instance it would be ridiculous to omit key doctrines from pen portraits in Part Seven because they have already been mentioned in the earlier political economy chapters. I have taken the opportunity to restore passages which have not appeared in print before, but which I think still add some value, and have felt free occasionally to change essay titles where this makes for greater clarity. I have also of course deleted material which is out of date in an uninteresting way. The deletion process has extended to acknowledgements of and tributes to various individuals in whose honour I was asked to lecture or write. I trust that this will be understood as an aid to readability and not taken as a discourtesy. I have discussed the subject matter of the material here with so many different people that it would be invidious to single out names and if I tried I would be in danger of missing out some of the most important. In a small number of cases a few remarks inserted later than the original date of publication have been put in square brackets.

The attributions at the beginning of each chapter are meant, where necessary, to thank the journals and reference books in question for permission to use my contributions and more generally to thank everyone who gave me the opportunity to air the ideas in the first place.

PART ONE

The International Scene

Shower upon him every blessing, drown him in a sea of happiness, give him economic prosperity, such that he should have nothing else to do but sleep, eat cakes, and busy himself with the continuation of his species, and even then, out of sheer ingratitude, sheer spite, man will play you some nasty trick. He would even risk his cakes and would deliberately desire the most fatal rubbish, the utmost economic absurdity, simply to introduce into all this positive good sense, his fatal fantastic element.

Dostoevski

Danger of Too Much Understanding

Financial Times, 27 September 2001

The resources of civilization are not yet exhausted.

Prime Minister Gladstone after the
Phoenix Park murders in Dublin, 1881

Many people love recalling where they were during traumatic events such as the assassination of Jack Kennedy. This is not normally my line. But the circumstances in which I learned of the outrage of September 11 were rather special. I was in hospital recovering from a non-threatening, but painful, operation. In many hotels and hospitals radio stations can only be obtained – at least by the electronically unskilful – by first turning on a television channel and then pressing a few buttons. It so happened that I was onto a television channel *en route* between two radio stations. Instead of the usual entertainment, we saw the World Trade Center on fire, followed by the collapse of the first tower. Maybe this huge atrocity ought to have put my own pain into perspective. But I am no hero. They continued side by side.

Predictably some commentator soon intoned that the world would never be the same again. My own reaction was 'you bet'. It did not take many minutes before every interest and single-issue pressure group was trying to turn the tragedy to its own advantage.

To return to serious matters. A few people vaguely remembered that I was opposed to the Falklands war of 1982, or that I am now against arms sales to dubious regimes, some of which have almost certainly ended up in Taliban hands. They were surprised by my hawkish reactions. But September 11, 2001, was not the Falklands. It was more like Pearl Harbor.

Yet it has not taken long for the appeasers to come out of the woodwork. Instead of discussing how to combat the terrorist scourge, commentators – and even friends of mine – were asking, 'Why do so many people hate America?' There is in fact little evidence that they really do. The hatred comes from religious and political zealots. They hate the USA because it is both free and rich. It so happens I feel far more at home in a central European *konditorei* than in a hamburger bar in middle America, where there is complete incomprehension between myself and the barman shouting something like 'Sunny side up!' But that is not the point. The book I would be reading in the *konditorei* would be highly likely to originate in America.

The USA is the most successful society the world has seen. The success is based on its material wealth, but is far from confined to business. If you are looking for the best scholarship on the English classical writer Jane Austen you go to a university in Texas. If you want the best studies of the Austro-British philosopher Ludwig Wittgenstein you will find them in North America. Indeed, if you are looking for serious analysis in any of the humanities, you will often go to American-based authors.

But none of this was of any interest to commentators who claimed that the root of the hatred was something called 'American backing of Israel'. Did they mean that the US was not putting enough pressure on the hardline Israeli prime minister Ariel Sharon to make concessions for peace? Bush can, should and will take care of Sharon [a false short-term prediction, but it may yet happen under Bush or his successor]. Or did they support those fanatics who wanted to roll back fifty years of history and wipe out the state of Israel altogether? They neither knew nor cared. 'Palestine' as an idiot headline would take them through the next few programmes.

I suppose I will be accused of being a racialist if I say that there are too many attempts to explain Islamic attitudes. The vast majority of Muslims, whether Arab or not, simply want to get on with their lives and use their mobiles and IT skills in a way I can only admire. It looks as if the United States and Britain will avoid the crass error of the early years of the Second World War when residents of German or Japanese origin were interned. Thugs who use the September 11 events as an excuse for attacking Afghan cab drivers – probably themselves refugees from the Taliban – are just like the football hooligans or the discreditable wing of the anti-globalization protesters who are simply looking for a rough house. They need to be treated with the full rigour of the law.

But can you imagine Winston Churchill in 1940 stopping preparations for the Battle of Britain until he felt he understood enough of the origins of the hostility of the German-speaking world to the West or of the appeal of Nazism to Germany and Austria or of Fascism to Italy? Does anyone think that he should have called off the war until he and his advisers had made a thorough study of German idealistic philosophy and how easily it became perverted, or of

Wagner's anti-Semitism or the cult of duelling in German universities? Indeed, a spate of studies has come out on all these aspects, many of them written in the USA, beginning late in the Second World War and continuing to this day. If somebody wants to blow you up, the most important thing is not to empathize with the combination of forces that has produced his attitudes but to do what you can to eliminate him. I question both the urgent need to understand Islam and the accusation that the West has never tried to do so. The foreign offices of Europe have not ceased poking their noses into Middle Eastern affairs for the last 200 years with disastrous results.

At this point of danger we cannot be too squeamish in our choice of allies. But for goodness sake let us remember that such alliances are based on ephemeral self-interest. General de Gaulle once wrote that countries have no permanent allies, only interests. Leaving aside the personification of countries – an unfortunate side product of the European romantic tradition – the General was right.

One of the most astonishing examples of prevailing softness towards Islamic inciters to murder was the long reluctance of an avowedly law and order Home Secretary such as David Blunkett to bring charges against self-styled Arab leaders who preached a holy war. No doubt he was advised that he might alienate moderate Muslims. I suspect that such moderates, if they felt free to speak, would be delighted to see such leaders deported or behind bars. Of course it is not only the appeasing left or the Arabists who are using the tragedy for their purpose. There are elements in the Home Office and in the police who have always wanted identity cards, and who are using the crisis, despite a lack of evidence that such cards would do anything worthwhile. And let us hear no more clichés such as 'We will never completely root out terrorism' as if that were an excuse for inaction.

It should not have taken this crisis to teach us the harmfulness of the saying: 'My enemy's enemy is my friend.' In practice the Taliban would not be there if US administrations had not backed them to fight against the Soviet Union in Afghanistan. How many times do we need to heed the warning of the great nineteenth-century liberal statesman Richard Cobden about the lack of knowledge with which we interfere in the affairs of other countries? The Afghans should have been left to deal with the Soviet army, as indeed they did.

When Hitler invaded Russia in 1941, Churchill said that as a lifelong opponent of communism, he would ally himself with the devil himself against Hitler. But it was not long before British sentimentalism took over and the mass murderer Stalin became 'Uncle Joe' and schoolchildren were contributing to Mrs Churchill's Aid to Russia Fund.

Of course, a network of alliances now needs to be constructed. But there is no need for clerks in the Foreign Office or the Quai d'Orsay to write hymns of praise to regimes which practise amputations and floggings and refuse to recognize the humanity of their female citizens. A novice UK foreign secretary (Jack Straw) ought to have known better than to allow some Foreign Office Arabist to draft a one-sided anti-Israel article for an Iranian newspaper in a pathetic attempt to curry favour with that country's rulers. Like most others, the Iranian regime will co-operate with the West to the extent that it pays it to do so.

Meanwhile, the best that the ordinary citizen can do, especially if we are in for the long haul, is to doggedly pursue normal activities. It is often forgotten that after an early phase of general shutdown during the Second World War, theatres, cinemas, concert halls and the like were encouraged to reopen; and the civilian population encouraged to think of non-war activities. We shall indeed overcome.

USA Is More Nearly Right

Financial Times, 1 August 2002

The characteristic American view of the world since September 11, 2001, is, although uncomfortable, a good deal closer to the truth than the European Union one.

Since September 11, millions of words have appeared on the related issues of international terrorism, the growing divergence between the United States and Europe, the Arab–Israeli conflict, the political aspects of globalization, the notion of a just war and other such topics. To have read them all would be incompatible with sleeping and eating, let alone doing anything else. Readers must therefore excuse some simplifications. The personification of countries has always been one of my pet bugbears. Still more so of continents. Just as 'society' is composed of individuals – as Lady Thatcher incurred so much odium by reminding us – so are nations and continents. There are as many American points of view on foreign policy as there are US citizens who think about such matters. The widely respected American journal *Foreign Policy* is full of articles closer to 'European' than to official US attitudes.

Nevertheless, the views somewhat crudely expressed by the Bush administration since September 11, 2001, seem to me more nearly correct than the appeasing and temporizing alternatives enunciated in European Union circles. One cannot choose one's allies. There are probably not many subjects on which I would agree with George W. Bush or Donald Rumsfeld – above all Bush's self-confessed incomprehension that there are people who have no religion. But they are nevertheless closer to the truth than European or East Coast American intellectuals whom it would be more convivial to meet at dinner.

The key 'American' doctrines which so annoy the European establishment seem to me three. First, the US is at war with international terrorism. As Philip Bobbitt, who, so far from being a

Republican, worked for the Clinton administration and is a nephew of Lyndon Johnson, wrote in the *Financial Times* on 13 July 2001, 'al-Qaeda is a virtual state'. It has a 'standing army, a treasury, a consistent source of revenue, a civil service and an intelligence corps: it even runs a rudimentary welfare programme for its fighters and their relatives and associates'. It declared war on the US in 1995; and, as at the time of Pearl Harbor, the US faces 'death and destruction on a scale associated with war – unlike states that terrorism has menaced in the past'. Second, controlling and diminishing the revenue stream to bin Laden's network emphasizes the case for international co-operation and consensus building. But if European allies will not or cannot co-operate, the US will go it alone with a 'coalition of the willing'. Third, the proliferation of nuclear military capacity, and still more the newer kinds of less expensive biological warfare in the hands of rogue states, is so dangerous that pre-emptive strikes can be justified.

On the other side is a characteristic, although not universally held, European view that terrorism must be tackled in its supposed roots in poverty and oppression and/or in the Arab–Israeli conflict. In the words of a controversial article by Robert Kagan in *Policy Review*, 'many officials and politicians in Europe worry more about how the USA might mishandle the problems in Iraq ... than they worry about Iraq itself'. See, for instance, any recent article by a retired British general.

Kagan unkindly points out that European legalism is based not on virtue but on weakness. Following the end of the Cold War, European defence budgets fell below 2 per cent of GDP, while US defence spending remained at 3 per cent. Europeans 'lack the wherewithal to introduce and sustain a fighting force in hostile territory, even in Europe'. They now 'hope to rein in US power without wielding power themselves'. In other words, the EU is as unimpressive on the diplomatic and miltary front as it is on the economic one.

An article by A. B. Krueger and Jane Maleckova in the 24 June issue of the *New Republic* provides the latest evidence 'that there is little direct connection between poverty, lack of education and participation in or support for terrorism'. Indeed, terrorists are more likely to come from better-off families with a relatively high level of education. There may, however, be indirect connections. Many Middle Eastern states have more graduates than their economies can accommodate. In addition, the more pro-western states such as Saudi Arabia tend to be feudal dictatorships which give no outlet to such people's political ambitions, although they support religious foundations that promote terrorism abroad. The moral is that the West should stop arming such regimes. If economic aid is given, it should be for its own sake rather than from a wishful belief that it will stop al-Qaeda.

As for Palestine, there are all too many regional conflicts in which both sides have an unending list of seemingly irrefutable debating points: Israel versus Palestinian Arabs; India versus Pakistan; Greece versus Turkey; Tamils versus mainstream Sri Lankans, and so on. Nothing is more pathetic than the stage armies of rival partisans of each side in western countries. There was a Cambridge-based letter in *The Times* (24 July 2002), many of whose signatories were former economists or economic officials in previous British governments, who have as little detailed knowledge of the Middle East as I have. Their key sentence was 'We believe that the welfare and self-respect of the Palestinians are as important as the welfare and self-respect of the Israelis.' They could with equal justice have said the reverse. The most sensible response to these intractable disputes is to keep one's distance, try to cauterize them so they do not become a systemic threat to peace and, if possible, intervene very cautiously to dampen down the worst atrocities.

I find myself somewhat surprised to be so much on the Bush side. I call myself a neo-pacifist because I do not believe in dying either for forms of governments or to have rulers of one ethnic or national origin rather than another. The choice between living under the Kaiser and living under Lloyd George was not worth the millions of deaths in the trenches, as Lloyd George himself came to appreciate. And I was old enough to have been opposed to the Vietnam war, as well as to the Falklands war, and was dubious about the Gulf one.

'Neo' because if our very lives and the right to exist are threatened, as my family's were by the Nazis in the Second World War, and as the whole western world is threatened by al-Qaeda and by rogue states, then I believe in fighting back with every available resource. The new wave of Islamist militancy is a self-confessed threat to the values, not merely of the United States, but of the European Enlightenment: to the preference for life over death, to peace, rationality, science and the humane treatment of our fellow men, not to speak of our fellow women. It is a reassertion of blind cruel faith over reason.

One does not have to be a scholar of Islam to say this. Evil men can find what they seek in most of the religious or philosophical texts of the world. In the Middle Ages it was the Christian Crusaders who represented intolerance, the murder of those of different faiths – or even different variants of one's own faith – and international pillage in the name of religion. Today the roles are reversed; and I leave it to theologians to decide which side has been truer at which time to the supposedly sacred texts.

Compared with the central issue of the struggle against terrorism and rogue states, doubts about the nature and style of the George W. Bush administration, the role of the UN, debates on the definition of terrorism, European quibbling on whether the war on it can ever be won, and even the Palestine conflict are side issues.

A Guilt-ridden Question
Contribution to International Economy Symposium,
January 2003

'Are you not satisfied to be doing an important and useful job, and one for which you are not badly paid. Do you need to be loved as well?'

These words were uttered some time ago by the late Harold Lever, a British financier and former member of the Wilson Labour cabinet. He was talking to bankers in London. But his remarks could equally apply to the US political and business elite.

The whole question is defensive and guilt-ridden. Since September 11, 2001, an informal coalition of Islamist apologists, wimpish European leaders and US public intellectuals have tried to switch the issue from the threat posed by fundamentalist terrorists to the question of: 'How likable is the USA, its leaders or its culture?' Its most nauseating aspect was the remark 'They had it coming to them'.

The West now faces a threat more difficult to deal with than the old Soviet empire. The latter was led by rational people whose ambitions could be deterred and with whom agreements could also be made. No such dialogue is possible with groups such as al-Qaeda. Any wishful thinking that their aims were confined to the United States should have been dispelled by the atrocity in Bali [and in Madrid in 2004]. But will it take similar atrocities in Berlin, London or Paris to bring the so-called intelligentsia to its senses? [I hope that this lesson will not be taught while this book is going to press.]

Of course much is wrong with US foreign policy. My advice would be to stop supporting the Saudi regime and to put pressure on the Israeli government on the issues of West Bank settlements and Jerusalem. But do not expect a model Saudi democracy to take over or be surprised if terrorist attacks continue to provoke Israeli over-reaction. The world is not a pleasant place.

My Enemy's Enemy Is Not Always My Friend

Hakluyt, New Year 2002

The terrorist attack on the World Trade Center on September 11 has brought renewed attention to a thesis by the political analyst Samuel P. Huntington, which first appeared in an article in *Foreign Affairs* in the summer of 1993, entitled 'The Clash of Civilisations', and was then expanded into a book (*The Clash of Civilisations*, Simon & Schuster, 1997).

His message was that western leaders were deluding themselves if they thought that they had won the battle of ideas with the collapse of the Soviet Union and that the world was now safe for liberal democracy, free market capitalism and the rule of law. It was a direct answer to Francis Fukuyuma who had appeared to assert just that in his thesis, *The End of History*, which originally appeared in 1989.

Instead Huntington predicted that we would be back in a world resembling that which existed before 1800, or even before 1600, when the West was only one of several contending civilizations. It would have been preferable to use the word culture, which surely evokes much better the differences, say, between the Orthodox and the Western Christian traditions than civilizations which suggest utterly different technologies, and populations which have little contact with each other.

The weakest part of his book is the attempt to enumerate the civilizations now in existence, as Arnold Toynbee tried to do for earlier periods in his *Study of History*. This leads to endless semantic arguments about whether Latin America belongs to western culture or is a separate world of its own; or whether to regard Japan as a separate civilization or part of an East Asian orbit. In fact a better title would have been *The Decline of the West* had not Oswald Spengler pre-empted it in a book published early in the twentieth century.

Huntington was at his least convincing in his encomium on Japan. This did not read so well after Japan's decade of economic stagnation.

The strongest part of Huntington's thesis is that, even though the US has emerged for the time being as the only world superpower, the West – defined as North America, Europe and closely related areas such as Australasia – has passed its zenith. The tables at the beginning of his book show convincingly that the West has constituted for some time a declining proportion of the world, whether viewed in terms of population under its political control or GDP, or proportion of European language speakers. It can only be a matter of time before the West's military supremacy is also threatened; and the author is fatalistic about nuclear weapons proliferation to the main power centres.

The real thesis of *The Clash of Civilisations* is the West against the Rest. Huntington was spot-on in his assertion that the main challenge to the West would come from a Muslim revival. As he remarks, it is not just a matter of Muslim fundamentalism but of one world outlook against another. Of course the majority of Muslims, especially those settled in the US and Europe, did not support bin Laden's raids. But a good many of the more passive majority did experience satisfaction with the embarrassment of the USA and expressed strong hostility to the Afghan campaign.

Huntington is on less firm ground when he identifies the West with a culture of democracy, toleration, reason and personal freedom, and Islam with more or less its opposite. People can find whatever they are looking for in canonical religious texts like the Bible or the Koran (or for that matter the writings of Karl Marx), which contain many passages ranging from the most bloodthirsty to the most humane. There have been periods when the Muslim world has been not only more scientifically advanced, but much more tolerant of dissent than the Christian West and indeed provided a home for Jews who had been driven out of Spain by the Christian reconquest. At the time of the Crusades it was the western European Christians who were aggressive and bloodthirsty – not merely against Islam but against the Byzantine Christians, whose capital, Constantinople, was pillaged more than once by western gangs on their way to liberate Jerusalem. The values which Huntington celebrates as western are really those of the Enlightenment which began in Europe in the eighteenth century and whose triumph has never been complete.

The new terrorism is indeed a challenge to the Enlightenment; or indeed to any kind of tolerable living. The world will not be safe while rulers of rogue states are free to develop nuclear and biological weapons of mass destruction; and President Bush would be well advised to ignore the advice of German intellectuals – or Arabists in the British Foreign Office or the French Quai d'Orsay – who shrink from the necessary confrontation.

There is now a network of militant Muslim organizations which will not disappear with the publication by the US authorities of the names of a few of the most prominent. It is indeed interesting that someone like David Roche, a London market strategist writing in the *Wall Street Journal* (28 November) to dispute Huntington, has a remarkably similar analysis to his of the planners of the September 11 atrocities. They were maladjusted, privileged middle-class youths who got sucked into a fanatical ideology – a more lethal version of the middle-class Maoist students of twenty or thirty years ago. Their identity kit looks like those who belonged to Baader Meinhof or the Red Brigade: spoilt middle-class kids, suicidal and brainwashed.

Huntington's advice that the West should above all stop interfering in other cultures and look to its own defences seems more realistic. This means, above all else, in my view, that we need to abandon the pernicious doctrine that 'My enemy's enemy is my friend'. This has involved western leaders in a dizzying successive embrace of rival dictatorships ranging from China to Iraq, Pakistan and Saudi Arabia and in the process selling arms to regimes which are eventually used against the West as well as their own people.

But he is too inclined to see western intervention as a campaign for human rights, which alas it is not except at the margins. The huge investment of the US and the UK in the royal despotism of Saudi Arabia has nothing to do with human rights and everything to do with the misplaced belief that the West will always need Saudi Arabian oil.

The Middle East and the struggle against terrorism are also the key to economic developments in the first decade of the new century. While in the past economics and international politics moved in separate spheres and practitioners simply made cross-references to show off, today the connection is very real.

Iraq: There Was an Alternative

Financial Times, 25 October 2002

The classical liberals of nineteenth-century England, whose spiritual heirs are now mostly to be found in the US, were divided on international affairs. One strand, associated with Lord Palmerston, advocated – rather selectively – intervention to help nations struggling to be free. The other strand, associated with Richard Cobden of anti-Corn Law fame, argued that such interventions were usually misguided and counterproductive, and that the first duty of states was to promote the peace, freedom and welfare of their own citizens.

My own sympathies are with the Cobdenites. But that does not mean we can neglect physical threats to ourselves and our own societies. An authoritative analysis of the Saddam threat has been published in the USA by Kenneth Pollack, who was long director for Gulf Affairs at the US National Security Council. Although subtitled *The Case for Invading Iraq*, the book[1] has had the opposite effect of making me sceptical about that case. Pollack believes Hussein is not inherently irrational but takes many risks and calculates badly. His case for invasion is that other strategies have failed – partly because many US allies have proved 'perfidious, feckless, or outright duplicitous'. He is nothing if not candid on the preconditions for a successful Iraq war. He is careful not to link Hussein with al-Qaeda – neither side wants to have much to do with the other. Nevertheless, the USA would first have to break the back of al-Qaeda at least to the point 'where we do not have monthly government warnings of possible terrorist attacks'. Moreover, Washington would have to line up the support of the Gulf states, Egypt and Turkey just to make the operation happen. To gain their support would require the US for good measure to 'take a more active role in mollifying Israeli–Palestinian violence'. Even then, if war plans did not go according to plan, 'we might suffer several thousand American military personnel killed' as well as tens of thousands of Iraqi civilians. After victory the US would have to remain in Iraq for years to come.

What I did not find in Pollack's book was any clear statement of the threat that Hussein poses to the West. He believes his goal is hegemony over the Arab world. The one wider threat is the oil weapon. Yet it is a conceit of foreign ministries to believe that countries need physical control over key supplies; Middle Eastern states need to sell oil even more than the West needs to buy it.

Of course, the possibility of a short-term embargo needs to be factored into our calculations. US oil imports from the Middle East account for some 14 per cent of US oil consumption. Net European dependence is similar. If the free world cannot cut consumption by these amounts in an emergency it hardly deserves to be saved. An investment in augmented strategic oil stocks and in an energy policy to reduce gas-guzzling would be a small price to pay for avoiding the potentially devastating fallout from an Iraq war.

I still have some hesitations about becoming a peacenik on Iraq. I have to allow for decisions being taken by people with different attitudes to my own. What I fear most is that if a Saddam-type regime does come to dominate the Middle East, many of the same establishment officials who are now most opposed to an Iraq war would then be banging the drum for military action. Pollack makes a telling comparison with the European appeasers of the 1930s, who had to fight a more terrible war as a result of not stopping Hitler earlier.

Meanwhile, the US should avoid what James Rubin, the former State Department spokesman, called 'gratuitous unilateralism', and try to build an international coalition to enforce Iraq disarmament, but not place too high hopes on it. As Pollack says, the main alternative to a pre-emptive attack is deterrence. This involves accepting the probability that Hussein will acquire nuclear weapons – between 2004 and 2008, he believes – as well as chemical and biological ones, and that western policy should concentrate on deterring him from using them as it deterred the former Soviet Union. We shall then have to leave it to time, his own people and his neighbours to enforce a regime change.

Note

1. Kenneth Pollack, *The Threatening Storm*, Random House, 2002.

This Is Not a Time for Boy Scouts

Financial Times, 24 October 2003

> In all my travels...three reflections constantly occur to me: how much unnecessary solicitude and alarm England devotes to the affairs of foreign countries; with how little knowledge we enter upon the task of regulating the concerns of other people; and how much better we might employ our energies in improving matters at home.
>
> Richard Cobden, letter to John Bright,
> 18 September 1847

George F. Kennan, the American diplomat and historian who developed the original Cold War doctrine of deterrence, also made a vigorous onslaught on what he called the 'moralistic-legalistic approach' to foreign policy. His strongest argument was that this approach brought more human hardship than a straightforward defence of national self-interest. He was reinforced in this belief by the work of Herbert Butterfield, the Cambridge historian. Writing from a Christian point of view, Butterfield warned fellow Christians of the dangers of rushing to make moralistic assumptions about international events that subsequently turned out to be wrong and inflicted more suffering than a more humble approach.

This modest view is now being challenged by two misguided forces. One is known as neo-conservatism. The other is liberal imperialism. Neither name is self-explanatory. It is easier to explain the liberal imperialists, who are to be found more in Britain than the USA. They observe the existence of sadistic dictatorships and their violations of human rights. They also notice the 'failed states', territories that do not have a stable government able to enforce the rule of law. The liberal imperialists believe that the West has a duty to intervene in these countries to impose better performance. They sometimes take these ideas to their logical conclusion and advocate the establishment of United Nations, Nato, US or other kinds of western protectorates, akin to those that existed in the closing years of the prewar empires.

There are two basic weaknesses in this Boy Scout attitude. The first is that the primary responsibility of any government is the welfare of the inhabitants of the area of which it is in charge. This does not mean placing a zero weight on the welfare of other people or being indifferent to the abuse of human rights elsewhere. Claims by some old-fashioned conservatives that morality has no place in foreign policy are mystification in a bad cause. But it is wrong to expect governments to have equal concern for all the inhabitants of the globe.

Even those who regard this as insufficiently altruistic need to pay attention to a second argument: we do not always have the *knowledge* to improve the affairs of distant countries. Because of this ignorance, dreadful mistakes are made and it is extremely doubtful that the welfare of those whom we purport to help is in fact improved. The assumption that US forces would be widely welcomed as liberators in Iraq and the failure to foresee the outbreak of tribal, religious and simple gang warfare after the fall of Saddam Hussein surely demonstrate the point.

The neo-conservatives start from a different position. Originally supporters of interventionist domestic social welfare policies, they eventually became disillusioned with President Lyndon Johnson's Great Society programmes. But they still wanted to 'moralize' the free market approach. After a period out of the public eye, they burst forth into the foreign policy field. They could not remain silent in the face of the proliferation of repressive regimes abroad and believed the US had a duty to export democracy wherever possible. In practice their desire to engage in 'nation-building' is almost indistinguishable from that of the liberal imperialists. A difference is that they put less emphasis on international organizations and exhibit a greater willingness to see the USA go it alone.

The alternative to both positions is a fairly simple one. It is that western nations have the right and duty to protect themselves not merely from traditional aggression across frontiers but also from terrorism, intolerant religious fundamentalism and other threats to their way of life. This may involve incursions into countries from which the threats emanate. But these should be as limited and as brief as possible.

Areas of tolerance, humanity and respect for disinterested learning are quite rare both historically and in geographical extent. The primary duty of western statesmen is to defend the elements of western liberalism that already exist and to concentrate on improving their own societies.

Poverty Not Root of Terrorism

Financial Times, 11 April 2002

There is a highly fashionable diagnosis of the causes and cures of international terrorism. It runs thus: 1. The root cause of terrorism is poverty. Or, as it is sometimes put, 'Violence is the only weapon of those who have no other way of making themselves heard.' 2. The best chance of alleviating world poverty is through a massive western aid effort – or 'a new Marshall Plan'. 3. Aid, however, is not enough. The world is full of 'failed states'. These will not use aid effectively without a concerted western attempt at what is called nation-building.

The three items of the creed are logically separate; but many exponents embrace them all. An example is a well-argued first article in the April issue of *Foreign Affairs* by Sebastian Mallaby on 'Imperialism's virtues'. Robert Cooper, foreign policy adviser to Tony Blair, also makes a plea for a 'postmodern imperialism' (*Reordering the World*, Foreign Policy Centre).

The evidence against terrorism being a reaction to extreme poverty is overwhelming. Many of the terrorists come from well-heeled backgrounds, are educated and proficient in information technology. The really poor are far too preoccupied with making ends meet. The appetite for violent change occurs after a take-off towards a higher standard of living.

It is, however, fair to say that there is some link between revolutionary activities and perceived differences of income and wealth. A widening of income gaps is inevitable if some countries or some sectors within each country take off into modernity before others do. But as more and more people and countries become involved in the growth process, the gaps start narrowing again. (The mathematics of the process are simply explained by Nobel Laureate Robert Lucas in *Economic Perspectives*, Winter 2000.)

It is untrue that countries cannot take off into self-sustaining growth without outside aid. Those who assert this might ask how the

Industrial Revolution ever started. A more modest claim is that aid, by adding to the resources of developing countries, can make the transition to modernity less painful. The main reason for helping people in poorer countries is humanitarian. It only detracts from the cause if its exponents try to add that it will also save the economies of the West or keep terrorism at bay. You can do more with $110 than you can do with $100 plus your own resources. But we then have to look at the practical record: how much government-to-government aid has been syphoned off either directly into the pockets of corrupt ruling elites or into prestige projects inimical to sound development. Or how much it has been used as a backdoor way for western countries to subsidize arms sales or prestige engineering projects.

My own preference is for direct aid to people or small communities who are hungry or impoverished or who can, with a little help, be supplied with clean water and remedies against disease. The problem is that there are so many hundreds of non-governmental agencies, all appealing to our consciences, that we do not know which of them will send help where it is most needed and which will waste the highest proportion on their own administration or on various kinds of anti-capitalist propaganda. If only some publisher would be brave enough to provide a good charities guide. (At least a start has been made by Luke FitzHerbert and Kathryn Becher in *The Major Charities*, Directory of Social Change, 2002.)

It is the third aspect of the new imperialism – nation-building – which most alarms me. There are, on United Nations estimates, more than 100 countries with oppressive governments covering 3.6bn people or 60 per cent of the world's population. Human rights do not stop at frontiers; and if there is an opportunity to introduce them abroad we should do so. The trouble is that, for the reasons given by Cobden, these attempts are often self-defeating.

A study by Gary Dempsey for the Cato Institute (*Policy Analysis*, 21 March) lists country after country, from the Lebanon to Somalia, where the US has entered in ignorance and retreated with ignominy. The worst example is Afghanistan, which was disrupted first by Soviet intervention, then by US support for the most extreme anti-Soviet and anti-modern elements in the country, and finally by Pakistan's internal security services which supported the Taliban faction. Generalizations are difficult. But as Dempsey writes, 'The security of the US does not require a multi-ethnic, liberal democracy in Afghanistan. It requires only that the governments there be deterred from harbouring terrorists as the Taliban once did.'

An Exit from the Middle East

Financial Times, 8 November 2001

I was privileged recently to hear by far the clearest statement so far of what western aims should be in the war against terrorism. It came, not surprisingly, from Henry Kissinger, the former US Secretary of State.

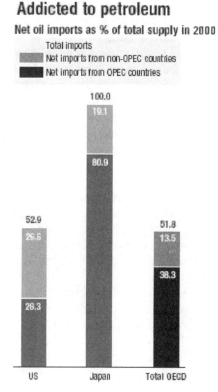

Addicted to petroleum

Net oil imports as % of total supply in 2000

Total imports
Net imports from non-OPEC countries
Net imports from OPEC countries

Source: International Energy Agency

He reminded us that, in the entire postwar period, the security of free people everywhere has depended on America's willingness to defend them. 'If America fails in its reaction to an attack on its own territory... the security of the postwar world will disintegrate.'

He argued that terrorism exists in many cells all over the world but cannot survive without some bases. The strategic objective has to be 'the elimination of these base areas, or at any rate the suppression of them by the host government'. He warned that if the alliance's aims were limited to victory in Afghanistan, terrorism would come back. Eventually all states that supported terrorism must be induced to stop, with no distinction between the global and local varieties. He did not advocate military intervention to settle old scores – but support for terror had to come to an end reasonably soon.

Kissinger looked forward to a concert of powers including the US, its European allies and perhaps Russia, China and India, which could agree on the definition of terrorism and a common response. He did not think this world concert could be postponed until issues such as Palestine, 'which have a long time-frame', had been tackled. He compared today's Nato with the quadripartite alliance existing at the end of the Napoleonic wars against any resurgence of French expansionism. But this never had to be invoked. Instead, the action was with a concert of European powers in which France participated – and which worked until Britain withdrew.

Kissinger rightly debunked some of the fashionable talk about allied military forces having the primary role to play in 'nation-building' in Afghanistan. This task has eluded many countries over many centuries. At most he favoured a United Nations contact group of neighbouring countries and western economic aid.

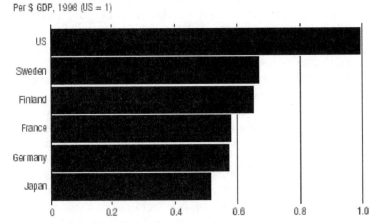

Energy consumption
Per $ GDP, 1998 (US = 1)

Source: International Energy Agency, National Bureau for International Research

Can the same detachment be applied to countries around the Gulf? In my view, not at present. The US and its allies will never disentangle themselves from the Middle East and establish Kissinger's wider concert while they are so dependent on Middle Eastern oil.

Until oil dependence is drastically reduced, the western powers are doomed to recurring intervention in the affairs of the region and to making unpleasant choices between unattractive regimes, nearly all contemptuous of human rights. From time to time they will back the wrong horse – as they did with the Shah of Iran and could easily do in Saudi Arabia now – and be blown from crisis to crisis.

Surely the West must seek a world in which it does not have to decide between the present feudal regime in Saudi Arabia and the fundamentalist radical opposition to it. Would we not all feel safer as well as more dignified if Tony Blair did not have to go looking for common ground with every unattractive Middle Eastern dictator? But we shall not escape from these begging missions while diplomacy is stifled by the need for oil supplies.

We have seen many maps showing how oil could be obtained from central Asia or Russia, bypassing the Arabian peninsula. But look at the areas through which the projected pipelines go. Some traverse the Caucasus and Turkey; others go through Afghanistan and Pakistan. These are some of the most turbulent and unstable areas of the globe. A medium-term escape from these dilemmas involves the US and its allies becoming, as a group, more self-sufficient in energy and particularly in oil. Let no one say that there is anything anti-free-market in paying an insurance premium to avoid dependence on a monopolistic seller.

A paper by the National Bureau of Economic Research[1] notes that most US federal energy initiatives were in response to emergencies following large increases in petroleum prices but were afterwards allowed to lapse. After the first 1973 oil price shock, President Richard Nixon launched Project Independence for energy self-sufficiency by 1980. But by the end of 2000 the US was importing 56 per cent of its petroleum. In the same year energy imports of all kinds surpassed the previous peak by 36 per cent. The failure of US energy-saving drives partly reflects the behaviour of real oil prices, which have remained far below the peaks of 1980.

Meanwhile US domestic refining capacity has been declining. Energy policy, like so much else, has been distorted by a running left–right battle. On the left it is argued that the problem lies in the failure of Congress to authorize petroleum taxes; so gasolene costs much less than in other western countries. On the right, the blame is put on excessive regulation. In the past ten years the refinery industry has had to respond to five sets of new environmental regulations. A serious policy will have to cut across these wrangles.

Environmental restrictions will have to be reduced to a minimum and shorn of their anti-business subtext. But Congressional leaders will have to perform a U-turn on gasolene taxes.

Faced with such problems, Paul Krugman, the US economist, is pessimistic about reducing dependence on Gulf oil. He accepts that strong conservation efforts could reduce US per capita oil use to European levels and make the country self-sufficient. But other industrial countries still account for two-thirds of oil imports from the Organization of Petroleum Exporting Countries.

For once Krugman may be too pessimistic – or too carried away by distaste for President Bush's desire to drill in a part of the Alaskan National Wildlife Refuge. There are in fact plenty of ways in which Europe and Japan could reduce oil consumption. American profligacy is mainly due to car and truck users. Hardly any electricity is generated by oil, in strong contrast to the position in other countries. If the US were to tax petrol sufficiently and its allies were to substitute other primary fuels for electricity generation, we could be almost home and dry. Faced with the alternative of continued dependence on countries such as Saudi Arabia, American and other voters should at last be prepared to accept the mixture of planning and the price mechanism so badly required.

Note

1. Paul Joskow, *US Energy Policy during the 1990s*. Paper prepared for the conference 'American Economic Policy during the 1990s' sponsored by the J F Kennedy School of Government, June 2001.

Small States are Sometimes Best

Financial Times, 14 March 2003

We do not yet know the future shape of Iraq. But every attempt until now by bodies such as the US State Department and the British Foreign Office to draw maps and constitutions for the rest of the world has ended in disaster.

The West has neither the right nor the knowledge to tell other people how to govern their affairs, or what their boundaries should be. Its primary object should be its own self-defence, which was achieved by Nato in its heyday. When western countries have become inextricably involved after military intervention, they should provide scope for boundaries and constitutions to emerge from the wishes of the local inhabitants. Where possible, the benefit of the doubt should be given to regimes with a less bad human rights record.

For much of the twentieth century, western foreign policy was governed by two principles. One was to favour federations and large areas of governments. The second was to try to preserve existing frontiers, even when they were entirely artificial. Both Iraq and Jordan were created by Winston Churchill, out of three former Ottoman provinces, when he was colonial secretary in 1921. He was talked out of creating an independent Kurdistan.

When the two principles have been in conflict, the preference for size has tended to prevail. One has only to think of the misguided efforts of British governments in the 1950s to impose a central African federation or to construct a Caribbean federation. Both of these had to be dismantled.

At the beginning of the 1990s, President George Bush Sr made a notorious speech in Kiev when he warned Ukraine against separating itself from the Soviet Union. Yugoslavia was put together after the First World War by the victors who forced all the southern Slavs into a Serbian-led kingdom. One reason for the poor showing of the European Union in the Balkans in the 1990s was the desire of some members, including the UK, to maintain the Yugoslav Federation when its reason for existence had gone. More recently still, despite the war undertaken to save Kosovo from Slobodan Milošević's rule, it remained a Nato aim to prevent a complete breakaway of that region from Serbia. Even now, when the Albanians predominate in all except the northern tip, the myth of its being part of Serbia remains.

I am not suggesting that policymakers should go to the other extreme and begin by carving up Iraq into Shiite Arab, Sunni Arab and Kurdish states. A glance at any map shows the difficulties. But let us at least learn some negative lessons from the past: not to force the Kurds in the north who have already established a *de facto* independence to go back into a larger whole; nor to make the 'integrity' of countries such as Iraq and Saudi Arabia into a plank of foreign policy.

It is a diplomats' myth that modern technology requires very large states. Look at the size of some of the new countries admitted to an enlarged EU to see that small states can be viable. Estonia has a population of 1m, Cyprus 800,000 and Malta 400,000. The greater the role of competitive markets, both internally and across borders, the less the exact size of the state matters and the easier it is for countries of all shapes and sizes to coexist. If the US were content to buy its oil on the open market it would not need to be so heavily involved in nation-building in the Middle East.

To say this is not to advocate a night-watchman state. It is precisely services such as education, health and transport that, if they are to be publicly financed, are best provided locally. The US does not try to provide all such services from Washington; and the UK is committed to doing so from Whitehall only because local authorities have become financially dependent on the centre.

There are of course other services, such as military defence and aspects of security, for which even the largest countries are too small. Many liberal thinkers have advocated a minimal world government with a monopoly of weapons of destruction and some authority to formulate rules for a free trading system. Should it also provide a world currency? Is it too heretical to provide freedom of choice? Cannot there be, as in the Middle Ages, one or more international currencies for large-scale trade and finance without abolishing local currencies?

This thumbnail sketch is meant only to provide a few pointers. No one has found a solution for the interpenetration of ethnic groups across the map that brought Woodrow Wilson's dream of homogenous states to grief. But if we cannot just say that 'small is beautiful', we have enough evidence that big is not always best.

An Ethical Foreign Policy?

The Hinton Lecture, delivered at NCVO Annual General Meeting, 24 November 1999

The subject of 'Morality and Foreign Policy' is one which has preoccupied me for a very long time. Indeed, it was the topic of my own first extended essay after I had ceased to be an undergraduate.[1] It was written in the aftermath of the Suez crisis of 1956 in which the Eden government and its French allies colluded with the Israelis to find a pretext for invading Egypt in the unfulfilled hope of overthrowing the government of Colonel Nasser which had seized the Suez canal.

At the time of Suez there was a fierce argument between those who thought that foreign policy should be concerned with the so-called national interest and those who believed that it should be governed by moral considerations as well, one of which included an inhibition on invading another country whose government had not committed physical aggression or embarked on gross violation of human rights.

Over the years the protagonists have changed position. At the time of Suez, it was the hard-boiled realists who were in favour of military intervention and the moralists who were against it . In later instances, such as Kosovo, the moralists of the centre left have been the greatest enthusiasts for such intervention, and it is the hard-boiled right who have been hostile, or at least very cautious. But although the protagonists have changed sides again and again, the underlying issues remain the same.

Successive circles

Analysis has been bedevilled by two extreme, but widely held, views. The first might be called universal moralism, to which I will come in a minute. The second is the view that foreign policy should be exclusively concerned with national interest. The French *raison d'état* conveys the meaning better. For it really has nothing to do with modern nationalism as such. It could equally be the view that foreign policy should have been exclusively concerned with promoting the interests of the multinational Hapsburg empire of the nineteenth century, or for that matter of the ancient Roman empire.

The second and opposite extreme might be called universal moralism. The best way into it is to re-examine the so-called golden rule, which is widely regarded as the foundation of good behaviour. I have seen this stated in different ways. One is: 'Do unto others what you would that they should do unto you.' The other is: 'Love thy neighbour as thyself.' I have greater problems with the latter. I am going to suggest that you should have some degree of love for your neighbour, but that it need not be the same as for yourself or your immediate family.

To elaborate just a little: there is nothing to be ashamed of if you give the greatest weight to your own family circle; a good deal of weight, but not quite so much, to your friends or professional associates; some weight to fellow citizens of your own country; and lesser but by no means negligible weight to other people in distant areas. I have called these the successive circles of obligation. They will vary from person to person. Some people, if they are being honest, would give more weight to members of their own profession or people with similar interests in other countries than they would to distant and unknown citizens of their own country.

My point is that we can live with these successive circles of obligation. The result is likely to be a more humane and altruistic world than if we pay lip service to a system of equal obligation to everyone, but are almost never able to live up to it in practice. What I cannot accept is that we replace the old diplomacy of non-intervention in internal affairs with some new principles of abstract justice to be pursued though the heavens fall.

What I am saying is thus opposed to the view that moral principles are universal prescriptive statements. Prescriptive yes, universal no. Some philosophers maintain that universalism is a purely logical thesis deriving from the meaning of moral terms. But if it is a purely logical principle, this means that it depends on the definition of words and nothing can follow about actual conduct. Many of the considerations which philosophers have in mind when they say that moral principles must be universal can be taken care of by less ambitious words such as 'general' or 'impersonal'. When we come to public policy, some such concept is necessary if those in authority are to do something other than just promote their own personal preferences.My argument is with those who do assert universalism as an actual substantive norm. They concede that human beings are often not able to live up to it, but insist that they should carry on trying. One danger is that people give up the effort as too difficult and lapse into indifference An alternative route – which leads to the greatest disasters – is to restrict its scope to fellow nationals and give zero weight to people in other countries. This is a bad moral position, but is sometimes disguised as a positive statement about the world, e.g. when it is said that foreign policy is only concerned with national interest.

Another way out is to stick with the universalist prescriptions; but to go on to say that the best way to observe them in practice is for people to carry out their local and immediate obligations; and if they do so human welfare will be served better in total than if they try vainly to give as much attention to Mongolian peasants suffering from war or famine as to their own children, parents or spouses. It is also said, that even if her objective is to promote equally the welfare of all children in the world, each mother would serve this purpose better by giving closest attention to her own children and promoting the welfare of others only as a subsidiary activity. This is better than either extreme of saying that other children do not matter or neglecting one's own children for the sake of the world. But, like most rules of thumb, it has severe limitations. To begin with, it is not entirely honest. The view that we have primary responsibility to our own children does not depend on the belief that we are also serving other children best that way.

The role of intervention

Let me now turn to the other extreme view, that foreign policy should only be concerned with national interest or *raison d'état*.

There are two very different justifications advanced for saying that foreign policy should be based on hard-headed calculations of national self-interest and not at all on supporting human rights or preventing atrocities. One is simply to assert that foreign policy has no concern with such matters. That is the traditional view of many diplomats and statesmen such as the French Cardinal Richelieu, the Prussian Otto Bismarck and even our own Disraeli.

But we do not need to go back to the eighteenth or nineteenth centuries to find examples of this attitude. For instance, Lord Bridges has told the House of Lords that he drafted a speech for Lord Home in 1963 'which took a strong line that there should be no connection between ethics and foreign policy'. To be fair this is not the attitude that Lord Bridges now takes; and even in 1963 the draft might have been tongue in cheek. It has also been said that Lord Home read these notes in the middle of a long air journey from Karachi to London and became so angry that he there and then produced the draft of an alternative speech. But whoever espouses it, the pure 'national interest view' is in fact a moral position disguised as some profound statement about the nature of international politics. It is a position that we are free not to hold; and it is in my view a reprehensible one.

There is another very different justification. This is to say that in practice the main results of trying to interfere in the affairs of other countries, when there is no pressing hard-faced reason for doing so, is to increase rather than diminish the sum of human misery. This was the view of the great nineteenth-century Liberal, Richard Cobden; and it has been forcefully restated by the distinguished US diplomat and historian George F. Kennan.[2]

In our own day, Lord Dahrendorf has taken a similar position that 'not everything that is morally unacceptable can be rectified by governments'. But he has added that non-governmental organizations, such as Amnesty, can do a great deal to assist the victims of oppressive regimes or to care for the victims of torture. Moreover governments can help create a climate that is friendly to such non-governmental activists. He also hoped that human rights could become civil rights entrenched in law. The UK, for instance, is committed to ratify the statute for an international criminal court. I feel sure that Cobden could have accepted these emendations of his original statement. But what do we do today if powerful governments do not follow Britain in accepting this new court? It is not only Russia or China that refuses to do so, but also the United States. We are then back to the Kosovo dilemma. Do we wait for an effective system of worldwide law; or should a smaller group of countries accept and enforce the court's findings?

There are numerous arguments that can be given to support the non-interventionist position. Historically, moral self-righteousness has led to doctrines such as unconditional surrender. These tend to prolong bloodshed and suffering compared with a willingness to negotiate a peace treaty at an earlier stage. They may even have played a part in establishing communist rule over parts of central and eastern Europe at the end of the Second World War.

There is also an element of self-deception. The late Professor Herbert Butterfield recalled the tremendous shock which Hitler's invasion of Norway in 1940 gave to people's moral susceptibilities. "A pupil of mine, who had been one of the most authentic of conscientious objectors, and had been exempted from military service, was so appalled by the attack that his whole attitude was shaken and he died not very much later in naval service. I have wondered sometimes what his reaction would have been if he had lived to know that Great Britain had had a prior intention of invading Norway – and this even irrespective of the desire to help Finland – and that Hitler, initially unwilling to undertake the adventure, had decided to forestall us."[3]

Another consideration is that it is presumptuous to suppose that we know enough about the affairs of other people to intervene successfully in their affairs. Often, with the best of intentions, we make matters worse. The pragmatic objection to high principled intervention can never be absolute. But it does suggest that we should be extremely careful before embarking on righteous crusades. The Crusades of the Middle Ages were themselves examples of actions, which were at least in part high-minded, but led to the pillaging and destruction of civilizations far more advanced than western Christendom.

Perhaps the worst example of the moralistic approach is that it tends to deprive diplomacy of its normal function of attempting to ease disputes without recourse to war and of negotiating a settlement when war has broken out. For once a dispute is seen, not as a conflict of interest but of struggle between good and evil, then bargaining with the other side is seen at best as an odious expedient, and at worst as a betrayal of all that is sacred. This process was at work during the seventeenth-century wars of religion. In the twentieth century its most disastrous fruits have included the war guilt clauses of the Versailles Treaty as well as the doctrine of unconditional surrender employed by the Allies in the Second World War.

There is an opposite kind of error. This is to smother with embraces an unpleasant dictatorship. We obviously need to deal with communist China; and it would not help either us or the Chinese dissidents to cut off trade or diplomatic relations. But welcoming these awful people to Buckingham Palace is surely an unnecessary act of self-degradation. It is reminiscent of the way in which the royal family were forced to embrace the rulers of the Soviet regime which had murdered the Romanovs, who happened to be their cousins.

There will always be exceptional cases when the evil being done is clear and obvious and the dangers of counterproductive action much smaller. An example of the moral absurdity of the conventional diplomatic view is the alleged reluctance of the British Foreign Office to take action to save Jews in Europe at the time of the Holocaust and the tendency to play down what was happening.

To come to more recent history. It is unrealistic to criticize the American public for not giving the same weight to the life of an American soldier as to a Serbian civilian or a Kosovan victim of Serb atrocity. But American policy could be criticized for behaving as if the lives of these non-Americans had zero weight by comparison with those in their own armed forces.

Blair's principles

The British Prime Minister, Tony Blair, has suggested five considerations which should govern intervention in favour of human rights (Speech at the Economic Club of Chicago, 22 April 1999).

1. We must be sure of our case.
2. We must have exhausted all diplomatic options.
3. There must be military operations which 'we can sensibly and prudently undertake'.
4. We have to be prepared for the long term, so as not to have to return for a repeat performance.
5. The case for intervention is strengthened if national interests are involved.

These considerations are an attempt to justify some military intervention without going to the extreme of 'trying to right every wrong that we see in the modern world, in which case we would do little else than interfere in the affairs of other countries'.

The first four considerations are to my mind broadly acceptable. The fifth, about the existence of national interest, is an attempt to offset the first four by more hard-headed considerations which could limit the degree of intervention. But there is some obfuscation on what national interest means. The Prime Minister interpreted it to mean that the Kosovo atrocities and expulsions were 'taking place in such a combustible part of Europe'. An alternative justification is that we have a special sympathy for people who are geographically close to us and with whom we can identify – but unfortunately this would not have been regarded as a 'politically correct' way of putting the matter.

Test cases

Let me try to draw some tentative conclusions about recent events. It is far too early to say anything final; and in any case I am not enough of a Balkan expert — and still less of a military expert – for any convincing judgements on the Kosovo war. [It still is $4^{1}/_{2}$ years later.] What I would really like to do is to offer a sort of template which could have been helpful at the time and which might help in judging other situations.

Let me start by saying that the murder and torture of ethnic Albanians in Kosovo was an international crime. If one were looking at the pre-history of the episode, the real Nato blunder was not to intervene much earlier, after Milošević started his campaign against Kosovan Albanians. It was the failure to act then which made the Serb leader suppose that he could get away with it and also led to the shift of support from the earlier moderate Kosovan leadership to the KLA guerrillas. I wish I could suppress the thought that these errors of timing had more to do with President Bill Clinton's domestic political agenda than with faulty Balkan intelligence.

But we need to tread carefully here. Earlier American blunders were water under the bridge: and continued US unwillingness to risk lives was a hard fact which the British Prime Minister was told in the strongest possible terms to take as given. Accepting this background, I will take a sample of the common objections to the military campaign, not in any particular order, and indicate what I think their force to be. The most basic objection is that governments should not interfere in the internal affairs of other countries. I have dealt with this earlier. It is a good rule of thumb. But it is not an absolute principle and can have exceptions. We have the word of UN Secretary General Kofi Annan that 'nothing in the UN charter precludes a recognition that there are rights beyond borders'.[4] If we are very confident that the suffering resulting from turning aside is greater than that of involvement – even when putting a higher value on our own fellow nationals – then the rule of thumb should be suspended.

But in making the assessments we have to allow for the damage done to the presumption in favour of non-interference and the danger that the intervention would encourage a crusading mentality in which various demagogues felt free to disrupt the peace of the world in the pursuit of their own proclaimed views of political justice. Intervention by regional blocs such as Nato has the advantage of bypassing the Security Council's veto, but has the danger in Annan's words 'of setting dangerous precedents for further interventions without a clear criterion to decide who might invoke these precedents and in what circumstances'. A more convincing principle is that we should not attempt to impose by force our own systems of western democracy on countries that reject them or are not ready for them. But what was at stake in Kosovo was not the absence of elections or free speech but a reign of terror over a whole ethnic group.

'No national interest was involved.' The Prime Minister obviously thought there was. Former Yugoslavia is opposite Italy, a founding member of both Nato and the European Union. If Milošević had been allowed a triumph first in Bosnia and then in Kosovo, his destabilizing influence could well have penetrated into western Europe. But my argument does not depend on Blair being right on this point. Even if we want to say, for the sake of argument, that there was no national interest at stake, that still does not give us leave to turn the other cheek. (Incidentally, it is entirely in accordance with what I have been saying about successive circles of obligation that Australia took the lead in East Timor just as western European countries should have done in the former Yugoslavia. The heavy American involvement came from the inability of the European Union countries to get their act together.)

The anti-interventionist argument that instinctively appeals to me most strongly is that there is so often an element of hypocrisy. East

Timor is perhaps a better example here than Kosovo. One of the most forceful comments I saw was a cartoon in *The Times* in which Tony Blair says 'We need a hawk. Here is one.' And he was shown piloting one of the Hawk aircraft which the UK had been sending to Indonesia for many years for the use of General Suharto, the unscrupulous dictator of Indonesia. As Amnesty International put it in a masterful piece of understatement: 'Despite the leadership of the Prime Minister...the Department of Trade and Industry, in particular, is not meeting its responsibility to promote trade in a manner which is not harmful to human rights.'

Such arms sales are utterly wrong. Perhaps it takes a market economist to realize that it is not even a regrettable necessity to safeguard British jobs. At this point I have to suppress my emotions. We need to make a distinction between our judgement of people and our judgement of actions. It is a distinction that I have only begun to appreciate properly in the course of preparing this lecture. The sale of arms to dubious dictatorships was a stain on the record of the previous government. Their continuation is a stain on the record of the present government, and one that is particularly difficult to take calmly after all the talk of an ethical foreign policy. But bygones are forever bygones. It would be far far better if Indonesian forces did not have British or any other western arms to shoot down opponents. We are where we are; and the question is whether more net harm or good is done by sending in an armed peacekeeping force.

The charge of hypocrisy is a valid reason for not embarking on a conflict, only if the hypocrisy relates to the effects of the action itself. It is for this reason that I am completely unrepentant about having opposed the Vietnam war. It was supposed to prevent a communist takeover of south-east Asia. Yet the only legitimate reason for using military force against communism was the suppression of human rights. The political or economic system of former Indo-China was the business of the inhabitants. In fact, so far from protecting human rights, the American forces propped up a corrupt dictatorship, which inflicted as much harm as the communists did; and in the course of the action villages were burnt, forests set on fire and atrocities committed, the total impact of which was in my view much more harmful than allowing a communist regime to take over – which, in any case, the war did not prevent from happening.

One instance of alleged hypocrisy is that there has been no intervention in Chechnya, where to assert the abstract principle of established national boundaries, and to prevent secession, thousands of civilians have been killed; but this is now justified even by moderate Russians as comparable to the Nato war against Serb terrorism. As the historian Norman Davies has remarked: 'After a decent interval the liberators of Chechnya can expected to be feted at Buckingham Palace like the liberators of Tibet.'[5]

The support that the West insisted on giving to the Yeltsin regime when it was long past its moral sell-by date well illustrates Cobden's dictum against ignorant involvement. Nevertheless it would not be possible to intervene in conflicts such as Chechnya without risking a Third World War – which is the reason General Sir Michael Jackson rightly gave for disobeying an order to remove the Russians from the airfield in Pristina at the end of the Kosovo campaign. But without going that far it would be possible for the West to stop treating the Russian regime as a friendly one, to whose misdeeds we can turn a blind eye. At the very least, while actions such as the Chechnya war continue, all western aid for that regime should be suspended – including aid from the IMF and World Bank, which in this case is just a front for American involvement.

The kid-glove treatment of the Yeltsin [and later Putin] regimes is an example of the biggest single error of western foreign policy since the fall of the Berlin Wall. This is to pick out a particular regime to back, as happened with Gorbachev and has continued with his successors. How much better would be a degree of disengagement; and if international organizations have to make decisions, for instance in the dispersement of aid, they should be based on clear principles rather than keeping in office favoured individuals.

I am more uneasy about the lack of decisive action in Rwanda, where far more people were probably killed than in any other of the cases. At least 100,000 people – nearly all civilians – were killed in the town of Butare alone in April and May 1994.[6] As they say in the playground, two wrongs do not make a right. The failure of the West to intervene in Rwanda – explained but not excused by an earlier US humiliation in Somalia – was not an argument for continuing the neglect in East Timor or Kosovo.

'The British bore a disproportionate share of the responsibilities and risks compared with other Europeans.' This cannot be decisive. The Good Samaritan in the familiar story could have said that he was taking too many risks in helping the man who had fallen among thieves and that others should have shared the burden. So they should have. But this does not make the Samaritan's act a mistake.

'The unwillingness of the Americans, without whom the action could not have taken place, to risk any serious casualties.' Early in this lecture I risked offending more rigorous moralists by saying that it was reasonable to put a greater weight on one's own circle than on those more distant from us. But this does not justify a zero weight on the lives of either Kosovans or Serbs. The US unwillingness to launch a land war in Kosovo probably did result in a prolongation of the conflict and a greater number of casualties, even though they were not Allied ones. The mass bombing of Serbia and the inevitable civilian suffering were a partial substitute for a land campaign.

To my mind there is only one genuine objection to the Kosovo undertaking. This is that it caused more suffering than it prevented. According to one of the most thorough studies of the war so far, 'had Nato not bombed, Yugoslav president Slobodan Milošević still would have moved against the Albanian population (as he had the previous year), but the Serbians might not have accelerated the killing or expanded their deadly reach to so many communities for fear of provoking Nato intervention.'[7] Exposure of the myths about mass graves should not lead us to minimize the extent of Serbian atrocities both before and after the Nato bombing. The head of the Spanish forensic team attached to the International Crime Tribunal, Emilo Perez Pujol, has frequently been quoted saying that he found a total of 187 bodies; but he did estimate that 2,500 Kosovans were killed altogether by Serb action – below the upper limit previously mentioned. John Pilger has probably got it right when he says that 'the numbers of dead so far confirmed suggest that the Nato bombing provoked a wave of random brutality, murders and expulsions, a far cry from genocide'.[8]

Nor can we ignore Serbian casualties. The Economist Intelligence Unit reported that Nato, during its eleven-week bombardment, produced an estimated death toll of 1,500 civilian deaths and 8,000 wounded. At least 450 of the deaths were due to admitted Nato mistakes. In addition there were the civilian casualties in Kosovo due to unexploded cluster bombs, estimated by *The Times* to number 14,000. In the first month after the bombing ceased such bombs are estimated to have killed or maimed an average of five persons a day. It is indeed possible that Nato killed more innocent civilians on both sides than the Serbs did.[9] As Davies has said: 'The smart way to wage wars these days is to ... bomb and blast the adversary from heights where tanks cannot be distinguished from tractors and Chinese embassies can be mistaken for command posts ... Sooner or later, one can claim victory amidst a sea of rubble and refugees.'[10]

While questions of cost should not be decisive when human rights are involved, it is at least worth noting an estimate of the cost of the war at almost $100bn. Of this some $60bn was accounted for by economic damage to Serbia. This means that the war cost the equivalent of $50,000 for every inhabitant of Kosovo.[11] A subsidiary question is whether the Kosovan Albanians wanted Allied intervention. My impression is that most of them did, despite the additional suffering. But this cannot be decisive. If you are going to take risks with your own life to prevent harm, you must be the judge of whether you are preventing it or not.

The question in Kosovo was: could the result have been reasonably expected beforehand? We are told that elements in the US government really did believe that Milošević would surrender after a few days of bombing. As we know from discussions of accidents in Britain, failure to brief oneself adequately, when human lives are at stake, is indeed culpable. For what it is worth, I never thought myself that a few days of bombing would be enough and was indeed surprised that Milošević retreated when he did; and the possibility, even if not the probability that the Americans might land after all was at least one factor in his final decision.

The Pinochet precedent

Let me come to a last uncomfortable example. For a long time General Pinochet could not be tried in Chile because of the settlement which restored democracy and civil rights to that country. One aspect of this was that neither right nor left would try to settle old scores. Did that give the authorities of any other country the right to try the general? In this specific case a Spanish judge applied to extradite him from the UK because of atrocities alleged to have been committed on Spanish citizens in Chile during his period in office.

I feel tempted to say it is a very good principle that anyone who believes that he may achieve his ends by torture should know that he cannot rely on being safe from justice wherever he goes in the world. The attraction should not lie in the pleasure at the thought of punishment but in the deterrent effect it might have on anyone contemplating atrocities in future.

Let me give another example of how the principle might work. Terrorist thugs have been let out of jail in Northern Ireland because the government believes that, however distasteful the process, it will help bring about a settlement which will lead to fewer killings and other outrages in future. Governments have always negotiated with terrorists, whatever they say to the contrary. Suppose, however – as is perfectly possible – that some of the Ulster victims were Australian nationals and one of the terrorists was rash enough to go to France. The principle would then suggest that, although the British government has decided to let bygones be bygones, the French should be prepared to extradite him to Australia. My own inclination would be to accept this implication. But we need to think this through carefully together with any other difficult implications.

Provisional conclusion

What I have been attempting to do in this paper is not to provide a cut and dried answer to every problem, but to suggest a few guidelines to aid the exercise of judgement.

I started off by querying one popular form of the golden rule: that we should love our neighbour as ourselves. Most attempts to follow it in practice lead to a very narrow definition of 'Who is my neighbour?', which only reinforces group conflicts and the terrible crimes committed in their name. It would be just as moral to say that we should have some regard for the interests of others, although this cannot be as much as for ourselves, our families, our immediate circle and our own nation.

I have rejected the metaphysical principle that foreign policy can have no concern with human rights or any other matters affecting the well-being of non-nationals. There is, however, a pragmatic argument for thinking many times before we try to introduce justice into the affairs of other people. This is simply that – even assuming our leaders are always well intentioned – they do not know enough to do so and the result is often more misery than following a presumption in favour of non-intervention. I do not know what has done more harm: the belief in the inviolability of national sovereignty, or the moralistic urge to intervene when we do not know what we are doing.

But a presumption is only a presumption. It can be overthrown by sufficiently compelling circumstances, such as genocide in Nazi Germany, and in the 1990s in the Balkans or Indonesia. My personal view is that the first priority in foreign policy, as in many other matters, is the negative utilitarian principle 'Do not do harm.' Let us start by putting a stop to the worst of British arms sales and refrain from entertaining at a royal level leaders of unsavoury dictatorships. If we did make a start here, we might then be in a better position to appreciate those occasions when carefully considered intervention might do some good.

Appendix: Ethical argument

How can one even begin to analyse ethical matters? The greatest of British philosophers, David Hume, explained that no proposition about what ought to be the case can follow from a statement about what is the case – or for that matter from any purely logical demonstration. How nevertheless can we argue about moral issues? This subject has been almost the main topic of academic moral philosophy for a century or more; and it would be impertinent for me to even attempt a definitive answer in this appendix. All I can try to do is to give a brief idea of how I have attempted to grapple with the problem myself.

The honest response might be to echo an Australian philosopher, who began his case for utilitarianism by saying 'I propose to rely on my own moral consciousness and to appeal to your moral consciousness...'[12] But one can try to be a little more persuasive! In the first place, statements of moral beliefs have to be embodied in language, which often traps people into stating more or less than what they really believe. My favourite example is adapted from Amartya Sen.[13] He takes the apparently highly liberal and humane attitude that people should be allowed to dress as they like. But supposing that certain forms of dress in certain places cause onlookers to faint and become violently ill – not necessarily such a far-fetched assumption? In that case most of us would wish to qualify, not our basic beliefs, but rash statements which appear to embody them.

There are everyday precepts of morality such as 'Do not lie' or 'Keep promises'. These are highly useful in benefiting our fellow human beings and making social life possible. Nevertheless there are all too many misguided people (including philosophers known as deontologists) who believe that such principles have to be followed to the bitter end irrespective of the suffering they inflict. Their motto is: 'Let justice prevail though the heavens fall.' Yet most of us know on reflection that there are occasions when telling a lie or breaking a promise is the lesser evil. In my biased view more evil is produced by those who believe there are objective moral values 'out there' than those who accept that moral judgements are inevitably subjective. The fact that we have to make up our own minds makes moral issues more serious rather than less.

There is yet another way of arguing about morality, which needs to be approached with great caution. This is the biological perspective. That is to examine human morality, not as it should be but as it is, and the function it serves in promoting the survival not so much of the species as of the gene. The tendency of evolutionary psychology is to suggest that human beings, like most other species of mammal, possess a limited degree of altruism. The antelope that stands on a piece of high ground to alert members of his flock to the arrival of predators, and thereby puts himself at risk, is nevertheless promoting the survival of the gene pool to which he belongs. The biologist J. B. S. Haldane once said that he should be willing to die to save eight first cousins who between them would encompass equivalent genetic material.

This approach needs to be used with care, because we still know all too little about the essentials of human nature and how behaviour can be modified by culture. We are logically at liberty to reject the traits which most human beings exhibit most of the time as being immoral. But we will not get very far. Most moral values would be better promoted if we accepted, even as a second best, behaviour which it would be realistic to expect human beings to conform to in some circumstances or other.

Notes

1. S. Brittan, "Morality and Foreign Policy", 1957. Reprinted as appendix in *A Restatement of Economic Liberalism*, Macmillan, 1988.
2. George F. Kennan, *The Realities of American Foreign Policy*, Oxford, 1954.
3. H. Butterfield, *Christianity, Diplomacy and War*, Epworth Press, 1954.
4. Kofi Annan, 'Two Concepts of Sovereignty', *The Economist*, 18 September 1999.
5. *The Spectator*, 12 November 1999.
6. *The Times*, 16 November 1999.
7. I. H. Daalder and M. E. O'Hanlon, 'Unlearning the Lessons of Kosovo', *Foreign Policy*, Washington DC, Fall 1999.
8. *New Statesman*, 12 November 1999.
9. Economist Intelligence Unit, Yugoslavia (Serbia-Montenegro) *Country Reports*, third quarter 1999.
10. *The Spectator*, 12 November 1999.
11. Op. cit.
12. J. C. Smart, 'Extreme and Restricted Forms of Utilitarianism', *Philosophical Quarterly*, vol. 6, 1956. Reprinted in *Theories of Ethics* (ed. Philippa Foot), Oxford University Press, 1967.
13 A. K. Sen, *Collective Choice and Social Welfare*, Holden Day, San Francisco, 1970.

The Flaw in the UN

Financial Times, 6 December 2002

In a few weeks' time a decision will have to be made on whether Iraq has complied with UN resolutions on disclosing and eliminating weapons of mass destruction or whether an invasion should be mounted to force it to do so. I have previously questioned whether Saddam Hussein was a sufficient threat to western interests to justify a war against Iraq . But that is not now the issue. On the pessimistic assumption that he is not seen to comply with the disarmament requirements there will be an attempt to push through another Security Council resolution permitting invasion, and in practice to enforce a regime change. A lot of arm-twisting and unedifying bargaining will go on to try to secure such a majority. But suppose that the USA fails in this, either because it cannot secure a sufficient majority or because one or more of the Great Powers exerts a veto? Public opinion then is likely to divide two ways: support for US or Anglo-US unilateralism versus 'Nothing without the UN'.

Both positions are deeply flawed and there really is here a third way. The critics of the Bush administration are right to say that the US should not throw its weight around to dispose of any regime in the world to which it takes a dislike or regards as a threat. But that does not mean that any action needs to fulfil the technical requirements of a UN vote. I am not referring to the arcane legal dispute about whether the original UN resolution provides adequate cover for an invasion. The more important point is that the UN organization is far from providing a satisfactory system of international law. There is a General Assembly which consists of nearly 200 countries, operating on the absurd system of one vote each for China and India, which have around a billion people each, and one vote also for Andorra, Antigua, Dominica, Grenada, Liechtenstein, the Marshall Islands, Monaco, Palau, St Kitts, San Marino, Seychelles and Vanuatu, all of which have under 100,000 inhabitants. An idea of its quality can be gained from the fact that Libya has been nominated to take over the chair of the UN Human Rights Commission. The fifteen-country Security Council, which does contain the Great Powers – except anachronistically those that were defeated in the Second World War – at least gives more weight to the larger countries and is ultimately more democratic as well as a more realistic reflection of power patterns.

But even that is hardly an international court of justice. It consists rather of a number of governments jockeying for position. They are, moreover, governments which often have interests at stake within an area of dispute. It is as if the US Supreme Court or the British High Court were selected not from highly qualified judges but from the heads of local government bodies. This scepticism about UN resolutions is not just a way of rationalizing force. Looking at a post-mortem I wrote on the Anglo-French Suez expedition, from a position of extreme hostility to that venture, I wrote that Labour and Liberal spokesmen put too much weight on particular UN resolutions rather than the general moral and strategic case.

I want to avoid misunderstanding. The UN is the only UN we have. If action is to be taken in Iraq it should certainly be put through the Security Council and it will be better if the Council approves. But in the last resort what matters are two features. First, action taken must accord with the general body of law, custom and approved behaviour which exists, in however tenuous a form, among countries even in the absence of a world government. Laws and resolutions are too rigid a terminology to describe the tentative gropings that the world has made towards an improved standard of international behaviour.

The rules we should do well to observe are related to UN principles, more than to UN votes. They are in nature midway between legal and customary restraints. They are important insofar that they provide an approximation to the rules of the game which governments endeavour to observe, although often with much backsliding in their actual conduct. It is particularly difficult to apply this body of thinking now, as the evolved body of international doctrine does not cover the case of pre-emptive wars which can hardly be ruled out a priori in a terrorist-ridden world.

This makes a second feature all the more important. That is to try for some kind of international consensus. This could not embrace the whole world any more than it did in the case of Kosovo or Bosnia. But it does have to be large enough to embrace countries outside the normal US ambit – in other words, much more than Tony Blair's UK. In the case of former Yugoslavia, Nato provided a degree of international sanction for intervention. General Wesley Clark, who commanded the Kosovo operation, believes that the labour of trying to get nineteen Nato members to agree to each new military strike in the Kosovo operation was well worthwhile, however irritating at the time. He stresses that every decision also generates pressure to agree. Greece, for example, never blocked a Nato action, although its people strongly opposed the war and the Greek government maintained a certain distance from operations. He believes that it is still not too late to enlist Nato in the fight against terrorism, to handle peacekeeping duties in Afghanistan, and to deepen its involvement in the fight against the proliferation of weapons of mass destruction.

The legalistic course of going by the letter of the UN Charter and Security Council votes is not necessarily the more moral or humane one. The US has already soft-pedalled its concern for the war in Chechnya and the suppression of Tibet for the sake of the Soviet and Chinese votes, or to avoid their vetoes. Is that really more moral than trying to secure a coalition of the willing, provided that that coalition embraces a sufficient number of countries with otherwise differing creeds and interests and is not confined to the US and the UK? In any case, making one's attitude to a war in Iraq or anywhere else depend on the vagaries of the UN vote is a sheer cop-out. I might be tempted to call it democracy run mad, except that it isn't even democracy.

An Inquest on the 'Terrible Twentieth Century'

Review of *Humanity: A Moral History of the 20th century* by
Jonathan Glover (Jonathan Cape, 1999)
Prospect, January 2000

'It is almost certain that, as you read this sentence, in some places
people are being killed and in others people are being tortured.' This
reflection may not be the most cheerful one with which to embark on
a new century, but it is all too realistic.

There have been many accounts of horrors of particular regimes or
episodes in the twentieth century, of which the best-known are the
mass killings of Hitler, Stalin and – as more people are forcing
themselves to admit – Mao in China, as well, of course, as Pol Pot in
Cambodia. It is all too easy to concentrate on whichever of these
episodes fits our political prejudices. One virtue of Jonathan Glover's
new book is that it is too wide-ranging to allow the reader such as
easy escape. Above all, he reminds us of unnecessary suffering and
killing emanating not just from these demonized regimes but from
what may be loosely called 'our own side'.

The author is not a pacifist. But he does make us realize that the
horrifying trench warfare on the Somme of the First World War was
not an unavoidable or unforeseeable by-product of the conflict, but
the results of a cold-blooded indifference to the human consequences
by the British officer class. One of the few to protest against so much
killing for so little purpose was Winston Churchill, whose memorandum was greeted with a rebuke from that awful authoritarian, King
George V. The same applies to offensives such as Passchendaele in
which 300,000 British and 200,000 German soldiers were killed or
wounded to gain a small amount of ground.

Then there was the blockade of Germany which continued until
March 1919, months after the end of the fighting and which led to
many deaths from starvation. Again it was Churchill who dissented
and wrote: 'These bitter experiences stripped their conquerors in
German eyes of all credentials except those of force.' The year 1919
was also saw General Dyer's massacre of 500–1,000 peaceful

demonstrators at Amritsar in India. This was only the worst of the 'fancy punishments' he and his fellow officers prescribed. Yet another example was the continued mass bombing of civilians in German cities by Air Marshal Sir Arthur Harris long after the Normandy landings when the Second World War was clearly in its closing phase. Later in the century there was the massacre by American forces of civilians in the village of My Lai in the Vietnam war. This was not an isolated incident but an all too likely outcome of the nature of that particular conflict.

Many of these episodes were accompanied by the 'cold joke'. An early example was the graffiti scrawled for Louis XVI to see before his execution, which were captioned 'Louis taking a cold bath in the air'. The killing of 2,000 people in Nantes around the same time was called 'the national bath'. But before dismissing these episodes as remote in time or space, how many of us cannot recall milder examples of such cold jokes in the playground or school or even in our own places of work?

Unfortunately Glover puts these shaming episodes from our own side fairly early on in the book. They would have had more impact if they had come near the end, just before the concluding chapters. In fact, the last historical episode analysed in detail is the Nazi Holocaust. Although there must be a new generation arising which still needs to be reminded of it, this lets the rest of us off far too easily.

Thus one arrives at a paradox. *Humanity: A Moral History of the 20th Century* is an imperfect book. Yet it is a book which as many people as possible ought to read. One never knows whether to blame authors or publishers for misleading titles. But the author does admit that it is far from a comprehensive moral history of the century just ended. As he himself writes: 'A more generous conception would also include changes in the family, in the way children are treated, and in the relations between men and women...It would also include attitudes to poverty, to sex, to animals, and to the environment.' Indeed, even in relation to the major man-made disasters, there is now probably more revulsion than there would have been in earlier centuries.

Yet such imperfections pale into insignificance compared with the substance covered. It is an indispensable work of reference. For instance, although I knew the substance of the material on the Holocaust, the Gulag and other Stalinist atrocities, much of the material on Mao was new to me; and it did clarify the story of Rwanda which has been treated so confusingly in the media.

There is also a novel analysis of two diplomatic episodes. The ineffectual attempts by governments to stop a European war after the assassination of the Austrian Archduke in Sarajevo in 1914 are compared with the statesmanship shown by Khrushchev and

Kennedy in handling the Cuban missile crisis of 1962. The author attributes the improvement to the impact on Kennedy of the briefings he received on the results of atomic warfare as he entered the White House and to the memories that Khrushchev had of the Second World War, which he was determined not to see repeated. But surely another factor was that the negotiations in 1962 were highly concentrated in the two capitals of Washington and Moscow, where there were clear lines of command. In 1914 not only was there a whole chain of countries linked in overlapping alliances, but in many of the key centres, including Berlin and Vienna, there was confusion and intrigue about who was in charge, which gave the military a chance to get into the saddle.

Not surprisingly the most valuable passages scattered throughout the book are on ethics itself. The author does not blame the events of what Churchill called 'this terrible twentieth century' solely on the decline of moral consciousness. On the contrary, he points out how over-rigid moral systems can themselves be the cause of harm. 'Those who led their countries into the First World War made an absolute out of a morality of national honour, regardless of the human consequences of obeying such a morality.' The US hawks of 1962 shared a similar absolutist view. This was in contrast to Jack Kennedy, who, after his briefings, remarked: 'And we call ourselves the human race.'

A sense of moral identity is only part of what is required. Franz Stangal, doing his duty at the Treblinka concentration camp, did not lack a sense of moral identity. Nor did Himmler when he said that SS men should not steal a single fur or watch from their victims. He speculates that many of the guilty men had a savage upbringing in the name of some rigid moral code. This was indeed true of Hitler and Stalin; and one suspects it was true of Dyer and the the First World War generals.

It is refreshing to see a philosopher, hailing from Oxford, avoiding the high-minded moral absolutism of so many Oxford philosophers over several generations. Glover supports John Rawls's idea of reflexive equilibrium in which moral principles are modified in relation to people's own feelings about humane and reasonable outcomes, and vice versa.

Human beings are creatures prone to group behaviour which can lead to great altruism and self-sacrifice towards fellow members combined with great callousness towards outsiders. Glover does have quite a lot to say about tribalism in this book; and he also reproduces the well-known analysis of tit-for-tat as a solution to a repeated series of prisoners' dilemmas. Yet his remarks on the human animal are scattered throughout the book and will not add much for those who have already dipped into existing popular evolutionary writing. Glover concludes by saying that twentieth-century wars, massacre

The Holocaust Industry

Review of *The Holocaust and Collective Memory: The American Experience* by Peter Novick (Bloomsbury, 2000) and *The Holocaust Industry: Reflections on the Exploitation of Jewish Suffering* by Norman G. Finkelstein (Verso, 2000) *Prospect*, November 2000

The horror felt at the Nazi crime of exterminating six million European Jews, simply because they were Jews, surely needs no explanation. The puzzling question is, in the words of Prof. Novick, 'Why now?' Why should so much more have been done to commemorate the Holocaust in the last twenty years than in the thirty-five years after the Second World War, when more of the survivors, and far more of their near relations, were still alive?

Norman Finkelstein is surely right to claim that commemoration has grown to the size of an industry with several thousand employees. Not only was a Holocaust museum inaugurated in the US by President Carter and subsidized by federal funds, but smaller versions have sprouted in many parts of the United States and a few in some other countries as well. Why do we not leave it to the genuine memorials on the spot? For instance, the Ninth Fort at the top of a green hill outside Kaunas, Lithuania. This was established by the Tsars, but is now mainly known as the place where the Nazis took tens of thousands of Jews and others to be shot. Against the skyline is a modern-style memorial of three jagged metallic pieces standing bare against the blue horizon. This is intrinsically more moving than anything that high-powered American publicity efforts can establish.

The two books have many themes in common. The authors often agree and Finkelstein acknowledges his indebtedness to Novick's research. Temperamentally I was more drawn to Novick's historical and philosophical reflections than I was to Finkelstein's two-fold indictment: of the state of Israel for using the Holocaust memories to drum up American support, and of Jewish representative organizations in America and their lawyers and advisers who have made a very good living out of their efforts to secure compensation and restitution from Germany, Switzerland, Austria and other countries. He understandably contrasts the $3,500 which his mother received in compensation immediately after the Second World War with the large sums obtained by those now leading or representing American Jewish organizations. But to discuss his angry accusations fairly and effectively one would need to know about the intricacies and in-fighting among American Jewish organizations and personalities. Alternatively, one would have to have knowledge and strong views about the minutiae of the Arab–Israeli conflict. On the latter I am not prepared to go beyond saying that the Israel 'doves' who would make concessions to attain an honourable peace settlement are acting in the best interests of Israel as well as the wider international community.

Neither writer can really tell us 'Why now?' Even if all Finkelstein's accusations are true, this does not explain why the evocation of the Holocaust did not take place over half a century ago. Indeed, although my own maternal grandmother and her family were killed by the Nazis, I do not remember the word 'Holocaust' coming into circulation until several decades later. Novick, as a good historian, knows that he cannot give a simple historical monocausal explanation of this or any other puzzling phenomenon. What he gives us is an illuminating partial history of organized American Jewry from the Second World War onwards, with attitudes to the Holocaust as its main focus. My own cynical view is that American presidents can now safely wax indignant because not only is the massacre of European Jewry a long distant event about which they are not called on to take any action; but so are many of its immediate consequences, such as the problem of the displaced persons who emerged from the camps and the arguments about whether to establish a Jewish state in Palestine.

Interestingly enough, Zionist leaders were initially very cautious about making too much of the problems of displaced persons, who found so many parts of the civilized world closed to them. For the fear was that if America or Britain or other western countries opened their doors wider the displaced would be less inclined to go to what was then Palestine, and the argument for establishing Israel as a state or refuge would be weakened. An additional factor – which perhaps both authors emphasize a little too much – is that when, at the height of the Cold War, when American leaders were concerned to enlist the German Federal Republic as an ally, they did not choose to dwell on Nazi crimes. In my own precocious youth I can remember being opposed to German rearmament – not because of the Holocaust but because I thought it a sin to snuff out the anti-militarist reaction that had developed in Germany in order to secure a few extra divisions which would, in any case, be of little use against an all-out Soviet attack.

In the early postwar years, Nato politics were not the only factor. Many of the concentration camp survivors wanted to rebuild their lives without dwelling on the past. Moreover, the emphasis was on Nazi barbarism which claimed many millions of other victims. Indeed, in the Second World War itself American Jews were anxious to rebut the accusation that the war had been entered into on their behalf. I myself could not imagine that the killings perpetrated by either side in a modern war could be justified by the usual disputes over frontiers and political regimes; and the only remotely plausible excuse for bombing German cities was that their rulers were responsible for barbarities extending far beyond any one ethnic group – as indeed they were, considering their treatment of the Roma, millions of civilians in the Slav countries and social democrats and trade unionists, not to speak of handicapped people in Germany itself.

According to Novick's account, the beginnings of the present focus on the Holocaust came during the Six-Day war of 1967. Although the Israelis won it and then secured their hold over the occupied territories, there was at the outset the fear that they might lose and that a new Holocaust would be perpetrated in the Middle East. The Yom Kippur war of 1973 was a shock of a different kind. Although the Israelis won, the unexpectedly good showing of the Arab countries made American Jews realize just how vulnerable even a strongly armed Israel was; and by this time American foreign policy had switched from fear of alienating Arab opinion to relying on Israel as one of its few dependable allies in the Middle East. In conversations both then and now, my Zionist friends have never ceased to emphasize how, for instance, German or Dutch Jews, who may have been remote from traditional observances and considered themselves solid citizens of their own country, were swept into the gas chambers. But, as Novick points out and a glance at a map of the Middle East will confirm, in today's world Israel is one of the places where Jews are least secure.

Subsequent events were not part of any coherent plot or story. The sensitivities of non-Jewish Americans were aroused by NBC's four-part series *Holocaust* in 1978, which was seen by a hundred million Americans. After that came the film *Schindler's List*, which reinforced the lessons. From then on events seem to have acquired a momentum of their own. In several American states the teaching of the Holocaust is compulsory; there are, as Novick remarks, many chairs in the subject and there is no early danger of it being forgotten. The impact of more recent events in the former Yugoslavia, in Rwanda and, a little earlier, the Pol Pot killings in Cambodia. pointed in two directions. It kept the propensity of human beings to genocide in the headlines; but it weakened Jewish claims to be unique victims.

An additional factor explaining the American Jewish emphasis on the Holocaust is the decay of traditional religious belief, the growth of intermarriage and the fading in many places of Zionist enthusiasm.

The Holocaust memories have thus emerged in the eye of the believer as the best available unifying factor to keep together the American Jewish community.

Both authors finds many aspects of the Holocaust industry distasteful. Novick's own views are given in his introduction: he does not pretend that they are 'lessons of history'. He notes that the cultivation of sacred relics of suffering is far more in the Christian than in the Jewish tradition. Both writers condemn the tendency to play down the suffering of millions of other victims of Hitler – and of Stalin and Mao for that matter. Yet those who query the uniqueness of Jewish suffering have been accused of being 'Holocaust deniers";
and legal actions have been taken over the matter.

Even while I write this, the British Home Secretary, Jack Straw, has been investigating whether 'Holocaust denial' should be an offence under British law. If it ever were to become an offence, there would soon be plausible demands by all kinds of other groups to make denial of their sufferings an equal offence. Before long the virtues of free speech and unimpaired historical enquiry would be cast aside in favour of the bogus virtue of the self-righteous, thus giving the philosophers of totalitarianism a posthumous victory.

PART TWO

Political Economy

How small, of all that human hearts endure,
That part which laws or kings can cause or cure.
Samuel Johnson, lines added to Goldsmith's *The Traveller*

Weapons Exports: The Bogus Moral Dilemma

World Economics, April–June 2003

Introduction

After Saddam Hussein invaded Kuwait in 1990, the arms-exporting governments belatedly realized that their weapons sales to his regime had been an enormous mistake. British equipment was used by Iraqi forces in 1991; and the French were unable to fly because Iraq's Mirage 2000 jets could not be easily distinguished from the French ones on radar screens. Indeed, ever since the Matrix Churchill arms for Iraq scandal and the subsequent Scott Report of 1996,[1] the attitude of western governments to arms exports has come under the microscope. After 1991 there was indeed an international embargo on arms exports to Saddam's regime. Nevertheless, rumours spread early in 2003 that a French company was supplying Iraq with spares for its Mirage jets and Gazelle helicopters. Fears that French troops would face forces using their own equipment may well have contributed to the French government's decision not to take part in the invasion, although other considerations were of course involved.

The belief of most heads of government, diplomats and business spokesmen is that it may be desirable to stop exports to dubious regimes; but that jobs and exports are at stake and a practical compromise has to be drawn between supporting a major industry and doing the right thing in foreign policy. There are indeed many occasions when an ethical policy is costly. We cannot all be heroes and a frequent human response is to strike some compromise between doing what is right and what is personally beneficial. Tragedy arises when the costs of

This article draws freely on a lecture published in the *Royal Society of Arts Journal*, August 2001, and, like the author's earlier work on this subject, has benefited from indispensable help by Paul Ingram of the British American Security Information Council.

an ethical approach are small or even negative, but we refuse to follow it out of a mistaken belief that they are horrendous. Official support for arms sales in the main western industrial economies is a prime example.

The circular flow

To understand the issue, it helps to stand back from the subject of arms and examine the basic fallacy of the common sense politician or businessman. This is to ignore the circular flow of income: a fundamental concept which many economists find too obvious to explain. The main idea is that there is a continuing flow of spending between final purchasers, the products which they buy and the incomes thereby generated, which in turn leads to still further purchases.

The process can be seen in the very first two tables of, for instance, the UK National Income Blue Book. This shows expenditure on consumption, government services, investment, exports and so on as one 'approach' to estimating gross domestic product. The second approach looks at the output produced. The third looks at the income generated in the process, which is overwhelmingly wages and salaries, but also includes profits and numerous miscellaneous items. These three approaches should all lead to the same total; and statistical discrepancies apart, they do. In the case of the UK, the result at the beginning of the twenty-first century is a gross domestic product of around £1,000bn per annum. There is a similar flow across the foreign exchanges. Here we have an outflow of spending on imports and on direct overseas investment as well as on portfolio purchases. There is an inflow from exports and inward investment. Under a floating exchange rate these two flows automatically balance.

Ignorance of the circular flow of income is probably the most important single source of perverse economic policies today. For instance, many alarmist writers worry about what will happen once China or India are able to produce cheaply vast quantities of products which are now made in the West. But few people go on to ask what the Chinese and Indians will do with their export earnings. Presumably they are selling these cheap goods to make a living and not to line their bank vaults with sterling, dollar or euro notes. (Even if they did, international payments would still balance, but by a more complicated route.)

'Lump of labour' fallacy

Similarly, it is frequently assumed that if Britain or France lose arms orders in pursuit of an 'ethical foreign policy', the workers in the arms industries would simply waste away in idleness. It is not asked whether there will be other purchases at home or abroad to make up the difference. Here is an extreme example of the widespread 'lump of labour' fallacy, which assumes that there is a fixed amount of work to be done in each industry and workers displaced by technological progress, or by a shift in demand away from their product, are doomed to the unemployment scrapheap.

The circular flow of income can be helped by sensible 'macro-economic' policies, such as efforts to maintain an adequate, but not excessive, flow of total spending. There are plenty of arguments about the relative roles of monetary and fiscal policy in providing this support and the form it should take. But the interested citizen needs to know mainly that there is, or can be, such a circular flow and there need be no fear of one country being undercut in everything by its competitors.

But suppose that there is a breakdown in this circular flow, whether on a large scale as in the Great Depression of the 1930s or on a modest scale as in the occasional recessions since the Second World War? Surely the remedy lies in general measures to boost total spending (in the jargon 'maintain aggregate demand') rather than to pump money into a few chosen industries whose leaders make most noise.

The root of the matter is the belief throughout the political and business establishments that exports are worthwhile for their own sake, irrespective of the terms on which they are sold and how much they have to be subsidized. It is for this reason that British prime ministers, whether Thatcher, Major or Blair, time and again come down against the Treasury in favour of controversial arms deals or dubious overseas capital projects.

Mercantilism

The balance of payments preoccupation goes back many centuries. Mercantilist writers in the sixteenth, seventeenth and eighteenth centuries campaigned for a favourable balance of trade and for an inflow of gold and silver. These writers were refuted as conclusively as anything can be in political economy by eighteenth-century members of the Scottish Enlightenment such as David Hume and Adam Smith. During the subsequent period of rapid world economic growth towards the end of the nineteenth century, huge current account surpluses and deficits built up, far greater than any of the imbalances which commentators have bemoaned in recent decades.

The origin of both the export drive and the reinvention of the so-called balance of payments problem was in the immediate postwar years when sterling, like many other currencies, was on a pegged exchange rate and also inconvertible. The financial policy regime was then one of suppressed inflation, which tended to spill over into the balance of payments, and which was held down by a mixture of controls and exchange rate overvaluation. It was, moreover, a world with strict restrictions over capital flows. These controls could not be severe enough to protect determined speculators from launching an attack on a suspect currency, but they were a deterrent to the regular flows of capital across borders which normally finance imbalances on current account. The post-Second World War generation of political and economic leaders was brought up on slogans and posters such as 'export or die', 'the dollar drive', and even on one occasion 'exporting is fun'.

By contrast, we are now back in a world of relatively free capital flows. There are bound to be large imbalances between countries with high savings ratios and relatively few investment outlets and other countries, such as the United States, which have had low savings but many investment opportunities. Moreover, we now have floating exchange rates. And advanced industrial countries with floating exchange rates need never have balance of payments problems. They may suffer from unwelcome downward pressure on their exchange rate due to financial markets' distrust of their policies or of fears about domestic inflation. If so, such fears should be tackled directly. In today's circumstances, export drives really amount to the diversion of public resources towards special interest groups under the guise of patriotic slogans.

The basic political and business fallacy is not to realize that exports, like investment, are a cost and not a benefit. If we could finance the imports that British citizens want to buy without any exports – say by interest-free loans from overseas on indefinite repayment terms – we would be better off. Of course, this would require a period of adjustment. But such adjustments are necessary after any kind of economic or industrial change. In the world as it is, exports are a waste of resources and serve no purpose if they are not paid for, or are paid for very late and on a heavily subsidized credit basis and with a strong political risk factor.

This is not the place for a long discussion of the euro. But even if the UK were to join, there would still be no balance of payments constraint. There would be no sterling parity to protect, as the pound would have been abolished; and so long as the European Central Bank and the Ecofin Council have the sense not to attempt to fix the euro exchange rate against other leading currencies like the dollar or the yen, the automatic balancing would take place at the euro level.

The 'York Report'

Does size make a difference? Of course it does. If a country is highly specialized in one class of products – say Hong Kong in textiles in the

1950s – then indeed a sudden closure of the market for this product would come as a shock and it would take time for workers and their supporting capital equipment to be relocated to their next best activities. This is the relevance of the empirical inquiries which have been made into the importance of arms sales for particular economies.

This article concentrates on the UK, on which I have more detailed information and which is one of the half dozen largest weapons exporters in the world; but similar arguments will certainly apply to other European countries such as France. The USA is more complicated. Its arms exports may indeed be the largest in the world, but it has a more flexible economy and a greater tradition of workers changing jobs or even moving geographically when the composition of demand changes. It is difficult to come by reliable figures on Russian weapons exports. The problem here is not necessarily their size, but the fact that the 'oligarchs' are more heavily involved than in most other sectors of the Russian economy. The greatest danger of an excessive concentration on arms exports, a reduction of which could lead to an adjustment burden, probably lies in the smaller former Soviet republics.

The magnitude of the British economy's dependence on the weapons business was recently investigated in some detail by a specialist group, including the chief economist of the Ministry of Defence. Its report was published in 2001 by the Centre for Defence Economics of York University.[2] Beforehand, the Ministry of Defence (MoD) was touting the report, which it expected would vindicate official support for British arms sales. Yet, despite a methodology which probably underestimated the subsidy provided by the Export Credits Guarantee Department (ECGD), the group concluded that the economic effects of halving UK arms sales would be relatively small and largely one-off.

According to the York Report, total defence export sales averaged £6bn per annum in constant 1999 prices at the end of the last century, or 2.6 per cent of all exports of goods and services. It also estimated that these had an average import content of 40 per cent. Defence exports also accounted for about 98,000 jobs or less than 0.4 per cent of total employment. For comparison, the study cited the net increase in total nationwide employment in the year 1999 alone as 284,000. The estimated number of engagements (that is, the gross number of people moving into jobs) during 1999 was nearly six million—sixty times defence export jobs.

The Report investigated a hypothetical 50 per cent halving of 'defence export jobs' as a proxy for a major policy change in this area. A halving of defence exports from recent levels would, it estimated, result in the loss of nearly 49,000 jobs in the defence sector and their replacement over a five-year period by around 67,000 new jobs, at somewhat lower wages, in civilian employment. The job loss is much less than the earlier loss of 150,000 jobs in this sector in the period from just before the end of the Cold War in 1985–6 to 1993–4. For comparison, 70,000 jobs were lost in metal manufacturing, and 180,000 in the coal industry between 1985 and 1993. I would add that the skills of coalminers are surely much more industry-specific than those used in weapons manufacture. Moreover, coalminers were surely much more heavily concentrated in specific districts. The Report suggested that the balance of argument about defence exports should 'depend mainly on non-economic considerations'.

The biggest quantitative difference of opinion was on the extent of government support and subsidies. A report by the Oxford Research Group and Saferworld estimated that there was a net subsidy to defence exports of £420m a year.[3] The York Report, on the other hand, estimated support in a range around £80m per annum, which it believed was slightly more than offset by items such as the contribution to the overhead costs of British weapons manufacture to provide a net benefit to the economy of around £140m or 0.16 per cent of GDP.

One bone of contention was the size of the offsetting benefits; but a much bigger difference was in the estimate for ECGD support (see Appendix). The main point, however, is that whether the direct cost of arms support slightly exceeds the benefits or slightly falls short of them, the amount is trivial in relation to a UK GDP of more than £1,000bn per annum, and supports the York conclusion that policy should be decided mainly on foreign policy and defence grounds.

When it saw how the report was shaping, the MoD ran a mile away from it. In the end it was published as a research paper by the University of York. The government left its response to the Defence Exports Services Organization – the part of the ministry that exists to sell arms – which cherry-picked among the findings to find reasons for continuing arms promotion as usual. For instance, it highlighted the total adjustment costs of around £1bn from the relocation of workers and the loss of shareholder capital in the arms industry. In fact, this sum was the cost spread over five years. As an annual average it amounted to 0.02 per cent of GDP. It is interesting that much of the pressure to support and subsidize British industry overseas comes from the Foreign Office and the Department of Trade and Industry – and does so from similar departments in other western countries. Yet it is the Treasury which has to take a view of the overall health of the economy which includes growth and employment; and the Treasury is against most of these projects. Indeed, it would have happily closed down the ECGD altogether. Unfortunately, it is all too often overruled in favour of departments that push specific interests.

There is only one respectable economic argument for trade intervention. This is to use a country's limited monopoly power as the sole seller of its own goods to improve the terms of trade on which its goods can exchange for imports. In any case, UK arms exports are such a small proportion of total UK exports that the terms of trade effects are tiny. The York Committee was prepared to contemplate adding another £1bn to its five-year adjustment cost bill to cover a temporary terms of trade loss due to the possible sterling depreciation and associated terms of trade loss required to replace lost arms exports. But it emphasized so much the 'speculative' and 'uncertain' nature of this effect that it looked as if it was divided over its existence.

There is, however, one other category of exports which has some similarities to arms. This is heavy capital projects, many of them involving schemes of a highly controversial nature and of dubious development value, but which are promoted by construction industries of western countries. They are illustrated by the Pergau Dam in Malaysia in the mid-1990s when the Conservative government overturned a publicly minuted reservation by the Permanent Secretary of the Department for Overseas Development and insisted on supporting credits for this dam. Over the most recent three years well over half of ECGD's total support has gone to defence exports and Airbus, which accounted respectively for 37 per cent and 25 per cent of its guarantees. An additional 18 per cent went to large power projects.

Table 1: One estimate of adjustment costs (£M in 1999 prices)

	1st year costs of 25% fall in exports (including multiplier effects)	Cumulative costs in MPV terms of 50% fall in exports (including multiplier effects)
Losses and gains to workers		
Defence workers	62–103	463–795
Other workers [benefits]	[12]–[17.5]	[280]–[437.5]
Multiplier effects	29–50	107–209
Net losses to UK shareholders		
Write-off and reduced profits	94	178
Multiplier effects	47	89
Exchequer		
Net loss of tax receipts and extra benefit payments	54–86.5	221–383
Net loss of receipts from shareholders	83	158
Total	357–446	134–1,357
Terms of trade	440	1,120
Total including terms of trade	797–886	2,054–2,495

Source: *The Government Costs and Benefits of UK Defence Experts*, Centre for Defence Economics, York, 2001.

One of the unstated arguments for going ahead with Pergau was that this would act as a sweetener to persuade the Malaysian government to buy other goods, including arms, from Britain. On the other hand, arms sales are justified because they are supposed to persuade governments that buy them to use British equipment in their capital projects. Thus one bad consequence is called in aid to support another; and Third World despots are encouraged to devote still more resources to military spending or prestige projects of dubious value.

The main contention

There are some who oppose all arms sales. But this is not a position open to anyone who supports Nato or any successor western defence organization. It would be absurd for each member of an alliance to try to make a full range of weapons, simply out of amour propre, when specialization would pay far better. In fact, the crying need is for more arms specialization among allied countries rather than less.

In 1998–9 the Ministry of Defence spent 13 per cent of its equipment budget on sixty-four co-operative equipment programmes involving nineteen partner nations. The most important of these, by far, were France, Germany, the USA, Italy and the Netherlands.[4] The Oxford Research Group study, drawing on the work of Keith Hartley, the defence economist, looked at a variety of ways in which the UK could maintain its alliances at lower cost. The key was to treat weapons, on the production and import side, like any other industry and to buy arms in the cheapest market. The greatest saving might come from a single European procurement agency. But I would not place too many hopes in this direction in view of the EU's disarray on foreign and defence policy. The most interesting option discussed by ORG was simply buying 'off the shelf', which it estimated would save nearly £4bn per annum.

Even before tackling the more general wastes of the export drive, we should make a start with overseas arms sales. These should not be subsidized or officially promoted in any way. Even where there are no subsidies, governments should be much stricter in enforcing bans on sales to dubious regimes. It should have been obvious even in the 1980s and in the context of the Iran–Iraq war, that the Saddam Hussein regime came under this category. There are strong arguments against export subsidies of any kind; but those for arms and heavy capital projects—which are often related—are a good place to start. Those who accept my thesis do not have to agree on which regimes are the most dubious. There is a pretty clear basic list of regimes that commit aggression, support terrorism or oppress large bodies of their own citizens; we can argue about how far the list should extend.

Subsidized credit for exports of arms or major capital goods have far worse effects than just the economic ones. Western nations are undoubtedly rich enough to waste some resources. As Adam Smith said, 'There is an awful lot of ruin in a nation.'

We cannot leave out of our account the enormous part that bribery plays in this trade. A forthcoming study by Joe Roeber concludes that: 'Because of the structure, complexity and capacity of the market, and above all, because of the secrecy that surrounds every aspect of its activities, the international arms trade is the most corrupt of all legal trades.' He asks: 'Can we justify bribing people to buy arms they may not need with money their taxpayers cannot afford, simply to inflate the number of jobs in a declining industry?'

Financial issues apart, there is surely something demeaning in using members of the royal family and Cabinet ministers to tout for arms sales abroad. In April 2002, Tony Blair squeezed in a lightning trip to Prague between a visit to the US to see President Bush in Texas and the Queen Mother's funeral. Its ostensible purpose was to discuss EU enlargement; but Downing Street made no attempt to deny that it was also concerned with the sale of twenty-four JAS-39 fighter planes made by a British-Swedish consortium, including BAE Systems. Unfortunately the public controversy, as in previous cases, concentrated on the nature of the links of the company with the Labour party rather than on the principle of the Prime Minister making such sales tours. Indeed, his spokesman emphasized, Thatcher-style, that he made 'no apology for promoting Britain and British business'. All these follies are supported by the myth that exports are valuable for their own sake, however small the return the British nation gets from them. Business lobbyists are able to persuade a succession of prime ministers, ranging from ultra-dry Conservatives to New Labour, that if the government does not support them, their overseas rivals will win the contracts instead.

We should follow the example of General de Gaulle. When he was told that if the French left Algeria the Russians would take their place, he replied, 'I wish them much joy of it.' The same applies to UK or other governments that want to throw away their national resources on projects which not only do not pay domestically, but which are detrimental to genuine Third World development.

The UK record

The recent UK record is not all bad. In July 1997 the then new British Foreign Secretary Robin Cook stated that the Labour government would 'not permit the sale of arms to regimes that might use them for internal repression'. It is the least he could have said after the arms for Iraq scandal.

The Blair government has fulfilled a 1997 election pledge to publish annual reports on the UK's strategic export controls. These have gradually improved in quality; and the third one, issued in July 2000, was described by Saferworld as 'the most transparent report published by any European country and one which offers a potential template for best practice throughout the EU'.[5] But even this latest report was criticised for failure to provide information on ultimate end users, the absence of summary information on licences refused, and lack of detailed information on actual deliveries, as distinct from licences.

The government inherited various international obligations such as membership of the 'Australia Group' of thirty countries aiming to discourage the proliferation of chemical and biological weapons. An international convention was reached in December 1997 banning the production and transfer of anti-personnel mines. This came too early to be attributed to the Labour government elected in the same year.

But the new government indeed took a lead in pressing for a European Union Code of Conduct on Arms Exports, which was agreed in June 1998. The Chancellor of the Exchequer, Gordon Brown, began the millennium by adding twenty-two new poor countries over and above the previous forty-one covered by the ban on export credits 'for unproductive expenditure'. Indonesia, however, remained off the banned list. And because the Chancellor's action was in the context of debt relief for poor countries, it did not affect Saudi Arabia, which recently accounted for close on 31 per cent of all ECGD's business. It is thus fair to say that there is still a long way to go. Amnesty International was also worried that the same department was responsible both for the licensing of arms sales and for their promotion.[6] A joint report of four House of Commons committees reiterated that a serious error of judgement was made in late 1998 and early 1999 in granting several open export licences for military equipment to the government of Zimbabwe, despite that government's heavy involvement in the fighting in the Congo and its domestic infringements of human rights. The same report urged considering a stricter interpretation of the arms embargo on China and also raised issues about licences for arms to other countries.[7]

Perhaps the worst example is that of the visits by Tony Blair and his foreign secretary Jack Straw to India both to discuss the Kashmir crisis and to try to clinch a $1bn Hawk deal that had been in negotiation for some years. The British government was obviously worried that India was also looking at Russian and Czech alternatives. Once again government spokesmen made 'no apologies for lobbying in support of the British defence industry', even though critics argued that the official sales pitch was at odds with Tony Blair's plea to his counterpart Atal Behari Vajpayee to reduce tension with Pakistan. India, large though it may be, is still a poor developing nation and there is no evidence that the UK Department for International Development (DFID) was allowed to decide whether the purchase of military hardware was a priority for Indian development.

Al Yamamah

There is a further category which is not overtly a subsidy, but is certainly a special arrangement. This is the very obscure Al Yamamah deal with Saudi Arabia under which weapons were bartered for oil. Full details have never been published, but a great deal of information has been collected in *The Arabian Connection*, published by the Campaign Against the Arms Trade, which is a useful source even for those who might not agree with all the objectives of the Campaign.[8]

The first Yamamah deal was negotiated in the middle to late 1980s and had its origin in the reluctance of the US Congress to sanction weapons exports to Saudi Arabia. American policies have fluctuated since then; but a second Yamamah agreement was negotiated in the late 1980s; and despite many difficulties it became operational in the early 1990s. Its biggest 'achievement' was to produce a market for the Tornado aircraft, which was said at one time to have 'saved' 19,000 jobs; and some would say that it saved BAE Systems itself.

The Labour government shows no sign of wanting to banish this kind of agreement, despite the distortions that the heavy investment in arms is producing in Saudi Arabia, the horrific human rights record of the country, and the basic instability of that regime. As for the argument about oil supplies, I have never seen why the US, Britain and France cannot – like other western countries – buy their oil on the international market, remembering that Middle Eastern countries often need to sell the oil even more urgently than we need to buy it.

Small arms

The problem, however, is not confined to officially supported exports of high technology equipment such as aircraft and missiles. It is most often small arms that have been used for domestic repression in the last decade – the vast majority of the victims have been civilians and most of them killed by small arms.

Clare Short's 2000 White Paper on International Development stated: 'Of the 40 poorest countries in the world, 24 are either in the midst of armed conflict or have only recently emerged from it. This problem is particularly acute in Africa...An estimated five million people have died.'[9] Sophisticated defenders of arms sales agree that there is a case for banning exports of small arms altogether except to the armed forces of western democratic states. For instance, Philip Towle argues that 'the profits Britain makes from this trade are very small' despite the benefits to some specialized manufacturers.[10]

The Scott Report of 1996 advocated legislation to put control on arms exports and arms brokering on a permanent non-emergency basis. The Labour government introduced such legislation to provide a licensing requirement for trafficking and brokering in arms between overseas countries. The legislation is undoubtedly a step forward. But there might still be loopholes if companies operate through overseas subsidiaries outside the control regime. Moreover, the government was still inhibited by two factors: its reluctance to move too far ahead of competitor countries, and its belief that small arms can legitimately be sent to official governments as distinct from so-called rebels.

Finally, I come to a question that I am often asked by friends in government circles. What additional measures would you like to see taken? Those who know more about the details of the arms trade than I do are best placed to advise on the specifics. But let me all the same end with a few suggestions.

1. DFID Intervention. One of the greatest safeguards against the irresponsible grant of licences for arms exports is the ability of the British Department for International Development (which it did not have under previous governments) to object to arms contracts on the basis that they are harmful to the recipient country's development. So far there is no known case where the UK government's criteria for sustainable development have prevented an arms export from being allowed.

2. Greater Transparency. Despite the improved UK Report on Strategic Exports, the criteria for approving them are still not clear. We need a list – covering military aircraft and dual use products as well as other arms – of countries to which complete bans apply, ones where there are no restrictions, and intermediate cases. In the latter, we need a clear statement of the criteria, covering the quantities and kind of arms which might be allowed. This recommendation involves moving away from the case by case basis which is dear to the hearts of so many government officials.

3. End subsidies. There should be absolutely no official export credit for arms exports of any kind. Even permitted exports in

uncontroversial cases should have to pay their way. The British government should lobby hard for such a ban internationally, but should not wait to take action itself.

4. Even unsubsidized arms sales should only be permitted to actual or potential allies.

5. Governments should use their influence on international aid organizations including the IMF, the World Bank, the EBRD and other regional banks on the following lines: (a) To take a much stricter line on excessive investment in military hardware at the expense of genuine development. To do this, these agencies would have to return to their original functions and cease to be arms of US and Nato diplomacy; (b) To insist on enforcement of a clampdown on small arms exports – other than in restricted and permitted categories – as a condition for receiving any aid at all.

6. Official export credit agencies such as ECGD, even when confined to civilian purposes, should pay a notional rate of return at the highest rate required for any other government agency. This follows on the recommendations by the economic consultants, NERA, for the ECGD.[11]

7. The ECGD itself should ultimately be abolished. This would appear common sense if the other steps were taken.

The most important thing is to keep going in the right direction in the face of the counterattacks to be expected by every kind of interest group and prejudiced viewpoint.

Notes

1. Report of the *Inquiry into the Export of Defence Equipment and Dual Use Goods to Iraq and Related Prosecutions*, HMSO, 1996.
2. *The Economic Costs and Benefits of UK Defence Exports*, Centre for Defence Economics, York, 2001.
3. *The Subsidy Trap*, Oxford Research Group and Saferworld, 2001.
4. *Maximizing the Benefits of Defence Equipment Co-operation*, Report by the Comptroller and Auditor General, March 2001.
5. 'Transparency and Accountability in European Arms Export Controls', Saferworld, December 2000.
6. *Human Rights Audit*, Amnesty International, 1999 and 2000.
7. 'Strategic Export Controls: Annual Report for 1999', HC 212, 6 March 2001.
8. *The Arabian Connection: The UK Arms Trade to Saudi Arabia*, Campaign Against the Arms Trade, 2001.
9. *Eliminating World Poverty: Making Globalization Work for the Poor*, Department for International Development, December 2000.

10. Philip Towle, *Ethics and the Arms Trade*, Institute of Economic Affairs, 2000.
11. *The Economic Rationale for the Public Provision of Export Credit Insurance*, ECGD, 2000 and 2003.

Appendix
ECGD Subsidies
by Paul Ingram, BASIC

In the words of the Export Credits Guarantee Department (ECGD) website, 'Our role is to help UK manufacturers and investors trade overseas by providing them with insurance and/or backing for finance to protect against non-payment.' Note that their mission is explicitly to help the exporters and investors, not the UK economy. They do this in several ways:

Buyer Credits and Supplier Credits (worth £1,185m in 2003–4); the Supplier Credit Insurance (worth £1,100m); protection provision of financing for the deal, with repayment terms, against payment default by the customer. Overseas Investment Insurance (worth £1,000m); security for UK investors in overseas projects £706m in 2003–4.

Fixed Rate Export Finance (FREF, worth $78m, £85m, €36.6m and ¥7,325m in 2003–4); guarantees on the exchange rate.

The claim made by the ECGD is that insurance available on the open market tends to be short term and weak in the 'emerging markets' (developing countries). This is true to the extent that the market that would be available is priced out by governments' subsidized export credit agencies (of which ECGD is one). With a portfolio capital base that dwarfs any government's, the international financial markets are perfectly able to provide spread insurance for exporters, at a price. But why go to the market if you can acquire the same cover for a much lower (subsidized) premium? It is this that is at the root of the debate raging at present between BASIC and the ECGD on how to account for the subsidies involved in the government's support for the ECGD. The different approaches can be summarized as follows:

The ECGD approach depends upon the concept of a lump of 'capital required' to back up the day-to-day operations of ECGD. This is often called the value-at-risk portfolio method. A notional rate of return to account for the cost of providing the necessary capital to back up the guarantees is added to the normal expenditure account. The problem with this method is choosing the appropriate rate of return (the ECGD understandably underestimated this at 6 per cent in 2002, when, for example, other government agencies may be required to return up to 13 per cent of capital invested), and identifying an appropriate value for the capital. It also does not account for what is called 'catastrophic risk', that is to say, the eventuality of many multiple defaults, perhaps caused by a general meltdown of the international economy in a region. Catastrophic risk is exactly the sort of circumstance the ECGD is designed to protect against, yet their methods of subsidy calculation take no account of this scenario.

Our approach seeks to measure the premium rates that the market would charge and compare them to those charged by ECGD. Our estimate of the total ECGD subsidy to arms exports in 2004 is £215m. This is a simple conceptual approach. As may be expected, there are several possible market mechanisms for taking on risk. In the case of arms exports, the customer is a recipient government, and governments issue bonds. Rates of return demanded by the market in the purchase of government bonds consist of two factors, the interest rate and the extra premium charged to account for the extra risk because of the particular government raising the finance. Comparing the bond rates with the dollar bond rate offered by the US government (deemed to be virtually risk-free) will determine the rate. Alternative market mechanisms may include options and credit derivative markets (where risks are traded explicitly). When such international finance mechanisms exist, questions are increasingly asked as to why the government is involved at all in distorting the market in the interests of a small number of arms exporters.

Paul Ingram is senior analyst at the British American Security Information Council. He is co-author, with Ian Davis, of *The Subsidy Trap: British Government Financial Support for Arms Exports and the Defence Industry* (Oxford Research Group and Saferworld, 2001).

The Globalization Argument

Evidence to House of Lords Committee, 15 January 2002
and *Financial Times*, 28 September 2000

Meaning of globalization

Globalization is usually used to refer to the free or freer movement of goods and services and also capital. It does not really mean anything different from an open integrated world economy. But such an economy ought also to involve the free movement of labour.

Globalization is certainly not a new phenomenon. In fact, capital movements in the main industrial centres were a higher proportion of GDP before the First World War than they are today. In the sense that I would like to use the word, there was also more globalization then, because movement of workers was relatively free.

Free trade and capital movements are supported by the so-called Washington Consensus which emerged around the early 1990s. This consensus arose largely as a result of the study of the varying experience of Third World countries and the lack of success of those that had tried to insulate themselves from the world economy, and devise, for instance, strategies of import substitution. The consensus was given a fresh wind by the collapse of the Soviet Union and its satellite regimes and the need to find ways of integrating these countries into the world economy. Nevertheless I do not think that the driving forces were mainly ideological. The framers of Bretton Woods envisaged a combination of trade liberalization and capital controls. But I doubt if it is possible to have free trade without relatively free capital movements. For once large payments across the exchanges are permitted for one purpose, it is difficult to stop them for other purposes. In exchange control days we had notorious 'leads and lags', which enabled international owners of capital to speculate against currencies which were overvalued. And if capital movements are going to take place in any case, why not admit them openly without having to resort to a complex set of loopholes?

Has the development of information technology added a new element – because any change in any part of the world can be viewed instantly on computer screens? Surely the bigger breakthroughs were made in the middle of the nineteenth century when we leapt from horse-drawn transport and sailing ships to the railways and transatlantic cable, which transmitted to the New York stock exchange news of the 1873 Vienna financial crash?

There is no particular difference between the way globalization affects the UK economy and other members of the G7. Both critics and supporters say that it makes it much more difficult to implement an independent economic policy or one which is disliked by those responsible for capital movements. In my view this is much exaggerated.

At the UK national level policies which made sense before the word globalization came into vogue make sense today, and policies which are vulnerable to adverse confidence movements today would have been nearly as vulnerable a few decades ago. Just to give two examples: extremely tight exchange and capital controls did not help Sir Stafford Cripps avoid devaluation in 1949. And the Labour government of the 1970s went through a notorious series of foreign exchange crises when international capital movements were at a much lower level than that of today's and when people spoke of liberalization rather than globalization. It is an exaggeration to talk about financial markets 'punishing' countries that pursue unorthodox financial policies. In fact they are merely asking for a higher nominal return to cover the risk of currency depreciation and debt repudiation.

A frequent complaint is that short-term transactions in the foreign exchange market far outweigh the amount directed to the finance of trade. But these very short-term transactions soon cancel each other out, sometimes within hours. In most of the cases where speculators appear to have brought down currencies, whether it was George Soros and sterling's departure from the ERM in 1992, or the crises in Latin American and Asian markets in the late 1990s, currencies were overvalued or artificially maintained.

Probably the main advantage of the free movement of all kinds of capital and not just direct investment is internal. A study by the US National Bureau of Economic Research suggests the cost to Malaysia of the recent controls may be not so much that foreign investors are wary of a repeat but that domestic financial institutions will merge in a non-transparent way during the period of control in a way that appears to favour the current political establishment.

Employment

Most advanced industrial countries are within reach of near full

employment. Their ability to get there depends partly on the level of
effective demand, but more fundamentally on the flexibility of labour
and product markets – in other words on people not pricing
themselves out of jobs. Developing countries on the other hand often
lack the capital equipment and business and social infrastructure
required to provide jobs for all. Anything which speeds up economic
development in these countries makes possible higher levels of
employment.

Effects on world economy

As Peter Jay has put it: 'The opportunity to combine capital and
labour, management, technology and markets in the most efficient
manner indubitably accelerates the growth and improves the
distribution of the prosperity of the globe as a whole.'[1] He adds, 'It is
an error in any way to regret what we have done and a misconception
to wish to recreate the predominant power of the autarchic nation
state in order to subdue the forces we have unleashed.'

Gainers and losers

Labour mobility ought to be part of a free and integrated world
economy. It would also be a powerful influence for narrowing
income differentials worldwide. If workers from North Africa could
migrate to European Mediterranean countries this would not only
increase the living standards for those who move. It would also help
those who stay at home by making labour scarcer than it otherwise
would have been.

Nearly all countries gain from the opening up of economic
frontiers. But within a particular advanced country those sectors
most directly open to competition from cheaper competitors – in
practice often unskilled labour – may lose relatively or even
absolutely. Such workers benefited in the past from the commercial
and political obstacles to large-scale investment in the developing
world, obstacles which imprisoned capital in the richer countries. As
a result of their removal the real price of low skilled labour may be
driven down. Differential impacts of this kind are best tackled by
redistribution via the tax and social security system and not by
erecting barriers to trade and capital movements.

Taken to its logical conclusion, completely free movement of
capital on its own or free movement of workers – let alone the two
together – might lead to an approximation of pay levels throughout
the world for particular types of labour. And so long as unskilled

labour remains plentiful worldwide this could lead to a drop in unskilled wages in advanced countries towards Third World levels. Evidence on the ground, however, indicates that such equalization is likely to happen, if at all, more slowly than the model indicates. This is suggested by studies of migrant workers in the UK who might be regarded as offering the most direct threats to indigenous workers.

Even in the extreme model, nearly all countries gain from the opening up of economic frontiers, but there is a shift in the distribution of income from unskilled labour in the industrial countries to the owners of capital, who presumably benefit from access to large supplies of cheap labour. The challenge will be, not how to isolate the home economy from global market forces, but how to recycle the income that should eventually be flooding in from the enhanced profitability of capital in its worldwide locations.

IMF and World Bank

The two major world economic institutions, the IMF and the World Bank, were created at a time when international transactions were mainly trade and when it was thought that capital movement should and could be controlled. In addition it was assumed that exchange rates would be fixed, but adjustable.

One of the IMF's jobs has traditionally been to supervise the setting of exchange rates to guard against policies such as competitive devaluation and – equally – to warn countries that were hanging onto overvalued exchange rates. Midnight oil was spent on matters such as defining a fundamental disequilibrium in a country's balance of payments. Much of this is now irrelevant.

In its early days IMF credits were an important part of the international capital resources available to a country in distress, especially one with a balance of payments deficit, and which helped to give it time to adjust. Nowadays IMF aid is a small proportion of the international credits available to governments that command confidence. IMF credits and standby facilities are much more a badge of good housekeeping to persuade private investors to support a country in temporary difficulties.

This task is made more difficult by the way in which the IMF is used for political purposes, especially by the USA. It has been too free in awarding its good housekeeping badge to countries which the USA wished to support – for example, Russia in the late 1990s, but possibly also Argentina in 2001. The USA is quite entitled to support countries or regimes for geopolitical reasons and to assemble international coalitions for this purpose. But it should do this on a government to government basis and not attempt to use international financial institutions as an instrument. One day there may be a managing director of the IMF courageous enough to assert the institution's independence.

As for the World Bank, the great expansion of international capital markets casts doubt over the World Bank's role in supporting international development. It has itself to borrow on international financial markets and all it can do is to provide a marginal amount of finance on marginally better terms. An apparently strange coalition of right and left recently emerged in the USA, urging that the World Bank should concentrate on poverty relief and on grants rather than loans. This shocked defenders of the international status quo. (The UK government will have nothing to do with it.) But I suspect that this rainbow coalition of critics is correct none the less.

If we believe that the free movement of goods and capital is beneficial, we should not focus so much on regulation. To a large extent excessive volatility in international capital markets arises because decisions are made by salaried employees in western countries who fear for their jobs unless they keep up with the herd, and who are therefore reluctant to stay away from bandwagons or to invest in unfashionable countries or sectors. The big problem for policy is how to help the victims of this instability without creating moral hazard which would encourage even more unthinking herd-like behaviour by investors.

Whatever one thinks of particular institutions and governments, the fact remains that the form of capitalism that has developed in the fifty-plus years since the Second World War has brought a bigger rise in worldwide living standards than anything seen before in the history of mankind. The first part of the period saw the freeing of trade and payments. The second part saw the rise of world capital markets on a scale not seen since 1914. One can argue about the timing of some policies – for example, whether capital account liberalization might have come too early for some countries. But the main thrust of the opponents of globalization is to say that the whole development has been wrong. The clearest rebuttal can be found in some information conveniently collected together in the winter 2000 issue of the *Journal of Economic Perspectives*.[2]

Richard Easterlin shows there growth rates since 1950. There is also a column giving the ratio of per capita gross domestic product at the end of the period to that at the beginning. This reveals that in the developed countries income per head in 1995 was three times as high as in 1950. The protesters may be surprised to learn that a ratio of almost three also applies to the less developed areas, with 80 per cent of the world's population. Sub-Saharan Africa, containing 11 per cent of the world's population, did not share in this prosperity. Here output per head at the end of the period was only 1.2 times as high as it had been in the beginning. This may have been due to bad luck, natural disasters or the way in which this part of the world has been governed. But it can hardly reflect on the international economic system, given what has happened elsewhere. Of course GDP per head can be a misleading guide to welfare; but Easterlin does have a close look at other indicators. Life expectancy, for instance, increased by more than twenty years in the less developed areas and even by twelve years in sub-Saharan Africa. Another index is adult literacy rates, which grew from 40 to 70 per cent in the less developed areas.

In the same issue of the journal there is a fascinating attempt by Professor Robert Lucas to look behind the growth numbers and speculate on what they might portend for the twenty-first century. He starts with the stylized fact that income per head in most of the world in about 1800 was in the neighbourhood of $600 at present dollar values. This is about the level that today brings out the anti-globalization protesters. But it is also the level at which the now advanced countries began; and if countries such as China and India are prevented from competing on the basis of their most favourable temporary asset – namely cheap labour – their whole development will be delayed. To be precise, if a 'decent wage' could be enforced in the emerging countries, then employment in their industries would be much smaller and a higher proportion of their population would be crowded into the subsistence or primitive agricultural sectors. Parity with the industrial West, instead of being approached by the end of the present century, could be postponed for a good many generations.

But to come back to Lucas: he assumes that one country takes off at a growth rate per head which averages about 2 per cent a year. This is followed by a series of further take-offs like a succession of rockets. His model cannot tell us which specific countries will take off at any particular time. But it does say that the probability of any country getting into a growth orbit depends on the distance between its own income levels and those of the leaders. Moreover, once a lagging country does get into orbit, it will temporarily grow faster than the leaders until it eventually catches up with them.

He mentions three possible reasons for this catch-up. One is that knowledge produced anywhere benefits everyone everywhere. The second is that the governments in the previously unsuccessful countries can adopt the institutions and policies of the successful ones. Third – and highly relevant to globalization – relatively high wages in the successful economies can lead to capital flows to emerging ones.

With these few stylized facts and bits of arithmetic, Lucas is able to come to some forceful conclusions. 'Sooner or later everyone will join the industrial revolution, all economies will grow at a rate common to the wealthiest economies and percentage differences in income levels will disappear.' As growth gets under way in the pioneering countries, the income gap between leaders and laggards ('the degree of inequality', if you insist) increases, reaching a maximum around the end of the twentieth century. But as more and more countries achieve developed status, income gaps start to narrow. Eventually we end up with most societies being roughly equal in income levels, as they were in 1800, but of course at much higher levels.

This story does not tell us much about the policies and institutions that produced growth. And it admittedly skates over short-term reverses and fluctuations due to wars, depressions or misgovernment. But it nevertheless gives an idea of what science and technology can deliver if only human institutions will allow them to do so. There is nothing inevitable about the process; and well-intentioned protest movements, which are radical about the wrong things, could bring this development down to a crawl.

Notes

1. Peter Jay, *Road to Riches*, Weidenfeld & Nicolson, 2000.
2. *Journal of Eonomic Perspectives*, Winter 2000, published by the American Economic Association, 2014 Broadway, Suite 305, Nashville, TN.

Let the Huddled Masses Go Free

Financial Times, 25 October 2001

For all the effect they have had on hostile opinion, the many books and articles showing the benefits of globalization might as well have been printed in invisible ink. Most people's reactions are based on their political prejudices or favourite newspapers.

What is needed is a dramatic gesture, which is worthwhile for its own sake and would demonstrate that the free movement of capital and labour is of benefit to the world's poor.

The trouble is that there is too little globalization rather than too much. There was far more economic free movement a century ago than there is today. The big difference is, of course, in migration policies. Many countries then allowed free inward and outward movement of labour. Today, migration is tightly restricted legally and, in practice, a focus of illegality and criminal violence. The resemblance to traditional drugs policy, where prohibition produces the very evils it claims to prevent, is all too obvious.

My proposal is to abolish the distinction between economic migrants and asylum-seekers – who in the UK are not permitted to work for the first six months and are provided with vouchers at sub-benefit levels – and allow anyone who so wishes to seek his or her fortune in any country of choice. This goes far beyond the ideas of David Blunkett, the Home Secretary, for merely extending the number of work permits.

Like nearly all economic liberalization, the free movement of labour would increase the world national income and would particularly benefit people in poorer countries, where even those who stayed behind would find a brisker demand for their services. Although the best results would be obtained at the lowest cost if this change were generally adopted, many western countries could move unilaterally.

Would there be any *quid pro quo*? Not as such. Recipient countries could impose a minimum qualifying period for state pensions. The main counterweight to liberal migration policy would be a relentless policy of exposure and punishment for anyone, irrespective of origin, who incited violence not merely against religious or racial groups but against any individuals, irrespective of the country in which they resided. Most human rights charters have provisions for amendment in emergencies.

The obvious European country to initiate a laissez-faire policy would be Ireland, which has a low population density and needs the safety valve of immigrant labour for a potentially overheated economy. But even the UK has a lower density than, say, the Netherlands, which is not obviously suffering from a low quality of life. Given the extreme hostility to immigration in Germany and Italy, a common European Union immigration policy is unthinkable except on highly restrictive lines; but one can live without it. It is hardly likely that immigrants will try to smuggle themselves from the UK and Ireland into some smoulderingly hostile German city.

The potential concession that an economic analyst has to make is that wages of workers competing with migrants could be relatively or even absolutely depressed. A high-quality and under-publicized research study[1] shows that native wages have not been depressed in the UK. Immigrants have tended to perform three types of job. They have worked in public services, especially health, where pay is determined by the government. Wages are well below market levels and the effect of newcomers is to reduce shortages. In London, 23 per cent of doctors and 47 per cent of nurses are non-UK born. At the other extreme, 'in relatively low paid and insecure sectors [such as] catering and domestic services, unskilled natives are simply unwilling or unable...to take the large number of available jobs...but it is not likely that natives are significantly disadvantaged: if migrants do not fill these jobs they simply go unfilled or uncreated'. An estimated 70 per cent of catering jobs are filled by migrants.

There are also the highly skilled information technology workers. According to the Home Office study, the inflow of these technicians has enabled the IT sector to grow faster rather than to depress pay in it. The study confirms that migrants are more polarized than the rest of the population, with larger concentrations of wealth and poverty and high and low skills. Not only are they highly concentrated in London and the south-east but there are also large clusters both in wealthy Kensington and in the impoverished East End. 'Levels of entrepreneurship in self-employment also appear to be high among migrants,' it adds. It is not only Pakistani and east African businesses that have been attracted to the UK: about 150,000 French entrepreneurs are said to have arrived since 1995.

In general, earnings behaviour follows what is known in the US as the 'assimilation hypothesis'. Wages in a particular age cohort start off lower for migrants but, as skills are acquired, eventually overtake those of comparable native workers. And, contrary to the popular view that immigrants are a burden on the public purse, they contribute 10 per cent more to government revenues than they receive in government expenditures.

The net effect of strict official restriction and feeble enforcement is, as one would expect, nightmarish conditions for those who depend on criminal gangs to enter the country. Harriet Sergeant, in *Welcome to the Asylum*,[2] explains how the process leads to 'slavery and child labour'. She advocates a government drive for better statistics and better control. But given that very few illegal immigrants are in fact sent back, the alternative laissez-faire policy might make surprisingly little difference to the net numbers but ensure that arrivals were recognized as human beings.

The present policy has reached a dead end. Why not try five years of laissez-faire, then review the strategy?

Notes

1. *Migration: An Economic and Social Analysis*, Home Office, 2001.
2. Centre for Policy Studies, 2001.

Time to Index the Retirement Age

Financial Times, 17 January 2003

Those whom the gods wish to destroy they first make mad. Most western countries face an ageing population. One would suppose that in these conditions governments would do their best to minimize the dependency ratio – that is, the ratio of dependants to the working population. In fact, they have done the opposite. Retirement ages have fallen. The proportion of younger people being 'educated' has risen and labour participation rates fallen.

An analysis in the December 2002 OECD *Economic Outlook* provides some fascinating insights. It starts off with a chart of participation and employment rates for workers aged 55 to 64. These both seem to cluster around 60 per cent. The worst showing comes from the core members of the European Union: Belgium, Italy, France and Germany. Nordic and English-speaking countries emerge rather better and best of all is Iceland.

Now look at the time series. The average effective retirement age in France fell from 64 years in 1970–75 to 59 years in the late 1990s. In West Germany it fell from 63 to 61. In the UK it has remained at 62, while in the US it has edged upwards to 65. Then look at it another way: employment rates of workers in the 55–64 age group. This was still 74 per cent in France in 1970. It is now 38 per cent. Even in the UK it has fallen to less than 60 per cent. At the same time life expectancy for men at retirement has risen dramatically.

If these changes were due just to people preferring to take out the fruits of economic growth in the form of a shorter working life, there would be nothing more to be said. But, as the OECD points out, there are perverse incentives. The French and German governments reacted to high unemployment by cutting hours, promoting early retirement and increasing holidays. This crudely arithmetical approach was the culmination of centuries of so-called French logic and German metaphysics.

The OECD acknowledges that there has been some policy reversal by some governments – but it does not go far enough to remove the perverse incentives. The organization has looked at two types of disincentives to continued working. One is the replacement ratio: the effective state pension as a proportion of average earnings. The other is the loss in pension wealth by those who postpone retirement and thus receive less for any given life expectancy.

At the age of 61 the greatest nationwide disincentives to continued work appear in France and the Netherlands, where the replacement rate is above 80 per cent. By age 67 only the US and the UK emerge without disincentives. So why are so few older people at work? It may be because some of them can draw early retirement occupational pensions as well as state benefits; or it may be because of weaknesses on the demand side resulting from an employer bias against older workers.

The straightforward way to tackle the state pension burden is to index the retirement age to life expectancy. The same medical advances that allow people to live longer have also made many of them healthier for much longer. The fixed retirement age is only due to fear of the pensioner lobby.

When it comes to voluntary pension plans, matters are complicated. If people want to retire early on a relatively low income, that is their choice. But the traditional defined benefit pension plans based on earnings in the last years discouraged people from staying on in a lesser role. The shift to defined contribution plans can only do good in the long run.

The hardest problem is how to prevent people financing early retirement with invalidity benefits. UK government moves to tighten up were met with parades of wheelchairs in Downing Street. But surely a civilized society should be able to make some distinction between people who are not capable of work through no fault of their own and those who – while no longer in their prime earnings years – may still have some contribution to make?

How to Tackle Europe's Baby Blip

Financial Times, 5 December 2003

My pet remedy for the adverse consequences of an ageing European population on the pensions burden has been to index the pension age to life expectancy. It goes without saying that this upward indexation needs to be accompanied by changes to make it easier for older workers to work at a different pace.

A study by David Willetts,[1] the clearest thinker in the Conservative shadow cabinet, has, however, drawn dramatic attention to another aspect of the rising dependency ratio – that is the ratio of older people to those of working age. Not only is the numerator of this ratio, that is the number of older people, rising. The denominator, that is the number of people of working age, is falling.

A rapid decline is foreseen in the proportion of the European Union population of prime working age over the next forty years. The most dramatic example is Italy where the number of Italians aged 15–59 is expected to drop from 35m to 21.5m. The age dependency ratio is accordingly expected to rise from 0.40 in 2000 to 1.03 in 2040. Even in the UK the age dependency ratio is expected to rise from 0.34 to 0.65. But demography is not all. The economic burden of providing for older workers has been much increased by the policy to encourage early retirement.

The argument becomes controversial when Willetts asserts that increased immigration will not help much. This is because the ten new members of the enlarged EU mostly have low fertility rates. Migrants, however, tend to be predominantly young. It will take some decades for their own low fertility rates to have an adverse effect on dependency ratios. In any case the greatest pressure for immigration is likely to come from north Africa and Asia, where fertility rates are much higher. It is neither right nor prudent to assume that this tide can be held back indefinitely.

The statement by David Blunkett, the Home Secretary, that there is no practical limit to absorptive capacity was correct. The number of people that can be supported on a given land mass is enormously variable, as it was not when the bulk of economic activity was traditional agriculture and trade was marginal. The one serious drawback to immigration is that it could increase population densities in some countries that are already crowded. But we need to tread carefully here. The Netherlands has a population density of 383 persons per square kilometre compared with 243 in the UK. In any case you cannot in the same breath complain of a prospective drop in population owing to falling fertility and bemoan the effects of an inflow of migrants who would counteract this. Where Blunkett, in line with most western political leaders, goes wrong is in trying to pinpoint sectors that are short of labour and to allow selective immigration to fill the gap. This is an example of the all-too-common 'economics without price'. There are rates of pay at which European countries can get sufficient native nurses and kitchen hands. But this would involve much higher wages that reflected their scarcity.

From the point of view of the recipient countries there are three arguments for immigration. First, it would avoid an increase in pay for those who do dirty jobs. Such increases may complicate the conduct of fiscal policy and irritate middle-class voters who would have to pay more for public and domestic services. But this is not an argument for a civilized person. The second argument is that more immigrants will improve the dependency ratio for some decades to come. The third and basic argument is that the movement of people is part of a global economy, just as is the free movement of goods and capital. Dare I add the claims of common humanity that apply to people in poor countries trying to better their lot, as well as refugees fleeing from torture and oppression?

Note

1. *Old Europe? Demographic Change and Pension Reform*, Centre for European Reform, 2003.

Shareholders, Not Stakeholders

Contribution to RSA and *Economist* debate, 6 February 2003

Competitive market capitalism has many faults. But as Churchill said about democracy, all the other systems that have been tried are far worse. Let me deal with the bad news at the beginning. First, anybody whose faith in market capitalism was based on the US stock market bubble of the late 1990s deserved to have his faith destroyed. All market systems have been subject to boom and bust since records began. In 1999, and a year before the bubble burst, I wrote an article describing the so-called new US paradigm as 'nonsense on stilts' (see 'Nonsense on Stilts' p.183 below). The run-up to the stock market peak of 2000 was remarkably similar to that leading up to the 1929 crash. Equity analysts based their conclusions on totally absurd predictions of annual rises in corporate earnings. Moreover, American consumers had stopped saving and were running down their financial balances: something which could not go on for ever. It is usually regarded as bad form to say 'I told you so', but as I am not normally any kind of stock market commentator I feel I should get away with it.

The corporate crisis

Secondly, there has been a crisis in the running of large corporations (I hate that horrible word 'governance'). Events such as the Enron fiasco cannot be dismissed as being due to the few bad apples found everywhere. The root of the problem is the separation of ownership from management – in modern economic jargon, 'the principal agent problem'. This has grown worse because of 'the decline of influential individual shareholders who align the longer term interests of owners and managers; and their replacement by essentially passive institutions who lack the incentive to hold corporate management accountable'. Such managements inevitably use their enhanced power for their own gain, often at investors' expense.[1]

One obvious weakness is that auditors are appointed by those whose performance they are meant to inspect. The threat of a takeover is – for all its messiness – the nearest approximation we have to a discipline over lazy or unscrupulous corporate executives. It has proved insufficient. The emphasis on short-term performance at the expense of the longer term is partly due to the brief tenure of fund managers who are expected to regulate the activities of chief executives.

The report from which I have been quoting has four main proposals for restoring effective shareholder control:

1. It should be stated public policy to encourage shareholder involvement in the running of corporations.
2. Pension fund trustees and similar agents must act solely in the long-term interests of their beneficiaries.
3. Institutional shareholders above a certain size should be made accountable for the exercise of their votes.
4. Shareholders should have the exclusive right and obligation to nominate at least three non-executive directors.

Whether these proposals are necessary or sufficient I do not pretend to know. But what I cannot sufficiently emphasize is that these and other reform proposals are designed to increase rather than diminish the role and power of shareholders.

The long view

Any judgement on competitive market capitalism has to be based on a longer historical span. Lord Keynes, writing in 1930 in the middle of the Great Depression, pointed out that in the 4,000 years up to around 1700 there had been no great change in the average standard of living: ups and downs, but no progressive improvement. But since 1700 average living standards had risen fourfold in Europe and the US. Since then, between 1930 and the year 2000, real UK GDP per head has again risen fourfold. In the last few decades there has been an even more remarkable rise in the living standards of many Third World countries, with notable exceptions such as southern Africa. To those who want to dismiss this improvement in human well-being as a rise in 'inequality' I have nothing to say. Let the statisticians argue it out.

The role of markets

There are only three ways of arranging human affairs: voluntary co-operation, markets and coercion. Voluntary co-operation is wonderful to the extent that it works, which seems to be most likely in relatively small face-to-face groups. State coercion has mercifully performed least well of all three methods. 'Mercifully' because to me the great virtue of the market system is that it is compatible with personal freedom. It empowers ordinary people who choose what to consume, where to work and how to make the various trade-offs between the good things of life, such as take-home pay and leisure. You do not need to tell me that none of this works perfectly and we could spend many days discussing how markets can be improved.

Attention is rightly paid to the role of incentives. But the role of markets in providing information on dispersed wants and opportunities is just as vital. And it is one that no computer system could possibly replace. The criticisms of the market system have been very similar throughout the centuries. First is the 'inequality' that it is supposed to engender. There are worse inequalities, especially of power, in feudalism, as well as in the 'real existing socialism' which came to an end in the former Soviet bloc in 1989. It is a matter for psychopathology that people who worry about high rewards for businessmen regard with equanimity the spectacular gains from gambling in, for instance, the National Lottery or the huge earnings of popstars and footballers. But I do not want to go too far along this road, which is paved with envy and jealousy. It is perfectly possible to redistribute both income and capital towards the losers, as British governments do, so long as we are careful not to kill the goose that lays the golden eggs.

Another indictment is the allegedly irrational pursuit of ever more fanciful and unnecessary consumer goods. But no one is forced to consume and it is not an indictment of an economic system that some of us cannot resist blandishment and temptation. The system could function just as well if the fruits of growth were taken in the form of more leisure or better public amenities. Admittedly greed is an unlovely thing. But given that it exists is it not better that it should be harnessed to providing the public with goods and services rather than to rob rivals or plunder in war? It was Keynes who said that it was better that a man should lord it over his pocketbook than over his fellow men.

Alternative capitalisms

We have seen a vogue for all kinds of alternative capitalisms: starting with the French planning model, then Scandinavian social democracy, then the German corporate system; and for a long time we were told to be more like Japan. All of these have proved big disappointments with the partial exception of Scandinavia, which retains more market-competitive elements than Old Europe does.

The primacy of the shareholder in the Anglo-US is not an accidental quirk. The essential point is that those who enjoy the residual gains also bear the residual losses when all contractual payments have been made. In most corporations this variable residual belongs to those who put up the equity capital. But it does not have to be like that. In employee share-ownership plans (ESOPs), employees enjoy the profits and losses and bear the responsibility of equity ownership. Worker-owned businesses have in some places achieved noteworthy results. One instance is the John Lewis Partnership; another is the Mondragon Group in the Basque region of Spain.

Whoever owns the equity, the role of the management is to promote the value of that equity. It is the task of the law, unwritten rules and of public policy to ensure that its efforts to do so benefit the general citizen. There is usually enough uncertainty about what will maximize long-term profits to justify many different approaches. Capitalism will not collapse if a business tries to produce a pleasant working environment or a playing field at the back of the establishment!

The present corporation is certain to evolve. But the stakeholder idea is a step backwards. If it means anything, it is that managements should do something other than strive for the best return on their assets. The losers are not just top-hatted capitalists but worker-owners, consumers and all the rest of us. The stakeholder idea is really a call for managers to take over the political task of offsetting market failures and even to lay down goals for their society. No wonder a few besotted managers embrace the idea.

The stakeholder approach is to promote a general mushiness. Everyone is supposed to pursue the interests of everyone and no one is really accountable for anything. A manager is theoretically responsible not only to shareholders, or even to workers, but to suppliers, customers and the public at large. This has no operational meaning. In practice it is simply a charter for management to do what it likes. How we are to decide in a relocation decision between the conflicting claims of employees, and other so-called stakeholders who would benefit from jobs nearer the site? One enthusiast advocates that every company should have a 'metaphysical director' who could supposedly resolve such conflicts of interest and value. This would indeed provide jobs for bogus philosophers.

The real German model

There are too many romantic notions about how businesses are run in supposedly stakeholder countries. A *Financial Times* reader remarked (David Morgan, 24 January 1996): 'It is a warm, comforting notion that a chief executive who stands before his shareholders could justify a big training initiative without being able to say he believes it would lead to profit now or in the future. I am sure that the chief executive would last no longer in Switzerland than in the UK, and rightly so.'

A recent investigation by a DTI steering group suggested that the issues affecting board members in countries such as Germany, Austria, the Netherlands and Sweden were little different from those who operate in the UK. For instance, although large German corporations are required to have two-tier boards with union representation on the top steering one, the chairman's casting vote has usually been enough to see that the interests of shareholders prevail.

A 1995 OECD report in Germany pointed out that so far from being stakeholder concerns, German companies accounting for 80 per cent of business turnover are run by small and medium-sized unincorporated companies 'with a close correspondence between owners and managers'. Many German companies escape the conflicts between owners and managers by making the two one and the same person. This explains far more about Germany than any amount of stakeholder theory. On the other hand, many US states have manager-friendly laws designed to dilute shareholder influence. They have mostly been the result of lobbying by managers trying to free themselves from activist shareholders and playing on the concern of state legislatures for local employment. European planners at a Brussels convention could learn something from the diversity of corporate legal structures that exist within the federation known as the United States.

A genuine stake for all

Where do we go from here? My own slogan has for a long time been the rather ungainly one of 'Redistributive market liberalism'. The idea is to allow the market system to function freely and competitively against a background of law and monetary stability. The Third Way element is cash redistribution of some of the rewards to those who would otherwise do less well in the lottery of life. This can go quite a long way, if done with care.

The main problem with unearned, investment income and equity ownership is that too few of us have them and are able to enjoy their benefits and risks. In addition to the redistribution of income through the tax and social security system, I have long advocated capital distribution to everyone at birth to make a reality of the slogan 'property owning democracy'. [Some proposals are discussed in the following chapters.] If some commentators want to call this 'stakeholder capitalism' so be it. But I would avoid putting much weight on so vague and contentious a word.

Unfortunately the financial and business worlds are not reformist in any of the ways at which I have hinted, but are simply wimpish in the face of their attackers – partly because they do not have the appropriate dialectical skills and partly because they are victims of various organizations who extract a sort of Danegeld in the form of membership and subscriptions.

Note

1. R. Monks and A. Sykes, *Capitalism without Owners will Fail*, Centre for the Study of Financial Innovation, November 2002.

Corruption, Moral and Financial

Financial Times, 20 June 2002

Few subjects dominate the media more than alleged corruption – even in countries such as the UK, once regarded as havens of correct behaviour. But it is difficult to say what is meant by corruption. It would be easy to devote a whole book to its definition. Even hard-core bribery is hard to define, although it is clearly connected with cash transfers to individuals not disclosed in official contracts. Corruption is wider and vaguer. In a wide-ranging study[1] the Cambridge economist Robert Nield defines public corruption as the breaking by public persons for private gain of the rules of conduct in public affairs. The difficulty with this definition, as the author acknowledges, is to distinguish between changes in the rules and breaches of them. But he does not allow changing standards to be too much of an excuse.

During the Cold War, illicit practices were a substitute for hot war. This left two legacies: the use of cover-up falsehoods by public officials and their involvement in corrupt arms deals. Neild provides a succinct economic analysis of the forces affecting the level of corruption in a democracy, from which it is clear that the outcome is indeterminate. The swing factor used to be Victorian public morality and its partial subsequent survival. But if the costs of corruption are too low, or the benefits too high, a strain is placed on the moral inhibitions.

The arms industry is a near-perfect example, in which contracts worth billions are placed by fairly low paid officials. This is also evident in highly regulated civilian economies. It is difficult to disagree that there was an increase in 'alleged wrong-doing' in Britain in the last years of the twentieth century. Market liberals would attribute it to the still-enormous size of the state sector. Yet global data do not suggest that government size correlates with corruption. The alternative analysis, to which Neild is more drawn, would put the emphasis on 'market behaviour and business models' fostered recently by both main British political parties and the denigration of old-fashioned public sector values. It is indeed difficult to imagine leaders such as Clement Attlee or Stafford Cripps indulging in either the excesses of spin or the proliferation of honours for political friends that we have seen recently.

My own suggestion would be that corruption arises in the West not just from the size of the public sector but from the increased interface between public officials and private business. If the state sector consists of professionally managed enterprises such as the old National Health Service, at arm's length from both ministers and private enterprise, the opportunities for corruption are limited to purchasing policy. But when the distinction between the public and private sector is said to represent outmoded ideology, and it is urged that the two should interact as much as possible, the floodgates have opened. This increased interpenetration came in with the more pragmatic post-Thatcher Conservative administrations of the 1990s with their emphasis on policies such as the private finance initiative. These ideas have, of course, been taken over and magnified in Tony Blair's Third Way and its equivalent in other countries. The risks incurred emerge from the latest report of Transparency International. This does indeed show that the most corrupt countries are in either the developing world, or former communist states. But the UK now emerges as only the thirteenth least corrupt country: less corrupt than France, Germany or the US but more corrupt than the Scandinavian countries, Canada or the Netherlands.

Nield does not analyse how harmful corruption really is. To my mind it is less odious than terrorism, cruelty to children or religious fundamentalism. Indeed, it may on occasion be positively desirable. It was mainly the use of side payments of various kinds that enabled the Soviet economy to function. Nevertheless, corruption is a second-best strategy. Its long-term harmful effects can be seen in the post-Soviet aftermath where too many entrepreneurs believe that successful competition consists in bribing or even killing business associates.

A last thought. Corruption in its widest sense often arises from over-passionate partisan politics. If the other side is seen as an unspeakable evil, stretching the rules seems a small price to pay to reduce the chances that it may ever regain office. Some friends of mine met a well-known Labour spin-doctor on a holiday in France and complained of government policies. The riposte was: 'Would you like to see a Tory government?' My friends were quick to reply: 'We have a Tory government.' Quips aside, if such a possibility is regarded as the ultimate evil, everything is justified to prevent it.

If we are serious about reversing the tide we need to go back to an arm's length relationship between the government and the private sector. Parliament would then make the rules within which the profit motive would be allowed to operate; and the number of face-to-face confrontations would be minimized. When the Blair government came into power in 1997, a sympathetic observer said to me: 'This government likes doing deals.' That is the trouble.

Note

1. Robert Nield, *Public Corruption*, Anthem Press, 2002.

The Case for Basic Income

Reviews of Philippe Van Parijs (ed.), *What's Wrong With a Free Lunch?*, Beacon Press 2001; and Robert van der Veen and Lock Groot (eds), *Basic Income on the Agenda*, Amsterdam University Press, 2001
Times Literary Supplement, 24 August 2001

One of the myths of New Labour is that paid work is the answer to most social problems. There is no need to argue about the miseries that arise when people able and willing to work are not able to find a job that makes them better off than being on the dole. Nor need anyone deny that people have become disheartened and, in the fashionable jargon, felt socially excluded through lack of work other than dead-end jobs. Some of these have had their self-respect and whole outlook on life transformed by appropriate job opportunities.

But it is a fatal logical slide to move from here to insisting that as many people as possible should work for cash, even if that is not what they want to do or that is not the best way of using their enthusiasms and skills. The obvious vulnerability of current policies is in the pressure placed on unmarried mothers to take up paid employment when in many cases the most useful thing they can do would be to look after their children.

The issue is wider. The mistake of Karl Marx was to thunder against private capital and investment income. The problem with them is not that they exist but that too few of us have them. One of the great advantages of the old professional classes is that they had some personal funds on which to fall back and were not completely dependent on wages and salaries. This gave them a degree of independence in dealing with employers or clients as well as a nest egg on which to fall back in difficult times. Last but by no means least, it was possible for younger or more unconventional people to take time off before or during their careers to travel around the world, follow an artistic bent on a modest income, give their time and energy to good causes, or engage in a little riotous living.

Unfortunately most defenders of market capitalism have chosen to ignore the existence of unearned income and shut their eyes to the ample evidence of its existence among affluent Americans as well as in the European upper middle class. Yet this easy way out was not taken by F. A. Hayek, Lady Thatcher's favourite economic philosopher. Hayek went out of his way to praise the existence of the person of independent means, who was responsible for much of the innovation of the last few centuries – whether in high culture, in the launch of good causes such as the anti-slavery campaign or the more mundane development of the art of living, including a great variety of hobbies and sports which were afterwards taken up by the mass of the population. Without the support of modest independent wealth we would not have had *Private Eye*; and without the Rowntree Fund British opposition parties would have very meagre research support. Indeed, Hayek went so far as to say that if there were no other way it would be better to grant an independent income to one householder in a hundred chosen by lot than not to have it at all. In the forty years and more since his *Constitution of Liberty* was published, productivity in the developed world has made great strides. Are we not now approaching a position where some non-wage income could be available not to one in a hundred but to all citizens?

There is also a very modern reason for advocating some form of non-work or property income for all. In recent times there has been a greater dispersion of market rewards for different types of work – usually labelled growing inequality. This could well be a passing phase in economic development; but even passing phases can last several decades. It is surely better that those without the skills required in the modern economy – including among the skills a street-wise instinct for market opportunities – should be able to do some low-paid work, supplemented by other sources of income, and not be forced into relying solely on the dole. Many elements of such an approach exist already in Labour's New Deal and social security reforms, which could be taken in gradual steps towards a universal minimum income and away from the present puritanical obsessions.

Indeed there is today an organized movement towards what is known as basic income. In Europe its support tends to come from left-Liberal and Green groups. It is especially strong in Ireland and Finland; but it also has a certain amount of support among the US Democrats. But it is not only among the unorthodox left that we find such ideas. They were inherent, even if he did not realize it, in the old slogan of Anthony Eden about a property-owning democracy. Milton Friedman was one of the pioneers of a negative income tax which would be received by those whose income fell below a certain threshold, instead of the present mass of conditional social security payments for pensions, unemployment and other contingencies. As one would expect, John Stuart Mill was sympathetic. Before the Second World War a thoughtful Liberal politician, Lady Rhys Williams, put forward the idea of a social dividend for all as an alternative to the Beveridge proposals.

There is now enough interest to warrant the publication of two series of essays on a proposal for a universal basic income (UBI) as defined by Philippe Van Parijs, who holds the Hoover Chair of Economic and Social Ethics at the Catholic University of Louvain, and who is at the intellectual centre of the contemporary movement. Much the most concise and clearest exposition is in the Beacon Press book. Van Parijs bases his advocacy on a specific theory of 'real freedom for all', which he has outlined in earlier works. Of course any kind of support for basic income must be based on a value judgement. But such a judgement is surely more persuasive if it can fasten on to a social form which has existed for many years, such as investment income, but which growing affluence provides us an opportunity of extending.

It has to be said, too, that such proposals have also attracted support for bad reasons from economic Luddites who believe that there is only a certain amount of work to go round, which needs to be rationed and shared. Such advocates see them as a sort of bribe for people to accept a compulsory shortening of the working week, work-sharing and other wealth-destroying ideas. Opposition comes from mainline social democrats whose trade union backers have traditionally thought in terms of paid work and statutory minimum wages as a principal weapon against poverty. In the US, opposition comes not only from instinctive conservatives, but also from radicals such as Prof. Edmund Phelps who is outraged by the idea of abandoning the work ethic and providing benefits to those who prefer to surf off Malibu in the afternoon and smoke pot all night.

Some of the Amsterdam contributors do their cause no favour by linking it up with the development of the European Social Charter and their assumption that a basic income scheme would require harmonization over the whole EU area. Presumably what they have in mind is that workers would otherwise move as free riders to countries which had such a scheme in operation. So far, however, the problem in the European Union has been inadequate rather than excessive mobility of labour. If worries of this kind are serious in an enlarged EU it would be possible to restrict the scheme to long-time residents and extend it if and when the fears turn out to prove unfounded.

The most persuasive way of putting the matter is in terms of what Winston Churchill once called a ladder and a floor. He espoused a minimum below which no one could fall irrespective of abilities, luck, training, effort or anything else; but above that there would be a ladder on which anyone could rise to whatever level their ability, luck and energy could take them. A minimum income in this sense needs to be sharply distinguished from a compulsory minimum wage which contributes to unemployment and is a breach of the human right to make a contract for services from which both sides benefit.

Persuasion is made more difficult because of the bewildering variety in which such proposals come. Some of the complexity is inherent in the subject. But it is aggravated by the confusion among many advocates between administrative forms and economic substance, and by the bewildering variety of labels for this set of ideas.

The conventional response is that if people can survive without working many will do just this, that the national income will collapse and the scheme therefore prove self-destructive. This was indeed the objection to the Speenhamland system introduced in the UK by some magistrates at the beginning of the nineteenth century under which labouring wages were made up to some conventional minimum. The political economists at the time rightly pointed to its disincentive effects, although that did not justify the harsher aspects of the New Poor Law which succeeded it in 1834.

There has been progress since the early nineteenth century. The reason why Speenhamland could not work was that the prevailing level of normal wages was hardly above subsistence. Therefore it really did not pay unskilled agricultural workers to take a job unless they were physically forced to do so. The hope today is that productivity and the general standard of living have reached a level well above even conventional subsistence. In other words, it should pay people to take a job. There is however no hope of reaching the goal of capitalism without the puritan ethic unless it is recognized that poverty is not just a relative concept. So long as we accept some compromise whereby there is both an absolute and a relative element, the gap between Churchill's floor and average pay levels can rise with national productivity. The majority of adults would want to do paid work as well. The Malibu surfers are not typical. Most of the old upper bourgeoisie also worked and regarded their own independent means as either a nest egg to fall back upon or as a supplement to their professional or business incomes. The late Nobel prize-winning economist, James Meade, looked forward to a time when the typical citizen would have three sources of income: a wage or salary, an unconditional basic income from the state and some assets other than their own homes.

Of course there are many distinctions to be made. One is between conditional and unconditional payments. In the UK, Keith Joseph, in his early incarnation in the 1970s as Secretary of State for Social Services, introduced the idea of an income top-up for workers in low-paid employment. This has been much extended by subsequent governments and especially the present UK Labour one to a fully fledged Working Families Tax Credit (WFTC). At present this is only available for families with children, but should be available to all adults in 2003 assuming that the government goes ahead with its proposed integrated Employment Credit. This kind of scheme has its parallel in the US Earned Income Tax Credit. It is in fact a negative income tax conditional on carrying out paid work.

A further distinction is whether the payments should be made on a household or individual basis. The household basis has the advantage of being less expensive and is used for present-day social security payments. The individual basis is, however, not dependent on probing into marital relationships and is more in keeping with the shift to independent taxation.

Another crucial aspect lies in the cut-off rate at which payments tail off as cash income from other sources rises. In their most limited form, which was probably what Friedman had in mind, there would be a 100 per cent cut-off. This would mean accepting a high poverty surtax which citizens could rise above once they had secured reasonably paid employment. In the most radical form, on the other hand, the cut-off rate would be no different to the normal rate of income tax. This would end the very high implicit surtax rates at the bottom of the income scale but at the cost of a higher marginal tax rate for all who pay positive tax.

Finally, minimum income schemes differ enormously according to which elements of the present welfare state they would supplement or replace. At one extreme they would simply plug gaps not covered by existing state pensions, unemployment pay and so on. At the other extreme (and this is what attracted the Friedmanites), they would replace not only all existing cash payments but also services in kind such as health and education.

Van Parijs's proposal is for a universal basic income (UBI) paid at a uniform level to each adult. The grant is paid, and its level is fixed, irrespective of whether the person is rich or poor, lives alone or with others, is willing to work or not. It is something on which a person can safely count. Any other income can be lawfully added to it. It need not however start by covering all basic needs. He argues that the easiest way forward is likely to consist of enacting a UBI first as a level below subsistence and then increasing it over time. Alaska already has a partial basic income income payment for all residents based on that state's well-known oil revenues.

Some BI supporters make a great deal of the fact that it would be paid to everyone over the counter or through the post. This would make it seem enormously expensive in conventional terms. It would seem much less so if it were given as a tax credit, i.e. a negative income tax. In that case most wage-earners would simply experience it as a deduction from their tax bill. The best solution would probably be to let the recipients themselves choose as in the case of the WFTC. If the payment is made in a tax credit form it is much easier to explode exaggerated ideas of what such a scheme would cost. Let us take a householder or a principal breadwinner who earns £500 a week and pays tax (including what are now called National Insurance contributions) of £100. If the minimum income is £100 he makes no payment and receives none. The perceived cost is zero. The net cost of the scheme will then be the transfers to those who will be receiving net payments; and it is only this element which could lead to an increase in the tax burden. As a rough order of magnitude a full basic income paid on an individual basis at the conventional subsistence rates laid down in social security provisions would add 10 to 15 per cent to marginal tax rates – now running at 32 per cent in the UK, including employee National Insurance contributions.

A compromise, known as a Citizen's Participation Income, has been put forward by Tony Atkinson, Warden of Nuffield College. It would not be unconditional but would be available for those engaged, for instance, in full-time education or training, intensive care work and approved forms of voluntary work. As Brian Barry notes, this opens up nightmarish prospects of bureaucratic probing to decide who is eligible. A former Cabinet minister recently spent the best part of a day helping a caretaker to fill in his application for WFTC. One can imagine how the complexities would increase with a Participation Income. Such an income might be a politically necessary initial move. But in the end we would see either a true basic income or the abandonment of the whole experiment.

A final issue concerns the pros and cons of a regular basic income versus a capital endowment. In some kinds of rational and far-sighted world they amount to the same thing. Lifetime basic income payments discounted at the appropriate interest rate are equivalent to a capital sum. And someone who receives this capital sum on achieving adult status would be able either to live on his or her capital at a steady rate or borrow on the strength of it. So on libertarian grounds the capital stake is to be preferred.

But obviously not everyone has access to credit markets at prime rates. Moreover, what do we propose to do about the prodigal son who spends his endowment at an early age and is not subsequently able to earn a market wage below the poverty level? It is most unlikely that a civilized society would let him starve; and as soon as this is conceded, the asset endowment looks the more expensive option. But an offsetting advantage of asset distribution is that it is politically easier to make it either universal, or general to those below a certain income, without the work test that is still insisted upon for income distribution schemes.

The British Labour government has in fact taken up the asset idea in small-scale proposals for a Child Trust Fund or so-called baby bonds. If the scheme is to make a more sizeable contribution to a wider distribution of wealth, some source of funds other than tax revenues will have to be found. An opportunity was missed when the revenue from mobile telephone auctions was devoted just to reducing the national debt. But there may well be similar windfalls for the government in future and we now have a ready place in which to put them. It is so difficult to convince a still puritanical public opinion of the advantages of either kind of reform that we should make progress wherever we can.

The Logic of the Baby Bond

Review of Will Paxton (ed.), *Equal Shares? Building a Progressive and Coherent Asset-Based Welfare Policy*, Institute for Public Policy Research, 2003
Prospect, August 2003

The nineteenth-century French anarchist socialist Pierre-Joseph Proudhon achieved fame with his dictum 'property is theft'. This has been one underlying socialist theme ever since. Karl Marx, who had contempt for Proudhon in everything else, took over the idea and envisaged that problems of poverty and maldistribution would be solved by some form of collective ownership of the means of production.

Marx may have been right in focusing on the ownership of capital and the unearned income deriving from it, but his diagnosis was wrong. The traditional European upper middle classes derived enormous benefits from not being complete wage slaves and having a nest egg to fall back upon.

These aspects help explain an alternative radical tradition based on distributing assets more widely. The Old Testament decreed that every fiftieth year should be a Jubilee in which all land would be returned to its original owners, debts cancelled, slaves set free, the land left fallow and transactions in the preceding half century annulled. There is no evidence that anything of this kind was ever attempted. But the injunction at least showed a recognition that capital ownership should not depend entirely on the accidents of heredity and past transfers.

The Peruvian Hernando de Soto has recently attracted attention by proposing for the Third World a form of popular capitalism based on granting full property rights to the many forms of de facto property, such as extra-legal small businesses and property owned by the poor in shanty towns.[1] There are not so many hidden assets of this kind in the industrial West. Property ownership for most people takes the form of home ownership and/or pension rights, whether in state or private schemes.

Indeed, the cheap sale of council houses was probably the most popular measure enacted by the Thatcher government, even though it was distributionally skewed and, as Paxton reminds us, did little to increase the wealth of those at the lowest end. One problem with home ownership is that, despite equity withdrawal, houses are there basically for people to live in and do not become available as a nest egg or reserve unless or until the owner moves down the market in late middle age when his children have moved away and he trades down. Similarly, pension rights are not usually tradable except at a substantial discount and are also a resource needed for later life.

The benefits of individual property ownership have been sung by writers throughout the ages. Such ownership was regarded by Greek and Roman classical authors as a precondition of good citizenship. But they did not investigate the problems of those who had no assets – they took it for granted that many people, including slaves and foreigners, could not be citizens. The debate in its modern form goes back at least to the late-seventeenth-century English philosopher John Locke. His vindication of the rights of property depended on the belief that men had 'mixed their labour' with it. I do not know how he would have replied to the observation that many of his fellow citizens did not have the opportunity to mix their labour with anything in his sense. My impression from his *Treatises on Government* is that his main concern was not with the distribution of property ownership but with laying a foundation for personal rights which despotic governments had no right to abrogate.

It was in America that the small stakeholder movement first took root. Jeffersonian democracy – notoriously to subsequent generations who lived in industrial society – was based on the concept of small proprietors, mostly owner-farmers for whose benefit the nation's affairs should be run. Around the time of the French Revolution such ideas took a more radical form in the Old World, for instance in the writings of Thomas Paine. Later on in the nineteenth century Gladstone supported an amendment to the 1886 Queen's Speech which advocated the goal of 'three acres and a cow' to help landless labourers. The slogan came from Joseph Chamberlain's 'unofficial programme' and was probably adopted by the Liberal leader as an expedient to vote the Salisbury Tory government out of office, which it temporarily succeeded in doing. Widespread citizen ownership was more seriously espoused by the political economist John Stuart Mill, who advocated an inheritance tax of a progressive kind, based on the size of the legacy rather than the wealth of the deceased. The object was to encourage people to spread their wealth on death as widely as possible. This proposal has since been backed by innumerable respectable political economists, including the late

Lionel Robbins, whom no one could have called a hellfire revolutionary. Yet even this modest change in tax and inheritance law has still to be made.

The Conservative Prime Minister Anthony Eden, best known for the Suez debacle, spoke about a 'property-owning democracy'. But the Tory governments of the 1950s and 1960s did little to promote it, apart from tax reliefs for mortgages and private pensions, which distorted the property market and the general economy far more than they effectively redistributed wealth. Left-wing thinkers have woken up very late in the day to the fact that property ownership is far more concentrated than earned income; and that it makes little sense to inveigh against corporate 'fat cats', or impose high marginal rates of tax on executives and professionals, when these people's wealth is trivial compared with the sums that still pass on at death in the face of estate duties, which still remain a voluntary tax for those who take legal advice in time or trust their descendants.

Recently, the idea of a citizen stake has attracted radicals across the political spectrum. Two US authors, Bruce Ackerman and Anne Alstott espoused it in their widely discussed book, *The Stakeholder Society*.[2] It has also been espoused by Julian Le Grand of the London School of Economics. David Owen canvassed it for the Social Democrats as early as 1984 and David Willetts, the current Conservative social security spokesman, has promoted it under the title 'Asset Based Welfare'. The natural home for asset-based welfare is surely, however, the 'extreme centre'. This was a name invented decades ago by *The Economist* journal to describe those political moderates who were not content to split the difference between extremes but were interested in more innovative ideas than either left or right felt comfortable with.

It is against this impressive, but not yet mainstream advocacy that Gordon Brown's scheme for a Child Trust Fund, introduced in the 2003 budget, needs to be viewed. The media assumption was that this was a gimmick to disguise the fact that the Chancellor could afford few goodies in this particular budget. What the commentators failed to notice was that for the first time a British government was committed to distribution of capital to citizens as distinct from welfare in kind, or social security payments. It was a first stab at distributing ownership of assets other than housing and pensions more widely. Asset-distribution proposals were incorporated in the 2001 Labour election manifesto. But as they did not have the backing of any powerful lobby, it would have been easy for the Chancellor to have postponed the project indefinitely; and it is to his credit that he has not done so.

It is now government policy that each new-born infant should be provided with a small capital sum – £500 for the poorest third of families, falling to £250 for the rest – that would be invested in the financial markets and which bearers would be free to draw from the age of eighteen. The Treasury suggested that with further modest contributions from the Exchequer at a later stage and a 5 per cent real return on equity, the capital stake could eventually be worth some £1,600 per head. The annual Exchequer cost of the scheme is put at £230m – less than a tenth of the additional sums provided for the Iraq war. Moreover it will not be a substantial drain on resources until the bonds become encashable in eighteen years.

Since the Budget the case for these baby bonds – and extending the idea much further – has been elaborated by Will Paxton and other authors in an IPPR paperback, *Equal Shares?* They consider the arguments for the idea and also how to finance its enlargement and extension. It is not surprising that they are more successful in the former than the latter. The beauty of the 'baby bond', as they explain, is that in contrast to pensions or outright home ownership, they come in at the young end of the adult age group when people may be healthy and optimistic enough to enjoy them.

The IPPR authors cite the usual statistics which exaggerate the concentration of wealth. For example, the top 1 per cent of the population is said, on the basis of Inland Revenue figures, to hold over 20 per cent of all personal wealth. The weakness of such figures is that they are snapshot rather than lifetime comparisons. Suppose that lifetime wealth was equally distributed among all households. Many of them would still tend to start off with little wealth, or even net debts, but would gradually build up assets in the course of their working lives. They would then run them down in retirement, even if they left something over to bequeath to their children. I do not want to exaggerate. The Office of National Statistics states that 'wealth is considerably less evenly distributed than income'; and a substantial proportion of the population is asset-poor, even allowing for the normal accumulation of debt for house purchase and the start of a career. But a good case can only be made better if supported by more sophisticated and less tendentious estimates.

It would thus be desirable to have some estimates of the distribution of wealth, taking into account lifetime and other complications. Impartial analyses of distributional issues were indeed carried out by the Diamond Commission, which was set up by the 1974—9 Wilson and Callaghan governments. It had as its senior economist a highly respected egalitarian scholar, the late Henry Phelps-Brown, who carried conviction when he explained how little there was to be gained at that time from the traditional Labour policy of soaking the rich. He concentrated mainly on income, but such a Commission today could carry out a very useful

job in examining the distribution of wealth. The Thatcher
government made a big mistake in abolishing this Commission, as
did the Blair government in not reinstating it.

Paxton provides four reasons for what he calls 'progressive asset
based welfare':

1. To create a more equal overall wealth distribution;
2. To create a more equal distribution of wealth among young adults;
3. To create a more equal distribution of, or access to, assets during
   times of change;
4. To provide more progressive incentives to accumulate assets.

Surprise has been expressed that some of us, for whom equality is a
false ideal achievable only in the graveyard, if there, nevertheless back
the baby bond idea and its possible extensions. In fact the arguments
of Paxton read well enough if the words 'wider distribution' are
substituted for 'equal distribution'. Indeed he admits that he does not
have in mind 'all citizens possessing precisely equal shares'.

The fourth of his objectives is more problematic. The case for wider
asset ownership is not helped by being so much entangled in the
savings drive. Some Treasury draftsmen are inclined to treat baby
bonds as simply one aspect of savings encouragement. But even
without bringing in Keynesian considerations of the dangers of
oversaving in recession, the appropriate attitude to savings versus
consumption should be one of liberal neutrality. In fact one of the great
advantages of baby bonds – enabling young people to 'do their own
thing' for a few years – would be associated with dissaving, i.e. drawing
on both baby bonds and quite likely some of their own savings.

Asset distribution is of course only one way of topping up the
resources of the poor. The other approach discussed in the previous
chapter is that of a basic income (not minimum wage) to ensure that
everyone has a source of income outside the market and is definitely
better off in moving from the dole to low-paid jobs. There has
unfortunately been something of a civil war between advocates of
state-paid income top-ups on the one hand and asset distribution on
the other. An advantage of asset distribution is that it is politically
easier to introduce without the work test still insisted upon in income
supplementation schemes.

The IPPR authors correctly point out how modest Gordon Brown's
present proposals are, compared with, for instance, Fabian proposals
to provide every eighteen-year-old with £10,000 worth of assets or
with the Ackerman plan for $80,000 per head. The weakness of the
Brown proposals is that they are to be financed entirely from revenue.
If such ideas are to make a big contribution to a wider distribution of
wealth, some other source of funds, preferably of a capital nature,
needs to be found.

I originally proposed in the late 1970s that state revenue from North Sea oil should be earmarked for citizen dividends which could be capitalized on the stock market.[3] No political party took the slightest interest. Another missed opportunity was the Conservative decision to sell privatization shares at bargain prices rather than distribute them freely to everyone – a proposal incidentally supported by Milton Friedman. Yet another missed chance was the capital receipts from the sale of mobile telephone licences which were unimaginatively devoted towards repaying the national debt.

Some experiments have been made in some of the former communist countries in distributing shares in privatized companies at a nominal price. But the lack of a capitalist culture has made these countries difficult soil. The allotments to citizens have sometimes fallen prey to Mafia financiers who have bought them up cheaply. Alaska has been much more successful in distributing to its inhabitants state income from oil extraction.

There will be other opportunities if only policymakers would look for them. An obvious one staring us in the face is the increment of land value resulting either from planning permission or the extension of public facilities, such as the Jubilee Line in London. Not far from the *Financial Times* in Southwark, South London, a property developer named Don Riley has an office which looks out over a site that was available for purchase in 1980 for £100,000. In January 2000 it was sold for £2.6m. The gain was 'money in the bank' for the owners but nothing was contributed to the general welfare'.[4]

Land taxation has the advantage over other forms in that it is in principle based on pure space and need not be a disincentive to either capital or labour. This was noticed as long ago as the early nineteenth century by the classical economist David Ricardo. Towards the end of that century the American social reformer Henry George advocated a single tax on land ownership as the main source of government revenue. The Attlee government attempted to nationalize development values, but its plans floundered in a morass of legal and political complication.

These matters will all need to be looked at again. But as a very simple practical proposal, why not auction planning permission? Many local authorities have approached this piecemeal by making such permission conditional on the provision of services such as leisure centres, approach roads and so on. Why not return this windfall to the taxpayer in the form of asset distribution and let citizens decide how to spend it? Meanwhile, anything which shifts public discussion from endless obsession with state delivery of services in kind to ways in which people could provide for themselves is highly welcome.

PART THREE

Some British Topics

It is surely time that Great Britain should...endeavour to accomodate her future views and designs to the real mediocrity of her circumstances.

Closing words of Adam Smith, *The Wealth of Nations*

The Changing Economic Role of Government

Contribution to *The Challenge of Change*, Profile Books for the Society of Business Economists, 2003

Introduction

At the risk of undermining my own subject, I will risk saying that the half century since 1953 has been excessively preoccupied with the economic role of government. We were at all times in danger of forgetting – until rudely awoken by the attack on the New York Twin Towers of September 11, 2001 – that the primary role of government is to look after the physical security of the population and that all else is secondary.

But even if we confine ourselves to traditional economic variables, the most impressive feature of British growth performance is how stable the underlying trend has been and how little affected by the huffing and puffing of governments. From 1870 until 1950 the best estimate is that UK output per hour grew by 1 per cent per annum. From 1950 to 1973 there was a temporary acceleration to 3 per cent. Much of this may have reflected postwar catch-up. In fact this temporary acceleration, so far from being celebrated, was denounced very widely by commentators for not being fast enough compared with continental and Japanese competitors who were overtaking the UK in some imaginary league table. Since 1973, when governments have become even more preoccupied with boosting productivity, its trend growth rate fell back to 2 per cent and indeed may have been slightly less in the final half of that period.[1]

Productivity is of course not the same as the overall growth rate, which can be affected by variations in activity rates as well as by demographic changes. The slight acceleration in the growth rate predicted in UK government documents for the first decade of the twenty-first century is due mainly to a faster population growth, itself largely the product of expected legal immigration. Although, for such reasons, growth trends have been more variable than productivity ones, even they have still proved pretty stable and resistant to attempts to change them.

Economic policy may thus make much less difference than those who argue about it like to think. That does not mean that we should stop criticizing and appraising it. Growth emerges from animal spirits and the human instinct to truck and barter. But it is always possible for policy to have an adverse effect on performance. Sometimes, however, mistaken courses have provoked reactions that have led to their own reversals. For instance, when union power was threatening in the 1970s to make Britain the sick man of Europe, there were first the sterling crises of the mid-1970s and then the election of Margaret Thatcher in 1979, both of which produced salutary shocks and associated policy changes.

The 1950s: half-hearted freedom

The year 1953 was a watershed. It was the first year of normality after the Second World War. The Korean war had come to an end, armaments were at last being run down; and most wartime rationing and controls had been lifted. It was also the halfway stage in the somewhat under-discussed postwar Churchill administration of 1951–5. By the time of his stroke of May 1953, Winston Churchill had abandoned his last remaining attempts to establish an overlord system. He himself retreated from the detailed conduct of affairs; and the pygmies took over.

But unfortunately the main chance of a real dash for freedom had already been thrown away. After the Conservatives returned to power, a bold scheme to float the pound and free the country from the throes of never-ending runs on sterling had been proposed – Operation Robot – named after the two civil servants and one Bank of England official who devised it. The Chancellor, R. A. Butler, was in favour, but Churchill overruled him on the advice of his wartime confidant Lord Cherwell – the way was thus open for twenty or more years of preoccupation with sterling and the balance of payments.

Meanwhile so-called league tables began to circulate, showing that continental countries were growing at a faster rate than the UK. The gathering discontent was not a matter of mere numbers. There was a widespread feeling that, despite the expansion of educational opportunity and increased prosperity, the country was still run in a class-ridden way and what mattered was not what you knew but whom you knew – and possibly how you held your fork. One best-selling book was Michael Shanks's *The Stagnant Society*. Some of these feelings emerged very clearly in John Osborne's play *Look Back in Anger* and in the early novels of Kingsley Amis.

They had their counterpart on the business side. The electrical industry was dominated by three vast bureaucracies. One of them, AEI, was run by Lord Chandos who gave his real name, Oliver Lyttelton, to part of the National Theatre. The interviewer approached him through a series of carpeted rooms, each larger than the other. A journalist knew that if he said or wrote anything that displeased, he might be reported to his editor, or more probably, the managing director whom Chandos was more likely to know socially. Indeed I was once so reported by a Bank of England director whom I had the temerity to ask for some factual evidence to back the observations he was making 'off the record'. If there is one word which summarizes everything against which the reformers were reacting it was fuddy-duddyism.

The decade of growthmanship

There was bound to be some sea change. The reformers were split between those who pinned their hopes on more competition and those who drew their inspiration from French-type indicative planning. Businessmen were just as split as economists or politicians, and probably in an even more muddle-headed way. The economy did need a competitive shock. The successive rounds of world trade liberalization had not yet gone far enough to make business anything like an international arena; the vestiges of imperial preference still provided soft external markets; and in many domestic areas restrictive practices abounded.

The reappraisal began well before Harold Wilson formed his Labour government in 1964. There were some earlier acts of liberalization, like the abolition of resale price maintenance by Edward Heath. There was also the first attempt at a forward look at public spending, following the Plowden Committee which reported in the early 1960s. Europe too put in its appearance. Having failed to take part in the negotiations which led to the Treaty of Rome, the Conservative government of Harold Macmillan applied belatedly in 1961 to join the EU (then called the Common Market) – only to have its application vetoed halfway through negotiations in the famous intervention by General de Gaulle. The latter was much mocked for announcing that Britain was an island; but he was not so far off the mark about the country's psychological unreadiness.

Unfortunately both the planners and the free marketeers had the ground cut off from under their feet by the return of sterling and balance of payments crises. The first three years of the Wilson government of 1964–70 were dominated by a futile attempt to prevent sterling devaluation and then, when that failed, by devaluing to another fixed exchange rate. Even after 1967 the Treasury could not divest itself of its balance of payments mentality; and when devaluation seemed slow to work, it threw up a ridiculous contingency plan, Operation Brutus, for going back to a wartime siege economy.

Domestically, governments' main form of intervention was devoted to futile attempts at prices and incomes policies. The hope was to keep down costs that way and avoid the need to devalue. Amazingly, neither the Macmillan nor the Wilson government could see any virtue in stable costs and prices other than in their effect in promoting British exports. There were any number of wage freezes, guiding lights and solemn and binding concordats. Perhaps the worst effect was the attempt to control prices to give the unions an apparent *quid pro quo* for wage restraint.

The traumas of the 1970s

The surprise return of the Heath government, which was in office from 1970–74, proved in retrospect an interlude in a decade and a half of Labour rule. Most British political commentators regarded a free market approach with horror and raised the spectre of Selsdon Man: named after a conference of Conservative leaders before the 1970 election after which the press was briefed in a slightly free market direction. The Prime Minister Edward Heath undoubtedly began with a belief that British industry needed a cold shower. But this was not accompanied by any deeper economic philosophy; and it did not take him long to decide that the road of 'free competition and all that' had been tried and failed and that the required bracing treatment would be applied through yet another attempt at incomes policy. He was not in fact enthusiastic about statutory wage controls, which he adopted as a fallback after he had failed to reach a voluntary concordat with the trades unions. Ideally he would have liked to govern by a corporate consensus in which agreements between civil service mandarins and the TUC, rubber stamped by the CBI, would take the place of normal Cabinet government.

The Heath government did have to cope with an unfortunate legacy. After the 1967 devaluation, inflation did not retreat to its earlier creeping 2 or 3 per cent level, but jumped to 6–7 per cent. Yet at the same time unemployment was a good deal higher than in the postwar period. In the 1971–2 recession, newspaper headlines celebrated the then horrific total of one million unemployed. The combination of unemployment and inflation, labelled stagflation, puzzled economists almost as much as it did politicians. If they had looked beyond their own backyard, they would have seen that the combination of the two evils was far from a rare event – it was normal, for instance, in Latin America from which they were too proud to draw lessons.

According to the accepted historical canon, it was the miners' strike of early 1974 which brought down the Heath government. But far more significant in fact was an earlier strike in the same industry at the beginning of 1972. The miners' victory then was more significant precisely because it took place in a recession and before there was any thought of a world energy shortage. The economic cards should have been on the government's side. But it was defeated by the violent new tactics of the National Union of Mineworkers symbolized by the flying pickets which roamed around the country preventing fuel from being delivered.

After its first defeat by the miners' union, the government moved back towards a dirigiste and supposedly expansionist approach. Despite the inflation figures, it began simultaneously to increase government spending and reduce taxes in an attempt to stimulate the economy. Bodies such as the PIB – Prices and Incomes Board – were expected to hold the lid on any inflationary consequences. Although there were some Conservative cynics who welcomed the second miners' strike of 1974 as a vote-winning way of bashing the unions, this was far from what Heath wanted. His government blundered into the strike because of wage and price guidelines which made no sense against the new international inflation and because it had completely miscalculated the genuine economic strength of the miners during a world fuel crisis.

The main economic event which affected British business in 1973–4 came from abroad in the shape of a fivefold increase in the price of oil following the Yom Kippur war. The proximate cause was that the Arab-dominated oil price cartel, OPEC, had at last got its act together. But it was only able to do so because of a simultaneous economic boom in the industrial world which was reflected to a more moderate extent in the rise of other commodity prices apart from oil.

Until 1971, world inflation has been held at bay by the Bretton Woods dollar standard. Under this system the main industrial countries tied their currencies to the US dollar under a system of fixed but adjustable exchange rates. The emphasis was on the fixed aspect with adjustment being regarded as a defeatist last resort. The counterpart was that the US itself acted as the anchor country and maintained reasonably sound money policies.

These were thrown to the wind during the inflationary financing of the Vietnam war in the 1960s. When Congress belatedly enacted a tax increase which failed to stem inflationary forces, political interest was for the first time kindled in the Chicago monetarist school which advocated domestic monetary control. Even the USA, however,

adopted the statutory pay and controls in 1971 just before President
Nixon floated the dollar and broke the last links of the US currency
with gold. There was one more attempt to fix a new dollar parity; but
by 1973 the world was on a floating exchange rate system
unconstrained by domestic monetary discipline.

Thus there was nothing to stop the main industrial countries from
over-reflating in 1972–3 and indulging in wishful thinking about the
rate of economic activity and economic growth which could be
sustained without accelerating inflation. A more perfect recipe for the
OPEC cartel was hard to imagine. Few countries deliberately sought
to inflate their money supply. It was much more that governments
such as those of Richard Nixon and Edward Heath – with some
support from their central banks – recoiled in horror from the
interest rates that they thought were necessary to contain the
monetary consequences of their own policies. Germany and Japan
were, however, more prepared to give priority to offsetting the
inflationary impact of the world oil price shock than were the English-
speaking economies.

When Labour came back to office first under Harold Wilson in 1974
and then under James Callaghan in 1976 it inherited an inflation rate
racing towards double digits. Its initial response was more of the
same: that is, pay and price controls which they hoped would more
easily be accepted under a party which had been created by the union
movement. Under governments of both persuasions, the leaders of
British industry proved far too compliant and accepted the wage and
price control diagnosis, concentrating mainly on trying to ease the
pressure on business at the margin.

During the whole Labour period of 1974–9, the Chancellor of the
Exchequer Denis Healey, who would have much preferred to have
been Foreign Secretary, poured out anathemas on all schools of
economic thought. He once declared that he wished to be to the
economic forecasters what the Boston Strangler was to door-to-door
salesmen. He came to share the alarm about the decline of the
profitability of British industry and claimed that at tripartite meetings
he had to make the case for industry himself. He was also prepared
to make some pragmatic gestures towards the control both of public
spending and of monetary growth. The monetary controls devised
under his regime were, however, too dependent on complicated
devices such as 'the corset', which attempted to control bank loans
directly and which the shrewder financial practitioners soon found a
way around.

The shift away from postwar full employment policies towards a
preoccupation with limiting public sector borrowing and a tentative
approach to monetary targets was thus apparent during the Labour
period. It was dramatized by a series of runs on sterling invariably

followed by public expenditure clampdowns, fiercer than anything attempted before or since. The conversion from demand management to a new sound money consensus was often attributed to the conditions imposed by the International Monetary Fund in its 1976 loan negotiations with the UK. In fact government policy had already moved most of the way before the IMF deal was done. The change was symbolized by James Callaghan's speech to the 1976 Labour party conference – widely and correctly attributed to his then son-in-law Peter Jay – in which he declared that governments could no longer spend their way into prosperity.

While the world inflation and the accompanying energy price increases of the mid-1970s posed genuine policy dilemmas, the British crisis of the late 1970s was an unnecessary one. Although the UK was well and truly on a floating exchange rate, policymakers still had the reflexes of a fixed exchange rate system; and whenever the pound weakened they were afraid that it would do something described in City dining rooms as 'going through the floor'. In retrospect, once appropriate monetary and fiscal policies were introduced, the government could have left the pound to recover in its own good time and not bothered with the IMF. Indeed, by 1977 sterling was already recovering too quickly for comfort and British policymakers experienced the first of a series of strange crises due to an excessively strong pound – crises which their predecessors would have given a proportion of their anatomy to have. The public sector strikes of early 1979, in which the dead were notoriously left unburied, reflected the boy scout-like desire of the government to use a policy of belt, braces and suspenders against inflation rather than any one or two of these alone.

The advent of Thatcher

Any assessment of the Thatcher government is still a matter of acute political controversy, which affects even the most academic attempts to be objective. In retrospect the two main innovations were the belated attack on union power and the privatization of state-owned industries. The latter was at first regarded as an impossibly utopian project, but was later copied by governments of many different political colours all over the world.

The attack on union power was spearheaded by a number of Acts designed to remove the legal immunities of these bodies and to introduce devices such as strike ballots before industrial action. But other aspects were just as important. The union legislation would not have been so successful had it not been for the government's courageous and successful resistance to yet another miners' strike in

1984–5, and one which had unmistakable political motives. But lest too much is attributed to government, one should also draw attention to the secular decline in manufacturing industry – much bemoaned at the time – a sector in which the unions were at their strongest (apart from public employment).

There were also important clearing-up measures. Wage, price and dividend controls were quickly removed and did not return for the rest of the century. In addition, confiscatory marginal tax rates of 80 per cent plus on higher earned incomes and 90 per cent plus on investment income were abolished. The two main tax cuts were in the Geoffrey Howe budget of 1979 and the Nigel Lawson budget of 1988. Although the last led to such an uproar that a House of Commons sitting had to be suspended, there has so far been no attempt by the Blair government to restore these confiscatory rates, whatever may be thought of the overall drift of the tax burden.

What the Thatcher government wished to be remembered for was its total impact in promoting what it called an 'enterprise culture'. It may have had some effect in doing so, judging by business reaction, though there was no productivity acceleration then or later. Indeed, the rhetoric about entrepreneurship was taken up again, in only slightly different words, by Gordon Brown, who became Labour Chancellor in 1997 and who was much influenced by US culture and academic writings, especially of the Harvard variety.

Money and the pound

Unfortunately much of the discussion among economists and economic commentators during the Thatcher period was on pseudo-technical questions of monetary control. The dilemma started from the very beginning in 1979–80, when the official broad measure of the money supply, sterling M3 (bank deposits plus notes and coins) was rising much faster than target; but this apparent monetary expansion was accompanied by a severe recession and a further rise in the pound about which British exporters complained bitterly. The renewed upward pressure on sterling was widely attributed to the impact of North Sea oil, which was then just coming on stream, on the British balance of payments. One industrialist remarked that he wished that 'the bloody stuff had been left under the ground'.

A more technical reaction to the rising pound was to argue that the British government had used the wrong measure of the money supply and should have used some narrower aggregate. This view seemed to be adopted in 1984–5, when, to the fury of another school of monetarists, the government abandoned targets for sterling M3 and moved over to a very narrow money aggregate called M0. This consisted of the bank balances with the Bank of England together with cash in the hands of the public. This aggregate was not however used as a form of monetary base control, for which the Friedmanites had argued, but as a rough guide to current economic conditions. The truth is that the government did not find any monetary indicator which conformed to common-sense observation of what was happening to the economy.

One effect of all this squabbling was to put off the general public – and even non-specialist economists – from anything to do with monetarism. Another effect was to build support for British membership of the European Monetary System, which had started without the UK in 1979. It was noted that some countries, notably France, had managed to import German price stability by tying their currencies to the German mark inside the European Exchange Rate Mechanism and realigning as little and as seldom as possible. The clamour to join the ERM was shared by far more people than chose to remember it afterwards.

There were two forms of the argument for a Deutschmark anchor. One was that the UK would have to follow a non-inflationary monetary policy if it was to avoid realignment; and the movement of the sterling market exchange rate would therefore send forth the right signals. Another argument was that the pressure of overseas competition, without the devaluation option, would put a lid on British costs and prices in international markets, and this would eventually percolate through to the domestic economy as well. Whether the external discipline and monetary control arguments were complementary or alternative, or amounted to the same thing, would take a lifetime of scholastic argument to determine. Business support for the ERM was based more simply on the hope of some exchange rate stability which would make life easier.

The case for the ERM as a monetary anchor was probably at its strongest in 1985 when the Chancellor Nigel Lawson first proposed it. Although it had a large amount of Cabinet support, it was vetoed by Margaret Thatcher, who was by then relying increasingly on the advice of her own personal economic adviser, Alan Walters, much of it given from across the Atlantic. There was another attempt at a more informal link with the ERM through the policy of shadowing the Deutschmark, which Lawson adopted in 1987 and which led to a much-publicized row with the Prime Minister in 1988 – a dispute culminating in the Chancellor's resignation in the following year.

The third attempt on the ERM was that of John Major, who succeeded Lawson as Chancellor and who managed to force through British membership in the autumn of 1990. By then the Treasury had no alternative policy to offer and Margaret Thatcher resigned near the end of that year after a disappointing leadership vote among

Conservative MPs. But by then the case for the Deutschmark anchor had been enormously weakened by the German reunification of 1989, which imposed a large budgetary burden on the German government. The Bundesbank, quite rightly in view of its mandate, maintained high interest rates to offset the inflationary effects. This interest rate policy was, however, quite unsuitable for the UK, which had entered one of its worst postwar recessions and one which was particularly resented because it hit the talking classes in the south-east of England. Thus by 1992 John Major, who was by then Prime Minister, was forced to take Britain out of the ERM and put the country back on a floating exchange rate which lasted for the rest of the 1990s and into the next century.

The more stable 1990s

The decade from 1992 witnessed first a gradual recovery from the recession and then a period of low inflation and moderate growth, with more stability than had been seen for many years past. The hallmarks of the new policies were inflation targets and a greater role for the Bank of England.

Probably the pioneering country in the use of inflation targets was New Zealand. But someone in the Treasury had the sense to propose them for the UK as part of the response to the post-ERM panic. These targets were accompanied by a new obligation on the part of the Bank of England to produce a regular inflation report. These innovations, which were introduced by Norman Lamont who had succeeded Major as Chancellor, were reinforced when his successor Kenneth Clarke surprised many officials by agreeing to the publication of the minutes of the monthly meetings on interest rate policy between the Chancellor and the Governor of the Bank of England. Operational independence of the Bank came with the Labour victory of 1997. It had first been advocated by Nigel Lawson and then by Norman Lamont, but proved unacceptable to both Thatcher and Major. Tony Blair, who had no ambition to control monetary policy personally, was more easily persuaded. The new policy regime, under which interest rates were set by a nine-person Monetary Policy Committee was more of an evolution than the revolution which Gordon Brown's supporters liked to claim.

The most interesting feature of the 1990s was not so much low and stable inflation itself, but that it was accompanied by a continuing drop in unemployment to much lower levels than in the 1980s. In economic jargon, the NAIRU – the rate of unemployment consistent with non-accelerating inflation – seemed to have dropped. Some of the credit can legitimately be granted to the Labour New Deal, which put emphasis on retraining and on pressure on the unemployed to take jobs and temporary subsidies to employers to take them on. Even more important was the belated effect of the reduction of union power to price people out of work arising from the Thatcher measures of the 1980s.

Labour leaders could not of course publicly admit this. But privately they were keen to emphasize how little of the Conservative union legislation they had reversed. Nevertheless there was some quiet backsliding. The minimum wage was more objectionable to libertarians in principle than in practice as the government was keen to keep it low to the chagrin of its own left-wing. Nevertheless there was a creeping movement back towards so-called social legislation which imposed high-cost obligations on employers. (At the time of writing, British employers are up in arms against a draft EU directive which grants all temporary workers the same conditions and terms as their permanent colleagues – thus closing one route for pricing workers into jobs. The British government was mainly concerned to delay this rule for the first six weeks rather than to stop it altogether.)

There were a great many specific domestic measures, which ministers undoubtedly believed were improving the supply side and making the economy more competitive; and it is true that most of them had been sanctioned by official economists as ways of tackling one or other externality which interfered with the optimal working of the market mechanism. *But what the new government found it difficult to appreciate was that the cumulative effect of a great many individual measures, which in themselves might have been desirable, produced an irritating and cost-increasing business environment.* Unfortunately the new government's academic praetorian guard was not as familiar with the US economic analysis of government failure as it was with the standard writing on market failure.

The argument about Europe rumbled on, threatening to split the Labour party as it already had the Conservatives. The economic argument no longer related to an exchange rate anchor. Many supporters of British membership of the euro had originally seen it as the best way to establish an independent central bank. But with the coming of the MPC arrangement, this argument had largely vanished. What was at stake now was the pros and cons of a more stable exchange rate against the disadvantages of a 'one size fits all' monetary policy. Or, to put it another way, would stability be better ensured by the MPC or the European Central Bank? No amount of technical analysis was likely to weaken the conclusion that it was half a dozen of one and six of the other. The famous five economic tests for euro membership could be interpreted according to taste and their application was delayed as long as possible. In any case public opinion remained for long resolutely opposed to dropping the pound;

and Tony Blair would have been well advised to put the whole issue on ice for his first two administrations. His reluctance to do so had little to do with euro technicalities and reflected far more the urgings of Foreign Office and Cabinet Office officials who wanted Britain to have a seat at some supposed European top table.

Conclusion: the new century

As the new century began there was a distinct possibility of old errors coming back in a new way. The most likely route was by means of the European Social Model, which was not social, not a model and did not deserve the name European. It was characterized by high labour overheads, wage arrangements which made it difficult to fire and therefore to hire workers, and which were too insensitive to market pressures.

The result was that an excessively low proportion of the EU population was at work, especially in the older age groups; and the coming explosion in the number of pensioners looked like having to be supported by an ever lower proportion of active workers. Too many people were being educated, were unemployed or prematurely retired. The simple step of linking retirement age with longevity, (discussed on pages 78–80 above), which might at least have eased the pressure on the European welfare state, was considered too revolutionary and reformers became obsessed with the minutiae of pensions arrangements.

The UK debate was muddled by an unhelpful dispute between the little Englanders and the euro enthusiasts. Yet for those of us who treated government as a device rather than a totem, it did not matter so much exactly where the centre of power was located. The British economy was equally capable of flourishing under a strong European federal government with appropriate decentralization and a single currency, or under a national government with an independent pound regulated by the Bank of England Monetary Policy Committee. The danger was that it would get the worst of both worlds: a weak European confederation, with enough power to stifle market forces and price people out of work, but without the power or drive for genuine reform.

Yet, for all these problems, most British people had a far higher standard of living than the vast majority of the human race in all past history; and the time could be coming for Lord Keynes's *Economic Possibilities for our Grandchildren*, in which attention would shift to more important matters. That is if the attempts of religious and other fundamentalists to destroy the European Enlightenment and the appeasing reaction of Europe's leaders do not derail us on the way.

Note

1. Nicholas Crafts, *Britain's Relative Economic Performance, 1870–1999*, Institute of Economic Affairs, 2002.

Black or White Wednesday

John Major, *The Autobiography*, HarperCollins, 1999;
Norman Lamont, *In Office*, Little, Brown, 1999
Prospect, December 1999

The sixteenth of September 1992 is not a date recalled in every pub in the country. But it is still etched into the brains of Britain's economic policymaking and talking classes. For it was the date on which the country was ignominiously forced out of the European Exchange Rate Mechanism – Black Wednesday or White Wednesday according to taste. Yet the government tried to pretend that nothing much had happened – except the exposure of mythical 'structural faults' in the ERM.

Few members of the wider public were turned on by the esoteric arguments about monetary regimes. Even among businessmen the day was remembered mostly for the shock when interest rates were temporarily raised from 10 to 15 per cent in a vain attempt to stop the rout. Nevertheless the main pillar of economic policy had collapsed; and some sense of this did eventually percolate through to the electorate. It could never be glad confident morning again for the Major government.

The ERM story is one of the main points of overlap between the Major and the Lamont books, which are otherwise quite different. Lamont's is an insider's story of some crucial years in economic policy. Major's is a much more extensive personal and political autobiography. Lamont is on the whole convincing that he was the first to realize that the UK might have to leave the ERM. Major's main efforts were devoted to a series of sad notes to the German Chancellor Helmut Kohl, pleading with him to lean on the Bundesbank to change policy to help out the UK. This was an area in which Kohl was out of his depth and not even sympathetic.

The speeches of both the Prime Minister and the Chancellor before Black Wednesday went much further out on a limb than the ritual 'no devaluation' protestations under a fixed exchange rate regime. It is normal in these circumstances for the chancellor to resign, if only to take over another portfolio. But in this case the policy was first and foremost John Major's. As he disarmingly remarked when Lamont offered to resign, his Chancellor was his 'lightning conductor'. When he had served that purpose, and the press was making him into a scapegoat for slow economic recovery, he was dismissed. If the Chancellor had gone in September 1992, the Prime Minister would quite likely have had to go too; and perhaps the reputation of both men would now be higher. No one came out of this episode with credit. Ministers such as Kenneth Clarke and Michael Heseltine – described as 'Big Beasts' by sycophantic journalists – were called in on that fatal day by Major to protect his own flank. They merely succeeded in adding to the reserve loss by insisting on holding out a few hours longer out of misplaced European sentiment.

Why, however, did John Major make the original decision to take Britain into the ERM in 1990, with such ill-fated political results? We need to go back quite a way to understand it. The postwar orthodoxy was that full employment could be secured and growth underwritten by maintaining the level of spending. It was called 'Keynesian' – but let us avoid an argument about whether it was what Lord Keynes, who died in 1946, would have meant or approved. Under this doctrine inflation could only be controlled by tackling wages directly, either by exhortation, or a pact with the unions, or legislation or some mixture of all three.

That was the principle. In practice, the link with the dollar, which was then a stable currency, ensured a low rate of creeping inflation. It was, in effect, monetarism by proxy. But by the 1970s this approach was in a shambles. There was a simultaneous deterioration in both employment and inflation, even before the Yom Kippur war triggered off a fivefold increase in the price of oil.

Meanwhile Milton Friedman had shown, on theoretical grounds, that there was no long-term choice between inflation and unemployment; and that inflation had to be tackled by monetary means. Under the influence of his then son-in-law, Peter Jay, Prime Minister Callaghan bravely embraced the Friedman doctrine at the Labour conference of 1976. How far he meant it no one will ever be sure. But for the Chancellor Denis Healey and his Permanent Secretary, the strongly Keynesian Douglas Wass, the new doctrines were mainly hot air, necessary to keep the financial markets at bay. Harold Lever described their attitude as one of 'unbelieving monetarism'.

When the Thatcher government came to office in 1979, believing monetarists took over from unbelieving ones. The question still remained: how was monetary policy to be guided to achieve the new aim of low inflation? Under both the last years of Denis Healey and the early ones of Geoffrey Howe (who became Chancellor in 1979), the answer was the pursuit of monetary targets.

The early 1980s witnessed a paradox. If inflation was to be regarded as the judge and jury, Conservative policy had if anything oversucceeded. The economy had been tightly – even excessively – squeezed, sterling had shot up, unemployment soared and inflation plummeted. Yet the professed monetary targets had been overshot and changed many times. Meanwhile a more theoretically minded Chancellor, Nigel Lawson, arrived in 1983 who was impressed by the way in which countries that had linked themselves to the German mark – then the currency of a very sound money country – had managed to reduce their inflation rates gradually but dramatically. This was a form of monetarism by proxy linked to the mark, just as Bretton Woods had been one linked to the dollar.

Readers of biographical memoirs – or even readers of reviews of them – will know of the struggles between Lawson, who wanted the ERM discipline for the UK, and Margaret Thatcher, who hated the idea of British policy being run by what she sometimes called 'Belgium'. The *faute de mieux* policy of 'taking everything into account' which guided events in the second half of the 1980s, did not convince anyone. By 1990 Lawson and Thatcher had fought each other to a standstill. The former resigned in 1989, followed a year later by the Iron Lady herself.

Major, who became Chancellor after Lawson, inherited the problem of how to set monetary policy. He also inherited a resurgence of inflation – exaggerated by absurd price indices and ultimately due to an unforeseen surge of bank lending and the associated boom in property prices. As Major candidly admits, this was a boom about which everyone was wise after the event. The highly unpopular 15 per cent base rate which Lawson had left behind was in fact squeezing out inflation pretty effectively. But how was the new Chancellor to convince the markets that sound money was here for keeps? He saw no alternative to taking up Lawson's policy of joining the ERM. He succeeded in getting membership past a by then demoralized Margaret Thatcher, six weeks before she left office herself; and it became the flagship of his own economic policy for the next two years.

What else could he have done? There are a few dedicated technical monetarists who still believe that all that was necessary was to reaffirm monetary targets. But as their professed allegiance was to different measures of the money supply which moved in dazzlingly different directions, they were easily – perhaps too easily – brushed aside.

A reader at the turn of the twentieth century might ask why inflation targets – which stated a clear goal but left the authorities with discretion on technical means – were not considered. The brief answer is that they had not yet become fashionable and there was perhaps one country – New Zealand – which had them at the centre of its policy during the time that John Major was steering Britain into the ERM. Moreover many Treasury and Bank officials would argue that an inflation target could only be credible once inflation was already down to low single figures.

Lamont, who had run Major's campaign for the Conservative leadership in November 1980 and then became Chancellor, had a different orientation. Although he had spent much of his ministerial career in the Treasury, he had not been involved in the exchange rate battles; and he writes that he himself would not have taken the decision to join the ERM. But once Chancellor, he soon came to see the ERM's value as an anti-inflationary constraint. Indeed, in 1991, the first full year of membership, it seemed to bring the best of both worlds. It was helping to bring down inflation; and, because it was partially credible, British interest rates could be cut. By 1992 the situation had changed dramatically. The earlier high interest rate policy had begun to work with a vengeance and the British economy was clearly in recession. Lamont had no doubt that on domestic grounds base rates needed to be reduced a good deal lower than the 10 per cent to which they had by then been cut. Not surprisingly, he began to see the ERM as an unwelcome constraint, probably well before Major did.

The fundamental reason why the ERM policy failed so dismally lay in the way in which Germany handled the economics of reunification. Just as the US could no longer be the anchor for a world system of semi-fixed exchange rates after the inflationary financing of the Vietnam war, so Germany could not be such an anchor in the years following the fall of the Berlin Wall. This should have been obvious not merely by 1992, but by 1990. In the summer of that year, well before the UK entered the ERM, the East and West German marks were unified at the ludicrous rate of one for one. Worse still, German employers and unions had committed themselves, with government encouragement, to a levering upwards of East German wages and social security benefits to West German levels, way ahead of any conceivable reduction in the productivity gap. To cap it all, Chancellor Kohl insisted that the budgetary costs of unification could be met without any substantial rise in taxes or cuts in West German spending.

The Berlin Wall came down a fortnight after Lawson had resigned; and the ill-fated currency unification announcement was made over three months before Britain's entry into the ERM. With hindsight all of us who urged entry, not as a step towards some federalist goal but as a practical monetary arrangement, should have seen the writing on the wall and shelved the idea. This applies to Major, Lawson and, I hasten to add, myself, as I became a staunch adherent of sticking to

ERM membership at the initial entry rate. My main reason was similar to that of Terry Burns, long-time chief government economic adviser, who asked what it would say for the determination of the British government, if after less than two years of a policy about which it had argued for ten years, it simply abandoned it.

By 1992 there was no strategy which could have kept Britain in the ERM without prolonging the recession, which – perhaps because it hit the talking classes in the south-east harder than any of its predecessors – provoked ferocious resentment. Lamont's own view at the time was that the combination of two years inside the ERM, followed by departure, was beneficial. Inflation would have been unlikely to come down, so far and so credibly, without the period in the ERM; but recovery from recession was earlier and more vigorous in the UK than in those countries which remained inside the system. The combination of entry, followed by forced exit, was nevertheless politically disastrous.

The former Chancellor should be given more credit than he usually receives for announcing an alternative within weeks of Black Wednesday. Indeed, most of the key features providing for transparency and accountability of which Gordon Brown now boasts were put in place by Lamont. It was he who installed the inflation target and the quarterly Bank of England inflation report, which lie at the heart of present policy. He would have gone the whole hog towards Bank of England operational independence – like Lawson before him – if the Prime Minister had allowed him to do so. The contribution of his successor, Clarke, was to publish the minutes of the Bank–Treasury meetings – which have now been replaced by the deliberations of the Bank's Monetary Policy Committee.

Unfortunately the story cannot end there. A common failing of both books is that they are too reticent and kind about the official advice that their authors received. This is explained, but not justified, by their need of Whitehall help in gaining access to documents after they left office. Is it unfair to expose the advice of officials who cannot answer back? Can't they just? A good deal of high-level economic commentary consists of unattributed comments by officials on the politicians whom they are supposed to serve. In some instances a franker account would indeed have been to the credit of official economists. The switch to an inflation target could not have come so quickly after the ERM departure unless officials had been thinking about it beforehand. And for all Gordon Brown's bluster to the contrary, his initial inflation target of $2^{1}/_{2}$ per cent, with a permissible range of one percentage point either side, was as near as makes no difference to the original Lamont target of 1 to 4 per cent.

Other episodes show officials in a less favourable light. If there is one matter on which tactics are suggested by officials rather than politicians, it is contingency planning against a run on the currency. The excuse for the undignified panic departure from the ERM was that the selling pressure on sterling took everyone by surprise. Surely, if there is one lesson that should have been learned from past crises, it is that the selling pressure when a fixed parity comes under speculative strain is dozens of times higher than any advance estimate. The standby credit which the Bank of England negotiated was enormous in terms of the kind of money with which normal people deal, but chicken-feed in the context of a far-from-surprising currency run.

At the time, the remarks of the Bundesbank president, Helmut Schlesinger, about the need for realignment, given in a press interview which was 'not confirmed', were more than a bit gauche and were blamed for the debacle. But the British side had no excuse for being surprised. In all my own contacts with the Bundesbank, long before Black Wednesday, the pressure for realignment was made quite clear. It is of course likely that the best of tactics could not have prevented sterling's forced departure. But at the very least wiser officials could have insisted that the only way of staying inside the system was to raise interest rates much earlier – probably by a good deal more than the one percentage point which Lamont had proposed and Major refused.

The biggest official deficiency of all was in the reliance on forecasts. Again and again, in the period of nearly two years up to Black Wednesday, an upturn was predicted but never materialized. In fact output stagnated in 1990, fell in 1991 and stagnated again in 1992. The 'green shoots of recovery' for which Lamont was so mercilessly castigated, did not really appear until 1993, about the time that he was sacked.

This over-reliance on short-term forecasts has been the bane of economic policy for getting on for fifty-five postwar years; and it has led governments down again and again. Lamont kindly quotes a prescient remark which I made, while the UK was still in the ERM, that officials put up hardline speeches to the Chancellor 'in the knowledge that the official Treasury would not hesitate to leave him as a scapegoat if it changed its mind about the appropriate policy'. The usual defence of these forecasting fiascos – and Burns himself has said that these forecasts do not improve with time – is to say that forecasts are inevitable in human affairs. This is just a debating point. If I have to make plans for holidays in January or February it would be best to assume that the weather will be reasonably cold, but with a wide range of variation; and I might be better advised to prepare myself for this variation by taking a range of clothing rather than rely on long-range weather forecasts.

Put Your Money Where Your Mouth Is

Financial Times, 2 March 2000

The best surprise that Gordon Brown, the Chancellor, could spring on us would be to announce that the next is the last traditional British budget – the last national sporting occasion on which the Chancellor produces tax changes like a rabbit from a hat and when analysts stay up all night to understand what is really meant.

The present Chancellor has already had his fun with these occasions. He could have even greater fun by bringing them to an end and saying that his real budget, like that of almost all commercial organizations and many other governments, will be the public spending plans to be unveiled in the summer.

Of course, there could be occasional finance bills. These would be used when the Chancellor wants to improve the tax structure, or needs to raise more revenue, or can afford to return some cash to the taxpayer. A year with no tax changes – which under the current arrangements would be dismissed as a 'boring budget' – would then count as a success story.

The virtues of stability, which Mr Brown constantly preaches, apply to the tax system as well. An essential preliminary to any such reform would be the indexing of all tax rates and starting points not merely to inflation, as many of them are now, but to the level of incomes. That would halt the insidious process of what economists call 'fiscal drag', by which the tax proportion increases even when tax rates are not increased.

Let me also put forward a second-best. Mr Brown should take heed of the recent conclusions of the Commons Treasury committee, on which Labour has a majority, and present the budget in a clearer, more concise and less propagandist way. For instance, one should not have to guess that tax remissions come under the heading 'Increasing Employment Opportunity'.

Above all, the financial effects of several budgets should be shown separately and not counted several times over. And tax and expenditure figures should be distinguished and shown on a single annual basis. 'New money' should be distinguished from existing commitments and Mr Brown should stop rolling up expenditure plans for three or four years together to give an exaggerated impression to Labour MPs, who are not as stupid as ministers suppose.

What else? Many economists would actually like the Chancellor to increase tax rates in the hope of encouraging interest rates and sterling to fall. Indeed, the European Commission has been lecturing the Irish government not to go ahead with plans for promised tax cuts to reduce economic overheating – almost certainly to no avail. Apart from their political unrealism, such pleas are based on economic assumptions that are often falsified by events. A more moderate view is that fiscal policy should support monetary policy to the extent of not attempting to remit most of any current budget surplus.

We have little true idea how much of this is structural and how much represents a cyclical boom effect. What we do know is how quickly surpluses can change into large deficits at the first whiff of recession.

How should the tax remissions be allocated when they are possible? There is one place in the tax structure where disincentives bite earlier and earlier, namely the starting point for the 40 per cent higher rate of income tax (equivalent to a consumption tax of well over 50 per cent). Although the higher rate has been unchanged since 1988, it has gradually bitten lower down the income scale. This has mainly been the result of Conservative chancellors trying to show their 'one nation' credentials by not adjusting the upper threshold in line with rising incomes. It was a futile gesture that gained them no political credit. But as a result, there are now 2.3m higher rate taxpayers, or three times as many as in 1980–81. Those affected are just the middle managers, the professionals and small businessmen on whom governments rely to spread the enterprise culture.

It would be best to combine a rise in this threshold with an increase in the upper earnings limit (UEL) for employee National Insurance contributions to the higher rate starting point. Doing so would eliminate the dip in the tax progression between the end of the UEL and the start of the higher rate.

Finally, I have a suggestion to make for all those dinner party conversationalists who say that they would rather not have the 1p income tax reduction already announced for 2000–01, and devote the sums to better public services. They should be enabled to do so.

Why should not income tax returns have a space in which the taxpayer could indicate his desire to forgo any tax relief (or any other relief on a future occasion)? The return could also contain an estimate of what the effects would be on his personal tax bill. There is no need to stop here. Why should there not be a structured ballot attached to the income tax form in which the public-spirited taxpayer could express his preferences between extra expenditure on different public services such as health or transport? Then the new expenditure could be divided among public services in line with taxpayer preferences.

So far from being 'right-wing', a move along these lines would reduce the biggest disadvantage of public over private spending, which is that the voter has to take a complete spending package from the winning political party and has no way of making his own choices as he can in his own personal shopping.

This reform might be called in the language of the spin-doctors 'An Opportunity to Put Your Money Where Your Mouth Is'. It would need to be carefully prepared months or years in advance of the actual announcement. But there is nothing impossible in it except to the bureaucratic mind.

A Dedicated Tax for Health

Financial Times, 14 March 2002, 7 December 2000

The government has benefited from several windfalls – above all from a falling share of national debt interest. But windfalls cannot continue for ever. For a time, total departmental expenditure can rise by 3 or 4 per cent per annum, even though the trend growth of national income is around $2^1/_2$ per cent per annum. There is little case for a tax increase now. But what Gordon Brown, the Chancellor of the Exchequer, has to do, if he wishes to adhere to his spending aspirations, is to prepare the ground for future increases.

Yet the government lost no time in putting clear water between itself and the report of the Tax Commission published by Labour's senior think tank, the Fabian Society ('Paying for Progress'). The Commission's most interesting and controversial proposal was for a fully hypothecated tax – that is, one that covers the whole cost – for the National Health Service. The earmarking proposal stemmed from opinion research showing that while people were, in principle, in favour of paying more to fund health or education, they were extremely suspicious of the links between the taxes they in fact paid and improved public services. The Commission's guiding idea is to 'reconnect' payments and services. This should be equally acceptable to people who differ widely on the desirable extent of collective provision.

If carried out carefully, earmarking ought to appeal both to those who want the state to spend much more and those who do not. Indeed, both left-of-centre and free-market think tanks have published papers in favour of earmarking. My own interest in the subject was restimulated in the run-up to the 1992 election when I saw militant, uniformed nurses arriving *en masse* at televised public discussions to insist that the NHS was 'underfunded'. I often wondered how much would have to be spent before such lobbies could ever be satisfied. (I am, however, a little suspicious that these militant nurses were no longer quite so much in evidence after the political colour of the government changed.)

The clamour for more spending is not of course really for health, which depends on many other things than the National Health Service. But as I am the last person to lecture anyone on diet or exercise, I shall concentrate on medical services and their finance. The only way citizens can know what is being spent on state medical provision, and whether they want to increase it, is to make it clear what they are paying for it. Of course earmarked expenditure has long had a bad name. A levy known as 'ship money', raised by Charles I, helped to trigger the British civil war of the seventeenth century. This was partly because parliament did not give its approval and partly because it was levied on inland areas even though the purpose was supposed to be to defend the coastal towns. In more modern times, earmarked taxes have been debased. For instance, taxes on road vehicles were supposed to go to a Road Fund, which was quickly raided for general revenue.

Earmarking is worse than useless if the earmarked taxes do not finance the whole of the service in question . The Liberal Democrats fought several elections on pledges to raise the basic rate of income tax by one percentage point to finance extra expenditure on education. This was tokenism. The net effect was to give the impression that a big improvement in education could be had on the cheap. There is nevertheless an overwhelming case for a hypothecated tax channelled specifically into the NHS. Such an earmarked tax would provide an automatic feedback. Voters would have to put their money where their mouth is.

It would be best to channel the bulk of the revenue from some clearly visible existing tax into the NHS. There are two taxes of roughly the right order of magnitude. They are social security contributions – which have long become a levy on payrolls far removed from any insurance principle – and value added tax. Social security contributions could easily be transformed into a payroll levy to cover health. The snag here is that about half the contributions are now paid by employers. Wage-earners, looking at the deductions from their own pay packets, would thus get a far too rosy idea of the true cost of the NHS. VAT, on the other hand, is clearly visible; and the trend towards itemizing VAT separately by many retailers and service providers will make it all the clearer. Moreover VAT is a pretty buoyant tax. Receipts here have risen remarkably in line with public health expenditure; but up to now they have always been a little higher, leaving some headroom for further NHS growth. In future, nothing could make clearer the cost of increasing NHS care than an automatic increase in the VAT rate or the extension of the tax to products now exempted.

Many of the objections to hypothecation are of a quibbling nature. For instance, receipts of individual taxes fluctuate with the state of the economy. But surely it would not matter if there were small amounts of topping up from general revenue in recessions, so long as it was clear that most NHS spending was financed from a specific fund, which might accumulate a surplus in times of boom. It is worth a little untidiness for the sake of greater transparency.

Earmarked taxes cannot remove all the inherent defects of the political market. They cannot enable different voters to have different sized health services to suit their individual preference as they can with supermarket purchases. But they can at least make sure that the service comes with a price tag and its expenditure is representative of what the middle-of-the-road taxpayer is prepared to finance. There is no need to be starry-eyed about hypothecation. Eventually even an earmarked NHS tax would go the way of the Road Fund. But for a few vital years it could segregate the NHS from the rest of the political debate and reduce the sanctimoniousness that surrounds the issue.

The Rise of the Inactive Man

Financial Times, 21 June 2001

In many parts of the world the unemployment statistics have proved a misleading guide to labour market performance and nowhere more so than in Britain. Between the bottom of the 1992 recession and the first quarter of 2001 the UK unemployment percentage, based on the count for those claiming benefit, fell from 9.9 per cent to 3.3 per cent. On the basis of the Labour Force Survey, the fall was slightly less – from 10.8 per cent to 5.2 per cent – but impressive all the same.

This improvement cannot be written off as just an aspect of the movement of the economy from recession to boom. For the remarkable thing is that the fall in unemployment has not so far been accompanied by any notable acceleration in wages or inflation. Something more than the upturn in the business cycle has been involved.

Conservatives may be inclined to attribute the improvement to the delayed-action effect of their own earlier measures to curb union power and other labour market reforms. Labour will naturally attribute the structural improvement to its New Deal for the jobless and to the maintenance of stable overall economic conditions. But before anyone seeks to judge between these claims, it is worth looking at other indicators that suggest that there is less to celebrate than meets the eye. People of working age are not only divided into those with jobs and the unemployed. There is a third large section who are not classified as unemployed but who do not have jobs either. The official statisticians call them 'economically inactive'. Here the picture looks very different. The economically inactive proportion of the working age population was 21 per cent in 1992 and is still 21 per cent, despite the economic upturn. So if we are looking at the success rate in placing people in jobs, there has been no improvement – there is even a deterioration if allowance is made for the business cycle.

Even more remarkable have been the different experiences of the two sexes. The overall behaviour of inactivity rates shows an actual improvement for women, where the ratio has dropped from 29 per cent in 1992 to 27 per cent today. The other side of the coin is of course an even greater deterioration for men. Here the inactivity rate has risen from 13 to 16 per cent – and this in a boom period.

Excluding students and those on training schemes, there are now 2.3m men of working age who are economically inactive compared with 400,000 twenty years ago. As might be expected, the rate is highest among men over fifty, of whom 28 per cent are outside the labour force. But the problem cannot be dismissed as confined to older workers who have retired prematurely. About 1m men under fifty, or 8 per cent of the total, are now inactive compared with fewer than 1 per cent in the mid-1970s, according to more detailed data unearthed in an article by three economists at the Centre for Economic Performance (Dickens, Gregg and Wadsworth, 'Non-Working Classes', *CentrePiece*, Summer 2001).

Early retirement has been highlighted by policymakers in view of the expected ageing of the population in most western countries over the next thirty years. An article by Philip Taylor in the April issue of the official *Labour Market Trends* lists policy shifts away from early retirement, as a wrong-headed means of reducing youth unemployment, and towards policies aimed at the participation of older workers in the labour force. The British government has published a code of practice on age diversity for employers; and the New Deal has been extended to the fifty-plus group. The government is now committed to implementing legislation proscribing age discrimination in employment. Other European countries have experimented with gradual retirement, so that older workers are not lost from the workforce altogether. In France and Germany there are wage subsidies for older employees. These may be early days yet; but so far there is little sign of a reversal of the trend towards lower participation.

One should be clear about what is a policy problem and what is not. There is no merit in paid work for its own sake. If older workers prefer to live on pensions that they have in some sense 'paid for' in their working lives, that is their right. Policy problems emerge if they have left the labour force because they believe that employers discriminate against people in their age group; or if their pension scheme or early retirement is publicly subsidized.

The CEP authors are sceptical of the idea that declining labour force participation is largely voluntary. If that were so we would see the highest withdrawal rate among groups with fallback incomes such as savings or private pensions. In fact male participation rates have fallen most among 'older, less skilled workers in depressed labour market areas'. Moreover the main reason given for inactivity by men under sixty is sickness rather than retirement. It is however possible that low-skilled workers are discouraged from looking for jobs by the low wages on offer for those re-entering employment. Re-entry wages for those coming back into employment have always been well below average but have fallen considerably in the last couple of decades. The CEP authors make much of widening pay differentials – which they call 'increasing inequality'.

But whatever one calls the phenomenon, it cannot encourage workers back into the labour force. There is indeed a probable connection between the low levels of pay for the unskilled and those re-entering employment and the large number of households where neither parent has a job. While UK unemployment rates compare favourably with other European Union countries the position is very different for the percentage of households without a wage-earner. This is nearly 20 per cent in Britain compared with 6 per cent in Germany and 9 to 10 per cent in France. The rise in female employment has not helped here because it has generally taken place where the male partner is already in work. On the other hand, men are more likely to have ceased employment if they are the only wage-earner.

The conclusion of the CEP authors is, predictably, that more official intervention is required and on a bigger scale than anything seen so far in the New Deal projects and other policies. How far one believes this is a matter of general political stance. But a reasonable middle-of-the-road conclusion is that, before embarking on massive new projects, government advisers need to trawl existing policies to ascertain how far they encourage early retirement or discourage participation in the labour force. This would be a big task for a single parliament, but one that should be completed before thinking of trying to improve the workings of an unimpeded labour market.

The Awful Lure of the Grassroots

Financial Times, 25 May 2003

Arthur Balfour, British Conservative leader a century ago, once claimed that he would no more take the advice of the Conservative conference on public policy than he would of his valet. He was right.

Political leaders are frequently advised to 'go back to the grassroots'. These voices are particularly loud after a period in which a prime minister has steered a course far removed from the instincts of his party members, as Tony Blair has done over Iraq. But long before Iraq, Peter Hain, the Welsh Secretary, was giving warnings about the need for Labour to regain its grassroots support. Recent middle-level Cabinet changes have been interpreted as a token gesture in this direction. For Labour, grassroots means constituency members and trade union leaders. In the Conservative party it also means constituency activists, especially those who come to party conferences.

Sometimes nourishing of grassroots is urged in the name of democracy. Nothing could be further from the truth. The views of activists tend to differ far more from the majority of the electorate than do those of Cabinet ministers and MPs. Nor is it that party activists are 'more extreme'. As Thomas Paine said: 'Moderation in temper is always a virtue; but moderation in principle is always a vice.' The trouble with the grassroots is not that they are undemocratic but that they represent beliefs which are too often outmoded, authoritarian or inhumane. One does not have to have a starry-eyed view of the capacities of modern electorates to see that even they often judge better.

It is mainly the activists who still take seriously the left–right political spectrum deriving from the seating of parties in the French Revolutionary Assembly of 1789. Labour activists are more suspicious of profits, more hostile to the price mechanism and more inclined to 'soak the rich' than the mass of Labour voters. The Third

Way may not be all that it is cracked up to be. But Tony Blair could never have weaned his party away from old-fashioned socialism if he had followed the grassroots instead of leading them, using as his weapon the supposed threat of never-ending Tory governments.

The dubious nature of grassroots pressure does not only affect Tony Blair. The Chancellor Gordon Brown has pursued some market-based policies much further than any Conservative chancellor has dared, most recently in his tentative espousal of market-based regional pay differentials in the public sector. He has been able to get away with it so far because he has a personal style which goes down well with party workers and seeks to maintain good relations with union leaders even when he is trampling their sacred cows underfoot. But style can only get one so far. Already there have been rumblings and some back-pedalling on the regional pay idea.

Conservative activists are not the monetarist fanatics of left-of-centre imagination. Their failings are different. They focus on distinctions between English people and foreigners, they are harsher on immigration and would never let supposedly Thatcherite free market economics stand between them and special subsidies to protect agriculture or 'the countryside'. It may be a cliché to say that they are keen on hanging and flogging. But both these barbaric practices have remained off the statute book mainly because successive Conservative Home Secretaries have either defied their activists, or at least not tried to reverse reforms introduced by Labour parliaments. The biggest mistake of the post-Thatcher Conservative leadership was to open the election of the leader to the mass party, with disastrous results. If the system had existed earlier, Disraeli would have stood no more chance of leading the party than Michael Portillo did later.

I do not know what to say about Liberal Democrats. The party is almost defined in terms of its grassroots. Indeed it started to recover its electoral prospects by embracing 'pavement politics', which were an extreme concentration on local issues which should have been the concern of municipal bodies. Yet it is the descendant of the nineteenth-century Liberal party, whose intellectual leaders, such as John Stuart Mill, were not only contemptuous of grassroots but were very cautious about extending the franchise too rapidly to people who would not know how to use it.

Elite groups can often be mistaken. For instance, I would not take the obsession of the British Foreign Office with a 'seat at the top table' – which has caused it to veer from Atlanticism to the European Union and back again – as the last word in wisdom. My thesis is unashamedly negative. Grassroots opinion would not have saved British governments from the mistakes of their official advisers but would often have embroiled them in additional ones.

One argument for paying attention to grassroots supporters is that they make the political system work by selfless efforts at constituency level and also by cash support. But it is mainly nostalgia that focuses on the devoted local loyalist licking stamps and serving rather good cups of tea. Elections are influenced by the mass media, above all television, and by general impressions the electorate have of particular leaders or the character of the government.

The cash problem is more serious. But the conventional view that state support should replace or supplement the grassroots as the source of party funds takes us along a dangerous route. Instead, donations of wealthy individuals should be welcomed as a way of freeing Labour from dependence on the unions and the Conservatives from constituency subscriptions. Some recent research has shown that, in the USA at least, the donations of corporations and rich individuals have not been enough to swing policy in favour of their financial interests.[1] The real charge against Tony Blair in this respect is not that he pursues orders for arms and dubious capital projects in the hope of receiving donations for Labour, but that he pursues such projects at all.

Let us examine a topical test case. What do you think would obtain a more considered result in a referendum on British euro membership? A franchise confined to party activists, a secret poll among the senior civil service, a free and secret vote of the House of Commons or the envisaged referendum? Surely the real choice is only between the last two.

It may be too late to revert to the system by which MPs alone elected the party leaders. But at the very least we should give three cheers when prime ministers go by their own instincts in the knowledge that, if they succeed, their partisan followers will have no choice but to accept.

Note

1. S. Ansolabehere, J. de Figueiredo and J. M. Schneider, 'Why is there so little money in US politics?', *Economic Perspectives*, Winter 2003.

A Frank Look at 'Labour Values'

Financial Times, 27 February 2004

Some months ago I wrote a column on the harm done by party leaders concentrating on their so-called grassroots supporters instead of the broader electorate. At that time the main examples were of the harm done by misguided Conservative reforms introduced to give more say to constituency party members. In the period ahead we are more likely to hear of grassroots Labour values and it is time to take a look at them without rose-tinted spectacles. What follows is a rule-of-thumb guide to policies and attitudes likely to meet with approval by Labour activists.

1. The group is more important than the individual. Tony Blair rewrote Clause Four of the Labour constitution, which formerly dealt with nationalization, to stress group values. The Conservatives are not free of this belief, which they tend to associate with the nation. Labour speaks more of the 'community' and of groups such as workers in manufacturing and in so-called public services.
2. National resources belong to a common pool rather than to individuals. It may be expedient to allow some people to keep some of their earnings, but no more than that. Therefore it is not taxation that has to be defended but 'tax cuts'. Under a progressive system, these will tend to benefit the better off and are best regarded as dirty words.
3. The French revolutionary slogan of 'Liberty, equality and fraternity' is cherished. But if there is a clash between them, equality must triumph. Sophists redefine true liberty to be identical with equality. It is not a very coherent goal as greater equality in some directions, such as income, is likely to mean greater inequality in other directions, such as power or prestige. Cynics paraphrase the doctrine as: 'If everybody cannot have something, nobody should have it.'

4. The supreme value is something called 'democracy'. This means that any brake on the people's will, such as an effective second chamber or judicial review of legislation, cannot be tolerated. But democracy has to be interpreted as first-past-the-post in a constituency system. Pedants who call this plurality, which enables a minority to rule, are written off as opponents.

5. There is a real sympathy for the poor and disadvantaged. But it sometimes clashes with another Labour slogan that policies should benefit 'the many, not the few'. As long as there was a pyramid-shaped distribution of income and wealth in which the poorest also formed the majority, there was no problem. But with the current diamond-shaped distribution, where the poor themselves are among the few, difficulties emerge.

6. The maxims of economics do not apply to labour markets. Wages and other elements of labour cost can be increased without affecting employment if the government keeps an eagle eye on cheating employers. Labour activists are therefore free to regard trade unions as the salt of the earth and to desire that pre-Thatcher legal privileges should be restored.

7. Rationing by price is evil. Public services should be 'free at the point of delivery'. This applies above all to medical services and education. It is never explained why this should not apply to food, which is even more important for maintaining health.

8. The public sector is to be preferred to the private one. While the belief in nationalizing further activities may be dormant, transfers to the private sector are seen as obscene.

9. There is a nostalgia for the Second World War, when individual aims were subordinated to a common purpose and we 'all mucked in together'.

10. There is a genuine dislike of repressive foreign dictatorships. But this is directed in a one-sided way at so-called right-wing dictatorships, such as General Augusto Pinochet's former regime in Chile. Visits to London by those associated with Soviet repression are not denounced or even noticed.

There are further subtleties. The toleration extended to the former Soviet Union does not extend to present-day China. Here the blind eye is mostly the prerogative of business people and Conservative leaders. There are subtleties within subtleties. Although it would have been the kiss of death for anyone in Labour circles to have had dealings with the Chilean military dictatorship, it was relatively easy to get away with being associated with the Argentinian one.

A problem in debating Labour values is that politicians of other parties tend either to share many of them or to be on the defensive if they do not. An example is provided by the contortions the

Conservatives have got involved in on tax and public spending.

Critics of Labour values can be disregarded as ultra right-wing or 'market fundamentalist'. This column can be dismissed as a 'gaffe' and its author encouraged to get back to inflation targets and exchange rates.

British Anxieties about the Public Service

Paper circulated at a Ditchley Park Conference, 25 April 2003

The old Whitehall culture

The UK is certainly not the only country to have suffered an undercurrent of anxiety over the performance of politicians, their advisers and the relations between them. But they have come into sharper focus here because we had for a long time a set of principles on the respective roles of the participants involved, which enjoyed cross-party consensus.

The peculiarity of the system in Britain, and to some extent in Commonwealth countries which have inherited British institutions, is a particularly sharp division between the civil servants, who have been called permanent politicians and who look after government departments as a lifetime career, and the political birds of passage who come and go with election results and prime ministerial whims.

The origins of this sharp division go back a long time – to the efforts made in Victorian England to remove the last vestiges of favouritism and corruption which coloured political life in the eighteenth century. The basic reforms were laid down in the Northcote-Trevelyan Report of 1854. These established the principle of an independent civil service appointed by merit – in practice competitive examinations. This was to a large degree a self-regulating institution. Indeed one interwar head of the civil service, Warren Fisher, spoke of the four Crown services: the army, the navy, the air force and the civil service. Ministers were there to take decisions and the civil servants to advise and to implement those decisions.

The relative importance of implementation and advice were never very clear; but it is pretty obvious from individual biographies that the path to advancement was not via the ability to run a tax office or to deal with unemployment claims, but brilliance in writing papers for ministers, helping them to keep out of trouble in parliament and elsewhere and in giving instructions to the genuine technocrats and administrators such as the parliamentary draftsmen.

The system was modified in the Second World War through the entry of academics, businessmen and others. Nobody would have called the late Isaiah Berlin a typical member of the higher civil service! But despite the election in 1945 of a Labour government committed to a more extensive role for the public sector, most of these wartime recruits went back to their former occupations and the traditional system was re-established.

Earlier discontents

The first rumblings of discontent first preceded and then accompanied the election of the first Wilson Labour government in 1964. Wilson did not talk about a Third Way, but the 'white-hot heat of the technological revolution'. He was looking for types of change other than the traditional socialist one of extending public ownership. The great cry of many of those who, directly or indirectly, gained his ear was that the civil service was technologically out of date. It had too few computers, had too few specialists and did not know how to use the ones that it had. It was then that we had the first influx of special advisers, who were then known popularly as 'irregulars'.

Unfortunately some of these otherwise desirable innovations were used as a way of avoiding awkward political decisions. It did not take a brilliant economic mind to see that the incoming government had the choice between devaluation and relying on deflation alone. (I served briefly in the short-lived Department of Economic Affairs, which was meant to provide a third way between these alternatives; but most of its economist members were vehement devaluationists and were told to keep their thoughts to themselves.) In the end devaluation was forced on Wilson by events in 1967.

The 1970s were a period of marking time. The Heath government of 1970–74 did not rely so much on irregular advisers, but continued to have some. Its main innovation was the Central Policy Review Staff, under Lord Rothschild, which was meant to give the Prime Minister and the Cabinet non-departmental views, especially on longer term issues. It was composed of a mixture of political and civil service appointees; but their bias was would-be technocratic and interventionist rather than partisan. It was abolished by Margaret Thatcher – largely, it was thought, out of pique when she blamed it for leaking a report. If it happened it was an aberration. For it hardly ever got into the job of news management. The various Number Ten policy staffs which succeeded it under both main political parties have been more short-term and more concerned with immediate trouble-shooting. The Labour governments of Wilson and Callaghan from 1974–9 were far too preoccupied with immediate threats to meddle with the civil service. There was the world oil crisis, the aftermath of the coal miners' strike and the excesses of rampant trade unionism – this was a time when top civil servants told their more trusted press contacts that the country was becoming 'ungovernable'.

Although Margaret Thatcher distrusted the senior civil service, she was not very interested in systematic reform when she came to office in 1979. Senior ministers had their special advisers, limited to two each; but her main involvement lay in the appointment of permanent secretaries and other senior figures. Indeed her war cry 'Advisers advise and ministers decide' could have come straight out of Northcote-Trevelyan.

Recent anxieties

The next phase of public anxiety occurred in the post-Thatcher years of the Conservative government (1990–97). The evaporation of the Thatcherite crusading zeal should have eased tensions but it did not. The main focus of anxiety in the mid-1990s related to 'sleaze', a shabby word to describe a shabby phenomenon. It mostly related to conduct which was not obviously illegal, but did not seem quite right, and where there was a suspicion of private gain. The scandals were mostly low level and did not affect the most senior politicians or civil servants. A typical example was the charge that MPs received payment for asking questions in parliament. It was these sleaze issues which led to the appointment of the Committee for Standards in Public Life, which has also been encouraged to consider broader and more interesting questions.

Having made so much of the sleaze issue in the run-up to the 1997 election, Tony Blair declared that his government would have to be 'whiter than white'. The sleaze issue has not been banished, but is now mostly subsumed under 'cronyism'. Most of the allegations under the present regime have related not so much to personal gain but to the treatment of businesses which have made donations to the Labour party. This has been a diversion from issues which are intrinsically much more important. It will never be possible to determine definitively whether the choice of companies to be supported in bids for overseas contracts is influenced by political donations. The more important and neglected issue is whether ministers should be canvassing for arms orders and dubious capital projects abroad at all. Am I a lonely idealist or am I corrupt in supposing that an ethical foreign policy is more important than a little bit of sleaze?

The two most recent causes of anxiety have been the role of special advisers and public service delivery. Anxiety over special advisers, who have doubled in number under the Blair government to reach nearly eighty, has emanated to a large extent from the civil service itself, but has been happily fanned by the media and could become a major political issue if the Conservative party came to life again.

Complaints have centred around two cases: Tony Blair's chief of staff and his principal adviser on media and communications [then Jonathan Powell and Alastair Campbell] who have been – as an exception to the normal rules – empowered to give instructions to permanent civil servants. This seems to me making a mountain out of a molehill. A prime minister is surely entitled to have a chief of staff and a head of media relations with whom he has a political and personal rapport. And it is difficult to see how people in such senior positions can operate without staff whom they can instruct. If one of the individuals concerned has behaved in an unnecessarily abrasive way, it is an *ad hominem* matter which hardly seems to raise great constitutional issues.

While all the attention has been focused on these two appointments, very few people have noticed how a similar situation has been handled smoothly and effectively inside the Treasury. When Gordon Brown became Chancellor he appointed a personal economic adviser with whom he felt at home [Ed Balls]. The fact that the latter was an economist in his own right, and not just a pamphleteer or spin-doctor, made a great deal of difference. In due course the person in question achieved the august title of Chief Economic Adviser to the Treasury, which had previously gone to non-political civil servants. It was said that he had to have a proper official rank and not be just an adviser if he was to represent the Chancellor at international discussions. (So I suppose he acquired the technical authority to require the assistance of permanent Treasury economists, whereas previously he would have had to ask them – or get the Chancellor to ask – the Permanent Secretary to instruct them!) But because of the human chemistry involved no one even noticed the difference. A lot of the credit for this smooth arrangement was due to the Treasury's top permanent economist, who saw no point in fighting the man on whose judgement the Chancellor relied. The adviser in question will probably fight a safe Labour seat in the next election, and his full-time services will be lost to the Chancellor without any offsetting constitutional gain.

Delivery

When it comes to the delivery of services I need to speak in a still, small voice. For I have very little feeling for practical operation and delivery. But I cannot help observing the fact that many of the people who write papers for the Prime Minister on the subject are no more obviously qualified than I am. Seen from a distance, we seem to have a series of brilliant undergraduate essays. And when one essay fails to convince, a different adviser is asked to write another one.

Aspiring civil servants are now told that delivery and implementation are at least as important as the traditional job of whispering policy advice into the minister's ear. But I suspect it is still the case that the brightest of new recruits will hope that they will be the exception and will be called upon to advise the minister on high policy or how to handle difficult political situations. It will be very difficult to overcome a culture in which the top ranks of the civil service, although called 'administrators', were really policy advisers, and the people who had to carry out the policies were one class below and known as executive officers. These class divisions have long been abolished and replaced by an incomprehensible system of numbered grades. The old administrative grade is still there under the guise of 'fast track admission'.

I cannot help noticing that the one area where UK implementation and delivery are internationally regarded as successful is the armed services. Is it a coincidence that in the defence department the top generals, admirals and air marshals are certainly not inferior to the senior civilian civil servants; and indeed as Joint Chiefs of Staff they have independent access to the Prime Minister. The lack of such people was surely noticeable in areas such as the BSE crisis and the mass fuel price revolt of a couple of years ago. The armed services have also prided themselves on their intelligence work – finding out what is going on among potential opponents, which is a different matter to forecasting or policy analysis. The occasional appointment of people who are billed in the press as energy czars or health service czars represents a groping in this direction. But even in a liberal society there is surely a case for a government having at its disposal genuine trouble-shooters with effective resources behind them.

Permanent politicians

Coming to more controversial subjects, is it not time to question the emphasis put on the political impartiality of civil service advisers. This is taken to fantastic extremes in a recent handbook (*How to be a Civil Servant*, by Martin Stanley, Politico, 2000). For instance 'it is essential that you give no sign that you oppose the principles and underlying thrust of the government's policies' and 'you must avoid saying anything that demonstrates that you personally agree or disagree with ministers' decisions'.

It is questionable whether someone so desiccated and so detached makes the best possible adviser. Supposed political impartiality works best in an era of simple left–right politics when an official can take a perverse pride in producing schemes both for nationalization and denationalization. It works much less well in the face of complex issues, which have both a political and a technical aspect – for instance the Thatcher government's desire to jettison the philosophy of economic management which had prevailed until the mid-1970s.

These matters can be left to evolve, which is one reason for being a little bit cautious about implanting present distinctions in stone in a new Civil Service Act. But I will dare to dissent from the Wicks Committee (on Standards in Public Life) on a specific point. As I understand it, the Committee reaffirms that both permanent and private secretaries should be chosen by departments rather than by ministers. (It does not even consider the Church of England's precedent by which the Church presents two candidates for Archbishop of Canterbury, knowing which one is certain to be rejected by the Prime Minister!) It is surely reasonable that a minister should not have to work with either a head of department or a head of his private office who is politically or personally uncongenial. In practice of course both prime ministers and other heavyweight ministers do get involved in such appointments, by giving their views privately to the top civil servants who make them. But can we not get away from these muddy waters by allowing the minister a formal say? British government did not break down when permanent secretaries were appointed from the outside world in the Second World War; and I doubt if it would if ministers could make such choices today.

Confidentiality of advice

Finally may I introduce a personal hobby horse? This is the emphasis put on the iron-clad confidentiality of advice given by officials, whether permanent or special advisers, to ministers. This is the rock on which the civil service establishment has made its stand over the last fifty years. It suits politicians who are not called to account if they reject official advice for insufficient reasons. But neither are officials called to account if this advice has been bad.

If civil servants may disclose advice, will it make them reluctant to give their honest opinions? It is equally arguable that their work would be improved if it had to withstand public scrutiny. I need not repeat what has been said over the ages about the privilege of power without responsibility. I have only recently learnt that the Fulton committee appointed by Harold Wilson originally intended to argue for greater openness in this respect, but was talked out of it by the Prime Minister and Permanent Treasury Secretary of the time.

Trust and the Public Services

Financial Times, 25 April 2002

'Trust' has been the theme of the BBC Reith Lectures given by Onora O'Neill, a distinguished philosopher and Principal of Newnham College, Cambridge.

Professor O'Neill is sceptical of the fashionable talk about the breakdown of trust in the professions, government, judges, police and so on. She finds little evidence that this is so, whatever people may say to opinion pollsters.

Trust is, however, a matter of degree. A patient might be more distrustful of alternative medicine than of the Health Service, but not have much faith in either. But let us settle for the lecturer's diagnosis that what we really have is a culture of suspicion rather than pure mistrust.

When it comes to remedies, she is suspicious of the cult of transparency. Perhaps too much so. While no sensible person would argue that the Cabinet should meet in the street, the availability of more information about how decisions are reached and of official advice reaching ministers is beneficial.

In my own neck of the woods the ascription of responsibility for interest rate changes to the Bank of England and not a confused amalgam of the Chancellor and the Bank Governor is pure gain. So is the publication of the minutes and votes of the Monetary Policy Committee. This is so, even if one takes with a grain of salt the econometric models on which so much emphasis is ostensibly placed. In other areas, such as the preparation of the UK budget, transparency is still very partial.

The Reith lecturer is at her best when she lays into 'the new accountability culture...Professionals have to work to ever more exacting standards of good practice and due process, to meet relentless demands to record and report, and they are subject to regular ranking and restructuring...Avoiding complaints becomes a central institutional goal in its own right...We are heading towards defensive medicine, defensive teaching and defensive policing...The real requirements are for accountability to regulators, to departments of government, to funders, to legal standards – indeed often to mutually inconsistent forms of central control...Performance indicators are chosen for ease of measurement and control...and even those who devise them know that they are at their very best surrogates for the real objectives.' As one general practitioner writes, all local managers 'want is to be able to report to the next layer of management that their own targets have been achieved. Thus a virtual NHS is created which has little relation to the real one.' (Dr Jonathan Reggler in *The Blue Book on Health*, Politico, 2003.)

Last week's British budget could have been designed to exemplify these warnings. Gordon Brown, and chancellors before him, have said that more cash for the NHS depends on evidence of improved performance. And sure enough that evidence is to take the form of even more tests and inspections. Two new 'super-regulators' are coming: the Commission for Health and Audited Inspections (CHAI) and the Commission for Social Care Inspection.

What, however, is the alternative? Professor O'Neill herself insists that trust must be earned and can never be unconditional. She wants to rely mainly on 'intelligent accountability', allowing 'some margin for self-governance', presumably exercised by institutions such as schools, universities, hospitals or professional associations. But here I have doubts.

A famous quotation from Adam Smith says that 'People of the same trade seldom meet together, even for merriment and diversion, but the conversation ends in a conspiracy against the public.' Public service professionals are not exempt from such temptations. How often have we come across scandals in local authority children's homes or in the behaviour of priests, which have been covered up by their brethren; and how often have whistle-blowers been given short shrift? Professional bodies are just as keen to restrict entry and control immigration to maintain earnings as any blue-collar trade union. The British Medical Association tried to prevent my own father from settling in the UK before the Second World War, because it was afraid that there would be too many doctors.

Much of the discussion after the Reith Lectures assumed that the culture of constant inspection and ultra-detailed targets comes from the private sector. The truth is that some firms behave like this and others do not. The culture of testing and inspection probably spreads from management consultants who persuade successive governments that these are the ultimate in modern business practice. There is an alternative both to professional self-government and to Whitehall invigilation. This is what is vulgarly known as the bottom line. A commercial concern which focuses on profitability does not need a myriad subsidiary tests *en route*.

In some of the best-managed conglomerates the component divisions are allowed to get on with their activities in their own way provided they can eventually show a reasonable return on capital. There is of course good reason why the purchase of medical services cannot be treated just like the buying of food and clothes. This is not the arrogant one that patients lack the knowledge to fend for themselves. The private medical service is far from ideal, but patients in it can get advice on where to go for treatment. Most people are affluent enough to purchase for themselves the procedures, medicines and consultations of everyday life. But beyond this medical needs differ by vast amounts from one person to another and cannot be taken care of by a negative income tax.

Many of the touted alternatives to tax finance lose their attraction on inspection. So-called social insurance turns out to be just a tax on payrolls, like the National Insurance contributions which Gordon Brown increased last week. Private insurance is full of snags in the small print. It works for one-off events like a broken leg or an appendix operation. But anything at all continuing or repeated is likely to be disallowed or excluded when the policy is renewed. This is quite apart from the cap which insurance companies have to put on benefits. New DNA techniques of investigation will inevitably discriminate against those who need financial help most. The heyday of medical and perhaps other kinds of insurance was reached when the likelihood of adverse events was a pure gamble and premiums had to be set on overall statistics.

The way to introduce genuine market forces into medicine is to recognize that there is a large element of personal choice in how much to spend on medical care. If we were starting from the beginning it might be best to regard medical expenditure as a personal discretionary item of spending, but with increasing state top-ups as crippling levels of medical expenditure are approached.

Starting from where we are, the best way of introducing market forces would be, as my colleague John Willman has suggested, to increase the element of charges, with a cap on how much anyone can be required to pay. (*A Better State of Health*, Profile Books, 1998.) Additionally, I would allow some of the fee proceeds to go directly to the providers of care. The combination would not only provide extra financial resources, but bring home to people that medical care cannot be free and make them think carefully before they spend. Meanwhile the Wanless Report on the NHS is fatally flawed as a classic example of economics without price.

Obviously, I have not described a complete alternative model. All I am trying to emphasize is that there must be and are alternatives to Gosplan-type targets or delegation to professional bodies. Nobody can be completely trusted; but we could trust the customer, patient or parent more and the bureaucrat or professional body a good deal less.

PART FOUR

Economic Management

Money can't buy friends, but you can get a better class of enemy.

Spike Milligan

There cannot in short be intrinsically a more insignificant thing in the economy of society than money...it only exerts a distinct and independent influence of its own when it gets out of order.

John Stuart Mill, *Principles of Political Economy*

The Forecasting Delusion

Financial Times, 4 January 2001

Winston Churchill said that a young person entering politics needs 'the ability to foretell what is going to happen, tomorrow, next week, next month and next year. And to have the ability afterwards to explain why it didn't.' Alas, only the last part can be done.

Ten or a dozen years ago many informed observers would have agreed on most of the following. Inflation is endemic to western economies; Labour is unelectable; the UK will integrate more closely with the European Union; full employment will never again be achieved; the USA is a sclerotic economy but Japan has the secret of rapid growth; British beef is the best in the world and organic farming will remain the preserve of a minority of cranks. This list is taken from a paper by an 'expert on social trends', Bob Tyrrell, just published by the Centre for Policy Studies (*Things Can Only Get...Different*, 2000). It must, however, be said that Tyrrell's own scenarios for the years ahead do not look any more convincing than the ones he is mocking.

The more interesting question is why it is so difficult to predict, and what we can nevertheless say in the absence of a crystal ball. Karl Popper, the philosopher of science, had a knock-out argument against long-range historical prophecy. This is that the course of human affairs is affected by new knowledge, which is by its nature unforeseeable. It is, however, unlikely that new knowledge will determine whether or not there is a recession in the US next year. Another Popper argument is relevant here concerning a misconception about scientific method. Some of the physical sciences have predictive power. But such predictions are conditional. They assert that certain changes, such as an increase to a certain point in the temperature of water in a kettle will, granted certain other conditions – for example a given atmospheric pressure – lead to boiling. But they cannot tell us whether the required conditions will be fulfilled or not.

The historical prophecies that practical men demand are unconditional scientific predictions. They can be derived from valid scientific theories, if, and only if, they can be combined with the correct assertion that the required conditions are in fact fulfilled. These requirements can only be fulfilled for systems that are 'well isolated, stationary and recurrent'. This happens to be approximately true of the solar system, which is why predictions of events such as eclipses of the sun are possible many years ahead. But contrary to popular belief such systems are not typical even of the physical world, let alone the rapidly changing society of human beings.

The problems of forecasting are rooted in the complexity of the phenomena under examination. Popper's friend, Friedrich Hayek, was virtually read out of economics for doubting whether it would be possible to discover simple, quantitative regularities between economic variables – which is what mainstream macroeconomists have been trying to do in the last half-century.

What then is there left to discover? Hayek's view was that the economist, like the biologist, was concerned with rules and patterns. A student of evolution can say something about the conditions in which new species evolve; but he cannot predict what these species will be or when they will occur. Economic theory can tell us that it is impossible to maintain a fixed rate of exchange and at the same time a national inflation objective. Nevertheless we cannot predict when the exchange rate will give way or where it will go when the chosen parity collapses.

Thanks to recent developments in mathematical physics it is possible to say more about such patterns, both in nature and in human society, than Hayek was able to do. A fascinating guide has been provided by a book entitled *Ubiquity* by Mark Buchanan, published by Weidenfeld and Nicolson, 2000. This book is not free of some of the faults of popular science books. The short table of contents consists of the usual cute headings which give little real guide to the structure of the book. A typical first chapter begins 'Hell Creek slips quietly out of one end of the Fort Peck reservoir in easternmost Montana and from there cuts a lonely meandering path into the hills'. Nevertheless it is not too difficult to find one's way into the arguments; and at least the book lacks the 'gee whizz' and 'wow' element so common to this genre.

We have already heard something of chaos and catastrophe theories. Buchanan discusses a third 'c' – complexity. He uses the analogy of a sand pile. If it is sufficiently steep a few extra grains can cause an upheaval; but without knowing the position of every grain it is quite impossible to say where or when the upheaval will occur. The sand pile is, however, 'in a critical state' – one that is vulnerable to disturbance – which he believes typical of much of social life as well, for instance, just as the earth's crust in certain regions is subject to earthquakes.

Nevertheless there is a 'power law' that can be given for earthquakes and similar phenomena and that seems to fit many human events. This says that the frequency of disturbances is inversely proportional to their size. Crudely, the bigger the rarer. Take a completely different event: the extinction of dinosaurs 65m years ago. The conventional wisdom is that this was due to a giant meteor hitting the Yucatan peninsula of Mexico. An alternative explanation is that such geological cataclysms are simply rare events liable to happen without any obvious 'cause'; and indeed the cataclysm of 65m years ago was only the latest, and not the biggest, of five such upheavals in the last 300m years.

Consider a single grain of sand falling on the western portion of a sand pile triggering a series of upheavals in the whole pile. Should the western authorities have been able to remove some of the sand from the initial spot and thus reduce its vulnerability? Alas no. To have foreseen the disaster the authorities 'would have needed near perfect knowledge of the position of grains over the entire pile coupled with unlimited computing power to work out the consequences of a grain falling'. Thus there is no way of knowing beforehand which grains should be removed and to where.

The simplest power law is based on the power 2. Earthquake B with double the force of Earthquake A is four times less likely to happen. For every city such as Atlanta with a population of 4m there are four cities having populations half that size, e.g. Cincinnati; and for every Cincinnati there are four cities half as large again. Thus there is no typical size for a city in the US or elsewhere and no reason to find any special cause behind the emergence of the very biggest. A different example relates to wealth. Find out how many people in the US have a net worth of a billion dollars. You will then find that four times as many have a net worth of about half a billion, and so on.

There are no deterministic laws of history relating to the causes of war: only the power laws which suggest that big wars are fortunately less frequent than small ones. Wars and revolutions 'don't come in simple cycles, and they don't telegraph their arrival in advance' any more than earthquakes do. Even the rough magnitude of the next stock market shift is unforeseeable. Great stock market crashes are simply ordinary events which occur infrequently.

Buchanan has the modesty to admit that we are only at the beginning of research. There are numerous problems of measurement.

Are there areas not in a critical state where we can plan ahead more confidently? I suspect there are at least two in macroeconomics. There is the very short-term outlook for say six to twelve months ahead, where something can be said by the economic statistician on the basis of typical lags between events that have already happened, such as oil price increases or wage explosions, and their path through to the rest of the economy.

There are also trends which tend to reassert themselves over five to ten years or more. For instance, British economic officials have found that almost whatever the period they look at in over a century the annual trend rate of productivity growth has been 2 per cent. Even this trend is only probable. It is likely that there will be rare upheavals leading to decades of above and below trend growth, the reasons for which will be explained after the event. Missing from the list, unfortunately, are the short- to medium-term forecasts, covering, say, eighteen months to five years, which are so much desired by central bankers for monetary policy or governments planning their spending over a parliament.

Inflation Targets Lose Their Glamour

Financial Times, 16 January 2004

The distinguished Belgian economist Paul De Grauwe has written (*Financial Times* on 8 January) that 'Central banking is not just about keeping inflation close to 2 per cent and praying the rest will be fine.' There are many straws in the wind suggesting that establishment opinion, even in the eurozone, is gradually shifting in his direction.

The head of the European Central Bank, Jean-Claude Trichet, the same day deplored 'exchange rate instability' – and not just for its possible effects on the eurozone price level. In an important speech in Leicester on 14 October, the Bank of England governor Mervyn King suggested that it was 'easier to measure the money value of spending and output in the economy than to split it into estimates of real output on the one hand and price indices on the other'. The latest data revisions, which considerably altered the picture of real UK growth over recent years 'have left estimated money spending and output broadly unchanged'.

There are numerous signs that inflation targets alone will not be a permanent regime like the gold standard or even the postwar Bretton Woods system. One sign of fraying at the edges is the arguments that have developed about how to measure inflation. The euro area has only managed to reach a common definition by using a harmonized index which excludes housing. Eurostat is now investigating methods of bringing owner-occupiers into the estimate, which could disturb the continuity of the series. The British Chancellor, Gordon Brown, has moved and slightly relaxed his target from RPIX to the UK version of the harmonized European index, which is now to be called the Consumer Price Index. In doing so he apparently cut inflation from 2.5 to 1.3 per cent at a stroke. Nobody believes this, but it has made it harder for the Bank to explain the likely need to increase interest rates. All this is coming on top of a long-standing critique of central bank neglect of boom and bust in asset markets – apart from their delayed effect on consumer prices.

A crude decade-by-decade history of macroeconomic policy in the second half of the twentieth century provides some context to current issues:

The 1950s. The dollar standard. Whatever governments said, policy was governed by the attempt to maintain the dollar parities of their currencies.

The 1960s. Growthmanship. Governments tried to boost growth rates by expanding demand. This produced:

The 1970s. The decade of *strato-inflation* with price increases in double digits which governments at first tried to control by 'incomes policies'.

The 1980s. Attempted monetary targets. Inflation did come down after painful squeezes; but the money supply proved difficult to regulate or even measure. Exchange rate pegs such as the European Exchange Rate Mechanism were also tried, with indifferent success.

The 1990s. Inflation targets and central bank independence came into fashion. The US Fed stood out against inflation targets, even though they have influential advocates on the Open Market Committee.

With hindsight, inflation targets are best suited to a period like the 1990s, when inflation has come down towards low single figures, but there is insufficient confidence that it will be maintained there. An objective of low but positive inflation helps build public confidence in a 'stability culture'. Inflation targets are less suitable if rapid inflation has become entrenched, as in the 1970s. A gradualist policy of reducing inflation by say 1 per cent per annum could lead to a very long period of depressed activity. On the other hand shock therapy could be very painful. In practice, policy relied then on unplanned shocks due to world events or policy errors to bring down inflation – sometimes called 'opportunistic disinflation'.

Inflation targets are also less suitable when inflation expectations are low and the main fears are of stagnation and recession. There is here the much discussed danger of the 'zero interest rate bound' which puts a limit on how far central banks can reduce the real price of borrowing. As both Mervyn King in his Ely Lecture of 3 January and Ben Bernanke of the Federal Reserve, in statements over several months, have reminded us, economic stimulation then requires cooperation between central banks and finance ministries, for instance for the monetary finance of budget deficits, rather than the arm's-length relationship suggested by the 1990s' model.

During the break-up of the monetary consensus of the 1980s I frequently urged a switch to the nominal GDP objectives at which King is now hinting. One virtue of such a nominal target is that when the economy is stagnating or in recession, it points decisively to expansionary policies so long as we are starting from a low inflation base. On the other hand if inflation takes off, the policy automatically acquires a restrictive bias and there can be no 1960s-type 'dash for growth'. Above all it avoids relying on estimates of the output gap which some recent studies have shown to be almost useless in the eurozone in recent years and excessively optimistic in the 1970s when they powerfully contributed to double digit inflation. The Fed under Greenspan can be said to have followed a rough and unannounced nominal GDP objective in that it has taken explicit account of output as well as consumer prices.

Why then have I said so little on the subject lately? When inflation targets appeared to be working there was no point in knocking my head against a brick wall. Moreover, some central bankers, such as King and Trichet, have always believed that a sufficiently flexible approach to such targets could make them approximate to nominal GDP.

Moreover, the promoters of any new objectives are likely to be crucified by the armies of short-term financial analysts. This is especially true for nominal GDP, which it would be neither possible nor desirable to monitor on a month-to-month basis but could only be sensibly tracked on a one-, two- or three-year moving average.

(And here is where I have shifted a bit.) Inflation and recession are not the only sources of instability even in western-type economies. We have yet to discover a simple and readily understood formula which would enable central banks to nip in the bud 'irrational exuberance' in asset and credit markets.

If we look at charts of the USA, the UK and the eurozone, we find that in the UK nominal GDP has followed a stable path of $4^1/_2$ to $5^1/_2$ per cent annual growth for the last few years. In the USA it has been in a 4 to 6 per cent band except for a sharp temporary dip in 2001. In the eurozone, on the other hand, nominal GDP growth has been in a much lower 2 to 4 per cent band in the last three years, with a pronounced downward trend. If M. Trichet and his colleagues were to inject enough money to raise this to 5 per cent, I do not believe that it would miraculously transform eurosclerosis, the main reasons for which are 'structural' – code for the stranglehold that union influence and inflexible labour costs impose. But it is still an olive branch which the ECB could honourably offer to its critics – and would be much better than tinkering with exchange rates. The worst that can happen

Unnatural Interest Rates
Financial Times, 1 March 2001

There was once an alternative theory of monetary policy different to both the inflation target version of monetarism and the Keynesian emphasis on stimulating output directly. This was the so-called 'Austrian' school, which in its turn drew on a Swedish economist of a century ago, Knut Wicksell. The latter distinguished between two rates of interest. There was the actual market rate; and there was also the unobservable 'natural rate' which would bring intended savings and investment into line if there were no distortions introduced by the monetary system.

The aim of monetary policy should be to be 'neutral'; in other words to try to minimize divergences between the natural and the market rates. The 'Austrians', in particular Von Mises and Hayek, emphasized that it was not sufficient to try to keep the general price level stable. Quite apart from index number problems – which they over-emphasized – the main harmful effect of inflation and deflation came, they argued, from distortions in relative prices which could occur even if the overall price index remained fairly stable. They emphasized particularly the malinvestment which would result if production became either too capital-intensive or not intensive enough.

One still controversial example is that of the behaviour of the Federal Reserve in the 1920s, leading up to the 1929 crash. While the monetarists believe that the Fed of those days was too tight, the 'Austrians' considered, even at the time, that it was from 1927 onwards too expansionary in promoting an investment boom which could not last. A similar controversy surrounds the period in the late 1990s, during which US inflation has remained low and stable, but when there were many signs of a rush into fashionable investments in IT and elsewhere.

During the interwar period the Austrian school discredited itself by insisting that the depression should run its course, to allow mistaken investment to be liquidated. Lionel Robbins of the London School of Economics, who had earlier supported such views, made a well-known recantation. Even 'assuming that the original diagnosis of successive financial ease and mistaken real investment was correct' to take no action against the ensuing depression, he remarked, was 'as unsuitable as denying blankets and stimulants to a drunk who had fallen into an icy pond, on the ground that his original trouble was overheating'.

Since the early 1970s there has, however, been a revival of Austrian economics, not anywhere near Vienna, but mostly in the United States where it is now a sufficiently important minority movement for respectable economic publishers to maintain sections of their lists devoted to it. Like all such minority movements the new 'Austrians' have their quota of fanatics and cranks. Indeed, when one of the more sophisticated of them attempted a semi-mathematical exposition of the school's teachings, he received hate mail from some who thought that he was being disloyal to the anti-mathematical gospel of Von Mises.

But at the other end of the spectrum there are 'Austrians' well aware of modern techniques, as well as of mainstream economics and of what is going on in the economy. One of the best examples can be found in a book with the unnecessarily forbidding title of *Microfoundations and Macroeconomics*, by Steven Horwitz, (Routledge, 2000). The emphasis is on the need to shift from monetary or inflation targets to some attempt at neutral money. He is less convincing on how to do so.

Yet we do not have to give up all attempt at a neutral policy. A starting point would be the research, stimulated by people such as de Anne Julius a founder member of the Monetary Policy Committee, on what a normal real short-term rate of interest might be. This would have to be based on the historical trend, abstracting from crisis years or periods of high inflation. Such an estimate will almost certainly come to somewhere in the range of 2 to 5 per cent.

This is only a beginning. Faced with developments such as a hectic scramble to invest in high-tech industries or a scramble for liquidity, it would be clear that the natural rate has moved. There is no avoiding judgement about how much, but it would surely be possible to do something better than just plough on regardless with rigid inflation targets.

For the time being, estimates of normal and natural interest rates are unlikely to be good enough to replace inflation targets altogether; and they will have to come in as a supplement. But anything that can replace the parrot-like incantations about price stability at every European central bankers' gathering would be a move in the right direction.

[In early 2004 real short-term interest rates were minus 1 per cent in the USA and above 1 per cent in the UK, and likely to rise if and when economic activity gathered pace.]

Taking Asset Prices Seriously

Financial Times, 29 August 2002

Inflation targets have now been in use for about ten years in many countries. The pioneer was probably New Zealand, followed not long afterwards by the UK. They have had a greater success than many people expected in keeping the inflation rate low while also reducing fluctuations in real growth. But rules for monetary policy in a paper currency world are not cast in stone. What was sufficient for the last decade may not be enough in the future.

The main original fear about inflation targets was that they would be achieved at the expense of growth and employment. That was one reason why some observers, myself included, would have preferred an objective that explicitly included a growth element, such as for nominal gross domestic product growth.

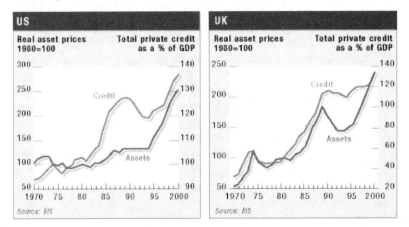

In fact, a regime of inflation targets alone has now come under criticism for a different reason. The fear now is not that real output has been neglected but that asset prices have been. There is a vigorous if rarefied debate about whether asset prices as well as consumer price inflation should be specifically targeted.

The riposte of central bankers is that asset prices are in fact taken into account insofar as they are expected to contribute to future inflation. The deputy governor of the Swedish central bank has suggested that policymakers should deal with the aftermath of an asset price boom but should not attempt to pre-empt it.

The critics argue, however, that this is not enough and action is needed to restrain an excessive rise in asset prices even if the inflation forecasts do not stray from the target range.

One of the more moderate statements of the case is made by Michael Bordo and Olivier Jeanne in a paper for the Centre for Economic Policy Research.[1] Inflation, they argue, is not the only danger from an unchecked boom in asset prices. Such a boom carries with it the risk of a bust that will destroy the value of securities held by financial institutions and thus induce 'a collateral-induced credit crunch'.

In their view the case for monetary restriction is greatest when the risk of a bust is large but when it can still be defused at relatively low cost. This means not delaying too long, as Alan Greenspan, chairman of the US Federal Reserve, did in the late 1990s. For, as the boom gathers momentum, more severe monetary restriction is required to puncture it. Central banks may then find themselves in the paradoxical position of having to induce a recession now to forestall the risk of a more severe recession when the bubble bursts.

To the ordinary person it seems odd to talk of low inflation when property prices are going through the roof and newlyweds cannot get their foot on the housing ladder. As Harvey Cole, an economic consultant, remarked: 'For those who doubt that asset bubbles are dangerously inflationary, the proof is simple. Does anyone deny that their bursting must be expected to have serious deflationary consequences?'

Bordo and Jeanne cite as their two main examples of a big stock exchange-induced boom-bust cycle the US depression of 1929–33 and the Japanese one of 1986–95. They agree with Milton Friedman that the depth and length of the depression were due to banking panics, which led to a collapse in the money supply. But the Wall Street crash contributed to this monetary contraction by reducing the value of bank loans and collateral. This led to a collapse of bank lending and the dumping of loans and securities, creating further asset price deflation. They argue that if the Fed had followed the views of Benjamin Strong, its chairman, and defused the stock market boom in 1928, the outcome would have been very different; and they conjecture the same for Japan in the late 1980s. The authors admit that assessing an asset price bubble is easier said than done. But is it, they ask quite reasonably, any more difficult than estimating the so-called output gap – how far output is from capacity levels – on which the interpretation of the current inflation target rules so often depends?

A Bank for International Settlements study[2] argues, with an eloquence rare in such research papers, that it is not asset prices themselves that pose a threat to the stability of the financial system but the combination of rapid credit growth, rapid increases in asset prices and, sometimes, high levels of physical investment. In any case, their charts show that for many countries there is a strong link between asset price growth and the growth of private credit.

The biggest policy problems relate to property prices. Bordo and Jeanne examine in detail experiences of OECD countries since 1970. They find that out of twenty-four boom episodes in equity prices only three were followed by busts: Finland in 1988, Japan in 1989 and Spain in 1998. On the other hand they diagnose nineteen booms in property prices in which ten were followed by busts (two of which occurred in the UK in 1973 and 1989). Property price bubbles tend to be localized. This suggests that central bank policy may not be the best way to deal with them in monetary areas as large as the eurozone or the US – or possibly even the UK.

Cole suggests decoupling mortgage rates from the rest of the market. But such segregation is difficult in a free economy. He advocates requiring all institutions lending on property to place variable special deposits with the Bank of England. Such a scheme for the commercial banks, which existed in the 1970s, was wound up because it introduced distortions without being very effective. Nevertheless, unless anyone suggests something more refined, we could well see a return to such methods.

In any case, policymakers will have to move on from targets aimed at inflation alone. The implicit model behind these targets is that all economic ills are reflected in inflation rates that are too high or too low – or are changing too rapidly or too slowly – and that, therefore, if these can be kept within sensible bounds all other ills will cure themselves.

If international events send the oil price soaring, so that we once again witness that combination of inflation and recession known as stagflation, the model will be tested to breaking point.

Notes

1. Discussion paper 3398, May 2002.
2. C. Borio and P. Lowe, BIS working paper 114, July 2002.

Take a Razor to the Deflation Debate

Financial Times, 4 July 2003

The fashionable shock-horror word is now 'deflation'. The European Central Bank in particular is often accused of pursuing deflationary policies. Faithful readers will know that I was intensely suspicious of this language long before the bond market shake-out indicated second thoughts in the financial markets on the deflation spectre.

Some years ago it was mostly the political and academic left that accused governments and central banks of following excessively deflationary policies. Today, however, the war cry is heard more loudly from some sections of the business community and the political right. It is difficult to suppress the unworthy thought that some of those behind the clamour are looking for a way out of unwise debts they have previously contracted.

It is as well to know just what we are talking about. Just as inflation is a general rise in the price level, so deflation is a general fall. Apart from Japan, the industrial world has not seen deflation for seventy years. Once there is a single currency and a single monetary authority, inflation and deflation refer to movements of the price level of the whole area. To raise the alarm about possible German deflation, because the rate of inflation in that country has fallen to 0.6 per cent – against a euro area rate of 1.9 per cent – is simply to ignore the advent of the new currency. To talk about German deflation makes as much sense as to talk about deflation in Texas or Cornwall, unless you believe monetary union is premature or still immature.

In any case it seems inherently absurd to believe that a $^{1}/_{4}$ per cent annual increase in prices is satisfactory, while a $^{1}/_{4}$ per cent decrease spells catastrophe. Very often the difference between these low rates of inflation and deflation will depend mainly on the price index used. A $^{1}/_{2}$ per cent rate of deflation based on the European Union's Harmonized Consumer Price Index usually translates into a $^{1}/_{4}$ per cent rate of inflation on the old British Retail Prices Index.

The problem is how to combat unhelpful deflationary panic without endorsing the frequently optimistic assurances of monetary authorities. There is a real danger ahead, but it is badly described by the deflationary war cry. It is that of a recession or slump in which nominal short-term interest rates are already near zero and cannot go any lower, even though the economy needs stimulation. It is this that has triggered a discussion, led by the US Federal Reserve, of 'unconventional policies'.

These policies may be required to prevent a decline or abnormally low increase in output and employment, irrespective of whether prices are slightly falling or slightly rising, as they often have been in past recessions. There have been periods, such as the 1880s in the UK, when prices fell by 0.6 per cent per annum, yet output grew by a highly respectable 2.2 per cent. Less happily, in the US in the years 1933 to 1937, after the Great Depression, the stimulatory effects of monetary expansion were syphoned off into wage and price increases by mistaken New Deal policies, thus retarding the recovery in output. When Keynes invented the 'liquidity trap', he made no mention of deflation but simply analysed the difficulty in some circumstances of getting interest rates low enough to stimulate output and employment.

The principle that is required for cutting through these complexities was provided by William of Occam, a fourteenth-century British philosopher. The principle, known as Occam's razor, states: 'Entities are not to be multiplied beyond necessity.' This is usually extended to mean that the simplest explanation should be preferred to more complex ones and that single encompassing hypotheses should be sought.

The simplest inclusive statement of the problem that may be facing monetary policy is that of the zero interest rate bound (ZIRB). This problem encompasses both the case when the need for stimulus is associated with falling prices and when it is not. It also excludes periods when prices are falling slightly owing to productivity improvements and there is no need for stimulus. The most thorough analysis has been provided by Ben Bernanke of the US Federal Reserve. Possible instruments range all the way from extending central bank operations to longer-dated securities to the finance of budget deficits by monetary creation, which Bernanke regards as the practical equivalent of Milton Friedman's helicopter drop of money from the sky. The bond market may now think it less likely that these devices will be tried; but fashions in financial markets change very quickly.

Let us suppose that nominal demand – or the national income in nominal terms – is rising by 3 per cent. Would you rather have a 4 per cent increase in output offset by a 1 per cent fall in prices? Or no increase in output but a 3 per cent rise in prices? The deflation-mongers implicitly assume the latter outcome would be better because there is a positive rate of inflation. This is no way to conduct a sensible debate.

How to Escape the Liquidity Trap

Financial Times, 28 March 2003

The hottest topic among highbrow financial analysts is: what can be done if official short-term interest rates approach zero but are still not low enough to revive an economy? Have the central banks then 'run out of ammunition'? The question has become serious enough for the Bank of England to include in its *Spring Quarterly Bulletin* an article by a senior official Tony Yates on the subject. Last November B. Bernanke, a new Fed governor, gave a well-publicized lecture entitled 'Deflation: making sure it doesn't happen here'.

The problem is quite easily stated. Short-term nominal interest rates cannot fall below zero, as no one would have any incentive to lend at negative rates. In fact the problem is worse. For most businessmen cannot borrow at the best prime rates but have to pay a couple of per cent more to allow for commercial risk.

In the 1930s Lord Keynes suggested that the lower bound to interest rates – which he called a liquidity trap – might prevent monetary policy from being sufficiently effective to restore normal output and employment. Milton Friedman in his postwar reply did not deny the theoretical possibility of such a trap. His view was that the Fed could have increased the money supply in 1931, but chose not to do so. The historical controversy still rages.

Yates is also anxious to play down the likelihood of such a liquidity trap. He tends, perhaps too easily, to dismiss the US in the 1930s and Japan today as suffering from conditions remote from the present-day UK, where interest rates could still fall several percentage points. He reinforces this by a consideration of various economic models purporting to show in what a small proportion of time an economy would be subject to the zero interest rate bound at varying, but low, rates of inflation.

But does he really expect his readers to be reassured. One tempting way, which he mentions only to dismiss, of preventing the liquidity trap from arising, would be to aim at substantial inflation rates, so that real rates could become negative during periods of recession and stagflation. This may indeed be one of the reasons why the world did not go into prolonged deep recession after the 1973 oil shock. But he dismisses the idea as bringing too many disadvantages as well as being politically 'not on'.

A popular course, frequently advocated for Japan, is pre-announced devaluation. This would both raise price expectations, and provide a direct stimulus to exports. The biggest problem with this remedy is that it would be quite inappropriate if the threat of slump were international rather than confined to one country. The zero bound to interest rates seems most likely to strike next in the case of Germany, where the single currency makes a national depreciation impossible.

Yet it surely ought not to be beyond human wisdom to prevent or at least treat a slump in a world of unmet needs that unemployed workers could be used to supply. Governor Bernanke remarks: 'If we do fall into deflation we can take comfort that the logic of the printing press asserts itself and a sufficient injection of money will ultimately always reverse a deflation.' Friedman indeed once contemplated dollar notes dropped from helicopters. A more respectable suggestion is that central banks, instead of limiting their pump priming operations to very short dated government securities, should buy a much wider range of assets, including private sector bonds. The Bank of England author discusses whether such operations could be reinforced by central bank guarantees to maintain near zero interest rates for some period ahead. But unlike Governor Bernanke he wonders whether such guarantees would be either credible or desirable.

The most unorthodox expedient he examines is a tax on money, if not spent by certain dates. This was proposed by academics a century ago, but is not as cloud cuckoo as it seems. When the Swiss were trying to repel short money inflows some years ago they imposed a tax on overseas-held bank deposits. This surely could have been extended to cover domestic deposits as well. Admittedly notes would have been a more difficult proposition, but not impossible with modern electronic means.

In discussing remedies the Bank of England analyst mentions first fiscal policy, that is tax cuts or public spending boosts. But this does not get the Bank off the hook altogether. For the effects of such stimuli would be controversial and uncertain unless they were financed by monetary creation rather than by long-term borrowing. As Governor Bernanke argues: 'A money financed tax cut is essentially equivalent to the helicopter drop.' Both EU rules and Gordon Brown's monetary and fiscal framework appear to rule out such expedients. But all these rules could surely be bent if the world was faced with utterly different dangers to those feared at the time they were drawn up. The real problem is that monetization of a flow of public debt requires, as Adair Turner of Merrill Lynch has reminded us, 'co-ordination between fiscal and monetary authorities, and that would be more difficult to achieve with one central bank and twelve fiscal authorities'. This is one further reason for countries outside the euro to stay outside for some time to come. My own preference would be for temporary cuts in consumer taxes, which would be reversed automatically at a stated date. This would be adequate to fight a temporary recession and not require unorthodox financing. In the face of more deep-seated stagnation or slump something more would be required. The obvious weapon would be public investment. The hole in the economy would arise because of the failure of private investment to keep up with attempted savings. So it would be sensible for public projects to take up the slack as Keynes originally suggested to Lloyd George.

There is an obvious danger of crying 'wolf' too soon and bringing back inflation or overblown government spending through errors of pessimism. But the best defence against such panic reaction is the knowledge that the authorities have in their cupboard weapons for coping with deficient as well as excess demand.

Is There a Consumer Debt Threat?

Financial Times, 10 October 2003

Neither a borrower, nor a lender be;
For loan oft loses both itself and friend.

These sentiments of Polonius in *Hamlet* express the personal instincts of many of us. But they are hardly the last word in a modern commercial economy. Although Margaret Thatcher never lost an opportunity to advise young people not to spend more than they earned, her beloved homebuyers were borrowing on a massive scale.

An irrational fear of debt lies behind the opposition to student loan schemes, even when repayment is strictly tied to income in later years. The shadow of the debtors' prison, which looms so large in the novels of Charles Dickens, still affects working-class culture. It would be better to switch to a graduate tax, which can have all the economic effects of a loan scheme.

The biggest source of controversy in the Anglo-Saxon countries is, however, the rapid growth of consumer debt. It has been rising in the UK at an annual rate of 14 per cent and stands at a record of nearly 120 per cent of disposable income. A coalition of Cassandras warns that the apparent success of Gordon Brown, the Chancellor, is based on an unsustainable mountain of debt. The coalition ranges from financial conservatives to left-leaning think tanks, such as Open Democracy, which has voiced fears for 'first world debt'.

The rise in the debt ratio is often explained by the boom in house prices. But that cannot be regarded as an independent force, to the extent that rising credit supports rising home prices, and the two could collapse together. The Bank of England's *Autumn Quarterly Bulletin* contains an analysis of the reasons for the jump in secured household debt – much the largest section of it. The rise in house prices relative to income plays a surprisingly small part. The biggest influences are the extension of home ownership, the reduction in inflation since 1985 and the associated fall in interest rates, which has reduced the burden of debt servicing. The author admits that his model does not explain the rise in secured borrowing since 2000.

The Bank of England itself is clearly divided. The most seriously argued alarmist analysis comes from Wynne Godley and Lex Izurieta of Cambridge, who argue that the consumer debt-to-income ratio has merely to stop increasing for UK consumer spending to be squeezed and economic slowdown or contraction to ensue. The most effective counter-argument comes from Goldman Sachs analysts, who maintain that most of the new credit has gone into the purchase of financial assets.

It is in any case clear that real UK consumer spending cannot go on increasing at the rate it did in 1997–2002, the first five years of the Labour government, when it rose by a cumulative 21 per cent on the revised national income figures, compared with a growth of 14 per cent in gross domestic product. The discrepancy can, however, be explained, without much reference to debt, by the slow rise in consumer prices relative to the prices of other GDP components.

What will replace the consumer as the main motor of expansion? Public spending will be in the lead. The arguments against this are the same as those against too much of our incomes being spent collectively. There need be no threat to economic balance if tax revenues also rise. The government hopes that investment and exports will also grow much faster than in the past. If they do not, the Bank of England will have to keep interest rates lower than they would otherwise be – even if higher than they have been recently – to sustain demand. Such a policy would also help exports by pressing down on the exchange rate, even if it delayed an adjustment in consumer credit. The inflation target might interfere with a smooth landing. But it is not possible in a free society to keep a free economy on an entirely smooth path.

The real rub of the Godley criticism is that the government has only one policy instrument – short-term interest rates – with which to meet its objectives. This is true if you want the government to have an instrument for affecting the components of GDP and, in particular, the balance of payments. But there is a second regulator, even if it is – wisely – not used as a policy instrument. That is the exchange rate, which is free to move whenever the financial markets start to worry about the size of the payments deficit. The foreign exchange markets may be inclined to overshoot. But there is little evidence that exchange rate management – which itself moves jerkily between reluctant adjustment and competitive devaluation – is any better.

Currency Competition: the British Debate

Speech to the Cato Institute, New York, 17 October 2002

Earlier history

It would probably be best for me to concentrate on the recent British debate. Not only do I know it best; but I do not think that the earlier debates on free banking in previous centuries in various countries have any very direct relevance. This is because, until some time in the twentieth century, it was generally assumed that money was based on an intrinsically valuable commodity, usually gold or silver, or some combination.

In earlier times freely floating paper currencies, not officially convertible into gold or silver or anything else, were regarded as emergency or temporary expedients. An example was the US dollar after the Civil War. During episodes of free banking, the privately issued currencies had an explicit or implicit bullion value; and their success was measured by how low the discounts on them were, relative to their stated metal value.

Hayek's proposals

The origin of the more recent British debate lies with some proposals made by the veteran Austro-British economist Friedrich Hayek. In a prewar work, *Monetary Nationalism and International Stability* (1937) he had come out in favour of a fixed international standard, which he thought would probably be gold. During the Second World War he published in the *Economic Journal* for June 1943 a proposal for 'A Commodity Reserve Currency' which would be convertible into a basketful of commodities on a predetermined basis, following on the lines of similar proposals earlier put forward by Benjamin Graham and Frank D. Graham. Such ideas faded from public view in the post-Second World War period, as the Bretton Woods system developed on the basis of national currencies linked by fixed but adjustable exchange rates.

The breakdown of that system after 1971, when President Nixon broke the last remaining link between the dollar and gold, was soon followed in many countries by the largest peacetime inflation of the twentieth century (leaving aside postwar hyperinflations.) In the 1970s Hayek started to investigate free competition between both official national currencies and privately issued ones as well. It started in his own words as a bitter joke directed against what he then thought was the chronic inability of governments to provide sound money. But it soon led him into the fascinating problem of what would happen if money were provided competitively.[1]

His preliminary analysis appeared in a short paper in 1976 and a much fuller treatment followed in *The Denationalisation of Money* (1978), which was his last contribution to monetary economics. A number of authorities contributed to the subsequent discussion. Milton Friedman, for one, was thoroughly sceptical, although he avoided the subject whenever he could out of deference to Hayek's standing and age, and in order to avoid a bitter internal war among free market inclined economists.[2]

Enter the euro

The issue arose again when the European Union began to develop plans for a single currency, later to be named the euro. Margaret Thatcher was bitterly opposed to the idea; but as an olive branch she suggested out of the blue at a meeting in Madrid in 1989 that the British would provide some alternative proposals for European monetary union. There had been no earlier discussion inside the British government. Indeed, the Treasury Permanent Secretary was so astonished when he heard the notion on his car radio that he nearly bumped into a tree.

This still left the Treasury with the job of fleshing out the proposal in some way. Part of the problem was that Hayek had long been considered an outrider by establishment economists and advisers, and his works were only considered if politicians pushed them down their throats. The lead was taken by the then Chancellor of the Exchequer Nigel Lawson, who had for some years been an avid reader of Hayek's later works. He took the opportunity to put forward the idea of currency competition, although he only then had in mind competition among official currencies; and just after he left his post in 1989 the UK Treasury published a paper on competitive currencies in the European Union.[3]

The problem with this paper, as with Hayek's original suggestion, was that there is nothing in British law to prevent people making deals or settling contracts in whatever currency they liked: dollars, Swiss francs, cowrie shells or anything else. The term 'legal tender', although sounding impressive, had little operational force. It mainly meant that if the currency in a contract was not stipulated, then it would have to be settled in pounds sterling. There was therefore nothing much to propose.

The competitive currency project was not accepted, or even understood, in most continental European countries. But the main trouble was that this – and later more complicated proposals for a so-called 'hard ecu' – came much too late when the EU countries, led by France and Germany, had already made up their mind to create a new common currency.

The Blair dilemma

We now have to fast forward to the more recent agonized debate on whether the Blair Labour government (elected in 1997), which had a different agenda, should propose adopting the euro in place of the pound sterling. Opinion polls over many years have shown a persistent public distaste for giving up the pound in favour of the euro. In the year 2000 I suggested that Tony Blair give the whole subject of euro membership a rest for five years, as endless discussions had not achieved anything and merely distracted attention from more important issues. For some time I had been suggesting that the most likely way for the euro to be adopted in Britain would be the parallel currency one: that is through its creeping use in ordinary business – or, as it is sometimes called, membership by osmosis.

Instead of just saying 'yes' or 'no' to euro membership, the British government has the option of leaving it to private citizens and traders to use the euro if they wish. Some, but not all, of those who welcome the idea hope that it will lead to increasing use of the euro in the UK. British exporters and financiers were perfectly free to make contracts in euros from the time the currency was launched in 1999; and, with the advent of euro notes and coins in 2002, visitors and returning tourists have been able to use them for payment to whomever will accept them. Many large London stores have done so with alacrity, as they had done for a long time with US dollars.

But we should have no illusions that genuine currency competition will be easy to achieve, even though there has been long experience of parallel currencies operating in border areas such as French-speaking Switzerland or western Austria. The Canadian dollar shows little sign of being relegated to the backyard despite a 3,000-mile frontier with the USA and the fact that most Canadians live within fifty miles of that border.

The acid test of whether the euro is functioning as a parallel currency will be if some wage contracts are denominated in it. There will be a strong case for this in corporations highly dependent on exports to Europe. If sterling rose, then wages would be automatically trimmed without the hard choice between negotiated wage reductions and job losses which now exist. If sterling fell, then workers in such companies would automatically share in the devaluation gain without having to engage in difficult pay negotiations. By similar logic, there is a case for other corporations, more heavily dependent on export to dollar-linked countries, paying wages in the US currency.

The most important single step the British government can take to encourage the use of the euro, without jettisoning the pound sterling, would probably be to make it easier for the euro to be employed for settling tax bills. And despite what I have said about legal tender being an archaic survival, it might make a symbolic difference if the euro were afforded that status along with sterling.

I have to admit that the currency competition idea has been seized upon by people who are extremely hostile to the euro, and even to the whole European Union, as a way of making a 'no' vote respectable in any future euro referendum. And it is true that even pro-European supporters of currency competition would have to vote 'no' in such a poll, as there could hardly be competition between the euro and a pound that had been abolished. This assumes of course that they are voting on purely economic grounds without considering the broader political implications of a 'yes' or 'no' vote – which will not be true in my case.

End of bank money?

So much for official currencies. But competitive private enterprise currencies might result from deep-seated trends in financial evolution which have little to do with government policy. The mainstream belief at present is that monetary policy exerts a big influence on output and employment in the short to medium run, and on prices in the medium to long run. Most central banks try to exert this influence by their power over short-term nominal interest rates, although some economists would prefer them to operate with targets for one or other definition of the money supply. They have such power because the greater part of the money supply consists of bank deposits; and banks are either obliged to, or find it prudent to, keep reserves at the central bank.

The result resembles some of the older cosmological theories in which the world rested on top of an elephant which in turn balanced upon a mouse. The supposed leverage is exercised by means of financial operations which are tiny in relation both to national and international monetary flows and in relation to total output. For instance, bank reserves in the USA account for only $1/2$ per cent of gross domestic product.

This influence can only continue if the commercial banks carry on accounting for the bulk of the effective money supply and if they themselves continue to hold reserves with central banks. Both these assumptions have been challenged, for instance, by a paper by Professor Benjamin Friedman of Harvard.[4] He suggests that the evolution of electronic means of payment will lead over a quarter of a century to the end of banks as we now understand them. The result is that even if the theory of how central banks influence the economy is now correct, ultimately they will lose all leverage.

Such developments were prematurely suggested when credit cards emerged some decades ago. But there is a difference this time round. In the case of most existing credit cards, at the end of the month you receive your dreaded statement, which is settled by a transfer from your bank to the credit card company. New forms of payment may not involve such transfers at all.

Smart cards – for example the single vendor advanced payment cards already used by many telephone services and the New York subway system – could develop into genuine private money. So long as issuers of these cards ask for settlement by transfers from bank balances, conventional sight accounts are still required. But firms and individuals might ultimately accept and swap balances on, say, the books of a transport or telephone authority. In other words they would be means, not only of payment, but also of settlement.

Another development is the proliferation of non-bank credit. At present when a bank extends credit, deposits are created on the other side of the balance sheet, which have to be backed by reserves at the central bank. But bank credit has been steadily contracting as a proportion of total credit. In the USA the combined share of banks and other depository institutions in the credit market has fallen from 50 per cent in 1950 to 30 per cent recently. Advances in data processing and the easier availability of information are likely to reduce still further the special advantages of banks in deciding on credit-worthiness. Moreover, even where banks still issue loans there is a trend to securitization. This means that the loans are sold to non-bank investors who are not subject to reserve requirements.

The combined results of all these developments could well be to reduce, perhaps to the point of elimination, the need for bank reserves and even the need for banks altogether. Benjamin Friedman is disarmingly frank about some of the further consequences. For instance, he cannot say what will determine the price level. Nor does he know whether national authorities will find an alternative way of limiting inflation and deflation or ironing out the worst of the business cycle. The Friedman prognosis is not completely novel and has been partially endorsed by Mervyn King, Deputy Governor of the Bank of England.[5] But I still admit to lingering doubts. They centre on what would be the means of settlement of last resort. There could well be money issued in the form of credits with, say, subway systems and telephone corporations. But these organizations are likely to have credits or debits with each other. How will these be settled?

One possibility is a return to a sophisticated form of barter. But even if this is the case for means of payment, I am sure that it will be convenient to have one, or a very small number, of standards of value for measuring indebtedness and wealth. In biblical times, a person's wealth was often measured by the number of heads of cattle that he held.

To peer much further ahead would take us into the world of science fiction. The future can be left to the evolution of normal market forces provided that the present freedom in monetary movements remains. This can by no means be taken for granted. Retrogression is always possible. The anti-globalization movements and hysteria about boom and bust and corporate misgovernment could easily lead to the partial resumption of exchange control or limits on capital movements by some of the countries which abandoned them towards the end of the twentieth century. Rather than squabble about the exact form that monetary freedom might take in future, it would be much better to concentrate on the defensive task of protecting the freedom we already have.

Notes

1. These and related writings are conveniently collected in Stephen Kresge (ed.), *The Collected Works of F. A. Hayek*, Volume 6, *Good Money Part Two*, Routledge, London, 1999.
2. Pascal Salin (ed.), *Currency Competition: A Sceptical View, in Currency Competition and Monetary Union*, The Hague, 1984.
3. 'An Evolutionary Approach to Economic and Monetary Union', London, HMSO, 1989.
4. *The Future of Monetary Policy, Social Science and the Future*, Centre for Economic Policy Research, London, 1999.
5. *Challenges for Monetary Policy: New and Old*, Bank of England Bulletin, November 1999.

Nonsense on Stilts

Financial Times, 13 May 1999

Let me start with 'an executive summary'. The 'new paradigm' is another name for what used to be called, with justifiable cynicism, the Goldilocks scenario. It has three elements. First, it is said, the US economy can now be run with a much lower level of unemployment than before without generating rising inflation. Secondly, it is suggested that there has been a pronounced upward shift in the underlying growth rate. And thirdly, Wall Street is supposed to soar to ever fresh heights for the foreseeable future.

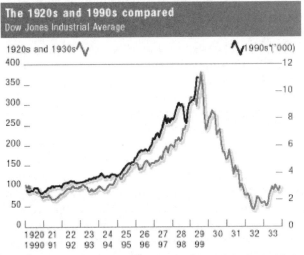

The 1920s and 1990s compared
Dow Jones Industrial Average

Sources: Dow Jones and Company, Thomson Datastream   * Proportionate scale

The first assertion – that the US can now be run with a tighter labour market than previously supposed without inflation taking off – is probably justified. The second – about a higher underlying growth rate – is more dubious. The third – about Wall Street's ability to reach the stratosphere – is nonsense on stilts.

The Fed chairman Alan Greenspan has just reminded us how the Fed's forecasts have chronically overpredicted inflation and under-predicted real growth. Unemployment has fallen to lows which nearly all models predicted would be associated with rising wage costs and accelerating inflation. Yet wage inflation has never seemed more subdued.

Even this most plausible part of the paradigm can be exaggerated. For there have been some favourable once-for-all influences on the inflation rate arising from falling commodity and oil prices. These may give a misleading idea about quite how far the sustainable rate of unemployment has fallen. We shall soon find out if oil and commodity prices continue their recovery or if the dollar experiences a setback. Another abnormality is the strength of the investment boom which has produced the rare coincidence of a tight labour market and a large margin of excess capacity. It is in any case nonsense to conclude that fundamental economic rules need rewriting. Those who say this do not know what these rules are. The estimates made of – forgive the jargon – the non-accelerating inflation rate of unemployment or NAIRU – are simply rough and ready guesses which, even if valid, apply only to limited historical periods. There is nothing in basic theory to expect the NAIRU to be unchanging. Indeed, Milton Friedman, who was one of the inventors of the idea, has always refused to guess its level. As Greenspan said in the same address, 'neither the fundamental laws of economics, nor of human nature on which they are based, have changed or are likely to change'.

The validity of the part of the new paradigm concerned with underlying growth depends somewhat on what you mean by 'underlying'. Greenspan sings the praises of the information technology and related revolutions. But he then points out that they are less important than revolutions around the turn of the last century, which saw the introduction of the automobile, the aircraft, the telephone and the beginnings of radio technology.

Charles Jonscher, who is an acknowledged IT expert, remarks on the lack of evidence that IT has increased US productivity growth.[1] Indeed, the average annual growth of business output per hour in the post-1992 business cycle has been less than in 1954–75.

Greenspan himself believes that the new technologies have indeed brought an unexpected increase in output over the last few years. But he considers it is invalid to project this increase into the future. For we do not have the knowledge to distinguish between a once-for-all jump and a change in long-term trend.

Now I come to Wall Street itself. Even if it does not crash and fluctuates around present levels, the US boom is highly vulnerable. For American consumers – the much-vaunted saviours of the world economy – have stopped saving and have been running down their financial balances. This cannot go on for ever. It only appears sustainable on the basis of a continuing rise in equity and other asset prices, which is creating the illusion of wealth.

Apostles of the new paradigm sometimes argue that income is understated because it excludes capital gains. But this is almost entirely circular. For the capital gains are only there because consumers think that they are wealthy enough to run down their financial assets and boost consumption, and thereby business turnover and profits. Surveys of equity analysts show expectations of 13 to 14 per cent annual rises in corporate earnings. But if these represent real profits and not just a resumption of inflation, they are absurd. For the average annual growth of nominal GDP is barely 5 per cent. And if any component of GDP continues to grow faster than the total, compound interest alone suggests that it would eventually almost swallow the whole of GDP.

But to me most impressive of all are the comparisons with the 1920s. Just as there are optimists today who talk about the Dow Jones rising from 11,000 to 20,000 or 30,000, their forebears in the 1920s spoke about a new era of everlasting prosperity. The rise in the Dow Jones between 1924 and 1929 was very similar to the rise from 1994 to date.

There is a recent story that a man in a dark suit was given a lift by a truck driver and asked him if he ever invested in stocks. The reply was that not only did he do so but that he had been able to buy a tropical island the size of a country, leaving the man in the suit to leave the truck, tail between his legs. This is the modern equivalent of the taxi drivers making fortunes in the 1920s and driving taxis only as a hobby or for pocket money.

Of course, in talking about 1929, it is important to avoid the error of identifying that crash with the Great Depression. That came rather later and was only partly the result of the 1929 Wall Street crash. The crash was only the beginning. It was followed by a moderate recovery which then gave way to further and much larger downturns which reached a bottom only in 1933.

One hopes that the Fed has learned enough to prevent a 1929-style crash being followed by a 1930s-style contraction in the money supply and economic activity. But it is doubtful if it can avoid at least some check to growth or even outright recession in such circumstances. Some Wall Street bulls point to falling bond yields – until a few weeks ago – which have been associated with rising PE (price to earnings) ratios over the last twenty years. They are supposed to reduce the rate at which future profits are discounted. Andrew Smithers has unfortunately spoiled the party by pointing out that in the earlier bull market in the two decades up to 1968, associated with accelerating inflation, there was an even stronger correlation between rising bond yields and higher PE ratios.

This is the first time that I recall expressing a view on stock markets anywhere. But if the pundits in any field seem to be in fantasy land one must say so. This applies whether they are military pundits making unrealistic claims for the results of bombing or stock market gurus projecting what Tim Congdon rightly calls 'a silly boom' for ever.

No one knows whether the break will come within one week, one month, one year, or five years. We must hope and pray that any Wall Street crash occurs after some combination of the eurozone, Japan and the emerging countries have got their acts together and can take over from the US the task of being the locomotive for world expansion. Meanwhile let us recall the remark of that stock market authority, Bernard Baruch, that no one ever lost his shirt from taking a profit.

Postscript

The Dow Jones Industrial Index averaged 11,108 in the second week of April 1999, when this article appeared. It reached a peak of 11,582 at the beginning of January 2000. It then started fluctuating with a downward trend. The serious fall occurred after September 11, 2001. But after an abortive recovery the index continued to drop to reach a low point of 7,534 in October 2002. A serious rally began in March 2003, which by April of the following year had taken the index back to 10,373. In other words, 70 per cent of the ground lost since the peak had by then been recovered.

Some of the more thoughtful analysts feared that the market was vulnerable at these recovery levels. But in any case market behaviour was a very long way from the 'new paradigm' of endless growth, let alone the 30,000 level that the Wall Street optimists expected the market to reach within a few years.

Note

1. Charles Jonscher, *Where Are We in the Digital Age?*, Bantam Press, 1999.

PART FIVE

'Europe' and the Euro

The chapter on the fall of the rupee you may omit. It is somewhat too sensational.

Miss Prism in Oscar Wilde, *The Importance of Being Earnest*

When the People Should Decide

Financial Times, 6 June 2003

The British debate on membership of the euro is being superseded by another debate on the new European Constitutional Treaty, drafted by a convention presided over by M. Valéry Giscard d'Estaing. The UK referendum debate is being distorted by two ridiculous extreme positions. Some of the opponents of the Giscard convention are presenting a hysterical picture of their fellow countrymen losing all their traditional freedoms and becoming subject to overseas rule in a way not seen since the departure of the Romans 1,700 years ago. But the British Prime Minister's response that there simply would not be a referendum, so 'you can put your placards away', was dictatorial and objectionable. It is therefore a good time to stand back from the details of current EU controversies and ask about the place of referenda in a liberal democracy.

Signed up free market economists will have no difficulty in responding. The commercial market is a continuous referendum in which voters make decisions every day. It has the great advantage over the political market place that minority tastes can be taken into account, and different citizens can buy different combinations to suit their individual preferences. Moreover, any tendencies for markets to produce unacceptable income differences can best be treated by cash redistribution via the tax and social security system. This doctrine is sometimes known as redistributive market liberalism.

It has enough validity to establish a presumption in favour of market rather than state provision. But admirable though it is, the doctrine leaves some big questions unanswered even if one excludes the charge that consumers are brainwashed into buying products they do not need. Messages which are literally subliminal, that is below the threshold of consciousness, should be, and I hope are, legally banned. But otherwise adult citizens should be free to make their own mistakes. However foolish some people look in the shopping mall, there are few who can be entrusted to make better decisions on their behalf.

The limitations of markets are different. Certain public services such as health and education have special characteristics which result in collective intervention – although not necessarily state supply – in nearly all countries. Most important of all, markets cannot function, and people cannot run their private lives, without police and law courts and a security apparatus to prevent citizens' lives from being disrupted by enemies within and without. Some collective decisions are thus inescapable, as are metadecisions on the best means of reaching them. In most western countries people elect representatives, or rulers, who make decisions on their behalf. But with modern electronics, it would certainly be possible to have frequent direct citizen voting, as was usual in the Assembly of Ancient Athens where the word 'democracy' was first coined.

The frank reason for being suspicious of frequent referenda is that people lack the knowledge to decide on complex issues. Even if one holds that the object of government is to pursue people's welfare in the way they themselves define it, most voters will not know how it should go about this job. Indeed, many of them are well aware of their lack and tend to reply to pollsters' questions by saying 'Aren't our politicians paid to decide these matters?'

There is another more subtle consideration. Citizens voting on each issue separately will be tempted to vote for expensive government services without necessarily being willing to pay the taxes required to finance them. The voter does not face the same budget constraint in the ballot box as he does in running his own household. The first and greatest American Secretary of the Treasury, Alexander Hamilton, declared that the people were fickle and seldom judged well. The Austrian-American economist Joseph Schumpeter wrote some sixty years ago, that even for a highly educated professional person political issues were a 'sub-hobby' to which he paid less concentrated attention than to his weekly game of bridge – and rationally so because the chance of his vote being decisive was negligible. The Swiss referenda, which are so often invoked, occur in a small country with its own unique and frugal traditions, and for the most part concern limited local issues. Schumpeter's own escape route was to say that the job of voters was to choose between teams of leaders who made the policy decisions; and in this limited way he restored the analogy with commercial competition.

By and large I am with this hard-boiled Austrian professor. But his competitive model comes up against its own limitations. Before rival teams can compete for our votes we have to decide the geographical area in which this competition should take place and the rules of the competition. If some big change in the whole arrangements by which they are governed is afoot, it is reasonable that citizens should be given a direct say. This brings us back to M. Giscard d'Estaing. He would like to be remembered for drafting a constitution which will govern the European Union for a long time to come. Tony Blair, on the other hand, claims that all that is happening is a tidying-up operation to make the rules of the European Union more transparent.

This leads to a paradoxical situation. To the extent that the former French president, and the integrationists urging him on, get their way, the case for a referendum is strengthened. To the extent that national governments succeed in limiting any changes, we are in the realm of detailed tidying-up amendments of an arrangement which British voters have previously accepted in Harold Wilson's 1975 EU referendum.

But we cannot just leave the matter here. Suppose we end up with a tidying-up operation plus a few extra elements? The fact is that each successive EU treaty has added new and little noticed powers to Brussels institutions, often involving majority voting. This was true of the Single Market Act signed by Margaret Thatcher herself, as well as the Maastricht, Amsterdam and Nice Treaties signed by her successors. It is arguable that the European Union now emerging is sufficiently different from anything approved in 1975 as to justify a fresh appeal to the voter. A referendum has already been promised in several European countries and is supported by M. Giscard d'Estaing himself.

Postscript

In the spring of 2004 Tony Blair bowed to political pressures and announced a referendum on the EU Constitutional Treaty. I have nevertheless retained the above essay, partly because EU-related issues have a habit of recurring in one form or another, but even more because of the attempt I have made to demarcate the sort of issues for which referenda are suitable from the many others where they are not.

The Dubious Political Case for the Euro

New Economy, June 2003

Politics versus economics

Many years ago, when I was on the committee of the Cambridge University Labour Club, Brian Redhead – who subsequently became a well-known British broadcaster – asked: 'Why is it that this one branch of policy, economics, is so dominated by obscure specialist studies which keep other people out of the discussion while everything else is decided by common sense argument in which we can all take part?'

This question has not been answered to this day. It has become all too topical in relation to possible British membership of the euro. Many British leaders believe that the political case has been made; and the only question is whether boring economic obstacles should keep the UK outside for the time being. In fact the political case has not been made and should not be taken for granted. It is simply asserted by the current generation of ministers and Foreign Office mandarins.

For the fullest explanation one is usually referred to Tony Blair's speech to the Polish Stock Exchange on 6 October 2000. Most of the relevant section is a generalized statement of the case for Britain 'being at the centre of influence in Europe'. On the euro specifically the Prime Minister merely said: 'The political case for Britain being part of the single currency is strong. I don't say political or constitutional issues aren't important. They are. But to my mind they are not an insuperable barrier. What does have to be overcome is the economic issue.'

What then would a true political assessment look like? The more I think about it, the less difference there is between the two kinds of assessment. The object of economic policy is surely to promote the welfare of the inhabitants of the United Kingdom, with some regard for the welfare of those outside, especially in poorer countries. But is that not an equally good description of the goal of political activity? We get bemused because the intermediate objectives seem so different. On the one hand the famous five UK tests referred to specifics including growth, employment and even the prosperity of one particular part of the economy, namely the financial sector. On the other hand the political case, so far as it has ever been made, centres around more nebulous matters, such as British influence in Europe or 'Who will be sitting at which top table?'

But surely all such specifics, whether on the so-called economic or political fronts, are intermediate objectives. Jobs and growth are only valuable to the extent to which they promote the welfare of inhabitants of these islands. Surely too, British government influence in international institutions is important only to the extent that it promotes the well-being of British citizens. Influence at European summits – or even the ability to 'speak for Europe' (this last, a rather remote goal) – may be important for their own sake to prime ministers and top-level diplomats; but for the rest of us they matter only insofar as they promote peace, security and prosperity.

'Economic' arguments

Many of the supposed economic arguments both for and against euro membership are extremely unconvincing. A frequent objection is that the core euro countries, and especially Germany, are suffering from low growth and high unemployment due to an over-rigid labour market and a bias against innovation. This has some truth. But why is it an argument against joining the euro? If other countries' economies are so rigid and ossified, this surely will give British businesses an opportunity to make gains at the expense of their competitors. The most successful single currency the world has known was the nineteenth-century gold standard. Under this, countries had complete independence over the whole range of fiscal and social policies and were even occasionally at war with each other.

There are indeed pressures from the European Union making for overunionized and overregulated labour markets which could price workers out of jobs. But they do not come from the euro. They come from the Labour government's decision to adopt the EU Social Charter when it came to office in 1997. There are further threats from the draft Constitutional Treaty which could give Brussels institutions an increased role in business and labour market decisions. It is a mistake to suppose that every unwise EU policy is an argument against the single currency.

I have never regarded the direct economic effects of euro

membership as terribly important one way or the other. The main reason why I formerly supported it was that it seemed for many years the most likely way of establishing an operationally independent central bank. The independence of the European Central Bank was established by treaty on the lines of the Bundesbank in Germany and seemed pretty safely ensconced. But since the incoming Labour government took many people by surprise in 1997 by unilaterally establishing operational independence for the Bank of England – and still more because of the favourable track record of the new regime – that particular argument for the euro goes out of the window.

The case I now wish to make is a positive one, not against the euro – still less against the European Union – but in favour of a floating exchange rate which the UK now enjoys and could not continue to have inside the euro. A floating exchange rate automatically balances a country's overseas payments – current and capital account taken together – without the need for cap-in-hand official overseas borrowing and without the need for inflationary or deflationary distortions of domestic policy.

A fixed rate of exchange produces two problems. The first is the threat of a balance of payments crisis and runs on the currency. The recurring feature for decades or even centuries of British economic history has been the needless crises brought about by futile efforts to maintain a fixed exchange rate. When in 1931 a Conservative-dominated national government floated the pound which its Labour predecessor tried so hard to save, the former Labour minister Margaret Bondfield remarked: 'Nobody told us we could do this.'

The foreign exchange crises which bedevilled British economic management through the 1940s, 50s, 60s and 70s are legendary. It would be foolish to argue that the UK has had a smooth ride since the pound floated in 1971. The last of the sterling crises, the 'IMF' one of 1976, took place when sterling was already floating. In retrospect, this was quite an unnecessary crisis, due to the fact that policymakers had insufficient experience of market-determined exchange rates. There were all kinds of fears that the pound would 'go through the floor', whatever that meant. But once the government had taken action to reduce the budget deficit and control money and credit, as it had largely done by the time of the IMF visit, the rest could have been left to the market, which indeed produced in 1977 a bigger 'recovery ' of sterling than anyone had bargained for. The then Chancellor, Denis Healey, actually used the IMF negotiations to gain support for policies that he in any case favoured.

It should in all fairness be said that the balance of payments threat is largely removed either by a floating exchange rate or by membership of the European Monetary Union. There cannot be a run on the pound if sterling no longer exists. The only run can be on the euro as a whole, which is a pretty far-fetched proposition – at least so long as the euro is managed by a cautious and independent European Central Bank. But there is a second problem which would not be removed by joining the euro. That is the possibility of unemployment due to money wages which make British goods uncompetitive compared with those of other countries. If the UK joins at too high an exchange rate many industries would become uncompetitive and unemployment would rise until wages were pushed down to a lower path than that of partner countries. An exchange rate adjustment to reduce them is no more possible in the euro area than it would be now for Yorkshire or Lancashire.

The dangers of entering at too low an exchange rate are more subtle. Instead of unemployment and deflation, the proximate consequence would be overheating and inflation. A euro enthusiast could argue that these would be once-for-all; but while the adjustment was taking place Gordon Brown's inflation target, into which so much political effort has been put, would be exceeded; and it could be very costly to regain credibility. Ireland has avoided this fate because its overvaluation within the EMU coincided with a world slowdown, which particularly affected Ireland's leading-edge industries. This is not the kind of 'luck' on which we can either count or should hope to achieve.

Today, the wide divergence of views on the exchange rate at which Britain can safely enter the euro shows how unsure we are of the correct exchange rate. Many of the businessmen who were campaigning to join the euro really meant that they wanted a sterling devaluation. A case can nevertheless be made for saying that the UK managed to live with a supposedly overvalued exchange rate for so long that it might have been a tenable rate after all.

Suppose, however, that the optimists are wrong and the pessimistic businessmen are right. Then under a floating rate the market will ultimately bring about a sufficient depreciation. But joining the euro forecloses the options. If the UK is already locked into the euro, the equivalent adjustment can only be made by a lengthy period of depressed demand and downward pressure on wages. There is of course no way of avoiding necessary adjustments in real wages. But there is all the difference in the world between adjusting them indirectly via the exchange rate and a pitched battle to bear down on money wages – as Winston Churchill discovered in the 1926 General Strike.

Some further advantages of a floating exchange rate were brought home to me at an international seminar. There was a session on the subject of left–right differences. Several of us argued that the terms had largely lost their meaning and mainly stood for rival tribes. But at this point there was a revolt by some British participants who insisted that there was still a left-wing agenda to be enacted in terms of public spending, union rights and so on.

Some of those who spoke regretted that globalization made an old left agenda impractical. This was wrong. Globalization is an excuse. A country inside the euro such as Italy has indeed to be very careful about anything that risks raising labour costs further. But there is nothing to stop a country like Britain that is still outside from taking these risks, knowing that sterling can take the strain from any cost-push effects. The argument against the old left agenda is that the electorate will not wear it or that in practice it has proved counterproductive. The issue should not be pre-empted by arbitrary currency mechanisms.

The embarrassments from locking in the exchange rate would not be confined to the left. Any experimentation with higher payroll or indirect taxes which raised nominal costs would be ruled out of court – whether the purpose was to reduce income tax or to finance the health service, as sometimes advocated on the centre and right. Or suppose that there were a serious move to tax energy? Any kind of experimentation from any part of the political compass would be extremely risky without the safety valve of a flexible exchange rate.

Some people will say that my exchange rate argument is too short-term. It is not. There is nothing short-term about a floating exchange rate as a permanent adjustment mechanism. The more conventional 'long-term' analysis also turns on the exchange rate. It comes down to weighing the advantages of exchange rate stability for over half of British trade against the disadvantages of a 'one size fits all' interest rate policy for the whole euro area.* It is difficult to become too excited about the issue. One is tempted to say that it is half a dozen of one and six of the other.

If the right entry rate is unclear and the positive advantages of being in the European Monetary Union are not overwhelming it would surely be better to stay with a floating rate for the pound as a safety valve which has served the UK so well in recent decades.

---

* The argument for interest rate independence needs to be made with care. The trend of interest rates over several years must reflect the international real rate of interest plus an allowance for expected inflation. If we no longer believe that tolerating a high rate of inflation will bring faster growth then we might as well converge on some common and modest European inflation rate. Once inflationary expectations are approximately the same then, inside or outside the eurozone, the UK does not have the ability to follow a completely different interest rate policy of its own, whether it is in the EMU or outside it. What the Bank of England can do if it remains independent is to pursue a different short-term trend around a common long-term average. It can then temporarily lower interest rates in a recession, as the Bank did in the early 1990s, and raise them again in the face of temporary overheating.

British overseas influence

The 'political' supporters of euro membership would say that this analysis ignores the increased influence it is supposed to bring for Britain. It would be foolish to deny that there might be a marginal increase in influence in some specialized areas. But would any such increase in influence carry over into less technical, but more important, issues such as British ability to pull France and Germany – the countries that Donald Rumsfeld aptly called old Europe – out of their negative anti-Americanism on the great issues of war, peace and terrorism? Or would it increase Britain's supposedly moderating influence on gung-ho Republican US presidents? The line of causation is very tortuous. The europhiles would have to say that joining the euro would be taken as a sign of positive involvement in EU affairs and thus help British spokesmen to 'take the lead' in Europe. But can anyone really argue that if Britain belonged to the euro, Tony Blair would have been able to talk President Chirac out of his unforgivable decision to invite Mr Mugabe to Paris? Let alone his threat to veto in the Security Council any military action on Iraq.

On transatlantic issues the argument is even more tenuous. The official British government line, from Vietnam onwards, has been to support the US in public, but privately to put its weight behind moderate State Department elements in their struggle with the 'hawks'. Whatever the pros and cons of this approach, is it conceivable that Chancellor Schröder and President Chirac would allow Tony Blair to speak for them too, just because the UK had the same currency as other western European countries?

The one plausible case is that British euro membership might be a step towards a European Federation in which there would only be one voice when the US president rang up (if he did) to enquire about European views. I do not dread a properly functioning European Federation based on limited government and effectively functioning markets. But a single currency is only a very small step in that direction. In any case we are many decades away; and for the foreseeable future we face a confusing confederation with at least two so-called 'presidents', not able to speak for governments when push comes to shove.

Finally, how important is it for the ordinary non-political British citizen that the British government should have a marginal increase in overseas influence? Naturally if you are working in the Foreign Office or advising the Cabinet, you would think that this could be only for the good. But a more detached historian would see the picture as far more mixed. He might ask, for instance, if official British insistence on the so-called independent nuclear deterrent has helped or hindered efforts to stop nuclear proliferation.

The most important task for British governments is to avoid disastrously wrong decisions on matters such as peace, war and terrorism. The welfare of British citizens will also depend on their ability to provide a reasonably stable economic environment free from the excesses of depression, runaway inflation and boom and bust. Beyond this basic agenda, there is room for argument on how far the governments should go in income redistribution or the provision of public services in kind. In any case, people's welfare will hardly depend on whether the Chancellor has to endure the boredom not merely of sitting on Ecofin but on the eurozone council as well.

At the most basic level of analysis the political and economic tests come to the same thing; and if there is no overwhelming economic case for British euro membership, there is no political case either.

The case for currency choice

Having said all this, I would find it difficult to voice any real enthusiasm for a 'no' vote in a euro referendum. The danger of euro rejection by the British electorate is that it would spill over into other areas. Much of the steam behind the anti-euro campaign comes from a jingoistic nationalism and impatience with any kind of international involvement in British affairs. To be quite specific: I fear that a 'no' vote would strengthen the voices that can already be heard – and not only from the tabloids – calling for Britain to pull out of the European Convention for the Protection of Human Rights and Fundamental Freedoms. This Charter has nothing to do with the EU and long predates it. It has already had a humanizing influence in many areas of British life.

My main hope now is that the whole euro membership issue will be shelved for as long as possible. Meanwhile there are several things that could be done to show a friendly British attitude to the euro without actually abandoning the pound sterling. (See pages 177 et seq.)

A Different View of Eurosclerosis

Financial Times, 28 February 2003

According to the conventional wisdom, Europe has been growing more slowly than the US for twenty years as a result of structural 'rigidities'. EU countries have themselves signed up to reform declarations at one EU summit after another, starting with Lisbon in 2000. Doubt is cast on this diagnosis in a recent paper, 'What's Wrong with Europe's Economy?' by the former CBI director Adair Turner.

At the very least his paper comes as a refreshing contrast to the dead and repetitive prose of EU communiqués and of the latest UK Treasury Paper on European Economic Reform. To start with, the facts are not as they are often made to appear. Over the twenty-one years 1980–2001 real growth per annum was indeed nearly half as fast again in the US as in the eurozone countries. But if you look at growth per head of population, nearly all the difference disappears; and the US lead represents mostly population growth.

Indeed, for a long time output per hour rose more quickly in the eurozone than in the US as European countries caught up with best American practice. If you look at the bigger picture, the differences between US and eurozone output per hour are now hardly visible. What is visible is a substantial remaining gap between British productivity and both American and eurozone levels, which has been impervious to over fifty years of productivity drives by governments of widely varying political complexions. We are however still left with some key questions. Why is US *output per head of population* nevertheless still larger than that of core eurozone countries? A related issue is: why has eurozone employment performance in these core countries been so poor? A lesser question is why has US productivity apparently begun to pull ahead again since the technological developments of the mid-1990s?

Turner puts under the microscope the difference between US and French GDP per capita, which put the US some 40 per cent ahead in

1999. There was virtually no difference between output per hour in the two countries. The differences were due to two factors. American workers put in nearly 20 per cent more hours than French ones and the employment ratio per 1000 of the population was 15 per cent higher in the US. Turner rightly argues that if French people are happier with a shorter working week and a shorter working life than Americans – so be it. Indeed it is American behaviour which is then more difficult to explain – 'a society getting steadily richer, but totally focused to take the gain in take-home pay'. Simply posing this question is sufficient to cast doubt on the *lumpeneconomics* of governments that put more stress on income than leisure. Turner concedes that shorter French working lifetimes may not be freely chosen. Some of the difference results from involuntary unemployment or involuntary early retirement, reflecting labour market distortions. There is room for disagreement with Turner's view that the greater part of the US–French GDP gap represents voluntary choice.

One of Turner's more surprising findings is that nearly all the differential US productivity spurt since the mid-1990s can be attributed to the distributive sector. His explanation is that the US, which is far more land-rich, can rationally allow more freedom for developments such as out-of-town shopping centres than land-hungry Europe. This diagnosis is corroborated by the fact that France, which is richer in land than many other European countries, had notable improvements in retail productivity in the 1970s and 80s, but has since clamped down for planning reasons.

Turner scores a bull's eye in belittling the 'Barcelona reform agenda'. This consists of five main items: strengthening European transport networks; liberalizing energy markets; further financial market liberalization; promoting education and research; and reforming labour markets. The first four of these items are undoubtedly desirable. But their contribution either to promoting growth or improving employment prospects is extremely slight. He is particularly scathing about the hopes placed in freer energy markets, a sector which amounts to no more than 2 or 3 per cent of European GDP.

The all-important item is of course labour market reform. He does not mention the political reasons why governments bury this instead of highlighting it. It is that an attack on union privileges or union-backed legislation is particularly sensitive, especially, but not only, for left of centre governments. They hope that they can get away with some freeing of labour markets if they bury this in a great many worthy declarations on other subjects.

When it comes to labour markets, Turner is rightly sceptical of the importance attached to social security contributions on their own. It is high time someone pointed out that if labour markets are reasonably flexible, 'workers receive a lower wage rate than they would if payroll taxes were lower'. What are so obviously too high in Germany are total labour costs: wages plus payroll contributions. It would be just as valid to advocate cutting German wages as cutting German payroll contributions. The truly liberal answer would be to give the choice to the workers themselves.

The conclusion that the former CBI director draws is that ideally Germany ought to achieve a reduction in labour costs through a lower exchange rate. But because it is part of the eurozone the devaluation option is closed to Germany. Rather oddly for a euro enthusiast, Turner is blaming the new European currency for a bit too much. I can see the advantages if Germany were allowed to depreciate. But in the last analysis, one has to ask whether the organized representatives of German labour would accept a reduction in real wages plus benefits through the exchange rate back door that they would refuse if offered openly.

In the heyday of discussions about European stagflation in the 1970s and 1980s, economists often spoke of 'real wage rigidity'. By this they meant an insistence on levels of remuneration which priced people out of jobs and which could not be overcome by any combination of fiscal monetary and exchange rate policies. It was instead partly overcome by Margaret Thatcher's efforts to weaken unions' monopoly power, and their pale imitators elsewhere, and – just as important – by the relative decline of the manufacturing sector where unions are particularly strong.

One final point. Let us suppose that Turner is wrong and the core European economies are as high cost and inefficient as British propaganda suggests; or at least that they are full of labour market inefficiencies. In neither case do we find a valid reason against British participation in the euro. The more rigid and sclerotic that European products or labour markets turn out to be, the greater the opportunity of British firms to make a killing. The main arguments against the UK joining the euro relate to the positive advantages of a floating exchange rate and the close relationship between stop-start in British economic policy and attempts to maintain a rigid exchange link. Euro opponents should concentrate on this positive case rather than regarding everything they do not like about the EU as an argument against adopting the euro.

The Pretence of Knowledge

Financial Times, 20 June 2003

The predictable political fudging surrounding the government's decision not to decide about the euro has detracted attention from the Treasury study of the subject. The eighteen or so volumes are actually of a high standard. Indeed, I would gladly hand over these documents to the proverbial nephew wanting to understand mainstream economics without having to do the mathematics or pass exams. Contrary to some anti-intellectual sneers, they are not full of equations. Such equations as there are can be found mostly in appendices, footnotes and similar places and are in the supporting studies rather than the main report.

The documents are best regarded as studies touched off by the proposal that the UK should adopt the euro. For they do not tell us whether the British economy will gain or lose from such a decision. The pro-euro lobby has focused on the long-term trade effects, which the Treasury judges could eventually increase UK trade with the euro area by 5 to 50 per cent. If the trade increase is at the upper end of the range, the effect could, according to the Treasury, be an addition of $^1/_4$ per cent to the UK annual growth rate, adding 9 per cent to GDP over thirty years. Needless to say, the euro lobby does not discuss the implications of the lower end of the range.

The opponents of the euro have naturally focused on other studies which outline the possible destabilization arising from a 'one size fits all' European monetary policy. The Treasury charts suggest that both growth and inflation would have been more unstable if the UK had joined in 1999. It is not good enough to say that there are long-term gains but short-term costs. Close readers of the Treasury paper will see that the authors are well aware that unnecessary stop-go or periods of unnecessarily high unemployment or inflation can themselves undermine the long-term growth potential of the economy. This is what they mean by the horrible word 'hysteresis'.

The reader of the documents is, however, left to judge for himself or herself the net effect of macroeconomic destabilization and the hoped-for long-term increases in trade. This is as it should be. For economic science is not advanced enough to provide the answer and probably never will be. It is thus right and proper to go by hunches or wider issues such as the political gains or otherwise of being inside the euro area or the pros and cons of the UK's floating exchange rate regime.

Having heaped all this praise on the Treasury documents, I come to the 'but'. For buried inside them is one suggestion which is, I believe, profoundly mistaken, and has implications for many economies apart from the UK. The fact that this dangerous proposal emanates from one of the more sophisticated and better studies (*Fiscal Stabilisation and EMU*) makes it all the more worthy of attention.

The authors start out from the fact that a country belonging to the EMU cannot have its own monetary policy. If there is a shock which affects one country more severely than others – or if the same shock has different effects because of different economic structures – then the worst affected country has either to grin and bear it or to find some other economic instrument. The favoured instrument is the revival of short-term discretionary fiscal policy, which has been out of fashion for the last few decades.

The Treasury authors faithfully discuss the problems which resulted in the discrediting of fiscal policy – including the lags between diagnosis and implementation and between implementation and the effects on the economy. There are also the more subtle distortions arising from politicians being more willing to provide a fiscal stimulus than to impose fiscal constraints. They correctly come to the conclusion that reversible tax changes are likely to be more effective than public expenditure variations, which are likely to be mistimed and to distort the supply side of the economy. They also favour the use of indirect taxes. But unless I have missed something, they leave out one of the key arguments for this preference. This is that if consumers know that a cut in say VAT is likely to be reversed, they will go out and buy while prices are temporarily lower. And similarly they will refrain from buying in the face of a temporary VAT increase. This is true even if taxpayers are forward-looking and realize that tax changes imposed for economic regulation are liable to be reversed. The same argument cannot be applied to income or other direct taxes. The Treasury authors have also reminded their readers that in the UK case there already exists a 'Regulator' power for the Chancellor to vary indirect taxes between budgets, that is implemented immediately after the announcement, with retrospective parliamentary approval within twenty-eight days. VAT, for instance, could be changed by up to a quarter on either side of the present 17.5 per cent rate. The fact that the Regulator power has rarely been used is not an argument against reviving it in more effective form.

So far, so good. But it is the precise form in which the Treasury authors would bring back discretionary policy that worries me. The proposal is that if the 'output gap' rises to more than 1 or $1^1/_2$ per cent of GDP, the Chancellor should either have to take action or explain in a report to Parliament why he has not done so. This is clearly modelled on the provisions by which the Governor of the Bank of England at present has to write a letter of explanation if inflation varies by more than 1 per cent on either side of the official $2^1/_2$ per cent target.

Whether such developments would be good or bad depends on what is meant by the output gap and whether it can be measured even roughly. In a sentence, the output gap is the difference between actual output and the sustainable level. If output is above that level inflation will rise and eventually an economic stop will have to be imposed. If output is below that level inflation will fall – perhaps even to negative levels, depending on where the starting point is.

An enormous number of assumptions are buried in that little word 'sustainable'. For it involves a judgement not just of the physical capacity of the economy but of how far output can be pushed without inflationary strain. It is the first cousin of a related idea, that of the non-accelerating inflation rate of unemployment or NAIRU. The idea here is that if we try to push unemployment down too far by expansionary policies the result would be an ever-increasing inflation. On the other hand if we allow it to rise too high, as in Japan in the last decade, we get a falling rate of inflation ultimately leading to the shock horror of deflation.

In my view, the NAIRU is the more fundamental concept. For businesses will eventually adjust capacity to the growth of demand. On the other hand unemployment can remain for a long time at very high levels if the rigidities of the European social model or the antics of the trade union brothers in the UK prevent adjustments to changes in economic conditions. Official analysts have more recently tended to focus on the output gap rather than the NAIRU, avowedly for technical reasons, but subconsciously at least aware that it is the less politically explosive concept of the two.

It is striking that Milton Friedman, who helped invent the NAIRU, has consistently refused to give any estimate either of its size or that of the output gap and has preferred to keep them as conceptual tools. A sensational vindication of this reluctance has been provided by a little-known Bank of England research paper.[1]

The authors have made a heroic effort to construct a series for what policymakers thought the output gap was in the 1970s and 80s, compared with what later data has suggested that it actually was. They have to confront the fact that in the 1970s official economists were not encouraged to estimate an output gap or anything similar. Policy at the time rested too much on the vain hope that an official wage and price controls could keep a lid on inflation without excessive unemployment. Nevertheless the authors have been able to estimate what policymakers implicitly believed from statements by ministers and officials and answers to parliamentary inquiries, in which they gave some views on the trend of output and whether the economy was in recession and by how much.

In the 1970s there was thought to be a very large output gap indeed. This was the period when postwar full employment disappeared and headline unemployment rates rose from the low hundreds of thousands to the low millions. No wonder then that governments were extremely reluctant to dampen down demand and that it took a sterling crisis and visits from the IMF to make them do so. But if we revisit these years from the perspective of the year 2000, it now seems that there was no output gap at all and that production was as often above as below its sustainable level. The average over-estimation of the negative output gap of about 7 per cent of GDP, a truly massive amount, gave all the wrong indications to policymakers. Some earlier studies have suggested that a similar overestimation was responsible for the US inflation of the 1970s.

The Bank of England authors try to allocate the UK misestimation between two causes: a 4 per cent underestimate of where output actually was – which was subsequently corrected by the revision of the national income figures – and a 3 per cent overestimate of where the trend line was. Perhaps more surprisingly, there was a $2\frac{1}{2}$ per cent overestimate of the output gap in the Thatcherite 1980s, despite the reduced ideological obstacles to hard-headed analysis. This time the problem was mainly an underestimate of actual GDP. Later revisions to the data suggest that recessionary forces had been eliminated by 1986, when the government was still being accused of holding back employment by overrestrictive demand management.

No doubt officials will say that we have now learned better and will make smaller mistakes. But the gap proposal goes in the face of all the lessons of the 1970s and 80s. The true revolution of ideas was the abandonment of the notion that it was possible to fix real variables such as output and employment by demand management, that is monetary and fiscal policy. Money supply targets, exchange rate targets, and later inflation targets, were all attempts to construct a 'nominal framework' which gave financial policy its due in combating cycles of inflation and deflation but no more than that. The roots of persistently high unemployment have to be tackled from the labour market side, whether the Thatcherite attack on union power or the concentration under Gordon Brown on work incentives. Attempts to use statistical estimates of the output gap for policy risk jeopardizing these hard-won gains.

It is quite true that the output gap plays a greater part than I would like in the deliberations of the Bank of England's Monetary Policy Committee. Nevertheless it occupies there a subordinate role as a forecasting tool and can be amended or put aside when not found helpful in implementing the Bank's statutory duty, which is confined to the inflation rate. The Treasury proposal, on the other hand, would make the output gap a prime policy target.

Behind the technical discussion there is a more human point. It is what Friedrich Hayek called in his Nobel Prize address, 'the pretence of knowledge'. By pretending we know more about the characteristics of the economy than we really do we actually throw away the more modest improvements which our limited knowledge makes possible. It took us the closing decades of the twentieth century to learn this lesson; I hope we do not spend the first few decades of the new century in unlearning it.

Note

1. E. Nelson and K. Nikolov, 'UK Inflation in the 1970s and 80s: the role of output gap mismeasurement', 2001.

PART SIX

Ideas and Reflections

Every scriptural canon has within it texts which, read literally, can be taken to endorse narrow particularism, suspicion of strangers, and intolerance towards those who believe differently than we do. Each also has within it sources that emphasize kinship with the stranger, empathy with the outsider, the courage that leads people to extend a hand across the boundaries of estrangement or hostility.

Chief Rabbi Jonathan Sacks, *The Dignity of Difference*

I confess I am not charmed with the idea of life held out by those who think that a normal state of human beings is that of struggling to get on; that the trampling, crushing, elbowing and treading on each other's heels, which form the existing type of social life, are the most desirable lot of humankind, or anything but the disagreeable symptoms of one of the phases of industrial progress.

John Stuart Mill, *Principles of Political Economy*

In Defence of Individualism

A paper delivered at the Royal Institute of Philosophy
Conference, St Andrews, 1997. Published in *Philosophy and
Public Affairs*, J. Haldane (ed.), Cambridge University Press,
2000)

Liberals versus communitarians

There are many writers and critics who regard what they call
individualist-liberalism as the root of many of the evils of the modern
world; and the emphasis of their attack is on the individualist half of
the term. Those who take this line nowadays often call themselves
communitarians. I would prefer to call them collectivists, as that
brings out their dangerous tendency to regard the group as more
important than the individuals of whom it is composed. But in what
follows I shall concede on labels and most often refer to them as
communitarians.

There are a number of slogans characteristic of communitarian
rhetoric. The most frequent of them is that 'Man is a political (or
sometimes social) animal'. The individualist-liberal is then accused of
an 'atomistic' view of society. Another slogan is that more emphasis
should be put on duties instead of rights. Here there would be no
difference between Tony Blair and Margaret Thatcher. In a lower key
there is a preference for teamwork as opposed to individual
responsibility (apparent even in the UK arrangements for monetary
policy).

But the emphasis of the attack is on modern market capitalism. The
historian of political thought, C. B. Macpherson, called this 'possessive
individualism',[1] an expression which has caught on with many who
have not read a single word of his work. The more low-brow version is
a contempt for the 'pursuit of the bottom line' which is said to
characterize our age. Ordinary citizens are accused of 'consumerism'
or of being obsessed by the psychology of 'me, me, me'.

In Britain the debate is confused because almost everyone on the
left and centre now adopts a communitarian rhetoric. Having
accepted much of the economic counter-revolution of the previous

decade and a half, the main issue on which Blairites dig in their heels is opposition to supposed Thatcherite individualism. This is based on a false chain of reasoning which identifies individualism with self-interest and self-interest with selfishness. The last is a howler, as can be testified by anyone who has laboured for a charity, for a good cause, or any of the arts or religion, or merely to improve the lot of his or her own family and intimates.

Many on the left will wonder why I am putting right-wing authoritarians together with benevolent communitarians. The American debate sheds some light here. A whole movement has arisen there to attack the liberal individualist foundations of western politics and culture. US communitarians dislike almost equally ultra-free market libertarians and the more left-wing liberals, such as the philosopher John Rawls, who support the welfare state and other forms of economic intervention. Communitarians condemn them both for regarding the individual person and his or her choices as the measure of all things in politics, and their failure to find a higher purpose for government.

The softer version of US communitarianism can be found in the writings of commentators such as Amital Etzioni, who is pictured with Vice President Al Gore on the dust cover of his book, *The Spirit of Community*.[2] Its harder version can be found in the Republican religious right, with its support of compulsory religious practices (of which school prayer is but a symbol), belief in savage punishment for retributive reasons and paranoid nationalist fears that foreigners are taking away American jobs.

The two kinds of anti-individualists come together in their advocacy of a year or two of compulsory national service to knock some patriotism and civic virtue into the American young. They have been answered by an individualist liberal, David Boaz, who replies: 'No group of people has the right to force another group to give up a year or two of their lives – and possibly life itself – without their consent. The basic liberal principle of the dignity of the individual is violated when individuals are treated as national resources.'[3]

Another tell-tale symptom is propaganda for so-called Asian values and admiration for the Singaporean leader Lee Kuan Yew, who justifies his brutal punishments by saying 'To us in Asia, an individual is an ant.' Are British Conservatives more tolerant? Almost every increase in personal liberty and toleration, from the legalization of homosexuality among consenting adults to the abolition of theatre censorship and more sensible divorce laws, has been brought about in the face of opposition from the majority of Conservative MPs and activists. In nearly every country the political right (with a few honourable individual exceptions) is adamantly opposed to any re-examination of the drug laws which have done so much to make money-laundering one of the world's biggest businesses. Their text is still that of Lord Hailsham in the 1960s when he hoped that the addicts of hashish and marijuana would be pursued 'with the utmost severity the law allows'. He hoped they would 'find themselves in the Old Bailey, where, however distinguished their positions in the Top 10, they will be treated as criminals deserve to be treated'. Unfortunately, too many Blairites rush to show their political 'moderation' by coming down like a ton of bricks on anyone on the Labour or Liberal side who opposes such Hailshamite blusterings.

The academic debate

The communitarian-liberal debate has been going on in the USA for a decade or more; and two Oxford philosophers, S. Mulhall and A. Swift, have recently written a textbook guide to it.[4] This takes as its starting point John Rawls's theory of justice, which has acquired a canonical status and which I shall not attempt to summarize here. Many individualist-liberals have criticized Rawls for making too many concessions to collective goals. But the communitarian attack is just the opposite. It is on the priority which Rawls says he attaches to personal freedom.

The debate takes place on several levels. What seems to motivate Alasdair McIntyre[5] and those who think like him is an intense hostility to theories in philosophical ethics such as emotivism, subjectivism and relativism. Such philosophers insist that some ways of life are preferable to others and are incensed by Jeremy Bentham's observation that Push-pin (an early nineteenth-century board game) was better than poetry if that was what people preferred. Today the argument would be in terms of Radio One versus Radio Three. But these philosophers are not necessarily committed to the specific proposals urged by more policy-oriented commmunitarians who are looking for some third way between socialism and market capitalism.

Metaphysical anti-individualism

In my experience, communitarians like to start from some metaphysical proposition. They say, for instance, that an individual is constituted by his or her social relationships. He or she is a grandfather, a doctor, a member of certain clubs, an active Scottish Nationalist, and so on. Without these relationships he or she is said to be 'nothing'. Even a hermit is identified by his decision to abandon the community from which he springs. (One often reads that the individual was an invention of the Renaissance and was unknown to the ancient and medieval world. I am not sure that this can be reconciled with the funeral oration of Pericles, as expounded by Thucydides.)

We soon get into an impasse. Groups are made up of individuals; but individuals form groups. A debate on which fact is 'primary' is the kind of dispute which never gets settled. As Stephen Holmes has pointed out: 'The social nature of Man is too trite to count as an insight and is worthless as an argument for or against any existing institutional arrangements. If all individuals are socially constituted then the social self cannot serve as a critical standard to praise some societies and revile others.'[6]

A biological perspective

Communitarians are inclined to say that the issue depends on the 'nature of Man'. To my mind this is a biological matter rather than one for armchair speculation. And you do not escape the biological nature of the problem by talking in seemingly more philosophical terms of the 'nature of the person' instead. It is a cliché to say 'Man is a social animal'. The statement can be given empirical content by noting that for the greater part of his existence on this planet he has belonged to clans of hunter-gatherers of not more than a couple of hundred people. It is, therefore, not surprising that people feel alienated, both in mass society and if left entirely to their own devices in nuclear families. This could be held to support the communitarian preference for relying on, whenever possible, local groups rather than the isolated individual or the nation state. Communitarians are, however, seldom specific about how this transformation can be undertaken.

Let us, moreover, not romanticize the small group. It can be very oppressive and stultifying; and even in primitive times there were those who left their groups to start other clans. Many of today's most vibrant communities are not people who are geographically close to each other. The most important communities for users of the internet in the Orkneys may consist, not of village neighbours, but other users with whom they form a professional link which can blossom into friendship and mutual support.

The worst side of group psychology is the hostility almost always generated to those outside the group. This long pre-dates modern nationalism. Byzantine emperors were able to generate artificial hostility between groups of citizens by dividing them by an arbitrary line into blues and greens. From here it is but a short distance to the bitter struggles in places like Bosnia, where people who had previously lived at ease with each other for generations, and indeed intermarried, went in for the barbarities of ethnic cleansing.

Many of the achievements of civilization are due to what Graham Wallas, the Fabian sociologist, called 'the great society'. This was the linking together through the market process of millions who have no chance of being personally acquainted. One interpretation of globalization is that the whole world is becoming a 'great society'. The problem ever since the Industrial Revolution, if not earlier, has been how to combine the benefits of the great society with the human ties generated by the smaller group.

Defensible individualism

In current political polemics, individualism is a pejorative term used by opponents of the concept. Few political writers call themselves individualists. They are more likely to say they are classical liberals, market liberals, old-fashioned liberals or something of the kind. But there clearly is an individualist component of their beliefs which is worth defending. The kind of individualism for which I will fight in the last ditch is ethical individualism. In its minimal form, it is the belief that actions should be judged by their effects on individual human beings.

How would I justify this judgement? It is individuals who feel, exult, despair and rejoice. And statements about group welfare are a shorthand way of referring to such individual effects. This seems to me a plain statement of fact, despite the numerous 'thinkers' who deny – or more usually – bypass it. Whatever might be said about sharing feelings with a close member of one's family, the rejoicing of a nation or a football club or a school is metaphorical.

The danger of collectivism is that of attributing a superior value to collective entities over and above the individuals who compose it. This disastrous error was made respectable by the teachings of Hegel and reached its apotheosis in the state worship of the Nazi and communist regimes. But it is lurking behind even the apparently more soft-hearted varieties of communitarianism.

Statements about large abstractions such as the interests of a country and the health of the economy must be translatable into statements about individual human beings. This translation cannot logically prevent the collectivist judgements I find so repellent; but such translations can nevertheless lead us to pose useful questions such as: 'How much suffering is justified by the gratification of my feelings of national pride as a Serb or a Croat?' Analysis along such lines would be likely to make people more self-conscious. It might even lead to a weakening of unreflective willingness to die for one's country, or the working class, and to a waning of nationalism and ideological enthusiasm in general.

Going beyond this reductionism, we do not find a single individualist creed. Benthamite utilitarianism does involve a commitment to individual welfare, but not to personal freedom. (The inhabitants of Aldous Huxley's *Brave New World* were made to take their soma pills.) Post-Bentham, individualists from John Stuart Mill onwards argued for the largest possible measure of individual freedom consistent with avoiding harm to others. They did so formally on the grounds that individuals were less bad judges of their own interests than governments, 'experts' or others who claimed to judge. But it is pretty clear from reading the classical liberals that they valued freedom for its own sake.

'What is so wonderful about individual choice?' One can only reply that it lies in the absence of coercion or man-made obstacles to the exercise of people's powers and capacities. In the final analysis, this judgement cannot be demonstrated rigorously against those with incompatibly different values. One can only try to remove misunderstandings and to display by anecdote, rhetoric and imaginative literature the virtues of the kind of society in which people have maximum opportunity to satisfy their preferences against societies where others make their judgements for them.

A particular misunderstanding is to pit the individual against the family. Anthropology and biology suggest that human beings are creatures who tend to live in one kind of family or another. The individualist is, however, more content to let the family evolve and hesitates to put a political imprimatur on the nuclear family in the state it reached among the middle classes of the late nineteenth century. However important the family, one is still allowed to write on other matters. And it is surely clear that it is not families but collective entities, from the state down to local collections of busybodies, from which the individualists want to protect us.

Self-realization

Individualists usually desire to go beyond liberating human beings from collectivist pressures and want to celebrate the achievements of particular people, whether in the arts or sciences or sports, or in the more mundane art of everyday living. This kind of positive individualism has its antithesis in the idealization of the team. Indeed, it is the British focus on team spirit which heavily qualifies the romantic continental notion that they are a nation of individualists. Recently I had occasion to congratulate an economist friend on some well-deserved professional promotion. He thanked me very generously, saying how glad he was that the work of his team had been recognized. But this is not what I meant at all. I was expressing pleasure that he personally had been promoted and that the choice had not been made on political grounds.

To go further into the more positive and indeed romantic aspects of individualism would take a separate paper. This would have to recognize the danger of this form of individualism becoming converted into worship of great men, such as Napoleon or Frederick the Great, for whom the lives and welfare of millions are sacrificed. Even in everyday life 'rugged individualism' sometimes means a craggy disregard for other people's interests, which is not a quality I wish to celebrate.

Political economy

A point requiring some emphasis is that an ethical individualist does not have to be an economic individualist. Generations of socialists have indeed argued that the collective control of economic activity would not only enable more individual citizens to satisfy more of their wants, but would enable them to flourish in a broader way. The argument against collectivist economic systems is that they utterly fail to fulfil their promise. Of course, it is a bonus to the individualist that allowing some rein to individual instincts for self-betterment will produce better results than centrally imposed direction. Nevertheless, the test of Adam Smith's view of the superiority of Natural Liberty must be that of experiments thrown up by events and not just of its psychological attractiveness or otherwise. Just as a philosophical individualist does not have to be an economic individualist, the same distinction works the other way around. An economic individualist does not have to share a wider individualist philosophy. He or she may simply accept that a market-based economic system brings better results without having a deeper belief in individual choice or in people 'doing their own thing'. Indeed, exponents of free markets often oppose freedom in every other sphere, especially in sexual behaviour and the behaviour of the young. This combination of economic individualism with authoritarian wider beliefs is all too common among many Conservatives, even in the so-called Thatcherite wing of that party.

Economic individualism

Despite these disclaimers, the type of individualism which is most under a cloud is economic individualism. It is associated with slogans like 'It's every man for himself and let the devil take the hindmost'. Or with Charles Dickens's Mr Gradgrind (his name, not the actual character in *Hard Times*). Or with thick-skinned City types who celebrate the rat-race in which they boast they are engaged. Even if the collapse of collectivist economic systems leaves people with no alternative, this fact is regarded as a necessary evil rather than anything to celebrate.

The greatest obstacle faced by economic individualism is the belief that it is based on, or encourages, materialism or acquisitiveness. In fact, self-interest in a market economy merely means that people follow their own chosen goals. These may be individual consumption; but they may equally be the acquiring of means to promote charitable, cultural or religious causes. Or they may try to maximize leisure to pursue some hobby or interest; or some mixture of all these. The altruistic businessman should indeed strive harder than his rivals to make profits and differentiate himself by what he does with his gain.

These necessary elaborations only take us a certain way. Defenders of market capitalism have rarely faced up to the shock with which many well brought-up people react when they learn that their job is not to feed or clothe, or even entertain, their fellow citizens directly, but to promote the profits of the company's owners. That is irrespective of how worthy or unworthy are the purposes to which the profits are devoted.

The most controversial aspect of economic individualism was expressed two centuries ago, by Adam Smith. No sentence in political economy has attracted more opprobrium than the passage in *The Wealth of Nations* saying: 'It is not from the benevolence of the butcher, brewer or baker that we expect our dinner, but from their regard to their own interest. We address ourselves, not to their humanity but to their self-love, and never talk to them of our own necessities but of their advantages.'[7]

The moralist is not appeased to learn that Smith also wrote *The Theory of Moral Sentiments*,[8] which emphasized benevolence. Nor is he or she appeased to learn that in *The Wealth of Nations* itself, a few sentences before the notorious ones just quoted, Smith stressed how much man was a social animal and 'has almost constant occasion for the help of his brethren' while a human being's 'whole life is scarce sufficient to gain the friendship of a few persons, in civilized society he stands at all times in need of the co-operation and assistance of great multitudes'. It is for this reason that he has to enlist their 'self-love' in his favour and cannot rely on their benevolence alone.

This 'self love' will be effective only if certain background conditions are fulfilled. There has to be a legal system and a political order which enforce contracts, protect property rights, and provide for limited liability or the equivalent. In other words, there is no private property without good government. Until the disillusioning experience of post-Communist countries, such background considerations were regarded by many modern economists as too obvious or insufficiently mathematical to be worth discussing. Their neglect has made it all too easy for former Communist bosses to flip over to being Mafia-style capitalists instead.

But it is not the incompleteness of 'invisible hand' statements which worries moralists, but their apparent reliance on the greed motive for the successful workings of an advanced civilization. (A generation before Adam Smith a similar shock was supplied by Bernard Mandeville's *Fable of the Bees*, which suggested that the vices of the few were essential for the prosperity of the many.) The two most common reactions are either to reject Smith's doctrine as outrageous or to accept it in a cynical spirit and say that Smith understood that the world was a jungle and that the animal with the sharpest teeth would inevitably win (which was not what he thought at all).

A rule utilitarian approach

There is, however, a third reaction which involves a little formal philosophy, although nothing more advanced than can be found in John Stuart Mill.[9] This is to explain both the strength and limitations of the 'invisible hand' doctrine in terms of a system of utilitarian morality. By utilitarianism I simply mean the view that actions are to be judged by their consequences for the welfare of other people. I do not have to argue whether utilitarianism can provide a complete system or whether it should be constrained by other ideas, such as those of Rawls, which I mentioned earlier. It is sufficient to say that public activities, whether in politics or business, are normally judged by utilitarian criteria; and it is difficult to see how this could be otherwise in a complex society.

Mill faced up to the problem of how to fit conventional moral rules such as 'Don't tell lies' or 'Keep promises' into utilitarian morality. He argued that we do not have the knowledge to assess directly on each separate occasion the effects of our actions on other human beings. What he called the *'prima facie* rules of common sense morality' arose from the common experience of mankind. The welfare of others will usually be better promoted by observing these rules rather than by trying to work out from first principles the effects of our behaviour on others on each separate occasion.

The 'invisible hand' doctrine is one of the more surprising *prima facie* rules to have been suggested. Surprising because of its apparently cynical flavour. For it does suggest that we will often do others more good if we behave as if we are following our self-interest than by pursuing more obviously altruistic purposes. (I suggested this interpretation of the 'invisible hand' in terms of rule utilitarianism several years ago. It has not so far attracted any attention.)

Prima facie rules of acceptable behaviour are by definition subject to exception and qualification. There will always be difficult cases in personal life which require reflection on basics. There will always be exceptional cases in which accepted rules should be overridden. So the maxims of Adam Smith do not enable businessmen to escape moral reflection – and were not intended to do so. The absence of laws or conventions prohibiting the dumping of poisonous lead would not excuse indiscriminate dumping. Nor do they excuse the sale of landmines to unscrupulous users.

In general, the closer to hand are the effects of business conduct the easier it is to know when to make exceptions to the 'invisible hand' doctrine. A takeover tycoon who shows an old retainer the door is a scoundrel and should not be excused by any market economist. The self-interest maxim comes in when we deal with remoter consequences. A business executive does not have the knowledge to estimate the remoter consequences of supposedly patriotic deviations from commercial self-interest such as 'buying British' when the overseas product gives better value. Nor is such knowledge available to MPs, officials or even academic economists. A manufacturer who keeps open uneconomic enterprises to 'provide jobs' is not necessarily promoting even the longer run interests of his immediate workforce. This is apart from the fact that, if he persists, he is likely to be taken over or abruptly closed down by successors, who may make the changes in a far more brutal way.

Information requirements

An economic system has at least five functions. They are to:

1. co-ordinate the activity of millions of individuals, households and firms;
2. obtain information about people's desires, tastes and preferences;
3. decide which productive techniques to use;
4. promote new ideas, tastes and activities which people would not have thought of without entrepreneurial initiative; and
5. create incentives for people to act on such information.

Only the fifth, incentive, function of markets could be abandoned in a community of saints. The others would still be required for the saints to know how best to serve their fellows. They might still be well advised to behave as if they were concerned with their own worldly well-being in order to create the market signals by which they could best serve others.

We know that the search for profit does not apply to large sections of activity. Institutions concerned with health and education are usually non-profit-making even when their services are sold for cash. A distinguished musician or surgeon will often have a strong sense of vocation and not just play or operate for the money. A doctor or teacher should have some responsibility to his patient or pupil over and above the search for fees. Here market rates of pay have their effects at the margin. They bring in the less dedicated who might have chosen a different field of endeavour; and they affect even the dedicated in their choice at the margin between work and leisure, or choice of profession. A hospital management need not be interested in profit maximization, but at least it should be interested in minimizing costs. So condemnation of the 'internal market' without examination is merely childish.

It is, however, time to query the pious belief that professional values are invariably superior to commercial ones. Professional bodies have their own inherent deficiencies. If left to themselves they often try to keep out new people and ideas and enforce restrictive practices. Many academics are opera lovers. Have they forgotten the professional guild of the Meistersingers of Nuremberg, which tried to keep out new influences and new types of song and verse from their guild? It was no free market fanatic, but Paul Samuelson, the Democrat Nobel Prize-winning economist, who long ago said that he preferred 'good clean money' to 'bad dirty power'.

Business culture

But let us descend to a lower level of abstraction. Part of the communitarian critique arises from an absurd idea of how a profit-seeking concern seeks to promote shareholder value. When I write an article for the *Financial Times*, the editor does not ask whether the article will increase the value of the Pearson equity. But he does know that, if the paper does not eventually make a return on its assets comparable to that of alternative investments, there is going to be trouble. As indeed there should be.

It is worth looking at the origin of the most criticized business attitudes, such as an exaggerated emphasis on the 'bottom line'. They arise not from profit-seeking or individualism as such, but from the separation of ownership from control. Modern economists have recognized something called the 'principal agent problem'. How do we make sure that appointed managers do in fact act as trustees for the ultimate owners and do not squander the resources for their own aggrandizement or alternatively just lead a quiet life? The problem affects state property as well as private corporations. It still arises for enterprises owned by their own workers or by local communities.

It was because of frequent abuses of managerial power that the takeover culture developed. On the Continent, and especially in Germany, this same function is performed for large enterprises by banks via the business establishment. It is far from obvious that a closed network is a better method of control than open bids for stock ownership. Admiration for German corporate culture is mostly found in English-speaking countries. Many of the tensions would be eased if there were a move to smaller units where the managers were also the proprietors. Ownership and control are combined in the German or Mittelstand or in the flourishing medium-sized Italian companies which are responsible for most of the real economic miracles in that country.

A manager who is merely a trustee for shareholders has to make his decisions in two halves. First, he has to earn as much as he can for the stockholders. Then he has to apportion the resulting earnings in a way which he believes the owners will approve. No wonder most top executives take the easy way out by some ploughing back, some dividend distribution and some token contribution, such as half a per cent of profits, to good causes. How much easier it is for an owner of a ceramics factory in the Italian Veneto to make all his decisions in one go; and, if he has a good year, to send an immediate cheque to a local musical society or to help the renovation of a Palladian villa. It is his affair and there is no conflict between profit-seeking and civic values.

The issue was brought home to me when, at a conference, I met a small American manufacturer whose main motive in life was to run a furniture factory profitable enough to give work to the disabled, who were paid something like normal wages. If he had been a mere manager, the shareholders could reasonably have demanded that he maximized his return on assets. As the owners, they could then decide what they wanted to do with the resulting profits, which might include providing work for the disabled at subsidized rates. But when the owner and the manager are the same person all these stages can be collapsed into one. It remains true that such an entrepreneur still does his best for the disabled or any other good cause by buying in the cheapest market and selling in the dearest.

The trend away from corporate dinosaurs towards smaller service companies which make separate contracts with individual purchasers could eventually lead to a much more dispersed pattern of economic decisions and a more personal form of individualism. But let us not pretend that everyone is going to like it. Salaried employees who are suddenly told to fend for themselves as consultants or suppliers of specialist services often find the process a shock – no matter how many books they have read or written decrying bureaucratic corporate management.

The true 'bottom line'

It is not difficult to summarize the economic argument. A stakeholder or communitarian would like to see social and ethical objectives pursued directly by corporations in addition to, or instead of, the search for profit. Market liberals prefer to provide for these objectives in the background conditions and rules which constrain the search for profit. In many particular cases two reasonable members of both schools might agree. But the market liberal will always worry that the stakeholder arrogates to business leaders the role of shaping society for which they are ill suited; and that they would serve us as well as themselves better if they stuck to specific and limited objectives and did not take on the role of Moses and the minor prophets as well.

The debate will not be decided by evidence or formal reasoning alone. To communitarians, selfishness is the most hideous of sins, and sometimes the only one. An individualist-liberal does not celebrate selfishness; but he believes that there can be worse sins, such as the sacrifice of individual human beings for the sake of some abstract doctrine or religious or other belief. If I may quote Holmes again: 'Communitarian anti-liberals suggest that, once people overcome their self-interest, they necessarily act in an admirable and public spirited way... but this leaves out of account the prominent place of selfless cruelty in human affairs. It is much easier to be cruel in the course of acting in the cause of others than while acting for one's own thing. Those who have homosexuals shot in the name of the Islamic revolution cannot be accused of anti-social individualism or base self-interest.'

My own conviction is that people in the grip of greed often do much less harm than people in the grip of self-righteousness, especially when that righteousness is harnessed to the supposed needs of a collectivity or given some theological or metaphysical justification.

Appendix on methodological individualism

One kind of individualism which creates much heat is methodological individualism. This is the desire to ground social

IDEAS AND REFLECTIONS

science in the behaviour and/or motivations of individual human beings. Neo-classical economic theory is based on this approach – although you would not guess so from the short-term forecaster in front of a screen who provides the public image of an economist. Most sociologists are hostile to methodological individualism; and indeed many economists write books denouncing the individualist foundations of their own subject.

Methodological individualism is itself a branch of reductionism, which seeks to ground explanation in the most basic units. But why stop at individual human beings? Why not try to reduce motivation to biology, biology to chemistry, and chemistry in its turn to sub-atomic physics? Freud, for instance, started off hoping that his analysis could be reduced in the end to biochemistry; and the inability to make this translation has counted against the scientific status of psychoanalysis. Nevertheless, the test of success in the social sciences is prediction or explanation. It is better to have a more successful explanation of business cycles, which starts with mere statistical regularities, than one which is well grounded in hypotheses about individual behaviour, but which tells us very little we did not know already.

Purely methodological individualism ought to be neutral in relation to morals and politics. It is a matter of finding from experience the approach which yields the most fruitful hypotheses in a particular context. There is, however, one reason why a social scientist might want to start from the individual human being rather than the group to which he or she belongs, or than the quarks of which he or she is composed. This is that the social scientist has an *advantage* over the physical scientist or the zoologist in being able to take into account motivations and intentions. And these exist at the level of the individual.

Notes

1. C. B. Macpherson, *The Political Theory of Possessive Individualism*, Oxford, 1962.
2. Amital Etzioni, *The Spirit of Community*, Crown Publishers, New York, 1993.
3. David Boaz, *Libertarianism*, Free Press, 1993.
4. S. Mulhall and A. Swift, *Liberals and Communitarians*, 2nd edition, Blackwell, 1997.
5. Alasdair McIntyre, *After Virtue*, 2nd edition, Duckworth, 1985.
6. Stephen Holmes, *The Anatomy of Anti-Liberalism*, Harvard, 1993.
7. Adam Smith, *The Wealth of Nations*, 1776; modern edition, Liberty Classics, 1981.

8. Adam Smith, *The Theory of Moral Sentiments*, 1759; modern edition, Liberty Classics, Indianapolis, 1982.
9. J. S. Mill, *Utilitarianism*, 1861; modern edition, J. M. Dent, London, 1948.

Ethics, Religion and Humbug
Speech to Oxford University Jewish Society, 3 March 2000

Some recollections

One of my earliest childhood enthusiasms was for the detailed observance of the ceremonies of the Jewish religion. My parents and many of their friends were mildly observant orthodox. Perhaps I should explain that orthodox Judaism of the kind in which I grew up required very little theological commitment. A person could be a good Jew who doubted the afterlife. ('No one ever came back to talk about it,' my father would say.) A devout Jew could be a logical positivist – it just showed that he was reading philosophical books. But if he did not carry out a bare minimum of observances he was beyond the pale.

As soon as I learned about the vast number of practices that were theoretically required, I became very dissatisfied with my parents' minimalism. Either these observances were the commands of God – in which case they should be observed – or they were not. There was some self-seeking here. For although I would not switch on the electric light on the Sabbath, I stood around waiting for other people to do so, rationalizing this by saying that they were going to do so in any case. This zealotry worried adults, even adults who were themselves observant, but who feared that I could easily go to the other extreme. Surely enough I did. For, within weeks, the concerns of my elders switched from worries that I was 'opening the synagogue' to how to cope with a precocious child that kept saying 'I do not believe in religion'.

There was, however, another aspect which was much less characteristic than my naive either-or logic. This was an attraction for aspects of ceremony – religious and otherwise – which has never really left me (ceremony rather than ritual, because ritual can be very cruel in the demands it makes on many unfortunate individuals). But to come back to my potted and partial autobiography: I was enchanted by the service of the Jewish High Holidays, the singing of familiar prayers to exciting new tunes and with insertions. There were other aspects which caught my fancy: how an otherwise unimportant old man became the key to proceedings when he told the blower of the Shofar (ram's horn) on New Year and at the end of the Day of Atonement which notes to play.

Indeed, I witnessed something similar when I happened to be in Venice on Yom Kippur many years later. I went to the old Synagogue. Unfortunately there was no cantor and no choir; and thus the proceedings took on the moaning and groaning form which puts me off so much. But there was one similarity which struck me from my early youth. In the congregation there were local personalities who did not know too much about what to do, but who were called up to the Reading of the Law because of their position. There was a man in a beard and trilby, who made sure that everyone came up to the platform on time and helped them through their blessings by pointing to each word as it came up. At other times he found every excuse for walking all around the synagogue. I could not help reflecting that this man was probably of no consequence during most of the year – probably much less important than the ignoramuses whom he helped through the proceedings. Here, however, was his moment of glory. The position maketh the man.

To go back to my youth. In my teens I was no longer a believer, but I would go to the synagogue on the New Year and Yom Kippur to avoid upsetting my father. The part of the whole-day service which I made a point of attending was in the early afternoon when other worshippers took a break and had a walk. I was impressed by the account of the Temple service when the high priest would sacrifice a goat, throwing it down from a rock after which it took on the sins of the congregation. There is indeed much to ponder about the roots of the word 'scapegoat'; but I never got round to looking it up in James Frazer's *Golden Bough*.

The fascination with the ceremonial-musical side continued in later life. Truth to tell, I often prefer a classical or post-classical setting of the Latin mass – in which the same words are set in ever differing ways – to the twists and turns of the operas which are much more fashionable to discuss. Indeed, I attended the last Christmas Midnight Mass at the Brompton Oratory before services changed to the vernacular. This change was an example of superficial reform by supposedly modernizing Popes who nevertheless obstinately stood by the rules which caused so much real misery, e.g. birth control, divorce and the celibacy of the clergy.

I would have returned more often in later life to the Jewish synagogue services except for the embarrassment of people saying 'What are *you* doing here?' But I read that the conductor Otto

Klemperer, who had undergone a superficial conversion to Catholicism, did make a return visit to the synagogue at least once before the end of his life. And quite recently I learned that the composer Igor Stravinsky remarked that the ceremonies, so far from being superficial, were the essential part of religion.

Ethnic religion

There was something else that occurred, which in retrospect is highly disturbing. The main reaction that greeted my childhood renunciation of religion – not, I hasten to say, from my parents, but from neighbours and friends – was to say accusingly 'Then you are not a Jew.' I did not then have the resources of linguistic analysis to give a proper response, but unconvincingly replied 'I am a Zionist'. This was not so much untruthful as feeble. I did not have the strength of mind to put everything into the melting pot at the same time and have been ashamed of my lack of robustness ever since.

The identification of religion with ethnic self-consciousness was perhaps understandable on account of mid-twentieth-century history. Nevertheless retrospection has given me a peculiar horror of the union of religion and nationalism which has become such a curse in the new millennium. Most people here will appreciate what I mean by the briefest of references to Bosnia or the militant Iranian clergy or the call of some fundamentalist Muslims for a Holy War against Israel. But we should be honest enough to see that there are traces of the same thing among Jews both outside and inside Israel. Surely one myth that it is time to jettison is that of the Chosen People.

The harm done by religion

The typical response of many non-religious people to religion is to say either 'It would be wonderful if it were true' or 'The trouble is that religious people do not practise what they preach.' This is far too easy. Most of the religions I know would be far from wonderful if they were true. And on the whole more harm is done by those who do practise what they preach than those who approach religion in a more opportunistic way. I cannot help noticing how in the operas of Verdi the religious characters are nearly always the most punitive and vengeful. When even Aida's rival Amneris pleads for mercy it is the pagan priests who insist on continuing the death by suffocation. And in *Don Carlos*, when the Flemish deputies are arrested by the royal officers, it is the lay population who plead for mercy while the Christian priests insist on death. Not to speak of the Grand Inquisitor who insists on King Philip being prepared to condemn his own son to death on pain of otherwise having to face the Inquisition himself.

And in case any of you think that I am in danger of taking opera libretti too seriously, the last execution in Spain for heresy was as late as 1826, when a schoolmaster was hanged for saying another prayer in place of the 'Ave Maria'. In 1766, at the height of the Enlightenment, when Gibbon and David Hume and Voltaire were already writing and Haydn and Mozart were composing and Gainsborough and Fragonard were painting, a young French aristocrat, the Chevalier de la Barre, was sentenced to have his hands amputated, his tongue torn out and then to be burned alive. His crime? Not to doff his hat to a Capuchin religious procession because it was raining.

Do not for one moment suppose that the Protestants were much more merciful than the Catholics. Both Luther and Calvin were enthusiastic supporters of the burning of witches. In Calvinistic Scotland some 4,500 supposed witches were killed in a one-hundred-year period. The Paisley Seven were executed for witchcraft as late as 1697, after the Glorious Revolution and when John Locke was already preaching toleration in England. In Northern Ireland today most pupils still attend either Catholic or Protestant schools, both funded by the state. We can only guess how much this division has contributed to the worsening of tribal warfare in that province.

It would be fascinating to have an attempt by one of the American school of quantitative historians to balance the good done by sects such as the Quakers and the early Franciscans or Rabbi Hugo Gryn, in our own century, against the savagery of the heresy hunts and crusades or those who killed an Israeli prime minister for betraying the faith. But in the absence of such attempts we must all rely on more subjective assessments. These episodes cannot be wiped out with the glib saying 'Christianity has never been tried'. Surely it has been tested to destruction. Today, perhaps because it is in retreat, Christianity seems a good deal gentler than Muslim fundamentalism. But it was not ever thus. In medieval Spain the Caliphs were a model of tolerance and civilization under which many cultures and religions flourished, while the Christians who reconquered Spain put to the sword those who would not accept their religion.

Even today not all Christians are so gentle. Who is it who threatens to take the British government to the Strasbourg Court of Human Rights, not for the ill-treatment of children, but on the contrary for banning beating in schools and thus going against the so-called convictions of so-called Christians? And who was it who held a meeting in a large hall in London to instruct parents how to punish their children more severely – to such an extent that secular human rights organizations tried to get the meeting stopped as a breach of the law? Of course, a group of fundamentalist Christians. And who was it, who at the time of the Profumo case, thundered against the private morals of a fellow minister and his own sin of having sat in the same Cabinet? The Christian Lord Hailsham. And who was it who strained Cabinet unity by responding about toleration? None other than the pretty irreligious Reginald Maudling.

Are not at least Christian moral teachings worthy of observance? Here one must remember that the Devil can quote scripture for his purposes. In St Matthew, Jesus is quoted as saying: 'The Son of Man is not come to destroy men's lives but to save them.' But in another verse he says, 'I come not to send peace but a sword.' In St Luke, he endorses the commandment 'Honour thy father and thy mother', but he also says 'If any man come to me and hate not his father and mother and wife and children and brothers and sisters, yea and his own life also, he cannot be my disciple.'

The God of the Old Testament

If Judaism seems less tarnished, it is probably because it has had so little power for the last 2,000 years. Even so, do I need to remind you that it is the religious parties in the Israeli Cabinet who have the most hawkish attitudes to peace negotiations with the Arabs: an attitude more than reciprocated by all too many Muslim fundamentalists.

To go a little further, there is no better source than the Old Testament. To refresh my memory I looked at the chapter on it in Ludovic Kennedy's book *All In The Mind, a Farewell to God* (Hodder and Stoughton, 1999). He reminds us that there are three kinds of passage in the Old Testament. There are places, full of 'A Begat B' or intricate details of sacrifices, where one finds the eyes glazing over, the head nodding on the chest. Secondly, there are passages of striking imagery or beauty, such as 'By the waters of Babylon we sat down and wept' (which Verdi nearly made into the Italian national anthem). Thirdly, there is a darker side: tales of treachery and betrayal, killings on a massive scale which crowd one another with sickening regularity. Elijah, having witnessed the triumph of his God, ordered 450 priests of Baal to be killed. Or 'Now go and smite the Amalekites and utterly destroy all they have and spare them not; both man and woman, infant and suckling, ox and sheep, camel and ass.' If that is not genocide, I do not know what is.

I did not want to be completely dependent on Kennedy. So I tried to check for myself by putting in five or six markers distributed at random throughout my copy of the Old Testament. My first marking was Numbers, 15. At first it looked like one of the boring passages dealing with sacrifices. Further on, the chapter appeared like a model of enlightenment, which should stand over the Home Office door:

'One ordinance shall be both for you of the congregation and also for the stranger that sojourneth with you.' But by the end there is a story of a man brought to Moses for gathering sticks on the Sabbath. The Lord's instruction was that he should be stoned by all the congregation; and stoned he was.

Next I came to the beginning of the first chapter of the Book of Joshua. This is mostly instructions about conquering (or reconquering) the land of Israel. But it ends with the sinister warning 'he that doth rebel against thy [Joshua's] commandments should be put to death'. After that I came to the Second Book of Chronicles, 2, which was about the building of the Temple. Solomon set to work 70,000 people to be bearers of burdens and 80,000 to be hewers in the mountain. Some 3,600 were overseers. It puts the Greenwich Dome quite into the shade.

Then I came to Psalm 72. This is one of the beautiful passages: 'The mountain shall bring peace to the people, and the little hills bring righteousness. He shall judge the poor of the people, he shall save the children of the needy, and shall break in pieces the oppressor.' (More like Old Labour squeezing the rich until the pips squeak than nice business-friendly Tony Blair.) The next passage was Jeremiah, 13. This is one of the more poetic books of the Bible with the passage about the leopard not being able to change his spots. Nevertheless God is made to say that the people of Israel, who had sinned, would be dashed one against the other, even the fathers and the sons together: 'I will not pity or spare nor have mercy, but destroy them.'

Finally I came to the fourth chapter of the Book of Daniel. This is about the three Jewish officials appointed by the Babylonian king Nebuchadnezzar. Because they would not worship an image of gold they were cast into the burning fiery furnace. When they walked out without a hair of their heads being singed, the king went to the other extreme and blessed the God of Israel and made a decree that anyone who spoke anything against these three Jewish officials should be cut in pieces and their houses made into a dunghill. The Old Testament God does nothing by halves!

Paganism and fanaticism

One affectation which was very fashionable in literary and artistic circles between the wars (e.g. Norman Douglas) was to say that they were literally pagan. This again will not do. By all means study the Greek and Roman mythologies, especially on a warm Mediterranean beach. But do not let us deceive ourselves: pagan actions were at least as bloody as those of the Christians. Among the Aztecs a huge image of a corn god was set up, made of dough and the blood of infants, which was supposed to become a god itself and was eaten. At the annual feast to celebrate another god, a victim was killed and his arms and legs eaten by the principal chiefs.

One of my colleagues, on being told the theme of my remarks, said that surely the evil was not religion but fanaticism. To which I can only comment: to some extent. The difference between political fanaticism and the religious variety is that the religious claim to have God on their side. This justifies everything. And even among the political sects it is those like old-style communism, that have so many of the characteristics of a religion, that have butchered most human beings.

The religious instinct

One of the lessons which I drew from Kennedy's book, which I do not think was intended, was quite how deep-seated the religious instinct is among human beings. Indeed he gives the game away by citing ceremonial incantations used by unbelievers, which read like parodies of standard prayers. Even Kennedy is unwilling to do entirely without the consolations of religion and joins those who, like Wordsworth or the Bloomsbury writers, look to nature or works of art to provide substitute spiritual nourishment. But I am afraid this is a cop-out. There is no way in which works of art, however great, can provide the bogus feelings of certainty about how the universe works or how we ought to behave that the world's religions claim to provide.

As Kennedy points out, the killing fields of Christianity are mainly in the past, while the legacy of the great cathedrals and Renaissance paintings remain. Of course we should enjoy this legacy. But if we could move the clock back who could suppose that any cathedral is worth the massacre of innocent people or the barbarities of the Crusades?

True, we cannot hope to gain a full understanding of the Jewish cantor, the Latin mass, or the Passions of J. S. Bach, without some knowledge of and feeling for the religious background. Nor can we fully understand medieval, Renaissance or Baroque painting. Indeed, I myself would get more out of visits to galleries if I were better acquainted both with the New Testament and with Greek mythology. I willingly confess to having some religious instincts myself. My two favourite vocal pieces are Mahler's 'Resurrection Symphony' and Beethoven's 'Choral Symphony'. The title of the first speaks for itself, with the opening words of the final chorus 'Auferstehen' (Rise again). And Schiller's *Ode to Joy* is full of vague but strong theistic references. But there is all the difference in the world between enjoying a quasi-religious wallow and treating any particular religion as the guide either to truth or to morals.

Morality

Finally, let us rid ourselves once and for all of the belief that without religion there is no basis for moral behaviour. I have found this most clearly stated by the Oxford philosopher R. M. Hare – himself a lay preacher – who explained that the concept of morality involved choice and that it was no more moral to behave well for fear of God than it was for fear of the policeman. I doubt if it is even psychologically necessary. Modern biological writers have suggested that, even in the world of the selfish gene, natural selection works in favour of at least some kinds of altruism, such as kinship altruism or 'tit for tat'. But we are only at the beginning of a scientific understanding of human nature, let alone of how to improve it.

The Bishop of Edinburgh, Richard Holloway, has published a book attacking the whole notion that we have to be religious to be moral and to believe in God to be good (*Godless Morality*, Canongate, 1999). He believes it is better to leave God out of the moral debate and find good human reasons for supporting the system or approach we advocate. The Bishop is especially interesting on the appeal to tradition which occupies such a prominent place in Jewish pleas to observe religious rituals. By the time we start appealing to tradition, in order to preserve some custom or practice, its days are clearly numbered, because traditions really only work when they are legitimated by widespread consent. Once we start appealing merely to the past, we have removed it from the circumstances that gave it logic and integrity. Traditions work by unconscious acceptance. While they are unreflectively fulfilling their role, they continue to have one. Once they have to be appealed to as a clincher in an argument, we can be certain that they have lost their role or are in the process of losing it.

Conclusion

In my view the best way to treat religion is as a cultural legacy. It can help to establish feelings of community much more genuinely than the appalling rhetoric of the Third Way. But even here let us avoid the trap of using it to strengthen solidarity among those in the group at the expense of hatred or indifference to those outside. It is this kind of exclusive group morality which is the curse of the human race. We do not yet know how to cope with this in-group, out-group dichotomy, but religion can make it worse.

Humanitarianism Without Illusions

Financial Times, 27 September 2002

Take two blindingly obvious propositions:

1. There is such a thing as human nature and this needs to be taken
   into account in all attempts to reform society. Theologians call it
   original sin, but you do not have to be religious to take the point.
2. There are also innate differences between individuals which cannot
   be wiped out by education, income redistribution or anything else.

You might think that these are hardly worth discussing. The
American cognitive psychologist Steven Pinker met this reaction
when he told colleagues that he was working on his just-published
book, *The Blank Slate*.[1] That was also my own reaction. Yet I was soon
disabused. The Standard Social Science Model which denies these
propositions has still not vanished. It still seems impossible to study
human behaviour objectively without being accused of every kind of
barbarity or of the distorted form of Darwinism which Nazi Germany
and the apartheid regime in South Africa used to justify their policies.

Direct evidence turned up the other night when I was listening to
a discussion of Pinker's book on the usually staid BBC Radio Three
programme, *Night Waves*. Pinker aroused the ire of the British
psychologist Oliver James, who espoused the widespread view that
children who had been brought up violently tended to become violent
parents themselves. Pinker argues that this could be because violent
tendencies are inherited. Of course, it is not all in the genes; but the
main environmental influences on children come from their peers
rather than their parents.

These contentions infuriated James, who tried to ask four times if
Pinker had read certain studies. Pinker had a methodological
objection to the genre on which James was relying. He also said that
James kept on interrupting him and did not give him a chance to

reply. As a listener, I put some of the blame for this embarrassing episode on the presenter who kept on trying to move on the discussion by saying 'Locked horns will get us nowhere.' The programme would have been better if the two had been allowed to engage directly. It all ended with James shouting that evolutionary psychology flourished in right-wing periods and exclaiming, 'You call Blair left wing!'

Of course, I am not an expert on statistical studies of twins and siblings, which involve controversies all too reminiscent of econometrics. But I have learned that a new study subsequent to Pinker's book showed that physically abused children are more likely to become anti-social. But this applies only to a minority who have a certain genetic mutation. So you cannot get rid of the innate factor. As a matter of fact, I have over several decades shown quiet but persistent opposition to the disgusting habit of corporal punishment still so rife in schools in parts of the English-speaking world – and I actually agree with the gist of James's own suggestions on child-rearing.[2] What however infuriated me was to hear Pinker accused of encouraging child abuse. Throughout his book he reminds people of the Scottish philosopher David Hume's demonstration that no 'ought' proposition follows from any factual or logical assertion.

The argument Pinker uses against cruelty to children is not just that they might in turn be cruel to their own children, but that it causes unnecessary misery here and now. What he writes is: 'Child rearing is above all an ethical responsibility. It is not OK for parents to beat, humiliate, deprive or neglect their children, because those are awful things for a big strong person to do to a small helpless one.' But if you want a more cynical reason, he quotes another writer: 'Be nice to your kid when he's young so that he will be nice to you when you are old.'

The Blank Slate is fascinatingly written with illustrations going well beyond biology. Pinker must have an enviably mastery of the internet to tap into so many different subjects. Although the publisher might have thought the title would make it a blockbuster, in my view it does the book less than justice. For most of it is concerned not with rebutting the blank slate, but with a positive attempt to synthesize research on mind, brain, genes and evolution. I was particularly attracted by the fact that Pinker has not confined his conclusions to feminism and sex differences on which so many writers on this subject concentrate, but has moved into areas such as political psychology and the anatomy of group hatreds.

He would probably accept that what he has to say does not differ from the wiser conclusions of experienced diplomats and historians. Evolutionary psychology has yet to make its distinctive contribution to a more peaceful world. But it does help to state the problems more clearly and to evaluate the rival theories of humanist scholars. Inevitably I have some quibbles. For instance Pinker reaffirms the right–left axis. Someone who favours a strong military is (in the US) likely to favour judicial restraint, be attached to religion, against sexual laxity, tough on crime and in favour of lower taxes. As the author asks, 'Why on earth should people's beliefs about sex predict their beliefs about the size of the military? What does religion have to do with tax?' Both left and right are full of contradictions. The left is permissive about sexual behaviour but not about business practices. Conservatives want to preserve communities and traditions but some of them also favour the free market economy that subverts them.

Moreover, these clusters of views have not always held together historically. In the early nineteenth century, for instance, free market doctrines were the province of radical liberals and it was conservatives who espoused – as some of them still do – agricultural protection and a strong state. It is indeed highly artificial to rank attitudes on a single dimension corresponding to the seating of delegates to the French Revolutionary Assembly of 1789. My own investigations some time ago[3] suggested that there are indeed left–right relationships, but that they are rather weak (the correlation coefficients are normally less than 0.5). So a free market supporter who is not religious or flag-waving need not despair. But he may find himself having arguments with his own side.

Pinker argues that the seemingly disparate attitudes making up the political right are linked by what he calls the 'Tragic Vision'. The ones making up the left belong to the 'Utopian Vision'. Adherents believe that human nature changes with social circumstances, so traditional institutions have no inherent value. Pinker himself, although he has some left-of-centre attitudes, believes that the 'Tragic Vision' more nearly conforms to human nature. This will do as a starting point, but does not apply in many cases. For instance Milton Friedman is put squarely among the upholders of the 'Tragic Vision'. Yet his best friends would concede that the 'Tragic Vison' is just what he lacks. His writings assume that if only we could abandon statist illusions and establish free markets, democracy and the rule of law, the human future would be bright indeed. On the other side of the Atlantic, Tony Blair, however much he may now be abused on the left, clearly has much more the Utopian-messianic than the Tragic vision of human possibilities.

Pinker himself believes that the left–right gap is narrowing because both sides are being forced to accept evolutionary psychology. The left-wing belief that human nature can be changed at will and the right-wing belief that morality rests on a god-given immaterial soul are giving way to more scientific attitudes. He therefore predicts that political differences will increasingly cut across the old divides and will instead depend on differing weights to different aspects of human nature or to pragmatic assessments of the consequences of alternative actions.

By an interesting coincidence, the 'Tragic View', in a highly non-religious version, has been taken to its ultimate by the English political philosopher John Gray in his new book *Straw Dogs*. No two writers could be more different in style. Pinker relies on experiments and statistics, leavened with extracts from his favourite writers and some old Jewish jokes. Gray relies mainly on quotations, not only from writers and philosophers, but also from neuroscientists. The result is more a French-type series of pensées than a consecutive argument. Normally I am allergic to such a literary form, but in this case it comes off. Gray relentlessly exposes the wishful desire of most philosophers to say that human beings are not animals – and violent ones – which they so clearly are. Indeed, he goes further than Pinker in asserting – quite correctly – that human beings are not alone in possessing consciousness. I would add that the evidence of its existing in, say, cats and dogs is very similar to that for supposing that it exists in human minds other than one's own.

In previous works Gray embraced in turn almost every modern political ideology, only to denounce them as vigorously as he had previously supported them. This time he spurns them all, including, I am glad to say, the moth-eaten eternities of the mystics. Voltaire argued that we should cultivate our own garden. Gray concludes 'Other animals do not need a purpose in life ... Can we not think of the aim of life as being simply to see?'

Pinker too exposes the moralistic fallacy that healthy, rational people will not injure others. Indeed, human violence does not have to be a disease for it to be worth combating. If anything, it is the belief that violence is an aberration that is dangerous, because it lulls us into forgetting how easily violence may erupt in quiescent places. Unfortunately anyone using the words 'violence' and 'biology' in the same paragraph may be put under a cloud of suspicion for racism. There have been well-known university studies which show how all too easy it is to get students to impose brutal punishments on each other even in an experimental situation. Pinker was particularly influenced as a teenager by the outbreak of criminal violence on a day when the Montreal police went on strike. From boyhood onwards men divide themselves into coalitions that compete aggressively. Worst of all they force others into an aggressive posture in self-defence. The question is not why children are aggressive but how they learn not to be so. The lion's share of US murders are committed by young men between fifteen and thirty. Moreover 7 per cent of young men commit 79 per cent of repeated violence offences.

People embrace a morality that usually does not embrace all human beings but only the members of their own clan, village or tribe. History and ethnography suggest that people can treat strangers the way we now treat lobsters. In early societies between 10 and 60 per cent of men died at the hands of other men. Studies of warfare in primitive societies have confirmed that men do not have to be short of food or land to wage it. One factor in why some countries are more willing to wage war than others is that they have a much higher proportion of the population consisting of men in that age group. Saudi Arabia is an obvious instance.

Pinker cites the English philosopher Thomas Hobbes, who speaks of human life in conditions of nature as being nasty, brutish and short. There is much evidence that the forces of evolution prepared human beings for violence. Far from being the friendly creatures of romantic imagination, our nearest relation, the chimpanzees, are even more violent than *homo sapiens*.Yet unlike Gray, Pinker remains an optimistic North American. He pins his hopes for a better future partly on the possibility that human beings will gradually expand their sense of group identity to a greater range of their fellows and partly on the resources of diplomacy and military deterrence.

He believes adjudication by an armed authority to be the most effective general violence reduction technique ever invented. He follows Hobbes in advocating a common power to keep them all in awe. But he adds that civil libertarian concern about abusive police practices is an indispensable counterweight to state monopoly of violence. He admits that no way has yet been found to establish a world authority with an ultimate global monopoly of violence. Meanwhile he supports devices like Mutually Assured Destruction (MAD) that prevailed in the Cold War. But how does one apply this remedy to terrorist organizations without a clear-cut base, such as al Qaeda?

Unfortunately I fear that the instinct of human beings to form mutually hostile groups is so deeply embedded that unconventional remedies will be required. If our race is to survive in an era of chemical and biological warfare we will need not just genetically modified foods, but genetically modified human beings. I am well aware that, if maverick scientists jump the gun, the attempt could result in monstrosities. Nor do I need John Gray to remind me of the likelihood that the process will be led by gangster politicians intent on producing robotic slaves. This is all the more reason for civilized people to take the matter seriously instead of mindlessly trying to banish all discussion.

Notes

1. Steven Pinker, *The Blank Slate*, Penguin, 2002.
2. Oliver James, *They F*** You Up*, Bloomsbury, 2002.
3. *Left or Right: The Bogus Dilemma*, Secker & Warburg, 1967.

The Poor Need Not Always Be With Us

Article in *Search* (a Joseph Rowntree Foundation journal), Issue 33, Spring 2000

According to the Bible, 'The poor will ye always have with you.' The Bible need only be right if poverty is seen as relative deprivation. In that case some people are always bound to be poorer than others. The search for a perfectly equal distribution – apart from being full of conceptual ambiguities – is in practice likely to lead to hell on earth, with much bigger disparities of power in exchange for relatively modest (if any) improvement in the relative possessions of the worse off.

On the other hand it does not quite work to define poverty only in absolute terms. It is of course worth knowing how many people there are who are hungry, or homeless or without clothes or heating or lighting. There is no need for anyone to be involuntarily in such a state in a moderately affluent western society. But on analysis this simplicity disappears. What do you do about people who would have enough to eat and could afford to do so, if their diet were planned by nutritionists, but in practice do not have enough to do so? Do we therefore want to extend this principle to include anyone of any income level who does not or cannot spend his or her income wisely?

The problems go further in an advanced industrial society. The kinds of cheap consumption available to a Bangladeshi are not available to us. An Englishman does not have the option of paying lower train fares and sitting on hard wooden benches. The very basic foodstuffs available in Third World retail outlets are difficult to find in a western metropolis.

One can go even further. There are such things as conventional necessities. A citizen who cannot afford a television set is in some sense deprived of a common point of reference with fellow citizens – of which he or she would not have been aware, living on the same income in 1850. But a line has to be drawn somewhere. To say that someone who cannot afford a holiday in the West Indies, or many meals at expensive restaurants, is poor is simply playing with words.

There seems to me no escape from the notion that poverty is in part a relative and in part an absolute concept. If you put all the emphasis on the relative part, then the main effect is to spread misery. For it means that however rich our societies become and however far-reaching the applications of science, social critics will always be able to complain of poverty; and, to the extent that their message is diffused, people will feel worse off than they need feel.

At root of much of the argument is the unanswerable question whether the riches of the wealthy or the more moderate affluence of the middle-income groups are the cause of the poverty of others. If someone makes or applies a new discovery, like Henry Ford, which benefits everyone but becomes rich from it himself, he is not causing poverty. On a reasonable use of language he is alleviating it. But for the mass of upper- and middle-income citizens with no such talents or opportunities, the question is much harder to answer. If there is some redistribution which could be undertaken, along Rawlsian lines, which really would make the poorest better off, it should be undertaken. But is the failure to make it a cause of poverty? We are here up against an ambiguity in the word 'cause', which we find in many other key concepts in the social and even natural sciences.

The acid test of whether someone who campaigns against poverty or deprivation is activated by malice against the better off or concern for the poor is the following: how does he or she react to an improvement in the income or wealth of the better off which has no adverse effect on those at the bottom or in the middle?Anyone who thinks such an improvement impossible should consider the following. A number of people have become rich through setting up internet companies. They have not become so by grinding the face of the poor; they have done so by venturing into a new form of activity which increases total national income, even if by not as much as the enthusiasts suppose. They have done nothing to harm the poor and may indirectly have benefited them, even though on some statistical measures the 'degree of inequality' has increased.

It so happens that, whether intentionally or by happy accident, the Rowntree definition of poverty passes the anti-resentment test with flying colours. On that definition, a poor household is one whose income is below half the median – the median is simply the mid-point, where there are as many households above as below it. The arrival of the internet millionaire has not increased poverty on this view – the changes have all been at the top end of the income distribution. But on the government view of distance from the average it almost certainly has. The Rowntree definition looks superficially similar to another definition of poverty as below half average income. But there is all the difference in the world between them and the difference should not be regarded as merely technical.

This is brought out very well in some of the tables near the beginning of the Rowntree survey, 'Monitoring Poverty and Social Exclusions, 1999'. They show that a reduction in the basic rate of income tax appears to increase poverty on the 'distance from average' definition. Even an increase in the work incomes obtained by the better-off half of citizens, without any government action, appears to increase poverty. The reason is that anything that happens which benefits the better-off sections of the population, or those in the middle, will increase average income. If the bottom quarter remains stable, then their difference from the average will increase, even if nothing has happened to increase poverty on a common sense view.

I have, however, mixed feelings about all the detail about what the poor cannot afford given by surveys such as Rowntree. There is of course a strong case for spelling out poverty in concrete terms. In the past it was easier to make out a case for redistribution by pointing to the number of households without inside lavatories or bathrooms than by abstract statistics of income distribution. And yet is it really so surprising or so disquieting that better-off people are healthier than poorer ones? There is more to health than medical care; and it would be both sad and astonishing if people on higher incomes spent all their extra resources on conspicuous consumption and overlooked the needs of their own person.

The figure that impressed me most in the Rowntree study was that it would be possible to abolish poverty on the Rowntree definition by a relatively modest expenditure of public funds – some £6bn to £10bn or 1 per cent of GDP. But the authors then go on to spoil their case by saying that the difficulty is to do this while diminishing reliance on means tests. I have long advocated the goal of a basic income (not minimum wage) adequate for a conventional subsistence for all. But this is not around the corner; and the elimination of poverty in the Rowntree sense will only be delayed if means testing is written off as inevitably carrying a stigma – the income tax has always been based on a means test.

Why, moreover, put all the emphasis on increases in income tax to fulfil this goal? The basic rate of tax is, as the Institute for Fiscal Studies often reminds us, one of the less important statistics in the tax system. But harping on it only increases popular opposition to redistribution, even if it gives a puritanical thrill to some. Why not talk in terms of increased VAT rates or petrol duties and the like?

I leave for last the doubts I have about the fashionable New Labour term 'social exclusion'. This adds nothing to what is conveyed by the simple word poverty. Of course we can use words to mean what we like; but they have connotations which affect how they are received.

Exclusion suggests that it is the action of other people who make some citizens worse off. Yet if someone is not able to drive a car, what is gained by saying that society excludes him, with its ridiculous implication that his car-driving friends should feel guilty on his account?

A black South African who was not allowed into an expensive restaurant because of apartheid was excluded in a meaningful way. If he cannot afford to go to the same restaurant today it is more accurate to say that he is poor without trying to make others feel guilty. As usual there are intermediate cases. A Jewish businessman who was not allowed into some prestigious golf club could say that he was suffering from social exclusion. But if there were plenty of other clubs he could join, he was only playing up to the anti-Semites by showing his resentment. He might have done better to wait until he could buy the club. Similarly for an Asian today.

My bottom line is that the poor lack money – that is income and capital. I would hope that more resources could be transferred to them by a reasonably generous electorate without guile or playing on guilt feelings. It would be even better if, by means of education and example, those who are now poor, or their children or descendants, could acquire more original income so that such transfers are less necessary. But do not let us fool ourselves about how much education can achieve. There will always be people – including some intelligent and sensitive persons – who will lack the particular skills which are in demand in society at any one time. To try to force them to perform according to some ideal yardstick is ultimately a threat to liberty (their liberty) which some of us value more than equality.

The Religion of Equality

Review of Adam Swift, *Political Philosophy: A Beginner's Guide for Students and Politicians* (Polity Press, 2001)
Prospect, January 2002

Some decades ago there was a temporary alliance of economic writers from across the political spectrum in favour of what we fondly called expansionist economic policies – although our opponents could legitimately have called them deficits and depreciation. At the height of this campaign I invited for lunch (at the expense of course of my then journalistic employer) the late Frank Blackaby, editor of the *National Institute of Economic and Social Research Review*.

To my surprise he spent the first part of the lunch sulking. My crime? To have conceded that, whatever one might have thought of Chancellor Selwyn Lloyd's macroeconomic policies, he was at least right to have made tax adjustments which effectively lowered some of the confiscatory upper marginal tax rates which had been inherited from the wartime period, and had become simply a penalty on those who did not know the tax avoidance ropes and a bonus for tax accountants. I tried to argue that there were more sensible methods of redistribution; but Blackaby was unwilling to contemplate the slightest praise for this minor Conservative rollback.

This was my first intimation of how strongly egalitarian gestures were valued even by members of the moderate left, who were not interested in other traditional issues such as nationalization. Equality serves as an ersatz religion for much of the academic left in Britain and the US Ivy League. The egalitarian religion will never be answered by the political right who are far too concerned with the boundaries of national jurisdictions and the allegiances which are supposed to follow from them to go into any detail on what these national authorities ought to be doing.

My second intimation came a few years later on a sabbatical at Nuffield College, Oxford, where I found almost universal acceptance of some kind of material equality as a goal, which maybe had to be traded off reluctantly against some incentive payments for the sake of economic efficiency. Even economists outside the left had to content themselves with contorted arguments to show that purportedly egalitarian policies did not achieve their proclaimed objectives. But they did not query the latter. Suppose, however, that the disincentive effects were modest or that economic growth was overvalued? In that case we would have to go back to the egalitarian paradise of equal chances to compete for equal prizes.

One might therefore welcome in principle a tract by an Oxford political philosopher (no prizes for guessing that he is at Balliol) for writing a defence of egalitarianism instead of simply assuming it. Unfortunately its potential value is negated by the author's pretence that he has simply written a neutral analysis and is not advocating anything. His method is a caricature of the early postwar books on moral philosophy, which purported to analyse moral language without imposing judgements.

Adam Swift's pretence that he is not advocating anything weakens the book even from his own point of view. Senior egalitarian writers, such as those who contribute to the publisher's puffs, agonize over whether equality should be considered at a particular moment or over a lifetime; between individuals or between families; and whether people with exceptional needs (e.g. due to illness) deserve more than a mathematically equal proportion. These and many more profound questions are overlooked. Even the issue of whether equality should be applied within national frontiers or all over the world is skated over in a few sentences; and there is nothing at all about equality between this and future generations. And Swift is so obsessed by equality of material conditions that he does not even take on the political right on subjects such as equality of status or respect.

Ideally Swift would like his book to be read by Labour politicians to force a more redistributive agenda onto the Prime Minister and Chancellor. But he reluctantly accepts his publisher's word that books like his are mainly read by students. So he adopts the second best tactic of hoping to influence the political world via the undergraduate route. His final chapter makes clear that he sees any backsliding from egalitarianism in terms of the influence of focus groups, spin doctoring and other concessions to ugly reality. He leaves his unfortunate undergraduate reader with no notion that there can be respectable non-opportunist opposition to egalitarianism – let alone for the view that philosophy is and largely should be a matter of analysis, which can only put forward policy ideas in a most tentative and Socratic form. One conclusion is that Tony Blair can expect little help from the academic left if he is looking for a third way. Nearly all its members (barring a few macroeconomists) were perfectly happy with Old Labour but were horrified that the electorate would not follow it.

By far the best chapter is the first one on the teachings of John Rawls, who relaunched political philosophy after a period of decadence, in the early 1970s. But like most left-wing Rawlsians, Swift is much more at home with Rawls's redistributive principles than with the primacy of civil rights and civil liberties which Rawls himself deliberately puts first. And he has little time for non-left-wing Rawlsians who stress the tool of the veil of ignorance as a method of reaching a degree of consensus rather than on Rawls's semi-egalitarian results.

The index is a giveaway. It has a whole column on equality but two lines on poverty. Swift does try to find reasons for preferring an income distribution in which everyone receives 20 units to one in which the worse off receive 25 and the better off 40. He ties himself up into knots in so doing. However ironically egalitarians quote their opponents as saying that equality is based on envy and jealousy, it does not make it any less true.

Swift then resorts to his first debating trick, which is suddenly to reduce the level of argument by suggesting that his reader might prefer equality of opportunity. He then has no difficulty in showing that opportunities cannot be literally equal when people come from different material and cultural backgrounds. But this is really a cheap ruse. An undergraduate can reply either that her initial choice of words was misleading and say that she really meant removal of the more obvious obstacles to the progress of the less privileged. Or she could reinterpret equality of opportunity in a slightly less literal way à la Gordon Brown.

His second debating trick comes in a later reference to Rawls when he considers the amount of inequality that might be required to persuade the well endowed to give of their best. He says that any such payments are a form of blackmail. Past political philosophers of all schools of thought tried to treat human beings as they actually were instead of admonishing them for not adopting a spartan form of sainthood. Even Plato confined ascetic practices to a handful of guardians. But is in fact a Lord Nuffield or a Bill Gates, who creates something which did not exist before and is rewarded for it, engaging in a form of blackmail? And what do we say about lesser businessmen or professionals, or sportsmen or pop stars who have the luck to possess scarce and valued talents?

There are two ways of looking at income and wealth. One is to envisage a pie to be divided up by a central authority, like a mother cutting a cake for her children. From this point of view it is departures from equality that have to be justified. The other is the entitlement theory. What each person gets, he or she receives from others as a legitimate transfer or in exchange for a service that he or she has provided. Neither theory entirely corresponds to the facts.

The weakness of the pie theory is that there is no fixed sum to go round, as individuals add to the pie by their activities. The final distribution of resources is the unintended product of many individual decisions. The weakness of the entitlement theory is that the very content of property rights and the rules governing their transfer, as well as their physical protection, are the result of collectively enforced rules which we are at liberty to change. To muddle through with a mixture of the two concepts ('Redistribution, yes, equality no') is better than the hell on earth which would prevail if either were carried through to its logical conclusion. What is wrong with the common sense conclusion, which the Nuffields of this world usually accept, that they have some claim to a high reward and also some duty to accept some redistribution towards the less favoured?

It is Swift's third debating trick that I find most unforgivable. Some readers will know that I am sceptical about the idolatry in which the late Isaiah Berlin was held. Nevertheless, he has never been forgiven by the left for by far his best piece of political philosophy, namely his essay distinguishing between negative and positive liberty. Negative liberty is what its name suggests: an area of life in which I can make my own choices without coercion. Positive liberty is, if you like, a richer concept covering a great many desirable states such as adequate nutrition, universal schooling as well of course as democratic voting rights and anything else of which the writer happens to approve. Berlin was no Thatcherite; and he did not believe that negative freedom was the sole guide to policy. His constant theme was that ideals were in inevitable conflict and that a painful choice might have to be made. He was very willing to accept that, for a starving Egyptian peasant, food might have a higher priority than liberty. But he did not think it served anyone's interest to confuse the different goals.

A variety of philosophers and politicians have refused to leave the matter there. Instead of accepting that social justice or economic growth or whatever are different – and occasionally more important – goals than freedom, they insist on using the word freedom to cover all desirable states of affairs, thereby contributing to general confusion. Swift's case against Berlin is that both his positive and negative freedom covered a great many different states of affairs and were not rigorously defined. But Berlin's whole method was to give hosts of examples which were put in contrasting families to indicate rival ideals and goals; and a commentator who cannot see that cannot see anything at all.

A similar confusion even permeates the penultimate chapter on communitarianism. Swift starts off by showing very effectively the erroneous nature of the most frequent metabiological attacks on liberalism. The question whether the individual derives from society

'Happiness' Is Not Enough

Templeton Lecture, Institute of Economic Affairs, 22 November 2001

The title

The title of this talk is 'Happiness is not enough'. It is important to emphasize that the word happiness is in quotation marks. This is not an ideal device to show what I mean, but I cannot think of anything better. The reason for the quotation marks is that I have no wish to put forward some puritanical, self-denying or ascetic alternative.

What I wish to question are statistical measures of happiness which have recently been put forward as a guide for public policy. Thus it is, I hope, a friendly discussion within the Enlightenment camp about alternative ways of stating objectives.

My talk has been sparked off by an excellent study of survey research into people's perceptions of their own happiness by two Swiss authors, Bruno S. Frey and Alois Stutzer (*Happiness and Economics*, Princeton University Press, December 2001; published in the UK by John Wiley & Sons). It is a good enough book to be worth disagreeing with its central contention, despite my being grateful both for its summary of existing research and for the stimulating ideas it contains.

Utilitarianism

I have an uphill task. The dominant outlook of English language political economy and quite a lot of political philosophy as well is utilitarianism. Its founding father, Jeremy Bentham, defined it as follows:

> By the principle of utility is meant that principle which approves or disapproves of every action whatsoever, according to the tendency which it appears to have to augment or diminish the happiness of

the party whose interest is in question…if that party be the community in general, then the happiness of the community: if a particular individual, then the happiness of that individual…The interest of the community then is, what? – the sum of the interest of the several members who compose it.

I hope you will notice the heavy emphasis on the individual and Bentham's disavowal of the idea of a collective consciousness, or of a state or nation being more important than the people who comprise it. I would count myself as a qualified utilitarian: the nature of the qualifications will be touched on in the remarks that follow.

After Bentham's time economists became more and more worried by the difficulties of assessing and measuring happiness. Instead they shifted towards interpreting utility in terms of the opportunity to satisfy desires – in technical terms being on the highest possible indifference curve. These desires are supposed to be revealed by observing people's act or choices in the market place and elsewhere, e.g. in voting. This shift of emphasis was originally the work of economists looking for a way of making utilitarianism operational. I have in earlier work suggested that this interpretation is not merely a fallback due to measurement problems, but actually a preferable objective to which I have given the name Choice Utilitarianism (*The Role and Limits of Government*, 1983, chapter 2 and *Capitalism with a Human Face*, 1996, chapter 3). It is preferable because it attaches a high value to individual choice and does not seek to peer into men's souls.

GDP fallacies

It is a common fallacy to interpret either variety of utilitarianism in terms of maximizing GDP or GDP per head. There are many components of utility which are excluded from conventional GDP measures. Well-known examples include the value of work undertaken in the home, leisure and environmental harm such as pollution and – less discussed – environmental goods such as the value of a well-kept front garden to those who just pass it by. Attempts have been made to construct more comprehensive human development indices which give weight to factors such as literacy, access to clean water, life expectancy and so on. One problem is that the further you go in taking these things into account the more the index reflects the subjective values of those who draw it up. The placing of a country in a human development league can alter radically if it is done by an economist who is obsessed with inequality than if it is done by one who is not. My own view is that adjustments to GDP should be confined to relatively straightforward matters, for instance working hours, and that other social indicators should be listed separately.

Happiness research

But a much more fundamental challenge to choice utilitarianism has emerged. This is the claim that human happiness can be at least approximately measured, coupled with the value judgement that this should be the goal of public policy. In a sense it is back to Bentham. This refurbished view is also associated with the use of questionnaires and opinion surveys, which have been common among empirical sociologists and students of politics, but which have late in the day been discovered by economists who have come upon them with all the thrill of the shock of the new. These researchers are of course aware that individual happiness levels depend to a large extent on temperament, which in turn depends on both genetic and early environmental factors. They hope, reasonably enough, that these individual differences will cancel out if they take national or group averages.

It is of course possible to advocate basing policy on some direct measurement of happiness, without relying so much on question-naire techniques. Who knows what direct physiological studies might one day be able to achieve? Even an untrained person can infer happiness among domestic cats by observing whether they are purring or not. But for the moment at least happiness advocacy is closely linked with these opinion studies.

Anything which extends the vision of empirical economics beyond those endless multiple regression analyses is to be welcomed. Too many of these regression analyses celebrate relatively small influences which are judged to be significant in the statistical sense. The variable being investigated is usually one of many; and an error in assessing any one of these other variables can throw out the whole study. I was first led to these criticisms by studies by American econometricians which purported to show that the death penalty either was or was not a deterrent. Even the most enthusiastic of the death penalty advocates had to take into their equations the effects of many other variables such as unemployment, poverty rates and so on. An error in assessing any one of these throws out the whole value of the study and condemns people needlessly to the electric chair.

Survey findings

But although I welcome the addition of survey studies to the all-too-limited toolbox of applied economics, I still have to question whether these happiness studies show what they are supposed to do. They are normally based on responses to questions such as 'Taking all things together, would you say that you are very happy, pretty happy or not too happy?' International comparisons of such studies produce some weird and wonderful results. Austria is rated as the least happy western country with an index of 6.51 and Denmark the happiest with an index of 8.16. Indeed, Nigeria comes out well above Austria. Countries such as Sweden and Finland with high suicide propensities also come towards the top of the European happiness league. Among the former Soviet republics the happiest is Azerbaijan, with neighbouring Armenia coming at the bottom.

The most striking single result from these subjective happiness studies is that reported well-being does depend on income, but only up to a point. Despite the offbeat examples I have cited, on the whole people living in poor countries become happier with increasing average per capita income. Within a single developed country, better off people report themselves as being more satisfied with life than their poorer fellow citizens. Nevertheless the contribution of income flattens out at a level which Frey estimates as $10,000 per annum. Above that level, increases in average income per head contribute little to well-being; even within a country such as the United States the reported happiness gains tend to vanish. Indeed, Frey has a chart showing that reported well-being peaked in the USA in the late 1960s, despite a large increase in real income per head since then. He explains this coming about as people adjust their expectations to the rise in income. Some of us will recall that quite similar results were reported from the early studies of savings behaviour. The rich saved more than the poor. But when average national income increased the savings ratio did not rise at all. Indeed, in the late 1990s US personal savings plunged dramatically with rising prosperity.

Misguided policy conclusions

Some economists have used these results as yet another debating point on an egalitarian agenda. If, beyond a certain level, people's well-being reflects their relative position, why not redistribute income so that those who are in the middle or at the bottom no longer feel such intense relative deprivation. As far as I know, no one has demonstrated that the gains to the median citizen from soaking the rich would offset any loss that he or she might feel from the levelling up of the poor, which might lower his or her own self-esteem.

But I am afraid that as a libertarian I would throw all these considerations out of the window. So-called 'interdependent utilities' have featured in economic writing well before people were asked questions about their happiness. Indeed, it is the admission of jealousy and envy which weakens all forms of utilitarianism, whether traditional or new-fangled. One of the qualifications I would make to any form of utilitarianism is to rule out all the satisfactions deriving from the discomfiture of other people. In the words of the Nobel Prize-winning economist, John Harsanyi: 'All clearly antisocial preferences, such as sadism, envy, resentment and malice should be excluded from the social utility function.' (Contribution to A. Sen and B. Williams, ed., *Utilitarianism and Beyond*, Cambridge University Press, 1982.)

Other results

It has long been known that unemployment makes many people unhappy; and Frey shows that this is not just due to loss of income but remains the case even if the responses are corrected for income effects. He also establishes that actual inflation is disliked, and not merely unanticipated inflation as many economic writers suppose. My interpretation would be that most citizens cannot easily distinguish between high and unexpected inflation and find that any substantial rate of price increase contributes to the uncertainty and tensions of life.

Frey even attempts to estimate a subjective trade-off between inflation and unemployment, suggesting that it would take an $8^1/_2$ percentage point reduction in the rate of inflation to compensate for a 5 percentage point increase in the rate of unemployment. This estimate is worth reporting but only just, as it nourishes the fallacy that such choices are available, except fleetingly.

A new result reported by Frey is that federalism and direct democracy contribute to personal happiness. The idea is that people enjoy being able to determine policies directly by referenda and by having small-scale government relatively independent of decisions taken in the national capital. It is hardly surprising that Swiss authors should come to such conclusions; and their results are based on a study of the different cantons which do have differences in the level both of local autonomy and the frequency and scope of referenda. Indeed they report that the inhabitants of Basel (Landschaft) are 11 percentage points happier on average than inhabitants of Geneva where direct democracy is at its lowest. The authors discuss another interpretation: living in a French-speaking canton means significantly lower happiness, whereas living in an Italian-speaking canton (Ticino) means significantly higher reported subjective well-being than living in a German-speaking canton!

More seriously, Frey refreshingly differs from many of the English and Eastern seaboard American economists in wanting to introduce corrective policies at the constitutional level rather than as immediate government measures. This might mean a focus, not on direct fiscal measures to reduce income disparities, but on a written constitution and voting rules other than simple pluralities. This would entail, in my view, making it difficult both to dismantle the welfare state and to attempt to tax the rich until the pips squeak.

A behaviourist interpretation

There is a different way of looking at happiness which derives from a book by the English philosopher Gilbert Ryle, *The Concept of Mind*, published in 1949 (Penguin Classics edition with introduction by Daniel C. Dennet, 2000). The tendency of that book is to reinterpret mental phenomena, which are usually discussed as subjective feelings open only to introspection, in terms of observable behaviour. Ryle does not deal with happiness as such, but he does discuss enjoyment and pleasure, which come close to it.

He gives an example of a person who is so absorbed in some activity, such as golf or argument, that he is reluctant to stop or even think of anything else. He is taking pleasure in or enjoying doing what he is doing, though he is in no degree convulsed or beside himself and he is not indeed experiencing any particular feelings. Another of his examples is of a person who enjoys digging in his garden. This is not to say that he has been both digging and doing or experiencing something else, as a concomitant or effect of the digging; it is to say he dug with his whole heart in his task, i.e. that he has dug, is wanting to dig and not wanting to do anything else. His digging was his pleasure, and not a vehicle of his pleasure. There are not two activities going on side-by-side: digging and an internal feeling of satisfaction.

Many philosophers do not believe that Ryle completely succeeded in banishing the subjective element. If one person who goes through all the motions of enjoying a game of golf but says he is in pain, then we can surely say he is less happy than another person who is not. And even if our subject is not in pain, he might be a grumpy individual who might believe that he would much rather have been a brain surgeon and is playing golf as a compensation. Nevertheless the first clue to how happy people are is to look at how they behave and regard their answers to direct questions about their feelings as no more than a useful supplement. The reported differences among happiness levels between countries may well reflect national cultures or even the exact meanings attached to happiness and related concepts when translated from one language into another.

Brave New World

If we take the happiness researchers seriously, it will not be enough to make a few mildly reformist suggestions, such as a Swiss-type constitution or fiscal transfers to reduce income disparities. We will have to go all the way towards *Brave New World*. This was, of course, a novel by Aldous Huxley, published as long ago as 1932. His new world differs from Orwell's in *Nineteen Eighty-four* because people are not made to conform by terror or fear of Big Brother. They are conditioned to do so by a selective breeding system applied when they are hatched in incubators. The population is divided into various categories ranging from the alphas, who give the directions, to the betas, gammas, deltas and epsilons – who do the world's dirty work. And just to top up the effects of genetic engineering, there is a drug, soma, to be taken at any sign of waning happiness.

This brave new world is presented as a nightmare or dystopia. To understand why you will have to read or re-read the novel. No plot summary can be a substitute. Many of the initial readers were appalled by the description in the first few chapters of how children were conditioned to reject any books that might tell them of a historical past in which they would have had more control of their own destinies. Looked at from where we are now or even were in 1932, the picture is indeed a horrible one. But we need to be careful. The inhabitants of *Brave New World* do not feel as we feel and are conditioned to enjoy their existence. The problem was previously aired by John Stuart Mill when he said it was better to be Socrates unhappy than a pig happy. I have always had a sneaking sympathy for the pig, so long as he can be bred to live as long as Socrates. But perhaps fortunately, we do not have that choice.

In all the seventy years that have passed since Huxley's novel appeared, genuine soma pills have not been invented. The hard drugs which some of the affluent young take to bring on a high seem in the end to produce squalor, suicides and other tragedies. Huxley himself was ambivalent. In a new preface written in 1946, he criticised his own novel for offering only the choice between an insane life in Utopia and the life of a primitive in an (American) Indian village. He rebuked himself for not having put forward a third possibility: simple human sanity. But he cannot keep up this optimistic vein. By the end of the preface he is talking in Orwellian terms of a choice between supranational totalitarianism and a number of national militarist totalitarianisms.

He is also ambivalent about soma pills or their equivalent. Throughout his life he was looking for drugs which could bring on delightful feelings without an unfortunate kickback. He ended up by recommending mescaline for the purpose. But to the best of my

knowledge there are still no happiness drugs devoid of unfortunate
side- or after-effects. What was to me conclusive was that the
conditioning in *Brave New World* was neither entirely painless nor
completely successful. Young children are given electric shocks to
induce distaste for flowers and books. And the action of the novel
depends on there being people who are incompletely conditioned and
who look back fondly to the world of Huxley's time and our own with
all its imperfections.

Conclusion

What then is the alternative? It might come as an anti-climax, but I
still think it is the choice utilitarian one of maximizing the range of
opportunities open to each individual. And I see the task of policy
largely in negative terms; to remove obstacles to the exercise of
individual choice rather than lots of fussy interventions on our behalf.
Even such negative policies involve in my view a degree of income
transfer towards the poor and less fortunate.

For about three quarters of the world's population a measure of
success will still be real GDP per head, corrected for the worst
absurdities, and supplemented by a few simple social indicators. But
for the more affluent populations of North America and western
Europe, economic growth in this sense is no longer a sensible
objective of policy. It is much better that the growth rate should
emerge from people's own choices. So it would not be a disaster if,
after the recent traumatic events, Americans adopted a quieter
lifestyle with more emphasis on leisure and reflection, and working to
live rather than living to work.

We should not throw out the baby with the bath water. GDP
statistics will still remain useful for economic management and for
looking at the way the national product is divided between different
activities and different groups. Information on these matters should
not take us along the road to serfdom. Indeed, I have heard American
friends observe that the social scientists who have been least tempted
by collectivism are those who have the most detailed knowledge of
the relevant facts and figures.

My conclusion is that the pursuit of happiness is and should remain
a personal matter; and the people most likely to achieve this are not
those who keep on asking themselves whether they are happy or
unhappy, but who find worthwhile purposes and activities and
concentrate on them. By all means make use of attitude surveys and
similar devices; but let us do so first and foremost to satisfy our
curiosity and not imagine that we have found the magic lodestar
which has eluded thinkers of the past.

The Many Failings of Postmodernism

The Spectator, 27 September 1997
Review of Richard Evans *In Defence of History,* Granta Books,
1977

Historians should stop behaving as if they are researching into things that actually happen. They should just tell 'stories' without bothering whether or not they are true. As we can never know anything at all about the past, we might as well confine ourselves to studying rival historians. Alternatively, we may dismiss all history as just naked ideology designed to provide historians with power and money in big university institutions run by the bourgeoisie. In any case, all the world is a text and time is a fictional construct.

Is it really worth refuting such views from the more extreme of the historians who call themselves postmodernists or occasionally deconstructionists? The professor of modern history at Cambridge, Richard Evans, evidently believes the effort necessary, so entrenched have such people become in universities.

Those of us fortunate enough to be distant from the scene of battle must respect his verdict. Evans certainly hammers the post-modernists into the ground by detailed consideration of their specific arguments and demolition of their logic. He is, however, willing to give them some due, saying that they have emphasized the importance of looking critically at texts for hidden or unintended meanings. Maybe he is even too generous, for some of the best historians have always employed such scepticism and been self-conscious about their own interests and political bias.

Most of the postmodernists regard themselves as being on the left. So too does Professor Evans, who castigates them for being so concerned with the deconstruction of texts that they ignore the reality of much suffering and oppression. He also points out how extreme deconstruction can provide comfort for the racialist right, as in various attempts to deny the reality of the Nazi Holocaust. I doubt, however, whether he will convince confirmed practitioners of the new ways.

For the rest of us, his deconstruction of postmodernism may be a little wearying with chapter after chapter and example after example. Indeed, the author can do the job in a few lines. For, as he points out, if there is no such thing as truth and we are free to tell what stories we like, then there is no particular reason to believe the deconstructionists, who are thus contradicted by their own doctrines.

Perhaps Evans is too much of a historian and not enough of a speculative thinker to ask about the basis of the absurdities which he condemns. They have at least three separate roots. The first is philosophical scepticism which reflects itself in traditional concerns about our knowledge of other minds, doubts about whether the world exists outside our sensations, and so on. Such scepticism is not as easily debunked as the postwar Oxford linguistic analysts supposed. But it exists on a different plane of discourse from history or the social sciences.

To talk about the Napoleonic wars or the Great Depression or the career of Frederick the Great assumes that there were such things. To investigate history, we have to suspend metaphysical doubt, just as we do in daily life. Nobody recognized this more clearly than the Scottish eighteenth-century philosopher David Hume, the greatest sceptic of all. But he set aside his doubts not merely when he wandered into society but when he went on to write a classic history of England, which he believed to be something other than a work of his imagination.

A second root of postmodernism is the desire to continue the Marxist critique of western society by other means. Most of the empirical claims of Marxism had been falsified well before the Berlin Wall fell in 1989. Intellectuals who half realized this had to find fresh structures of oppression, whether of race or gender, to replace the old typologies. (Hence pejorative expressions such as 'dead white males'.) But they also needed to immunize themselves against empirical criticism. Whereas the most endearing feature of old-fashioned Marxism was its belief in a happy ending, many postmodernists are mired in a permanent pessimism which will always give them something to deconstruct and undermine.

A third element is the retreat from reason, discernible also in New Age fashions, the indulgence given to medical quacks and the contemporary kind of religiosity stretching from revived fundamentalism to the more fantastic Californian cults. Alas, we do not have any good general theory explaining these periodic revolts against enlightenment and telling us in which conditions they flourish or wither.

Fortunately Evans does not confine himself to postmodernism. The most interesting part of his book is the first third, in which he outlines the history of history as a discipline. The rival historical schools of the last generation were represented by E. H. Carr and Sir Geoffrey Elton.

At this distance they seem beyond caricature. Carr, the historian of the USSR, believed that history must be governed by a vision of the future, which he took to mean that of Soviet-style collectivism. But he also prided himself on his realism and did not consider the activities of ordinary people merited investigation until the last century or two, when organized socialist movements appeared.

Elton, by contrast, was a refugee from central Europe who admired not so much English democracy as English order and became a great fan of Thomas Cromwell, the ruthless agent of Henry VIII. Elton asserted, however, that the political views of historians were irrelevant and that the study of sources could be as objective as the analysis of chemical elements.

The author holds the more balanced view that the interests and beliefs of the historian inevitably affect the story he or she tells. Thus many interpretations are possible, but the honest historian cannot say just what he likes and is confined by evidence.

Evans touches on, but does not fully explore, the relationship between history and the social sciences. He mentions the early ambitions of the cliometricians who wanted to make history a science by applying a mixture of economic theory and modern statistical methods. One notable example was *Time on the Cross*, Robert Fogel and Stanley Engermann, Little, Brown & Co., 1974, which its authors believed demonstrated that slavery was an economically viable way of life in the American South, although that could not in the least excuse it morally. But other qualified investigators believe that they have torn the whole edifice to pieces. Modern techniques have thus in no way banished old-fashioned controversies but have reinstated them in more complex form.

The most perplexing problem raised in *In Defence of History* (1997) has little to do with postmodernism. Conventional political and diplomatic history is now only a small fraction of the vast amount being written. History may be breaking up into thousands of different specialities, which no one person can hope to grasp. The most he or she can learn to do is to tap into selected parts on the internet. A historian of epidemics is likely to have more in common with a medical student interested in this subject than with a student of politics at the time of the accession of George III.

We can say that there is still a common historical core based on political events in one's own country, to which a selection from other specialities can be added. Or we can say that there is no longer a single subject – history – but a historical aspect to many different disciplines. The choice is a semantic one, but will inevitably be influenced by contemporary politics, whether of the academic variety or the hubris of Ministers of Education who purport to lay down common curricula.

A Rational Response to Insecurity

Financial Times, 30 August 2000

Despite the fall in unemployment levels in North America and some European countries in the last few years, the sense of job insecurity has, if anything, heightened. Many researchers have found it difficult to unearth statistical evidence that labour turnover is higher or that periods in particular jobs are shorter than in earlier times. In Britain, redundancy levels fell after the 1992 recession and have since remained remarkably stable at 10 per 1,000 employees a year, according to official estimates. Moreover, two fifths of those made redundant were in employment again, usually within three months of losing their jobs.

One of the most thoroughgoing attempts to reconcile the data with subjective impressions has been made by Stephen Nickell (*A Picture of the Job Insecurity Facing British Men*, Centre for Economic Perform-ance, London School of Economics, December 1999). He finds an objective basis for job insecurity in the increased chances of a drop in pay rather than a higher chance of becoming unemployed. The prospects of pay losses have become greater even for those who stay in the same job without an intervening spell of unemployment. This change is explained for most workers by the decline in the growth of average UK real pay in the 1990s compared with the 1980s. But highly skilled and older workers seem to face a greater risk of pay losses.

Nevertheless, the effects reported are rather modest. The percentage of highly skilled men facing a one-yearly earnings drop of a tenth or more rose from 5.2 per cent in 1982–6 to 8.8 per cent in 1992–6 for those who did not change jobs. For those who did, without an intervening spell of unemployment, the percentage rose from 10.6 per cent to 14.4 per cent. It is difficult to believe that such wage changes explain the whole of the increased feeling of insecurity. If shorter job tenure is a very recent phenomenon, it may not yet show up in official records of spells in employment. Even if it exists only in the mind it is still a fact of life. The 'end of lifetime employment' has become a modern cliché.

Indeed, fear of job loss has been cited by central bankers and academic analysts alike as an important reason why a number of countries are able to sustain relatively low levels of unemployment, which in the past would have been associated with rising wage inflation. In other words, even the workers who have jobs hesitate to press for more pay for fear of the possible employment consequences. The euphemistic name for job insecurity is 'labour flexibility' – in one of its many meanings. It is this aspect that Alan Greenspan, chairman of the US Federal Reserve Bank, highlighted in an address in Pennsylvania in July and again last weekend. He stated that advances in information technology had benefited the US economy more than Europe or Japan. He attributed this discrepancy quite directly to the 'inflexible, and hence more costly' labour markets of these other economies. The rates of return on investment in the same new technologies are 'correspondingly less in Europe and Japan because businesses there face higher costs of displacing workers'. In the US 'labour displacement is more readily countenanced both by law and culture'. But because the costs of dismissing workers are lower, 'the potential costs of hiring and the risks associated with expanding employment are less'. The result of this 'significantly higher capacity for job dismissal has been, counterintuitively, a dramatic decline in the US unemployment rate'.

But although the consequences for productivity and the unemployment–inflation relationship may be favourable, other aspects of job insecurity are not. Excessive anxiety hardly makes for an increased level of welfare. Indeed, it may help explain why rising incomes have not produced increases in reported levels of happiness and satisfaction. But do we have to accept such high human costs? The first clue to improving the trade-offs is that people differ in their attitude to change and risk. Some people see the need to retrain and change jobs as a positive challenge. There is a New York-based 'Five O'Clock Club' that instructs its members in the art of changing jobs; and US business magazines contain many articles about 'why it pays to quit'. The chance to cease being a wage slave and sell services directly to business has been viewed by some as a more human kind of capitalism operating on a smaller scale than the huge corporations that emerged early in the twentieth century.

For others, however, the challenge is one they would rather not face. They regard the tendency of corporations to reduce their permanent staff and to 'outsource' their supplies as a threat. This diversity of attitudes to risk is a theme of a paperback by Richard North, *Risk: the Human Choice* (European Science and Environment Forum). Some people are risk-averse and would be prepared to make sacrifices in take-home pay for the sake of greater security.

Here one sees the outlines of a possible compromise. According to the high priests of new technology, it is out of date to offer workers job security. But why not give employees a choice? Let them decide between labour contracts with high prospective rewards, but which may not last very long, and more secure jobs that pay less. One should not pretend that the suggested solution is an easy one. A difficulty is that many of the past 'jobs for life' were not guaranteed as such. There was rather the unspoken assumption that employees could expect to stay where they were, if their work was satisfactory. But it was always understood that a big shock, for instance a trade depression, or a technological revolution, might bring their employment to an end. So in advocating the possibility of trading lower take-home pay for more security or shorter hours of work, I am not suggesting going back to something entirely old and familiar, but am really advocating a new and more explicit kind of employment contract.

The immediate response of some people is to ask: what should the government do about it? Not all problems can be solved by state action; and clumsy intervention often makes matters worse. There is plenty for policy analysts to do, but in this instance it would be best to examine existing policies and legislation to see whether there is anything in them that impedes a greater diversity of labour contracts.

The Rules Need Fixing, But Greed Can Be Good

Financial Times, 4 July 2002

The biggest obstacle faced by proponents of a competitive market economy is the belief that it is based on, or encourages, selfishness, materialism or acquisitiveness. This belief will have been powerfully reinforced by recent US corporate scandals. Capitalism has always been subject to boom and bust; there have always been human beings who break or stretch the rules. Such scandals have been a feature of the late stages of a high-powered boom. At the height of the South Sea Bubble in the early eighteenth century, fraudulent promoters were able to sell shares in ventures, 'the nature of which will be later disclosed'. The boom of the 1920s saw the activities of Clarence Hatry, the British financier jailed for fraud. A few years ago the American financier Ivan Boesky, who was jailed for insider trading, declared 'greed is great'. The same belief could have been behind the activities of American corporate leaders who falsify accounts or bury their activities in hosts of off-balance-sheet ventures.

None of this destroys the fact that competitive free market capitalism has been the biggest engine for growth – and for the reduction of poverty – that the world has ever seen. We should never rule out superior alternatives; but they have yet to be discovered. Moreover, the wrongdoers often get caught and the rules are subsequently tightened – which is more than one can always say about the misdeeds of governments.

Does that mean that greed is really good? My dictionary defines greed as a never satisfied longing, especially for wealth. It is obviously a loaded word. If you approve of an activity you talk about people's honourable desire to better themselves and their families and not to be a burden on their fellow citizens. If you disapprove you call it greed. A more neutral description would be the pursuit not of selfishness, but of self-interest, which can have many motivations. It can be the desire to found a dynasty which could motivate people like

Rupert Murdoch or Tony O'Reilly. Or it can be the desire to be
remembered by posterity, which is often best accomplished by
endowing a museum, a concert hall, an academic institution or a
sports ground. And there are some souls like Scott Fitzgerald's Jay
Gatsby who frenetically pursue more and bigger automobiles, more
and bigger residences to attract a particular female.

We can be too preoccupied with motivation. Some people,
especially leaders in business or fashion or sport, want to amass far
more wealth that they can possibly use even on the most self-
indulgent and sybaritic basis. What does not receive enough
emphasis is that the rest of us can benefit from this seemingly
irrational fetish. If the Medici rulers of Florence had stopped
acquiring wealth when their personal needs were satisfied, we would
not have had much of the art of the Renaissance. If Henry Ford had
stopped developing the motor industry when his own personal wants
had been satisfied, the cheap mass-produced car would have been
long delayed. If Bill Gates had left off when he became sufficiently
rich, the development of household computer technology would have
been delayed. The desire to pile up endless treasures beyond rhyme
or reason would not be a healthy basis for the great mass of human
activity. But we all benefit from the fact that some people are made
that way.

The point is not motivation but the framework of rules, conventions
and assumptions within which market activity is carried out. Reading
accounts of what has gone wrong with the many attempts to establish
a free enterprise society in the former Soviet Union, I am stuck by
some similarities with New York at the beginning of the twenty-first
century. With all the wisdom of hindsight, many western economists
now emphasize that it was not enough for Russia to remove controls
on prices and wages, to privatize state industries or even to balance
the budget and introduce currency convertibility. None of these
things will work without a whole lot of other institutional changes,
such as an effective legal system, the rule of law and a state which can
police it, clear and secure property rights and a social safety net. Not
to speak of the introduction of standard western accounting and
banking techniques.

I originally supposed that these were less and less known the
further you moved from Germany's eastern border towards Moscow.
But now they do not seem to be all that well known if you move
towards the Atlantic seaboard of the United States. A clear conclusion
is that we need a tightening up of accounting rules to reduce the gulf
between ownership and management. If I might throw my own
suggestion into the ring: it has long seemed anachronistic that boards
of directors should choose their own auditors – whether these
auditors give them other management advice or not. It is like schools

appointing their own inspectors, or, as one taxi driver put it to me, like criminals appointing their own policemen. The auditors should be there to represent the interests of shareholders. It is admittedly not easy to say who else should appoint them. To say the government would bring in further temptations to corruption or political favours. Maybe it should be some body such as the Stock Exchange Council or, in the UK, the Financial Services Authority.

There is in fact a growing body of knowledge about the conditions in which competitive markets will bring socially beneficial results and these in which they will not. By far the most readable book I know on the subject has just appeared. It is by John McMillan, entitled *Reinventing the Bazaar, a Natural History of Markets*. The book covers far more than the title suggests. The author is enviably up to date on matters such as the internet and modern auction theory. But he writes simply and directly without talking down. At long last I have found a book that I can recommend to the proverbial nephew who desires to find out about economics without wanting to pass an exam or become a practitioner himself.

Although McMillan is enthusiastic about markets, he has far from the messianic belief found in some circles; and he insists that markets require careful construction, which may come from the bottom upwards, but may also need a vigorous steer from the top downwards. He gives five conditions for well-functioning markets: a smooth flow of information; trust that people will fulfil their promises; competitive, contestable markets; the protection, but not overprotection, of property rights; and that side-effects on third parties must be taken into account.

There is clearly a long way to go before these conditions are even approximately fulfilled. But let us avoid an overreaction towards, if not vindictiveness, at least overcaution. It would be so easy in a bout of anti-corporate frenzy to slay the goose that lays the golden eggs.

Economic Possibilities for our Grandchildren

Financial Times, 3 January 2002

After the destruction of the New York Twin Towers last September 11, the immediate advice of the American administration to their US citizens was to carry on spending. This was good emergency counsel. An economic depression in the West would have been a triumph too far for Muslim fundamentalism. But the official advice might not look so good from a longer term perspective. If western citizens became less keen on buying more and more goods and services and earning enough to pay for them, the development might not be entirely bad.

To see why, it is worth going back to an essay completed in 1930 by John Maynard Keynes, entitled *Economic Possibilities for our Grandchildren*. It could equally have been called 'The Miraculous Properties of Compound Interest'. The essay was published as the Great Depression was gathering force. But Keynes asked his readers to stand back and note that in the 4,000 years up to around 1700, there had been no great change in the average standard of living. There had been ups and downs and golden intervals, but no progressive improvement. The Industrial Revolution transformed the picture. Despite the enormous growth in population, average living standards had risen fourfold in Europe and the US since 1700. Compound growth could, he propounded, make us four to eight times better off still in a further hundred years.

Keynes concluded that mankind was well on the way to solving its economic problem and thereby ending the struggle for subsistence which had hitherto been its most pressing problem. He viewed this prospect with delight. Eventually we would realize 'that avarice is a vice, that the exaction of usury is a misdemeanour, and the love of money is detestable, that those walk most truly in the paths of virtue and sane wisdom who take least thought for the morrow...We shall honour those who can teach us to pluck the hour and the day virtuously and well, the delightful people who are capable of taking direct enjoyment in things, the lilies of the field who toil not, neither do they spin.'

Keynes believed that the pace at which we could reach this destination of economic bliss would be governed by four factors: success in limiting the growth of the population, avoiding wars and civil dissension, willingness to entrust to science its proper role, and an adequate rate of capital investment. The last would easily look after itself given the first three.

He anticipated the criticism that human needs were insatiable and divided such needs into two classes: the absolute ones, such as food and shelter, that do not depend on what other people are achieving; and the relative ones which we feel only if their satisfaction 'makes us feel superior to our fellows'. In the future to which he looked forward there would still be people under the influence of the second kind of artificial need who would blindly pursue wealth. 'But the rest of us would no longer feel under any obligation to applaud and encourage them.' His real worry was that little thought had been given to educating people for this new world of leisure; and there was a danger they would not be able to use their opportunities.

On the arithmetic Keynes has proved right, despite the Second World War, rearmament drives and occasional slumps. He probably took as his base year 1929, the last before the Depression. Between then and 2000 real UK GDP per head grew at a compound annual rate of nearly 1.9 per cent; and the actual level of output per head was about 3.8 times as high in the later year. If growth continues at this rate, output per head in 2029 will indeed be around six or seven times the 1929 level or bang in the middle of Keynes's estimate.

Keynes did not of course envisage the many new applications of science and technology which would give people fresh material aims, quite apart from the drive to feel superior. Some of these, such as television and compact discs, provide not merely opportunities for emulation but the possibility of mass access to the arts which meant so much to him. Nevertheless the appetite for such gadgets may have its limits. There could yet be a change of tastes away from the ultra-consumer society and towards a quieter lifestyle with more emphasis on leisure and personal enjoyment and less on take-home pay and what it can buy. This has not happened yet.

A slowdown in economic growth which reflects a change in taste is a very different animal to one which reflects a deficiency of purchasing power. If people want to buy less, they should – ultimately and rationally – also want to work less. A structural growth slowdown need not therefore be accompanied by a large increase in involuntary unemployment. Instead of balancing at a high rate of growth, the economic system would balance at a low rate or at zero. In the extreme case people would enjoy the benefits of technological progress entirely in the form of reduced working hours rather than in increased take-home pay. The efficient organization of production would mean supplying static wants with the minimum of working hours.

The real difficulty is that, coming in response to shocks, a structural slowdown would hit different industries very differently. We have already had a foretaste of that in the misfortunes of the aviation and travel industries, far exceeding those of the rest of the economy. The policy problems are the familiar ones of how to compensate the victims of economic misfortune without putting a brake on all structural change. There will be for a long time opportunities for business expansion in meeting the growing needs of the Third World. And even in a static western economy there might still be a good deal of investment and entrepreneurial action. Consumer desires, even if modest, might still be subject to changes of taste; the fashionable clothing 'gear' might change; or trips to old coalmines might alternate with visits to the Himalayas, or painting one's home in a novel manner, as ways of spending leisure.

Even in a world of slow or zero growth a competitive market economy would still be best for satisfying people's choices. A profit-making businessman need not be interested in the private values of his workers. If they wish to work fewer hours for less money or only one week in four, it is their affair. If irregular and unpredictable working habits impose difficulties in keeping up a smooth flow of production, the rate for the job would simply be less than for workers willing to work in a more regular way. Although the resulting system would not look much like capitalism as we know it, there would still be great advantages in retaining competitive markets. People who did not share the anti-consumption, anti-work ethos could – as Keynes indicated so long ago – opt in to the consumer society without disturbing their neighbours; and there could still be luxury hotels or ocean cruises for those who wanted them and who were prepared to work more than average to obtain them.

John Stuart Mill, rather prematurely, looked forward to this state of affairs in the middle of the nineteenth century when he wrote that a 'stationary state', so far from being a tragedy, would be highly desirable. He considered that 'elbowing and treading on each other's heels' were only a stage in human development and not the final end of civilization. The transition will not be an easy one and will be accompanied by slumps and booms of a traditional kind. But it may help our sanity if we discern in them the silver lining that Keynes and Mill so long ago discerned.

Get Thee to an Ivory Tower and Stay Put

Financial Times, 2 February 2002

Judge Richard Posner occupies a unique position in American intellectual life. He started off as an academic lawyer who pioneered the application of economic analysis to his subject. He has since become a judge in the Federal Appeal Court; but in contrast to others who have taken this route he has continued to pour out a stream of books. He has also been in the forefront of public affairs; for instance, he was appointed to try to mediate between the US anti-trust authorities and Microsoft. When I knew him for a brief spell he was learning classical Greek to pass the time.

He has now turned his attention to what he calls the 'public intellectual'. By this he means a writer who speaks in an accessible way on political or ideological matters. They may be people like Milton Friedman, or Galbraith, or Posner himself, who try to popularize their own academic work but then branch out in more opinionated directions. More often, however, they are pontificating way outside their own expertise, but use their authority to pronounce on every subject under the sun.

The archetypal example is Noam Chomsky, who uses the distinction he has achieved in linguistics to denounce US society, which he regards as worse than Stalin's Soviet Union. Posner, not surprisingly, has a low view of the breed. Their comments tend to be 'opinionated, judgmental, sometimes condescending, and often waspish'. They are controversialists, with a tendency to take extreme positions, and are often careless of facts and rash on predictions. They can be novelists, literary critics or journalists; but to a large and growing extent they are moonlighting academics, a fact which Posner regrets. The more public they become the less intellectual they get.

There is nothing new in this line of attack. Friedrich Hayek and Joseph Schumpeter, conservative Austrian economists who settled in Britain and the US, came out with very similar analyses in the 1940s and 1950s. They despised this whole class of writing, even though they had to enter the arena themselves to express their dislike. The Austrian critiques appeared mainly as asides in volumes devoted to other topics. Posner has brought the role of the academic media superstar to centre-stage in a book devoted exclusively to the subject.

Posner would regard his contribution as taking the debate beyond Hayek and Schumpeter in the statistical analyses he has made of the relationship between frequency of media and of scholarly citations. Some of his tables show no correlation whatever, others a modest negative correlation. European readers should be tolerant of this exercise in Chicago positivism, as it has produced lists of names in which we can all wallow, some of the most frequently cited being dead or European. But I found far more convincing his verbal reminders of the false predictions made by these eminent men and women, which in many cases have not in the least reduced their prestige with the lay public. George Soros is a rare example of a pundit admitting his error – in this case his 1998 prognostication that global capitalism was about to collapse.

Posner accepts the need for public intellectuals – his ideal is John Stuart Mill who died in 1873 – but regrets their low and deteriorating quality. He has an economic explanation for this, similar to that of his Austrian predecessors. Public intellectuals operate in markets without quality control. The public has no means of judging the gurus' credentials and their academic peers do not deign to monitor their work. As Schumpeter once put it, a highly educated lawyer quite rationally treats public affairs as a sub-hobby, which he can do little to influence, and he brings to them less critical intelligence than he would to a game of bridge.

Like so many of its kind, this book is far too exclusively based on the USA. His remarks about pundits moonlighting from the leisure and status of the tenured university post will make European academics green with envy. Although he notes that two thirds of the public intellectuals enumerated from media mentions are on the left, there are various corrective forces. For instance, he concedes that the think tanks, which are on a par with universities as a source of these intellectuals, are predominantly right-wing, which would hardly be the case in Europe.

Moreover, the US media compensate for the preponderance of left-wing intellectuals by giving them relatively fewer mentions. Any despairing conservative fearing that the list of mentions would be headed by people such as Galbraith or Chomsky might be reassured to find that the largest number of mentions in 1995–2000 is achieved by Henry Kissinger. The second, third and fourth positions are occupied by the late Senator Daniel Moynihan, a Democrat who delighted in puncturing left-wing preconceptions, the conservative columnist George Will, and Larry Summers, the outgoing US Treasury Secretary – a Democrat all right, but one who came to personify globalization in the eyes of the left-wing protest movements.

What I enjoyed most were Posner's more personal essays on particular writers. He is just as severe on the right-wing cultural critics of American society (the Jeremiah School) as he is on the knee-jerk left. He dismisses George Orwell's *Nineteen Eighty-four* as prophecy but reinstates it for its literary and human qualities. He is less kind about Aldous Huxley's *Brave New World*. This is because Posner's conservatism is of the optimistic, individualist kind that celebrates business and technology, and not that of the doom-mongers who look back on some mythical golden age. These latter, although classed as conservative in US parlance, sometimes sound almost identical to the French intellectuals who arrived in London for a Royal Academy Paris Exhibition and who said they would like – I hope only figuratively – to explode a bomb over the modern city.

Posner believes that his anti-heroes have little influence, citing other empirical studies to this effect. But he obviously has a nagging worry that their discourse affects the climate of opinion and what may or may not be regarded as politically possible. He has also an aesthetic distaste for seeing capable academics going slumming for the sake of their egos or political prejudices. As a reluctant interventionist, Posner's suggested remedies are relatively mild. He would like universities to compel faculty members to put on the internet all their non-academic utterances, in the hope that they will then be more critically inspected. But I suspect that once they get the hang of the technology they will need little further urging.

The sad thing is that his book will mostly be read by people who already agree with the message, such as the present reviewer, rather than those who would benefit most, but who are more likely to read the attempted rebuttals which have already been proliferating in the USA.

Over-education
Financial Times, 8 June 2000

There is an old story about an American billionaire, who, it was discovered, was unable to read or write English. One brave interviewer asked him, seeing that he had achieved so much, how much more he could have done if he had been fully literate. His reply was: 'I would have got the job of lavatory attendant; maybe today I would have been a superintendent.'

The story should not be taken too literally. A working group chaired by Sir Claus Moser concluded not long ago that 23 per cent of adults in Britain have low literacy or low numeracy. ('Improving Literacy and Numeracy', Department of Employment and Education, 1999). One in five adults in England, if given the alphabetical index to the *Yellow Pages*, cannot locate the page for plumbers. Most of these people are not going to become millionaires or even attain anything like the average standard of living. Both their careers and their personal development will be frustrated and they will contribute disproportionately to the long-term unemployed and the prison population. The place to look for over-qualification is at the other end of the spectrum, namely higher education in universities and similar institutions. It is here one can find evidence for querying the role Tony Blair has given to 'education, education, education' as his three priorities.

Financial constraints apart, can there really be such a thing as over-education? Surely knowledge is always better than ignorance? This is right as a slogan for personal development, even though there are other values apart from the pursuit of book learning. The real worry is not so much about the pursuit of knowledge but 'credentialism'. This means the multiplication of paper certificates and qualifications as a condition for more and more kinds of professional and other employment. When education in this sense is being promoted by so many governments and international organizations as the key to economic growth, it is time to ask critical questions.

Some researchers at the eminently respectable Centre for

Economic Performance, at the London School of Economics, have unearthed some evidence of what they call over-education, which they define as 'people with more educational qualifications than they need to do their job – such as estate agents with PhDs'. Such a person will be no better at being an estate agent because of his doctoral thesis than someone with an ordinary degree – or perhaps no degree at all. It does matter that some people are over-qualified. Sample data suggests that the majority of those who were in a first job for which they were still over-qualified 'have still not moved in to a graduate level job six years later'. So it is not just a matter of a graduate starting off as an office assistant or factory hand, pending promotion to higher things.

These results need to be linked to an ongoing debate about the return from higher education. The mainstream view among economists is that education is an investment in human capital that increases the productivity of both the individual and the society of which he or she is part. But there is a more heretical 'filter' view. It has long been known that employers who formerly recruited school leavers at sixteen or eighteen now look for graduates. One possibility is that they simply use the university system as a filter to sort out the abler people, who nowadays tend to go to university. But they might have been just as good if they had gone straight into employment.

In the survey results, it is not surprising that the degree of 'over-education' is much greater among graduates in the humanities than in the sciences. The fact that a degree, higher or lower, may not always be strictly necessary or lead to a financial reward is not of course an argument against taking it. Much of education may be a consumption good, that is something that people purchase for their own edification rather than as a contribution to a career.

If the activities of universities are regarded as partly the promotion of learning for its own sake and partly as a consumption good for students, rather than as just career training, then a different approach to the finance of higher education becomes attractive. Lord Owen has recently suggested that universities should fund themselves from teaching charges that they should be free to fix and to vary between subjects (*A World Class University Education?*, Social Market Foundation, May 2000). In return the government would switch all the teaching contribution, now almost £3bn a year, to a bursary fund for which all students would be eligible subject to a means test, and from which they would pay their fees. Lord Owen's motivation – he is now chancellor of Liverpool University – is not fear of over-education but a belief that universities must find new sources of funding if they are to free themselves from financial penury and government control. But the net result of this change – to which less radical reformers are moving in fits and starts – would be to undo the confusion between education and training that bedevils so much of government policy.

A Swiss Morality Play

Financial Times, 16 August 2001

The expression 'nimbyism' – after the phrase 'not in my back yard' – became notorious a few years ago to describe a hypocritical attitude to social improvement. Most people support the building of new homes to cater for a greater number of families. But any idea of new housing in the countryside is vigorously opposed by local residents, who worry about the effect on property values.

There are many other forms of nimbyism. In theory people can see the effect of over-severe planning legislation in raising house prices and land values, reducing growth and employment and increasing income disparities. But the same people, even if they are economists living in the country outside a university city, do not find it easy to accept an industrial or office block in their own vicinity. A particularly controversial example concerns the siting of units for disposing of atomic waste.

Some economists believe they have a way of dealing with such questions. This is to offer the localities affected a sum of money to accept the required changes. The edifices can then be put up where the inhabitants believe that the monetary incentive is greater than the environmental disadvantage; as a result everyone could be better off. Bruno Frey, a Swiss economist, has studied how such schemes have worked in relation to the disposal of Swiss nuclear waste.[1] A preliminary investigation took place in Wolfenschiessen, a small village in central Switzerland with a population of 2,100. But to the consternation of the economic advisers, the offer of cash to the villagers, whether in the form of individual payments or cash to the municipality, only increased the opposition. The villagers were certainly not going to be bribed into accepting a nuclear disposal plant in their backyard. But then a strange thing happened. In the course of a year or two opinion mysteriously swung round and the process was approved by a three-fifths majority. The plant now stands there.

Frey draws an analogy with a play by the Swiss dramatist Friedrich Dürrenmatt, entitled *The Visit*. It is the story of a woman who returns after many years to her impoverished home town after having married a series of millionaire husbands and become the richest person in the world. It was made into a 20th Century Fox film, starring Ingrid Bergman and Anthony Quinn. The play begins with her arrival at the station of Gullen, where the express has been halted especially for her benefit. She is given a ceremonial welcome by the town's dignitaries, who are dependent for their hopes for restored prosperity on an expected benefaction of $5m from her. I had expected the Old Lady to be someone in her seventies with a veil hanging from her hat and layers of chalky make-up. In fact she is an ostentatious woman in her sixties, travelling with exotic effects, including a black panther, and a retinue of servants and ex-husbands.

She is indeed prepared to oblige – but on one highly embarrassing condition. This is that they put to death a citizen named Ill, who jilted her as a young girl and bribed his way out of a paternity suit. Of course the townsfolk are outraged by this suggestion. Nevertheless they start spending money lavishly, buying new clothes and revitalizing their shops in the expectation of bounty to come. By the final act they have decided to dispose of Ill. Their excuse is that his behaviour all those years ago was highly immoral and a blot on their good name.

Frey is halfway there when he makes a comparison with nuclear waste disposal. In conventional economics there is no difference between a bribe and an offer of compensation, except for the distributional effects. If the inhabitants on the western fringes of Greater London are bribed to accept a new Heathrow runway, this is seen as similar to what would happen if the government compensated those affected on the basis of a fall in property values, or any other factor. Frey realizes there is more to it than that. Compensation is regarded as morally acceptable, while a bribe, however politely disguised as a cash inducement, is a matter for outrage. In his interpretation, the inhabitants of Gullen gradually come to see the terms they are offered as legitimate compensation.

Although I know much less about Swiss drama than Frey, I do not think he has penetrated to the heart of *The Visit*. The reason why the citizens engineer the death is not because they see the Old Lady's cheque in slightly different economic terms but because they work themselves up into moral outrage at Ill's behaviour all those years ago. The result is that his behaviour, which did deserve some penalty and perhaps even some atonement, becomes an excuse forty years later for an undeserved death sentence.

The lesson seems to me to transcend any normal economic calculus. It shows how cruelly people can be induced to behave when

PART SEVEN

Some Twentieth-century Luminaries

If all mankind minus one were of one opinion, and only one person were of a contrary opinion, mankind would be no more justified in silencing that one person, than he, if he had the power, would be justified in silencing mankind.

John Stuart Mill, *On Liberty*

All plans of government, which suppose great reformation in the manners of mankind, are plainly imaginary.

David Hume, *Idea of a Perfect Commonwealth*

The Political Philosophy of Maynard Keynes

A version of this chapter also appears in the *Cambridge Companion to Keynes* (forthcoming), and is included here by permission of Cambridge University Press.

The works of Keynes have this resemblance to the Bible or the publications of Karl Marx. People of many different schools of thought can find chapter and verse to back up their views if they look hard enough. This is not necessarily bad. His writings cover over forty adult years in which a great many events occurred and in which his own views developed and changed.[1] This variability has often been trivialized by those who imagine Keynes to have said 'When facts change, I change my mind.' There is no suggestion in Robert Skidelsky's authoritative three-volume biography that he ever said anything as banal. What he is more likely to have said is: 'When I change my mind, I say so. What do you do?'

There are four aspects of Keynes relevant to this essay:

1. Keynesian economics. I have to insist that Keynes's principal contribution to economics was the theory of effective demand. Without it he would still be remembered for his contributions to public life and for *The Economic Consequences of the Peace*, 1919, the best-seller which denounced the Versailles Treaty of 1919, but he would not have had the giant status which he has occupied for so many years.
2. Keynesian economics as developed by followers after the Second World War.
3. Keynes as seen by politicians, academic and otherwise, sociologists and modern historians. He is here identified, often with little direct citation, with the welfare state, income redistribution and government intervention in industry.
4 The beliefs of Keynes the man.

This essay naturally concentrates on the last, but his belief can only be understood in relation to these other clusters of ideas. Keynesian economics has gradually merged into what is often called the Keynesian-neo-classical synthesis. As such it has become almost a branch of applied mathematics with a highly technical apparatus, leaning very heavily on formal models and econometric forecasts. Nevertheless there have remained differences between those who emphasize the Keynesian and those who emphasize the neo-classical aspects of this synthesis. Moreover, some Keynesian economists have tried from time to time to remedy some of the deficiencies in the policy models by stratagems such as 'incomes policy' which they hope will make them more closely fit the facts.

Perhaps the best way to get into the subject is to contrast the personal beliefs of Keynes with the market liberal school of thought which re-emerged in the last two decades of the twentieth century. This school was often labelled 'neoliberal', 'market fundamentalist' or even 'radical right' by its opponents, while some of its supporters would have preferred the title 'classical liberal'. Its teachings were popularly associated with the governments of Ronald Reagan in the USA and Margaret Thatcher in the UK, but the relationship was highly approximate. As their name suggests, market liberals emphasized the benefits of market forces and the pitfalls of discretionary government intervention. But just as important was the search for policy rules. Heads of government were never so keen on having their hands tied by such rules as were their supposed academic inspirers. But these were nevertheless a central plank of the revived doctrines.

The most famous of these was Milton Friedman's advocacy of a fixed growth of some specified version of the money supply. There were also rules for the allowable amount of the budget deficit related to the state of the economic cycle. Indeed Nigel Lawson summarized his idea of a medium-term financial strategy even before the Thatcher government was elected with the slogan 'Rules rule'.

So far from withering away, these rules had a new lease of life when the political pendulum swung to the left. The euro was launched with both an independent European Central Bank committed to price stability and the ill-fated Growth and Stability Pact which aimed to limit budget deficits. In Britain there was no firmer advocate of government by rules than the Labour Chancellor, Gordon Brown, who came to office in 1997 and who kept on republishing a fiscal strategy which aimed to lay down strict rules for government borrowing over the whole of a carefully defined business cycle. Another aspect was the operational independence of the Bank of England, which devised some rules of its own in implementing the inflation targets laid down by the government.

Market liberalism did not have to be nearly as hardhearted or as inflexible as its opponents claimed or as appeared from some of the more doctrinaire think-tank pronouncements. For instance, it was consistent with a considerable degree of income redistribution and also government intervention where there were glaring market failures, but always bearing in mind that there could be government failures too. The distinguishing feature of classical liberal doctrines was that intervention should be bound by rules and not depend on discretionary deals between governments and interest groups.

Those market liberals who were interested in the history of ideas had a varying attitude to Keynes. In some American Republican circles he was regarded as the fount of all political and economic evil. But there were others who tried to distinguish between Keynes and social democrat versions of Keynesian economics (2 and 3 above) which they regarded as a distortion of his teachings.

I hesitate to disillusion this last group with whom I have a temperamental sympathy; but my own reading suggests that he himself was far from a classical liberal. It is true that he had little sympathy with what came to be called 'Labour values'. Beatrice Webb qualified a eulogy written in 1926 by remarking 'he is contemptuous of common men, especially when gathered together in herds...He has no desire to enlist the herd instinct on his side. Hence his antipathy to trade unions, to proletarian culture, to nationalism and patriotism...' He was not very interested in equality and his support for the redistributive welfare state was perfunctory. All he would say on wage push under full employment was 'One is also, simply because one knows no solution, inclined to turn a blind eye to the wages problem in a fully employed economy.'[2]

Keynes is rightly identified with what was called in his time 'the Middle Way'. Indeed, he wrote a favourable review of a book of just that title by his friend and publisher Harold Macmillan. But it must be remembered that the interwar Middle Way was in between laissez-faire capitalism and state socialism. The contemporary Third Way, as proclaimed for instance by Tony Blair's government in Britain, was meant to be in between the Thatcher-Reagan model of competitive free enterprise and 'Rhenish' corporatist capitalism.

Obviously Keynes died too soon to pronounce on this Third Way. Nevertheless, to the extent to which the issues developed in his time he was a corporatist. This comes out clearly from his excursions into current issues and in his support for the Liberal Industrial Inquiry of the 1920s. He was a strong advocate of both public corporations and large private concerns that were ready to do deals with the government and look beyond shareholder value. From the 1920s to the 1940s he frequently referred approvingly to the two thirds or three quarters of fixed investment which he regarded as already effectively under public control or influence. This was pretty far removed from the privatization of later governments. He was indeed an early exponent of what have come to be called public/private partnerships; and their role in keeping public investment out of the budget arithmetic was seen by him as a positive advantage.

The reader will have noticed that I have been discussing so far the political economy of Keynes rather than anything that might strictly be called political philosophy. In fact, although Keynes read mathematics at Cambridge as an undergraduate, his main academic interests were in philosophy and they continued to be so until the First World War. He had a few economic supervisions from Alfred Marshall, the father figure of Cambridge economics, who urged him to take the Tripos in that subject. But he resisted and took the Civil Service exam and went into the India Office instead. It is possible that if he had obtained a King's Fellowship when he first applied in 1908 on the basis of a dissertation on probability his interests might have turned permanently to philosophy. But the fellowship was delayed until 1909, by which time he had already taken up the offer of a lectureship in economics. It is not entirely clear why he did so. Skidelsky suggests that he discovered an aptitude for the subject, having worked on Indian currency and finance which became the subject of his first book. But in any case he devoted almost all his spare time to his probability study – which was held up by the World War and eventually published as the *Treatise on Probability* in 1921.

Although Keynes published very little on philosophy after 1921 he maintained his interest between the wars. He was a close friend of Frank Ramsey, the genius who died tragically in 1930 at the age of twenty-seven. He also saw quite a lot of Ludwig Wittgenstein. Indeed, some have seen a parallel between Keynes's abandonment of classical economic theory, with its occasionally counter-intuitive conclusions, and the shift of Wittgenstein to ordinary language philosophy.

Nevertheless Keynes was not a political philosopher in the sense that Hobbes, Plato or Michael Oakeshott in the twentieth century can be said to have been. The closest he came was in an unpublished, hundred-page paper on Edmund Burke as an undergraduate; but he never went on to formulate an explicit scheme of his own. The most extensive study of Keynes's philosophy I know, that of O'Donnell, does not discuss political philosophy until the thirteenth of its sixteen chapters. His primary philosophical interests were in ethics, logic and probability.

By far the most important formative influence on Keynes was his membership of a highly selective Cambridge society known as the Apostles. It was founded in 1820 and Keynes joined in 1903 as Apostle number 243. Its objectives were summarized as 'the pursuit of truth in absolute devotion and unreservedly by a group of intimate friends'. The society later became notorious because four of the Communist spies later unmasked were members, including Blunt and Burgess, and many others became Marxists of one kind or another. These young men – oblivious of Keynes's own work – came to despair of western capitalist nations either finding a cure for unemployment or poverty or confronting the rising menace of Nazism. But that was all three decades ahead. In the twelve years from 1903, in which they had their greatest influence on the young Keynes, the Apostles were marked by a deliberate unworldliness. One feature that many members then had in common was a strong homosexual or bisexual element.

Those whom Keynes particularly recalled in his memoir included Lytton Strachey, Leonard Woolf and the economist Ralph Hawtrey. But the dominating influence was the philosopher G. E. Moore who was ten years older than Keynes and who attended as an 'Angel', the name given for members who had already graduated but were free to return. (The slightly later Bloomsbury Group was, in Skidelsky's words 'a London extension of the Apostles'.) In his famous memoir of 1938, *My Early Beliefs* (vol. X) Keynes admits that 'what we got from Moore was by no means entirely what he offered us'. The greater part of Moore's *Principia Ethica* consisted of an analytical examination of the meaning of 'good'. It became famous for its exposure of the 'naturalist fallacy'. By this Moore meant identifying goodness with some other quality such as happiness. In Keynes's words, goodness was 'a matter of direct inspection, of direct unanalysed intuition about which it was impossible to argue'.

The Apostles were, however, influenced mainly by the final chapter on 'The Ideal'. Here Moore asserted that 'the most valuable things which we know or can imagine are certain states of consciousness which may be roughly described as personal affection and the appreciation of what is beautiful in art or nature'. One might wonder if Moore did not himself commit the naturalist fallacy in identifying goodness with these aspects. Moreover, he provides little argument for identifying the enumerated states of mind as the ideal, simply saying 'once the meaning of the question is clearly understood, the answer to it in its main outline appears to be so obvious'. Fortunately, however, my concern here is not with Moore but with what Keynes derived from him. He described it as a religion 'altogether unworldly – in which wealth, power, popularity or success... were thoroughly despised'. Even three decades later Keynes believed that it remained 'nearer the truth than any other that I know... It was a purer, sweeter air by far than Freud cum Marx'. In the halcyon pre-First World War days the Apostles were mainly concerned with their own feelings and treated politics and the outside world with contempt. But anyone with experience of such societies knows that however much they profess individualism, there is an enormous pressure to conform with the prevailing ethos. As Keynes confesses, 'In practice of course at least as far as I was concerned, the outside world was not forgotten or foresworn.'

How did he get from there to justifying his later activities as a political economist, inevitably concerned with promoting welfare in the Benthamite manner? In his memoir he puts the emphasis on there being worthy categories of human emotion other than Moore's, including 'spontaneous, irrational outbursts of human nature' – of a kind that interested D. H. Lawrence, who hated the Apostles and Bloomsbury. I am not sure that this brings us any nearer to political economy. A more formal reconciliation, not mentioned in the memoir, was that certain attributes such as happiness, or even material wealth, could enhance the value of the more basic qualities, as explained in Moore's doctrine of the 'organic unities'. Keynes himself came to regard success in tackling the economic problem as a prerequisite to a better society in which most people – and not just a tiny elite – could concentrate on the matters of supreme value. This was one, but only one, element in his desire to accelerate investment, as discussed in the Appendix.

There is a respect in which Keynes came closer to Moore, as he matured. The latter had accepted the duty of the individual to obey society's rules as an indirect way to promote his form of Ideal Utilitarianism. This was initially repudiated by Keynes and his friends, who utterly disregarded 'customary moral conventions and traditional wisdom'. After his experiences in the political world, Keynes came to doubt that the human race consisted of 'reliable, rational, decent people' who could be 'safely released from the outward constraints of convention and traditional standards, in flexible rules of conduct, and left to reliable intuitions of the good'.

Looking back in 1938, he said, 'We were not aware that civilization was a thin and precarious trust, erected by the personality and the will of a very few, and only maintained by rules and conventions, skilfully put across and guilefully preserved.' This brought him closer to the respect for rules and conventions he had found in Burke and which Hayek was to regard as a necessary constraint on the freedom he espoused. Keynes never quite resolved the issue, remarking, even in 1938, that he would always remain an immoralist and still insisting that 'it is only states of mind that matter'. Some would say that his immoralism consisted mainly of a continuing rejection of the somewhat hypocritical Victorian constraints on sexual and other personal behaviour which carried over for a surprisingly large proportion of the twentieth century. (The 'trial of *Lady Chatterley*' took place as late as 1960.) Moreover, his references to 'guile' would hardly have been echoed in the writings of Burke and Hayek.

There are indeed three themes to which Keynes stuck fairly consistently throughout all his changes of outlook and interest. These were:

1. A suspicion of fixed rules, although he sometimes reluctantly accepted the case for them.
2. An intense dislike of what he called the money motive. This was not just a contempt for those who had an anal fixation on the accumulation of wealth for its own sake rather than what it could buy. It was a hostility to the whole idea of material gain as a motive. Indeed, what attracted him to his first great hero, the philosopher G. E. Moore, was that he believed that the latter had for the first time disposed of the Benthamite calculus of pleasure and pain as a guide to conduct. A contempt for business and money-making was fairly common among comfortably off Oxbridge intellectuals. What marked Keynes out was the combination of this contempt with a strong personal interest in the detailed processes of money-making in the City, going far beyond anything possessed by most mainstream utilitarian economists.
3. An interest in non-conclusive inference. That is the logic of drawing tentative conclusions from facts or propositions which could not be known with certainty. It was this which formed the basis of his work on probability.

These interests were interrelated. He was quite content to accept Burke's suspicion of revolutionary change. But he could not accept Burke's insistence on fixed rules of conduct any more than his reverence for established property rights. And in contrast to both conservative and revolutionary theorists he was always suspicious of arguments for enduring present suffering for the sake of future benefits. He was not one of those who identified bourgeois civilization with postponed gratification.

Was he an individualist? At the personal level he was so to an extreme degree. In my view the most valuable part of the ethic of the Apostles and Bloomsbury consisted of a dictum of William Paley quoted in *My Early Beliefs*: 'Although we speak of communities as sentient beings and ascribe to them happiness and misery, desires, interests and passions, nothing really exists or feels but individuals.' When Keynes in 1938 qualifies this by saying that 'we carried individualism...too far' he probably had in mind his later strictures on economic individualism, as well perhaps as the need to identify with a wider group than particular coteries of close friends.

Although no formal political theorist, Keynes had a pronounced and surprisingly stable political outlook. He was himself politically engaged in the 1920s and 1930s. He took a prominent part in the deliberations of the Liberal party and was instrumental in merging

The New Statesman and *The Nation*. Indeed, he became the first chairman of the merged journal, and in this capacity he was a considerable thorn in the flesh of the more conventionally left-wing editor Kingsley Martin, berating him for his opposition to rearmament in the 1930s.

A recherché argument has developed on whether Keynes was one of the New Liberals. This was a group of intellectuals who, in the period 1870–1914, exerted their influence towards weaning the Liberal party away from free market economics towards more state intervention. Many of them were Oxford-based and included the philosopher T. H. Green, the sociologist Lionel Hobhouse, and the radical economist J. A. Hobson on whom Lenin drew for his work on imperialism. Keynes was not personally a member of this group. Nor would he have sympathized with the Hegelian view of some of them which exalted the collective above the individual. (In fact Hobhouse himself vigorously repudiated that notion, if he had ever held it, in his magnificent First World War polemic entitled *The Metaphysical Idea of the State* in which he blamed the war partly on the influence of such doctrines in Germany.) The short answer is that Keynes was not associated with this group either in terms of personalities or high theory but accepted many of its interventionist conclusions – although even there he put more emphasis on the inefficiencies of capitalism, as he knew it, and less on its inequities than they did.

Keynes regarded one of his main roles in the Liberal party as being to wean it away from the last vestiges of Gladstonian free market doctrine, emphasizing that 'the world is not so governed from above that private and social interest always coincide' (*The End of Laissez-Faire*, 1926, vol. IX). Indeed, he was most struck by cases where they did not. Although he was best known at the time for his opposition to the return to gold in 1925 at the prewar parity, he was also heavily involved in Lloyd George's plans for public works to reduce unemployment, and he took a personal part in schemes for a Lancashire cotton cartel.

Some have detected a shift back towards economic individualism after he had completed his *General Theory*, published in 1936. He himself wrote that once government had assumed responsibility for managing effective demand, some of the other implications of his teachings were 'moderately conservative' – by which he meant liberal in the classical sense. Indeed it is difficult to imagine that the hymn of praise to individualism, which seems to mix together personal individualism with the economic variety, at the end of *The General Theory* could have been written at any earlier time during his career as an economist. The swing had its limits. During the Second World War he took a great interest in ideas such as commodity stabilization and buffer stocks; and even his proposed rules for an international monetary system, partially realized in Bretton Woods, left a strong element for discretion in defining notions such as 'fundamental disequilibrium'. He also envisaged controls over capital movements as a permanent feature of the international scene.

Keynes had such a well-known flexibility of outlook and susceptibility to newly emerging facts that it is easy to imagine him changing his mind on many of the issues on which his followers clashed with the market liberals and monetarists in the decades after his death. It would not have been at all surprising if he had, along with some of the American Keynesians, given a greater role to monetary policy; and he might even have become disillusioned with public investment. On any of these specifics he would have been pretty pragmatic. But trying to work out in detail what he might have said if he had lived longer but maintained the intellect of his prime is a futile exercise.

The fundamental reason for his remaining disagreement with Hayek after the publication of *The Road to Serfdom* did not have so much to do with technical economics as with his belief that a much higher degree of intervention and planning would be compatible with personal liberty if carried out by 'right-thinking' leaders. He carried over from his Apostles period a belief in the importance of disinterested elites. At the back of his mind was the assumption that politicians of all main parties were still to some extent enlightened amateurs with sufficient means and independence to resist democratic pressures, while bureaucrats were, for similar reasons, able to resist the pressures of politicians. And neither group was under financial pressure to continue at their posts unless they believed in the tasks they were carrying out. It would have been difficult for Keynes to have persisted in his idealized view if he had lived long enough to see the way in which democratic politics developed as an auction for votes and in which crude personal rivalries and political spinning have come to dominate.

But there is another respect in which it is difficult to see him moving very near present thinking. This refers to the doubts which Keynes expressed about rigid rules for public policy throughout his career; and it is here that he might, had he lived, have had a profitable dialogue with Hayek. (Keynes's partial and unenthusiastic re-espousal of rules in *My Early Beliefs* probably referred mainly to private conduct.) The issue is far from settled. The expression 'rules' can have many different applications. They may, for instance, mean rules of personal conduct, constitutional and political rules or operational rules for policy. Keynes's scepticism applied to varying degrees in all spheres. But the contrast drawn with Hayek is incomplete. Hayek, for instance, was always pretty sceptical about anything like a money supply rule, a scepticism which was expressed as early as his magnum opus, *The Constitution of Liberty*, in 1960. Nor was he optimistic about central bank independence, remarking that whatever the legal form, the central bank would have to be closely intertwined with the finance ministry of the day.

An innovation of the 1990s was the idea of constrained discretion under which the Bank of England and other central banks were given operational freedom to fix interest rates, but subject to an overriding inflation target, laid down by the government. It would be stretching the analysis of 'might have been' too far to guess what Keynes would have made of this concept, although doubtless he would have been happier with the discretionary than with the constraint part of it.

Indeed, there may well have been too sharp a swing back to rules in reaction to the monetary failures of the 1970s. The fiscal and monetary framework both in the euro area and in the UK may be hampering government ability to respond to asset bubbles, systemic failures, or, should they arise, deflationary threats.

The problem in talking about trends and tendencies is that they are not the same in all directions. We may now be too rule-bound in certain limited areas of financial policy – so much so that they may discredit themselves – yet as far as ever from the old classical liberal idea of a government of laws rather than of men in which there are limits on what a temporary majority can achieve or on a concept of law which goes beyond the whims of individual ministers or their advisers and appointees. In the end the main interest of the Keynes–Hayek debate may well lie in the perennial argument about rules versus discretion rather than in the technical areas from which, to use a New Labour phrase, 'we ought to move on'.

Appendix: Keynes and investment

Some aspects of Keynes's political beliefs require one to go a little further into his economics. The main heresy in *The General Theory* was the doctrine of oversaving. He explained how attempts to save more could in some circumstances lead not to increased investment and faster growth but to a slump with lower output and employment. This collided with the conventional wisdom that savings were always virtuous. This tension was still present nearly seventy years later, when a Labour chancellor was on the one hand trying to stimulate private savings to help with the pensions problem, and then on the other hand boasting of his flexible fiscal rules which allowed a deficit – i.e. public dissaving – in recessions or periods of slow growth.

This fundamental heresy could be kept under the carpet by concentrating on policy implications. These were in terms of what was known in the jargon as 'aggregate demand'. If this rises too quickly the result is sure to be inflation. On the other hand, a sudden or unexpected drop in total spending – or even its rate of increase – is likely to produce not merely lower prices, but recession and unemployment. These two assertions taken together are compatible both with Keynesian policies and with the monetarist counterrevolution. The greater importance attached by the latter to monetary policy was an empirical matter of a kind on which Keynes was always prepared to adjust his views to changing evidence. What Keynes did insist upon as far back as his 1923 *Tract on Monetary Reform* (vol. IV) was that aggregate demand would not manage itself. But this was not really so very far from the original Friedman policy of using control over the money supply to promote sustainable growth without inflation or deflation.*

Keynes himself had a more radical interpretation from the 1930s onwards. He did not then see economic management merely as a matter of smoothing out the business cycle. He believed it was quite easy – indeed historically likely – for an economy to get stuck in a state of underemployment which would take a long time to cure. The absence of a great depression since the Second World War has fortunately made this a difficult matter on which to adjudicate. The nearest approximation to a long-lasting Keynesian depression has been the decade and more of stagnation which Japan suffered in the 1990s and after. But despite premature alarms about more widespread deflation, the possibility of longer term stagnation is sufficiently real to be prepared for it.

Keynes might not have quarrelled with present-day central bankers who regard low nominal interest rates as the first line of defence against stagnation and slump. But he was concerned with situations where interest rates as low as practicable would not be enough to shift the economy out of a rut. It was here that he saw a role for fiscal policy.

The question raised for political theory is why he attached such importance to public investment as a way of raising expenditure both in relation to deep-seated stagnation and to more conventional business cycle recessions. After all, if a recession or slump is due to attempted savings exceeding investment why not then tackle the savings side by stimulating consumption, if necessary by means of a budget deficit? Why then did Keynes himself concentrate almost entirely on the investment route? The question was put to him several

---

*It is not well known that late in his career Friedman modified his views on money supply control by saying that once inflation was low and stable the money supply would have to fluctuate to offset short-term changes in velocity. He thus accepted pragmatically the success of central banks in holding down inflation from the mid-1980s onwards. 'Reflections on a Monetary History', *Cato Journal*, Winter 2004.

times in correspondence during the Second World War (vol. XX). He did offer various answers, even though the question seemed to irritate him. The empirical mainspring of his attitude was the view that past business cycles had been touched off by fluctuations in investment. Therefore stimulating investment artificially to make up for shortfalls seemed a natural route and involved less structural dislocation.

He also believed that it was much easier to win over public opinion to investment promotion than it was to stimulate consumption through budget deficits. This came over very clearly in his interchanges with James Meade, who in the wartime economic service was more consistently Keynesian than the master, arguing for instance in favour of variations in National Insurance contributions according to the state of the business cycle, even if it meant current budget deficits, which the public was very far from accepting.

Keynes was reinforced in his bias by the fact that Parliament had in Victorian times provided governments with the authority to borrow for certain projects, then called 'below the line', and which would nowadays be called 'off budget', and which did not contribute to official estimates of the fiscal balance. More important, however, was his belief that three quarters of fixed investment, not merely of the public corporations, but also of the larger private businesses, was, or could be, influenced by the government – in his view more predictably and effectively than consumption could be. He also made a great deal in his interwar calculations of the return flow to the exchequer, which would arise from investment promotion schemes which led to higher economic activity. He usually fell short of saying that the expenditure would pay for itself, although he had some hopes from the use of public money to top up schemes in transport and construction, the greater part of which could be privately funded. He was thus in a sense a spiritual father of today's public/private partnerships.

Nevertheless some of Keynes's wartime correspondents did probe him on what would happen when investment was pushed as far as what was practicable. It was only last in his line of reasoning that he brought in the hope of saturating the economy with capital and bringing forward the situation in which the economic problem would be solved and men and women could concentrate on nobler pursuits.

Even then he did not espouse anything like permanent postwar credits or helicopter money. Indeed, he once said in reply to a letter from the poet T. S. Eliot (vol. XXVII) that the remedy would then lie in shorter hours. He did not make it clear whether he was thinking of compulsion or a natural drift. It is no slur on Keynes that in the midst of his wartime preoccupations he was unable to think the matter through. But nor, I suspect, has anyone else subsequently. Rather than engage in hermeneutics about what Keynes really meant, should have meant or might be saying today, it is more useful to have a shot at the substance of the problem.

I would suggest examining it by imagining possible reactions to a continuing drop of helicopter money from the sky or some equivalent. Three possibilities occur to me:

1. People might simply bank it or buy financial assets which by hypothesis would already be providing a very low yield. They might rationally do so if they regarded the windfall as temporary and believed the government would later have to raise taxes. This is what American economists have called 'the Ricardo effect' on account of a one-sentence footnote in the works of the early nineteenth-century British economist. If they are right, we would not be dealing with a Keynesian underemployment problem at all but mundane political bribery, to which the whole discussion about credibility and fiscal and monetary rules would be relevant. There would only be a problem of policy if a long-term excess of desired savings had really arrived, but the public did not believe it. I then leave it to the reader's imagination whether the best response would be to increase the amount of helicopter droppings or to invite economic spin-doctors to popularize the General Theory; but there is nothing of great philosophical interest in this case.

2. People would use their helicopter wealth to increase voluntary leisure, or to work in a more congenial and less stressful manner, or to take more breaks and sabbaticals for any purpose they chose. This would be akin to Keynes's 1933 *Economic Possibilities for our Grandchildren* (vol. XIX)) or what George Bush Sr had to say about a kinder, gentler form of capitalism. Demand management to secure optimal output without inflation would be trickier because of the assumed structural changes; but there would not in my view be any reason for compulsory reductions in working hours, forced early retirement or any of the other illiberal ideas that appeal to the management mentality.

3. People would simply throw away the helicopter money or give it to charity (included among this aid to the Third World). This is the saturation case. So far from being a disaster it would be a sign than nirvana or economic bliss had really arrived and we could almost forget about the economic problem altogether. It is just possible that in such a world what we now call work would be more like a hobby and people might pay for the opportunity to undertake it. Many years ago I sketched out my own fancies on the subject.[3]

Pure cases rarely occur in real life and reactions would be a mixture of all three cases explained above and perhaps some others.

There would be quite a challenge to practical policymakers to differentiate between a recession or slump requiring an injection of purchasing power and a shift in fundamental values requiring more subtle help in adjusting to increased leisure and voluntary reductions in paid work. But adapting to a world with such problems of success would be a much more cheerful prospect than a world governed by the Wall Street imperative of 'grow, grow, grow' and cries of disaster whenever the GDP change in the most recent quarter was found by analysts to be disappointing.

Notes

1. I do not claim to be an authority on the immense amount of primary, secondary and tertiary material on Keynes. My main sources are Skidelsky's three-volume biography, its abbreviated one-volume form, *John Maynard Keynes (1883–1946)*, 2003; and R. M. O'Donnell, *Keynes: Philosophy, Economy and Politics*, 1989. I have also tried wherever practicable to go back to Keynes's original texts. I have benefited from G. C. Harcourt and Sean Turnell, *On Skidelsky's Keynes* (Cambridge mimeo). I am also grateful to Prof. Harcourt for drawing my attention to John Coates, *The Claims of Common Sense*, 1995, which examines the role of Keynes in the deliberations of Cambridge philosophers up to the Second World War. It should in all fairness be added that my earliest knowledge of Keynes came from Sir Roy Harrod's *The Life of John Maynard Keynes* (1951). Although to some extent superseded, this pioneering work provided valuable insights. Bracketed Roman reference numbers in the text refer to the Macmillan collected edition of Keynes's works.
2. Letter to an Australian correspondent S. G. Macfarlane, 5 June 1945, vol. XXVII.
3. S. Brittan, *A Restatement of Economic Liberalism*, Macmillan 1973, 1988, Chapter 3.

Milton Friedman – A Portrait

Milton Friedman is the last of the great economists to combine possession of a household name with the highest professional credentials. In this respect he has often been compared to John Maynard Keynes, whose work he has always respected, even when he has challenged it.

Moreover, in contrast to many leading economists, Friedman has maintained a continuity between his Nobel Prize-winning academic contributions and his more popular work. The columns he contributed to *Newsweek* every third week between 1966 and 1984 were a model of how to use economic analysis to illuminate events.

Both his admirers and his detractors have pointed out that his world view is essentially simple: a passionate belief in personal freedom combined with a conviction that free markets are the best way of co-ordinating the activities of dispersed individuals to their mutual enrichment. Where he has shone has been in his ability to derive interesting and unexpected consequences from simple ideas. As I know from my postbag, part of his appeal has also lain in his willingness to come out with home truths which had occurred to many other people who had not dared to utter them. Friedman has then gone on, however, to defend these maxims against the massed forces of political or economic correctness; and in the course of those defences he has, almost unintentionally, added to knowledge.

Those who have wanted to write him off as a right-wing Republican have been disabused by the variety of radical causes he has championed. I was not impressed in my own student years by the claims to a belief in personal freedom of the pro-market British economists whom I first encountered. It was not until I came across Friedman, and learned that he had spent more time in lobbying against the US 'draft' than on any other policy issue, that I began to take seriously the wider philosophic protestations of the pro-market economists.

Friedman's iconoclasm has endured. He regards the anti-drugs laws as virtually a government subsidy for organised crime. Even in the financial sphere, he has espoused causes – such as indexed contracts and taxes, as a way of mitigating the harm done by inflation – which have not endeared him to natural conservatives.

But there is no self-conscious balancing of the political ticket in these positions. He reaches them by following the argument wherever it leads. Unlike his fellow exponent of free market capitalism, Friedrich Hayek (see next chapter), he has no great patience for hidden truths that might be embedded in inherited attitudes, rules and prejudices.

There is, indeed, nothing of the Herr Professor about Friedman. A small voluble figure, he prefers the spoken to the written word, and he took to television as a duck to water. He came to add a good many subtleties to the book *Free to Choose*, which he wrote with his wife Rose, which were not in the broadcast version. But there is no systematic treatise – only some written-up lecture notes – outlining Friedmanite economics or even Friedmanite monetary theory.

Those won over by his charm sometimes underestimate his resolve. He would not give a millimetre where his convictions were at stake. Although an unassuming and essentially democratic personality, he is human enough to be aware of, and enjoy, his hard-earned reputation.

His professed attitude to the political process is that of the critical Public Choice theorists. The latter believe that legislators follow their self-interest in a highly defective political market place in which geographical and industrially concentrated special interest groups gain at the general expense. But Friedman's ingrained belief in the power of reason and persuasion tends to get the better of any such theoretical misgivings. Although he occasionally professed gloom about the future of freedom, such forebodings were best left to the central Europeans whom he met at the Mont Pélerin Society. Friedman himself has been an optimistic American to his fingertips.

Early years

His own career was an archetypical American success story. He was born in New York in 1912 to poor immigrant parents and his father died when he was fifteen. He nevertheless studied at Rutgers and Chicago. In the 1930s he was on the staff of various research organizations and began an association with the National Bureau of Economic Research, which lasted until 1981 and which sponsored some of his most important work.

In 1938 he married Rose Director, herself an economist, who has been the co-author of some of his more general books. The closeness of his family life is an important clue to the man. His family circle included his wife's brother, Aaron Director, an economist who published little but whose wisdom was much cherished in the Friedman circle. His son David, in an attempt to avoid following in his father's footsteps, became at first a physicist, but eventually found the lure of socio-economic argument too difficult to resist. His father has been highly tolerant of David's excursions into anarchocapitalism – preferring deviations in that direction to lapses towards the conventional left.

During the Second World War Friedman not only worked for the US Treasury on tax, but had a spell in the statistical war research group at Columbia. He became professor of economics at Chicago in 1946, where he remained until his retirement. Friedman's own earliest work was in mathematical statistics, where he helped to pioneer some methods, for instance in sampling, which are still in use.

His first work of wider appeal was a study with Simon Kuznets, published in 1945, of income from independent professional practice. The authors found that state control of entry into the medical profession kept up the level of fees to the detriment of patients. These findings never ceased to get under the skin of the profession. Friedman's next book, *Essays in Positive Economics*, published in 1953, contained a famous essay on method. While many other economists were embarrassed by the oversimplified view of human nature in much economic theory, he was characteristically non-apologetic. The fruitfulness of a theory, in both the physical and the social sciences, he declared, depended on the success of the predictions which could be made with it and not on the descriptive realism of the assumptions. One of his famous examples was the proposition that the leaves of a tree spread themselves to maximize the area of sunlight falling upon them. The value of the theory depends on whether the layout of the leaves corresponded to this prediction and not on whether the tree made any such conscious effort.

This essay generated a still-running controversy which has consumed many acres of forest. But Friedman, having issued his manifesto, has left others to argue about it and has been more concerned to apply it in practice. Similarly, in his later expositions of the case for capitalism, he has stated his own values, and cited corroborative evidence, but resisted the temptation to argue about theories of freedom, justice, the state and so on.

Friedman's methods came as a breath of fresh air to many of the academic defenders of market capitalism who had previously felt themselves to be beleaguered armchair thinkers – in contrast to the econometricians and other quantitative researchers who claimed to be the wave of the future and wanted to use their methods for planning and intervention. Here at last was somebody who could hold his own with the most advanced of whizz kids and was quicker on his feet than most of them, but who was on the side of the market – indeed, with far fewer reservations and qualifications than most of its other supporters.

Despite the unfashionable nature of his policy views, Friedman spoke the same language as the postwar Keynesians, fitted equations to time series and provided a new field for economists in the investigation of 'demand for money' functions. Indeed, his contribution was essential. For if age-old verities about the relations between money and prices, or the futility of nations trying to spend themselves into full employment were to be rehabilitated, it had to be in modern statistical dress.

Friedman in Cambridge

I first met Friedman in the 1950s when I was a second-year undergraduate at Cambridge where he had come on a sabbatical. Unfortunately, I had to share supervisions with another student who had no difficulty in deflecting him into general political conversation. Friedman once arrived early and started to read a copy of Shaw's contribution to *Fabian Essays* which was lying on the table. 'There are three mistakes in the first few pages,' he said, referring to Shaw's excursion into marginal productivity theory in which he thought he could instruct his less well-read fellow Fabians.

For all Friedman's charm, I received from him one of the best put-down remarks I have ever encountered. He mentioned to me a letter he had received from Arthur Burns (later chairman of the Federal Reserve) saying that Eisenhower was turning out well as President. I expressed surprise, to which Friedman responded: 'First, Burns has much better knowledge of Eisenhower. Secondly, given equal knowledge I would prefer his opinion to yours.'

In the 1950s, Friedman was much better known for his advocacy of floating exchange rates than for monetarism. The background was the widespread concern about a supposed dollar shortage, which Friedman believed entirely due to overvalued exhange rates in Europe and elsewhere. 'Sure,' he would say, 'there is a dollar shortage in Britain – in exactly the same way as there is a dollar shortage for every US citizen.' He had the last laugh, as within a few years the supposed dollar shortage had turned into an equally mythical dollar surplus.

What I did not discover until many years later was that Friedman had been spitefully frozen out of much of the intellectual life of the Cambridge Economics Faculty. For instance, there was an absurdly named 'secret seminar' that discussed capital theory, where Friedman could have helped very much by cutting through some of the mathematical problems and bringing out the essentials, but from which he was excluded.

What dismayed him most were the illiberal attitudes of some in the faculty who were theoretically on his side. An example was the late Sir Dennis Robertson, who always maintained reservations about Keynes and who advocated near-zero inflation decades before that became fashionable. But he shocked Friedman by defending vigorously the right of County Agricultural Committees to dispossess farmers they deemed inefficient. The Chicago professor's admiration for the founding fathers of British economics became tinged with perplexity at what so many contemporary English people were inclined to assert.

'Permanent income' and money

During the rest of his career, Friedman was largely occupied with the empirical testing of economic ideas. His most widely praised achievement was his *Theory of the Consumption Function*, published in 1957, which was the work prominently mentioned in the citation for the Nobel Prize which he won in 1974. His investigation was touched off by a well-known paradox. Cross-section data appeared to show that the percentage of income saved increased as income rose. On the other hand, time series data showed much less change in the savings proportion over the years. The resolution of the puzzle was that spending and savings decisions depended on people's views of their long-term ('permanent') income; but they were much less inclined to adjust to transitory income variations in either direction.

These findings had at least two implications which Friedman cherished. One was that capitalism did not after all suffer from a long-term tendency to stagnate because of under-consumption. Another was that fiscal fine-tuning would be very difficult, as consumers would ignore temporary variations in disposable income due to government budgetary tightening or relaxation. Friedman's *Consumption Function* was so thorough and convincing in its marriage of theory and data that it convinced many economists who far from relished the political implications.

It was in the late 1950s and 1960s that Friedman developed the monetarist doctrines for which he became best known. He treated money as an asset. The public desire to hold this asset depended on incomes, the rate of interest and expected inflation. If more money became available, the effect would be initially to raise real output and incomes, but eventually just to raise prices more or less in proportion.

Here was where the famous 'long and variable lags' appeared: typically nine months before real output and income were affected and a further nine months before the main effects on prices came through. These time periods have been much cited and much derided; but they are not the heart of Friedman's message.

The stock response of the anti-monetarists has been to say that the money supply adjusted passively to events such as wage explosions or government deficits. Although this sometimes occurred it was important for Friedman to establish that this was not always the case. Sometimes money was the active agent, whether because of an inflow of gold, an official easy money policy, an attempt to maintain a particular exchange rate, or other impulses.

Monetary history and monetarism

The book in which he tried most fully to demonstrate money's active role was *A Monetary History of the USA, 1867–1960*, published in 1963 and written jointly with Anna Schwartz – it is one of Friedman's skills that he has always found the right collaborator for a particular work. The *Monetary History* is Friedman's masterpiece. Containing hardly any equations, it has been read with profit and pleasure as history, even by people who have disagreed with, or been indifferent to, the doctrines it was designed to advance. Characteristically, it began as a by-product of an attempt to establish the factual record of the US money supply, which turned up so many problems and brought to light so much new material that the more ambitious volume more or less suggested itself.

A later attempt by the same two authors at a more formal equation-based approach, concentrating on cyclical averages and covering the UK as well, was not as successful. There were so many snags that the results did not appear until 1982; and the authors themselves admitted that they were hardly worth the effort. They particularly regretted the time spent on extending the analysis to the UK, which had not yielded much extra light. The scholarly debate on the new work was itself delayed for nearly another decade, partly because of the attempts of British anti-Thatcherites to harness the analysis of Friedman's critics for their own political purposes. One day the full story will be told.

The policy conclusion Friedman drew was his famous money supply rule – a stable growth of the money supply, year in year out. He accepted that this was not the only policy that could be derived from monetarist findings. But nearly all suggested monetarist strategies have become embroiled in difficulties as financial assets have proliferated and with them the number of rival definitions of money. In the early 1990s some monetarists were accusing the Fed of depressing the US economy with too tight a policy at the same time as other monetarists were criticizing it for expanding too much.

Friedman himself sometimes gave the impression that whatever a central bank did, it could do no right. To gain his favour it had not only to pursue monetary targets, but pursue them by a particular method known as 'monetary base control'; and when the Fed attempted such a method in 1979–82 it was damned for getting the mechanics wrong. But more recently he has expressed – occasionally puzzled – admiration for the more eclectic achievements of Alan Greenspan.

No inflation-jobs trade-off

Some economists would argue that Friedman's most important contribution to macroeconomics has been not his technical monetary work, but his 1967 presidential address to the American Economic Association. Here he demonstrated that the idea of a stable trade-off between inflation and unemployment, which held a sway under the name of the 'Phillips curve' and which seemed to give policymakers a menu of choices, was invalid. Suppose that a government or central bank tried to raise output and employment at the expense of accepting higher inflation. Once market participants started to take into account inflation in their behaviour, the economy would eventually end up with the same rate of unemployment as before but a higher rate of inflation. If the authorities none the less persisted in trying to achieve an over-ambitious target unemployment rate, the result would not be merely inflation, but accelerating inflation, with which no society can live for long.

This family of Friedman doctrines was sometimes called the vertical Phillips curve, sometimes the accelerationist hypothesis, and sometimes the 'natural rate' of unemployment. This last was the level at which the economy would settle once any stable rate of inflation had been established. The name was later changed by some users to the NAIRU – the non-accelerating inflation rate of unemployment – to banish the idea that there was anything natural or inevitable about it.

It was in fact these ideas related to the NAIRU which caused my own shift away from postwar Keynesianism rather than any of Friedman's more technical monetary ideas. The basic propositions are now quite familiar. But at the time they were explosive stuff for the British economic establishment and also for many American economists on the Eastern seaboard.

Some economists have treated the NAIRU as a new technocratic concept which they set about estimating and using for still more sophisticated forms of demand management. This is contrary to the spirit of Friedman's address, where it was obviously intended as a warning against governments' attempts to spend their way into predetermined levels of employment. The Friedman ideas achieved popular currency in the UK – amazingly enough as a result of Prime Minister Callaghan's address to the 1976 Labour party conference when he warned against believing that governments could spend their way into full employment.

All the same it was a little disappointing to those who were interested in macroeconomics rather than monetary technicalities that Friedman did not make more use of the NAIRU in his more popular writings. Indeed, he sometimes seemed to stretch his own doctrines in attributing to short-term variations in monetary growth the responsibility for recessions – about which he could be as critical as any Keynesian.

Relations with Thatcher

Friedman's direct influence on Margaret Thatcher was much less than often supposed. Although they got on together at a private dinner before the 1979 election, the two did not know each other well and Friedman is only mentioned *en passant* in the former prime minister's memoirs. Her own inspiration, as she relates, came from Hayek.

Nevertheless, Friedman had an obvious, if indirect, effect on many of her advisers and ministers. The Medium-Term Financial Strategy of the 1980s, with its target of a gradual reduction in the growth of the money supply and the abandonment of fine tuning, obviously stemmed at one remove or another from the Chicago economist.

But the master himself disowned the MTFS because the Bank of England continued to regulate the money supply indirectly through interest rates rather than via the 'monetary base'. Moreover, he did not believe that reducing the budget deficit would have much effect on interest rates or in any other way deserved the prominence given to it in the MTFS. On a broader front, however, without Friedman's writings and television expositions, the Thatcher government would not have enjoyed even that very limited degree of approval that it did among a minority of the intellectual elite.

A working retirement

From the late 1970s onwards Friedman has lived in San Francisco. He obviously enjoys his working retirement in this more clement climate, within easy reach of his office at the Hoover Institution in

Stanford. Rose has been even more obviously delighted with the move.

The very modernity of Friedman meant that he has been vulnerable in his technical findings to new researchers claiming to refute his work by still more up-to-date statistical methods. Indeed, Friedman has lived long enough to see a reaction against basing economics on discoverable numerical relationships and the revival of so-called 'Austrian' methods, which concentrated on predicting general features of interacting systems on the lines of biology and linguistics (see next chapter).

In the last few decades of his life, Friedman has also kept his distance from the New Classical Economics, based on rational expectations and rapid market clearing. He fears that economists are being trapped into a search for mathematical rigour and elegance for their own sake instead of as tools for investigating what is happening.

Outside monetary matters, Friedman has remained a mainstream economist. As he himself wrote in *Capitalism and Freedom* (a book published in 1962 which went deeper than *Free to Choose*), he could offer no hard and fast line for the limits of government intervention. But he believed that an objective study of the facts, case by case, combined with an underlying belief in personal choice, would usually swing the argument in favour of private provision in the market place.

Friedman himself has attributed the spread of both free markets and monetarist ideas to belated recognition of the consequences of soaring government spending and high inflation in the 1970s. But so far as the reaction was coherent and rational, much of the credit must go to him. The very success of free market policies has, of course, led to fresh problems; and what would one not give for a reborn thirty-year-old Milton Friedman to comment upon and analyse these new challenges?

Hayek's Contribution

Entry in *Oxford Dictionary of National Biography* (Oxford University Press, 2004) by permission of OUP

Friedrich August von Hayek (1899–1992), economist and political philosopher, was born in Vienna on 8 May 1899, the eldest of three sons of August von Hayek (1871–1928), physician and botanist. His mother called him 'Fritz', an appellation also used by friends and contemporaries, but which he never liked.

Hayek was mainly known in the 1930s for technical studies of monetary, business cycle and capital theory. These were subsequently overshadowed by the 'Keynesian Revolution', but were being re-examined towards the end of the twentieth century (e.g. by John Hicks, *Capital and Time, a Neo-Austrian Approach*, OUP, 1973). He had a brief period of fame in some circles and notoriety in others for *The Road to Serfdom*, his 1944 tract against centralized economic planning in time of peace. He was held to have inspired a controversial election broadcast by Winston Churchill a year later, in which the latter warned of a socialist 'Gestapo'. Hayek re-emerged in the public eye in the 1970s and 1980s at a time of widespread disillusion both with Keynesian methods for securing full employment and with the apparently relentless expansion in the role of government. The breakdown of the postwar boom, triggered off by the oil price explosion of 1973, was no surprise to Hayek – except that he had never expected it to last nearly as long as it did. In the last twenty years of the twentieth century many dozens of books and articles on Hayek appeared, although mostly by political theorists and historians of ideas rather than economists. His most important contribution to political and economic philosophy will almost certainly turn out to have been *The Constitution of Liberty*.

His own personal story starts with his great-great-grandfather, Josef von Hayek(1750–1830), who gained a minor title of nobility as an enterprising steward for an aristocratic landowner of Moravia. In later life English language opponents of the economist insisted on calling him 'von Hayek'. In fact such titles were abolished in the interwar Austrian republic. The 'von' only got back into his name by an accident when he submitted his birth certificate for British naturalization in 1938, and was in too much of a hurry for a passport to correct it.

Hayek's father never achieved his ambition of holding a university chair, which helped to account for his son's belief that that was the most desirable of all positions. He afterwards remarked that the decisive aspect of his own student years was that 'you were not expected to confine yourself to your own subject'; and indeed he wavered between psychology and economics, which at the time had to be combined with law. He once said that he might well have become a biologist had not his father given him two 'heavy volumes' by August Weismann (the biologist who rediscovered Mendel's genetics) at a time when Hayek was too immature to appreciate them. He later remarked that the qualities he had admired in the University of Vienna had disappeared by the Second World War and he avoided returning to the city.

His first job after graduating was with an agency concerned with clearing debts arising from the First World War. But his real opportunity came when he gained a research assistantship in New York in 1923–4. While there he investigated statistical time series and, more characteristically, wrote a critique of proto-Keynesian underconsumption theories. He also unearthed from American accounts facts about the First World War which had largely been kept from the Austrian population. This may well have been one of the origins of his scepticism about government and all its works.

The London School of Economics

Back in Austria he became a participant in the seminar organized by the economist Ludwig von Mises, who secured for him the post of director of a newly established institute for business cycle research. Some of Hayek's papers caught the attention of Lionel (later Lord) Robbins, professor of economics at the London School of Economics, one of the very few British economists who could read German, and who invited him to give a series of lectures in London in 1931, subsequently published as *Prices and Production*. Recalling his arrival, Robbins subsequently wrote: 'I can still see the door of my room opening to admit the tall, powerful, reserved figure which announced itself quietly and firmly as "Hayek".' The same year Hayek was appointed Tooke Professor of Economic Science and Statistics, a post he held until 1950. As he subsequently remarked: 'If you are offered a chair in the University of London at the age of thirty-two you take it.'

Robbins himself was appointed in 1929, at the age of thirty the youngest economics professor in the UK. He wanted to establish the LSE as a centre for economic theory, to counteract the insular emphasis of Cambridge, and to combat the influence of Keynes with whom he had already clashed on an official committee in 1930. He believed Hayek could help on all three fronts. Hayek did indeed bring many cosmopolitan contacts to the LSE. He was, for instance, instrumental in the appointment of Karl Popper, the philosopher and author of *The Open Society*. He subsequently looked back on his own work at the LSE in the 1930s as intellectually the most satisfying of his life.

His technical work there had three main but related aspects: capital, monetary and business cycle theory. He promoted the 'Austrian' capital theory which emphasized that lower interest rates promoted a more 'roundabout' structure of production – in today's language a capital-deepening one. But he eventually abandoned the earlier Austrian concept of an 'average period of production' in favour of the more complex idea of the 'structure of production'. He was himself dissatisfied with his final effort in this direction, *The Pure Theory of Capital*, which appeared in 1941 and which he subsequently said he had rushed out too quickly under the erroneous belief that the war would soon make such publications impossible. An intended sequel covering money and business cycles was never written.

American writers who attempted to relaunch 'Austrian economics' towards the end of the twentieth century tended to treat *The Pure Theory of Capital* as an unfortunate diversion and preferred to base themselves on *Prices and Production* and related works. The issue of 'Austrian economics' did not loom large in the 1930s because during that time the differences between the Austrian and other branches of neo-classical economics were less than at any time before or since. The main intellectual battle line was between neo-classical economics of all kinds and the increasingly heretical work of Keynes at Cambridge. By the time that the large divergences between postwar mainstream economics and the Austrian tradition had emerged into daylight Hayek had largely switched his interest to political philosophy and broad questions of economic policy. Nevertheless his policy recommendations still had their roots in his earlier work on capital and monetary theory; and he did write the occasional short clarificatory paper well into the 1960s, sometimes in response to queries from John Hicks.

It was ironical that media critics later described him as the 'father of monetarism'. From his early studies of business cycles onwards he emphasized how difficult it was to define the money supply and that, in any case, variations in velocity were at least as important as changes in the quantity. But the special characteristic of his cycle theory was his stress on the divergent movement of different prices during the business cycle, so that general price indices could not convey useful information for policy. (This is best explained in vol. 6 of the *Routledge Collected Works of F. A. Hayek*, especially 'Introduction' and 'Correspondence with John Hicks'.)

In view of his insistence on the importance of changing relative prices in so many contexts, and throughout his career, it is surprising that he never sought to measure or estimate such relative price changes. This cannot be completely explained away by his distrust of index numbers. His insistence that, while inflation is a monetary phenomenon, there is no such thing as 'the quantity of money', and no sharp boundary between money and other financial assets, has, however, stood the test of time. The experience of the British governments in the 1980s, which changed their monetary targets so much and to so little avail, was much less puzzling to a Hayekian than to a true monetarist believer. So, too, was the high unemployment cost of reducing inflation, which Hayek insisted was inevitable while labour markets were dominated by the collective bargaining mentality.

Hayek's own business cycle theory started out from the 'natural rate of interest', a concept invented by the Swedish economist Knut Wicksell. This was the rate at which savings and investment were equal and the economy was in equilibrium. In an upturn or downturn the market rate of interest diverges from the natural one and the economy becomes uncoordinated. In the boom phase banks expand credit, and consumption goods are pushed up in price; and thus 'forced savings' are extracted from consumers. A neutral monetary policy would attempt to smooth out the cycle by keeping the market rates equal to the natural rate. But as the latter was unknowable this would, in Hayek's view, be an impossible undertaking. Moreover, any attempt to use monetary policy to keep the general price level stable would make matters worse – for instance central banks would raise interest rates near the top of a boom, thus aggravating the ensuing recession. During the 1970s, when the main questions were no longer those of smoothing the business cycle, but double digit inflation that threatened world prosperity, Hayek changed his views, at least by implication. For he roundly castigated governments, central banks, and, above all, economists for having allowed inflation to soar out of control, from a misguided 'Keynesian' desire to give priority to output and employment.

Hayek and Keynes

During his 1931 visit to Britain, Hayek was invited to Cambridge. Richard Kahn, Keynes's closest collaborator, asked why if in the middle of a slump he went out and bought an overcoat he would not help to increase output and employment. Hayek replied that it would take a long mathematical demonstration to explain why not; and according to local reports this incident destroyed Hayek's chances of a Cambridge chair.

Looking back after seventy years from the beginning of the twenty-first century the analyst is struck by the similarity rather than the differences of the business cycle theories of Hayek and Keynes at the time of the latter's *Treatise on Money* of 1931. The controversy is admirably set out in volume IX of the Routledge edition of the collected works of Hayek. This contains papers by Keynes and others as well as Hayek; and the editor, Bruce Caldwell, contributes a lucid and non-partisan introduction, concluding that both men promoted theories with specific application to particular times and place but that neither produced a general theory of the trade cycle. (The Cambridge economist Dennis Robertson quipped that what Hayek called a boom Keynes called a slump.) Ironically, Hayek's over-investment theory of the cycle was least applicable to the depressed 1930s when it was launched, but could have found its application in Japan in the 1980s and 1990s when excessive investment helped trigger off a long-lasting recession. Any attempt, however, to revive the theory in a globalized economy would require an analysis of the effects of supporting investment by overseas capital inflows as well as by forced domestic savings.

The underlying divergence between Hayek and Keynes was rooted in the latter's growing conviction that a frequent and perhaps normal condition of capitalism was one of unused resources, a doctrine which was not fully set out until *The General Theory*, published in 1936. Hayek, on the other hand, tended to assume as a first approximation full employment of resources. Keynes's rapid victory was above all due to the fact that his theory was primarily directed to explain severe and persistent unemployment during one of the worst depressions of all time. In addition Keynes's theory was more easily translated into mathematical models which bore the hallmark of what was regarded as serious economics. Last but by no means least, Keynes was able to promote *The General Theory* by various means (including offering the book at an especially low price). By the end of the 1930s even the LSE was largely Keynesian.

Hayek wrote a long review of Keynes's earlier 1931 *Treatise on Money*, only to be told by the author (who was by then working on *The General Theory*): 'Oh, never mind; I no longer believe all that.' Hayek often declared that his greatest regret was his failure to write a critique of *The General Theory*, which after his earlier experience he was initially inclined to dismiss as a mere 'tract for the times'.There is nevertheless in the last few pages of *The Pure Theory of Capital* a sketch of Hayek's unwritten critique. In a section entitled 'Mr Keynes's Economics of Abundance', Hayek insists that abundant reserves of all resources are unlikely except in the depths of a severe depression. This still left open the question of where between the two extremes an economy would tend to be. The answer did not appear until Milton Friedman launched the concept of the 'natural rate of unemployment' (later rechristened the 'non-accelerating inflation' rate of unemployment or NAIRU) in 1967. The implicit answer was that the sustainable limit to economic activity was the point at which inflation began to accelerate.

Prices as signalling devices

Hayek himself came to regard a different and less technical essay, 'Economics and Knowledge', first published in 1937 (and usefully collected together with related papers in *Individualism and the Economic Order*, 1949) as his 'most original contribution to the theory of economics'; and it does indeed form the link between his economic ideas and his wider social philosophy. It set itself to answer the question: 'How can a combination of fragments of knowledge existing in different minds bring about results, which if they were to be brought about deliberately would require a knowledge on the part of the directing mind which no single person can possess?'

According to Hayek, a market system is a discovery technique. No computer can predict the emergence of new knowledge, original ideas, or innovations – and people's reactions to them. His scepticism about the use of econometric relationships was based on a wider epistemological view. For he insisted that the most important kind of knowledge was not of propositions or theories, but of practical skills and dispositions governed by rules which we may imperfectly discover afterwards, but not formulate in advance.

Contrary to popular repute, Hayek always believed that mathematics had an important role to play in economic theory as 'a beautiful way of describing certain patterns'. But he remarked that mathematical economists usually understood so little real mathematics that they believed their subject had to be quantitative and numerical. Unlike many mainstream neo-classical economists, Hayek saw the market as an example of human institutions, like language or law, which have evolved without any conscious plan on anyone's part. Whereas mainstream economists were preoccupied with the optimal allocation of resources in given conditions, Hayek was concerned with the effect of the market system on the evolution and stability of society. He insisted that wants, techniques and resources are not given, but are constantly changing – in part because of the activities of entrepreneurs who open up possibilities which people did not know existed before. (The dynamic and entrepreneurial aspect was also emphasized by another economist of Austrian origin, Joseph Schumpeter, thus providing a so-called 'Austrian' critique of mainstream neo-classical economics, which overlaps with the objections of 'radical' political economists.)

It was this turn in his economic thinking, quite as much as any politicial differences, which was responsible for Hayek's growing estrangement from the mainstream economics profession. It was not that they disagreed with his depiction of the market as a signalling and incentive device. It was much more that it was difficult to formulate it in terms of the models fashionable among the new generation of economists. A more legitimate criticism was that just as there could be market failures in traditional economics, due to the divergence of private from social costs, so there could be failures in signalling systems, which policy might try to improve. But Hayek had little to say on these, apart from his specialized work on business cycles which he did not revisit. Another problem was that his depiction of markets did not seem to lead to a research programme for further work. (A reasonably sympathetic critic described it as 'poetry'.) This deficiency was beginning to be remedied at the end of the twentieth century by researchers developing the mathematical theory of complexity, originally derived from physics and applied to phenomena such as earthquakes or biological cataclysms, but which they felt could be developed for the study of social events.

During the war years the LSE was evacuated to Cambridge; and Keynes took care that Hayek had comfortable rooms in King's College. Keynes himself would spend weekends in Cambridge and the two became friends, despite differences of outlook. Unlike Keynes, Hayek was in no sense a charismatic personality. But they had many shared interests, for instance in antiquarian books and biography. It was then that Hayek 'came across' the correspondence between John Stuart Mill and his future wife Harriet Taylor, which he subsequently published in 1951.

The Road to Serfdom

Contrary to widespread belief, Hayek did not suddenly 'leave economics' to write a political polemic. His inaugural lecture at the London School of Economics in 1933 was partly devoted to what he saw as the error of socialists who, from the best of motives, were liable to bring about results the very opposite of what he intended ('The Trend of Economic Thinking', reprinted in vol. III of the Routledge series). But he was no more happy with conservatives 'who never felt the urge to reconstruct the world and who frequently supported the forces of stability only for reasons of selfishness'.

The basic idea that a planned economy could not work because it would provide no basis for deciding what to produce and by what methods (the so-called 'calculation problem') was due not to Hayek but to his mentor von Mises. Hayek became involved through his role as an editor of a book on this debate (*Collectivist Economic Planning*, 1935) which also contained essays by socialists who wanted to use the market mechanism. Hayek's main contribution was to explain why it would not be possible for socialist enterprises simply to copy private enterprise principles, while remitting their profits to the state. The unexpected collapse of the Soviet Union and its satellites in 1989–91 supplied a belated vindication of his thesis.

The genesis of *The Road to Serfdom* was a memorandum he wrote in the late 1930s for William Beveridge, then director of the London School of Economics, protesting against the frequent depiction of Nazism and Fascism as forms of capitalism. He viewed them as collectivist systems, much closer to Soviet Communism than to anything in the USA or Britain. This memorandum was enlarged in 1939 for the 'public policy pamphlets' series of the University of Chicago Press. Hayek was induced to expand it further as a tract for a wider market by his alarm at the number of well-intentioned English writers who naively wished to continue wartime planning systems to direct the economy for conscious purposes in times of peace. He saw such centralized control as a threat not only to prosperity but to freedom. He did not pretend that most people enjoyed choice. The question was rather whether people should be left themselves to make inescapable choices or whether the decisions should be made for them by someone else.

A reader several decades later would have had to make some allowance for the historical circumstances. But that would have been all to the good. For Hayek had indeed seen all the supposedly progressive ideas he castigated advanced a generation earlier among German militaristic as well as socialist circles. Although central planning fell into dispute among political elites in the last twenty or thirty years of the twentieth century, there is always a danger that, faced with seemingly intractable problems, there will be a cry for a strong government 'to take a lead'. Hayek afterwards regretted that, because of the wartime alliance with the Soviet Union, he had to choose all his examples from German thinking and policy. But it was fortunate that he did so. He thereby removed his work from Cold War polemics and also provided a perennially needed reminder of the roots of collectivism in German metaphysics, which exalted society over the individual and poured scorn on the selfish and commercial motivation of the Anglo-Saxons.

The Road to Serfdom was far and away the most eloquent and straightforward statement of his political and economic outlook that Hayek ever achieved. It also seemed something of a miracle, given the sometimes tortuous nature of his other writing. Perhaps the greatest miracle was his choice of title, which is so important to the success of any popular work of political economy. The historian of ideas would give a lot to know who exactly suggested the title – the author, the publisher or some third party?

Apart from anything else, *The Road to Serfdom* is a very clear statement of certain economic verities, which mainstream economists would find it difficult to deny, but which rarely come out in their work. For instance it analysed what would happen if a planning authority tried to regulate the numbers in different employments by adjusting pay and other terms of work. Is not this an enlightened application of market principles? No, it is not. When a government authority fixes remuneration for a category of worker and supposedly selects them by merit 'the strength of people's desire for the job will count for very little. The person whose qualifications are not of the standard type, or whose temperament is not of the ordinary kind, will no longer be able to come to special arrangements with an employer.' Someone who prefers irregular hours or even a happy-go-lucky existence with a small and perhaps uncertain income to a regular routine will no longer have the choice. People will 'no longer be free to be rational and efficient, only when or where they think it worthwhile'. The individual would be used by authority to service such abstractions as the social welfare or the good of the community. These few sentences are worth more than all the 'research-based' studies of minimum wage laws of later decades.

In his preface to the 1976 edition Hayek explains that he subsequently 'tried hard to get back to economics proper' but he could not free himself of the feeling 'that the problems on which I had so undesignedly embarked were more challenging and important than those of economic theory; and that much more remained to be said.' Not all of those who criticized Hayek for leaving 'economics proper' were political opponents. Some just did not believe that such questions on the borders of politics, philosophy and economics lent themselves to academic study and that they were best discussed over coffee when economists were challenged by sociologists, politicians or journalists.

With *The Road to Serfdom* Hayek achieved what the editor of his collected works subsequently called his 'fifteen minutes of fame' and he was invited in 1946 to give a lecture tour of the United States where he was not always as politely received as in Britain. Although the book became an international best-seller, Hayek dated his ostracism by many fellow economists to that work, which they shunned as a popular polemic. Nevertheless his critique of 'planning' was more sympathetically received in Britain than it was in America. For instance, one leading British Fabian, Barbara Wootton, took pains to try to show that democratic planning need not be a threat to freedom. Some of Hayek's disciples have however made too much of Keynes's letter in which he said that 'morally and philosophically' he was 'in deeply moved agreement' with *The Road to Serfdom*. More indicative of their underlying differences was Keynes's remark: 'Dangerous acts can be done safely in a community which thinks and feels rightly, which would be the way to hell if they were executed by those who think wrongly.'

Although no politician, Hayek did indeed try to rally intellectual support. With aid from Swiss and American sympathizers he founded in 1947 the 'Mont Pélerin' group of scholars dedicated to the revival of classical liberalism and of which he was president for the next thirteen years and which continued to meet for the rest of the century and beyond. His most lasting practical legacy was probably the network of free market 'think tanks' he helped to inspire all over the world. He later remarked that if he had followed his natural inclination he would eventually have become active in public life; but his migration from one country to another made that impossible.

Chicago and after

To add to his problems, Hayek remarried in controversial circumstances. Owing to some misunderstanding, his youthful first love, Helen Bitterlich, had married someone else and Hayek himself went on to marry in 1926 Hella von Fritsch by whom he had a son and a daughter. But when he returned on a private visit to Vienna after the Second World War he found that he was then free to marry Helen Bitterlich, which he did in 1950, after divorcing his first wife. This led to estrangement from many of his closest associates in London, and especially Lionel Robbins, whose actions have been condemned by some as an example of 'illiberal liberalism' and explained by others as sympathy for Hayek's first wife. It was in any case this combined personal and professional distancing which helped to explain his move to Chicago, where he went in 1950 to take up a chair of social and moral science established by the interdisciplinary Committee on Social Thought, a post he held until 1962. (He had earlier been turned down by the economics faculty.)

His initial years in Chicago saw the publication in book form of two earlier works. *The Sensory Order* was the final form of a thesis he had developed in Vienna in the 1920s on philosophical psychology. In oversimplified form, the thesis was that there are inherent limits to the human mind's capacity to understand itself and that human beings know much more than they can ever explicitly explain. The second book, *The Counter-Revolution of Science* (1952) was based on wartime papers attacking 'scientism', by which he meant the pitfalls which arise when the social sciences believe they can ape too closely the methods of the natural ones. His scepticism was initially based on the 'Austrian' belief that the data of the social sciences were inherently subjective. In later papers, reproduced in *Essays in Philosophy, Politics and Economics* (1967), he shifted his ground – partly under the influence of Popper – somewhat away from subjectivity towards the more persuasive one of the complexity of social phenomena. He maintained that the social sciences – in common with biology – dealt with complex phenomena which are susceptible only to predictions of pattern and not to specific forecasts. For Hayek the cardinal sin of his time was something known by the ungainly label of 'constructivism'. This was akin to what Michael Oakeshott called 'rationalism', and is the error of believing that any order we find in society has been put there by a designing mind – and can be, accordingly, redesigned from scratch. His continuing concern was 'with the results of human action but not of human intention', a phrase which he took from the Scottish philosopher Adam Ferguson (1723–1816). This led him away from the Benthamite utilitarianism, which he had originally imbibed from von Mises, towards a version of rule utilitarianism.

The main achievement of his Chicago years was *The Constitution of Liberty*, published in 1960. His concern in that book was for 'that condition of man in which coercion of some by others is reduced as much as possible'. However, he did not in fact provide any easily recognizable criteria for identifying state interventions of the harmful type. The free-market arguments in *The Road to Serfdom* were based on the incompatibility of central planning with personal liberty. But now Hayek approached the issue indirectly. He argued that the main condition for a free society is what he called 'the rule of law'. By that he meant a presumption in favour of general rules and against discretionary power. He attempted to derive from this conception not only the fundamental political and legal basis, but also the economic policies, of a free society. Many writers of the most diverse political persuasions accepted that general rules were an important protection – perhaps the most important single protection – for freedom. But Hayek was criticized for suggesting that general laws were a sufficient condition for a free society. Many policies involving a high degree of coercion can be imposed by general rules – for example, a ban on the teaching of evolution or on any literature or music which flouts the principles of Marxist-Leninism.

There is no one philosopher's stone for minimizing coercion in society. Hayek's concern to restore a government of laws rather than men can be seen from his later writings, which warned of the degeneration of democracy into a struggle for spoils among competing groups. He saw the source of interest-group domination in what he called 'majoritarian' or unlimited democracy. This is the belief that a government elected by a majority of voters (usually a plurality) should be able to enact what it likes without any check – a system which Lord Hailsham was to call an 'elective dictatorship'. Some of Hayek's own later constitutional proposals struck even his admirers as far-fetched. But their underlying aim was important. It was to recover an older idea of a state, which has no purposes of its own, but provides a framework of rules and arrangements under which people can pursue their own individual aims without getting in each other's way. This ideal – which is a long way removed from the practice of any modern government, even of the radical right – has been labelled by Oakeshott as a 'civil association', as opposed to the more usual idea of the state as an 'enterprise association' with its own aims and purposes. The close similarity of the later work of both Hayek and Oakeshott, pursued in relative isolation, is a theme which deserves a study of its own.

Politics apart, Hayek ascribed his isolation from postwar economics partly to the fact that he never sympathized with either macroeconomics or econometrics. At a time when most go-ahead economists were raring to equip themselves with forecasting models and computer print-outs, Hayek, in contrast to Milton Friedman, seemed an armchair thinker, preoccupied with problems such as the limitations of human knowledge. But in the longer haul the contrast did not necessarily tell against Hayek. A disadvantage of late twentieth-century methodological orthodoxy, carefully explained in *Studies in Philosophy, Politics and Economics*, is that many economists acquired a vested interest in the existence of stable, discoverable numerical relationships between phenomena such as income and consumption, or short-run changes in the money supply and the price level. Hayek warned that one could not guarantee the successful discovery of such relationships, but that scientific method could still be applied to predict certain general features of interacting systems – as it is, for instance, in biology and linguistics. Despite his friendship and ideological sympathy with Milton Friedman, he regarded the stress on prediction in Friedman's *Essays in Positive Economics* as quite as dangerous as anything that Keynes had written.

Although Hayek spent over a decade in Chicago he never really felt at home in the United States. He was also growing increasingly deaf and had ceased to go to the theatre – thus leaving mountaineering as his main extra-curricular interest. In 1962 he accepted a professorship of Economic Policy in Freiburg in Breisgau in Germany where he enjoyed a pretty free rein. This was followed by a less happy period as a professor in Salzburg from 1969 to 1977; and he then returned to Freiburg where he spent the rest of his days.

The Nobel Prize

Hayek suffered more than one fit of depression in later life. The first was in 1960, which he ascribed to his cessation of smoking because of a false medical alarm. A subsequent depression occurred in the early 1970s, which he attributed to a doctor erroneously treating him for diabetes. But his disappointment with the initial reception of *The Constitution of Liberty* and his self-observation that after his seventieth birthday in 1969 his mental powers 'began noticeably to decline' could also have been relevant.

The award of a Nobel Prize for economics in 1974, jointly with the left-inclined Swedish economist Gunnar Myrdal, was followed by a rejuvenation. Even that award had its bitter-sweet side. For his Nobel address, *The Pretence of Knowledge*, was rejected by *Economica*, the journal of the LSE of which he had previously been editor; and it was eventually published by the free market Institute of Economic Affairs. But among political theorists and sociologists, even those critical of the New Right, he was studied more seriously than the more fashionable economic technicians. (A good example is Andrew Gamble, *The Iron Cage of Liberty*, 1996.)

Hayek's last major work of social philosophy was entitled *Law, Legislation and Liberty* (1973–9). He originally described it as a tailpiece to *The Constitution of Liberty*. But what attracted most attention was a postscript in which he ascribed the success of certain institutions to their evolutionary success in the struggle for survival. This came dangerously near to justifying whatever system happened to exist – including by inference the Communist order which still prevailed in Russia. Some of his strongest earlier supporters, such as Norman Barry (*Classical Liberalism in the Age of Post-Communism*, 1995), complained that his previous critical rationalism had been 'almost completely jettisoned in favour of a curious, neo-Darwinian form of social evolutionism'.

There were thus great ultimate differences between Hayek and some others who shared a similar outlook. Unlike most classical liberals, Hayek's espousal of liberty turned out to be based neither on ultimate judgements, nor on considerations of welfare, utility or happiness. He did not even accept the methodological individualism of most mainstream economists. For him, the key to institutions was natural selection among competing traditions. This evolutionary approach remained in the background in the classic politico-economic works of his middle period. But its roots went back to his student reflections on biology.

Meanwhile, in the world of public affairs, Hayek's return to public attention also owed something to the proclaimed adherence of Margaret Thatcher, British 'radical right' Prime Minister from 1979 to 1990. One Hayek obituary remarked that if she was, as she proclaimed, 'a conviction politician', the convictions were those of Hayek. Yet the conclusion was not quite fair to either. Although the former UK Conservative leader was an admirer, Hayek mainly provided articulation and confirmation of convictions she had already reached. The admiration was reciprocated, yet there was much in his writings that some saw as at variance with Thatcherite practice.

Competitive money

Hayek never ceased commenting on topical economic issues. He had always been distrustful of purely national currencies floating against each other. In a prewar work, *Monetary Nationalism and International Stability* (1937) he came out in favour of a fixed international standard. This would probably be gold, but he had no particular preference for that over any other reference point. During the Second World War he published a proposal for an international currency which would be convertible into a basket of commodities on a predetermined basis. ('A Commodity Reserve Currency', *Economic Journal*, vol. 53, 1943.) He was here supporting and amplifying similar proposals put forward earlier by Benjamin Graham and Frank D. Graham. Such ideas faded from public view, as the Bretton Woods system developed at the end of the war came to be based on national currencies linked by 'fixed but adjustable' exchange rates. It may or may not be a coincidence (most likely it was common causality) that the breakdown of Bretton Woods coincided with the great inflation of the 1970s, probably the largest peacetime inflation of the twentieth century, apart from the hyperinflations following the two world wars.

In the 1970s Hayek went on to propose free competition, not only between national currencies, but between privately issued ones as well. This started 'as a bitter joke' directed against what he regarded as the chronic inability of governments to provide sound money. But it led him into the 'fascinating problem of what would happen if money were provided competitively'. His analysis of this topic proved to be his most detailed pronouncement on monetary matters for several decades (*The Denationalisation of Money*, Institute of Economic Affairs, 1978). A number of economists devoted serious attention to these proposals. Indeed, competition between different official (but not private) currencies was the main alternative put forward by the British government in various guises to the plan for a European currency – the euro – which was finally launched in 1999. (See chapter on Currency Competition, p. 177 et seq.) Notions of competitive currencies enjoyed a certain vogue, especially but not only among opponents of European monetary union. But what their exponents could never explain was what prevented this competition from developing in countries such as the UK, where legal tender laws were not restrictive and people could contract in whatever currencies they chose.

Much more was likely to be heard of competitive private enterprise currencies in the course of the twenty-first century. The progress of electronic money and instant communication via the internet was a long-term threat to the central bank monopoly of base money – cash and bank reserves. Electronic transactions could reach a point where the private sector might make settlements 'without the need for clearing through the central bank'. This threatened the whole concept of an official national money, a possibility outlined by none other than the then Deputy Governor of the Bank Of England, Mervyn King ('Challenges for Monetary Policy', *Bank of England Bulletin*, November 1999).

An iconoclast to the end

In 1988 Hayek produced a final book, *The Fatal Conceit*, which some readers have found a refreshingly straightforward guide to his teachings. It needs however to be stressed that this book emerged near the end of his life, and after an illness, and that it was heavily edited by W. Bartley with the aid of a host of scholars apart from Hayek himself.

Whatever the status of this last volume, Hayek remained to the end much more iconoclastic than his more conventional supporters would have liked. He could, for instance, never subscribe to any religious belief; and late in life he reiterated in an interview that he found monotheistic religions more objectionable than some others because they tended to be more intolerant of competition and dissent.

As far as the economy was concerned, he never imagined that there was anything just in market rewards. These depended on an unpredictable mixture of effort, ability and luck. Quite apart from the adverse economic consequences, it was not desirable even to try to reward merit through public policy, which would involve some authority deciding how much pain and effort a task had cost and how much of a person's achievement was due to outside circumstances.

Hayek's own inability to resolve the ultimate conundrums of

human conduct should not obscure the range of his achievements. His writings have asserted the case for general rules over discretionary authority. They have exposed the misleading identification of liberal democracy with the divine right of temporary majorities. They have demonstrated the connection between economic and personal freedoms. They have shown that the domination of both the political and economic market place by interest group struggles is a source of evil; and they have explained why pecuniary rewards neither can nor should reflect merit. In presenting him as a revered thinker with a complete system, his followers may have made his work neater, simpler and less interesting than it really was. In all these matters Hayek, like Keynes or Friedman or the American philosopher John Rawls or other such seminal figures, is best treated as an intellectual iconoclast rather than a pundit with all the answers.

Bibliography

N. Barry, *Hayek's Social and Economic Philosophy* (Macmillan, London, 1979).

N. Barry, *Classical Liberalism in the Age of Post-Communism* (Edward Elgar, Cheltenham, 1996).

A. Gamble, *Hayek: The Iron Cage of Liberty* (Polity, Cambridge, 1996).

R. M. Hartwell, *A History of the Mont Pelerin Society* (Liberty Fund, Indianapolis, 1995).

F. A. Hayek, *The Collected Works of F. A. Hayek*, (ed.) Bartley *et al.* (University of Chicago Press, Chicago, 1988–92).

F. A. Hayek, *Hayek on Hayek: An Autobiographical Dialogue*, (ed.) S. Kresge and L. Wenar (Routledge, London, 1994).

J. R. Hicks, *Capital and Time: A Neo-Austrian Theory* (Clarendon Press, Oxford, 1973).

L. Robbins, *Autobiography of an Economist* (Macmillan, London, 1971).

Why Be Interested in Ayn Rand?

To the typical left-of-centre English intellectual, the free market school is a mass of repellent wrong-headedness. But to anyone with sufficient curiosity to look a little further, this school is ridden with as many internal differences of opinion and personality conflicts as Marxism, New Labour or any other body of thought.

Take the late Friedrich Hayek. He is best known in Britain as Margaret Thatcher's frequently cited intellectual guru. But for his own mentor, Ludwig von Mises, who was a purer advocate of laissez-faire, matters stood very differently. At a dinner they both attended Hayek remarked that it was a pity that there was no longer any intellectually worthy exponent of socialism with whom one could engage. To which von Mises replied: 'There is one sitting right beside me.'

But even von Mises was regarded as philosophically unsound by the high-profile American writer Ayn Rand. For he based his support of free markets on the same utilitarian grounds that many British Fabians advocated socialism – crudely summarized as the greatest good for the greatest number. Ayn Rand regarded him as philosophically incorrect, being stuck in the groove of altruism.

Added to all this, she was, like all too many advocates of freedom, intolerant of the slightest dissent and quick to excommunicate people from her circle. A notable example was Nathaniel Branden, at one time her closest collaborator. But when he declined to renew an affair with her when she was sixty-three and he was twenty-five years younger, he was utterly cut off. All later editions of their joint works contain the disclaimer that Branden was no longer associated with her or her 'objectivist' movement. Her appointed intellectual heir, Leonard Peikoff, writes at the beginning of his guide *Objectivism – the Philosophy of Ayn Rand*: 'Our discussions were not a collaboration; I asked questions; she answered them.'

One of the few people who were allowed to develop in their own way without being excommunicated was Alan Greenspan, later the world-renowned chairman of the Fed. In Greenspan's essays, published in the 1960s when he was working with Rand, you can find an attack on the Anti-Trust Acts as destructive of enterprise and an onslaught on all regulation, including bodies such as the Securities and Exchange Commission with which he now has a lot to do. He also endorsed the gold standard as indispensable to economic freedom. I suspect that he still hankers after gold and regards the paper money system he is running as second best. Rand, of course, always rejected the second best with contempt.

This bald recital will put many people off Rand altogether. I have not been able to find, even among the most Thatcherite of Conservatives, anyone whose attitude to her is other than ignorance, hostility or indifference. She died in 1982 and I would not be able to write even this qualified appeal to take her seriously without embarrassment if she were still alive. For she shared the early Communist attitude of 'He who is not with us is against us.'

Yet I found three reasons for investigating her thought further. First, although her following is very largely based in the United States, she was not at all the Waspish Daughter of the American Revolution that some might suppose. She was born in Russia as Alice Rosenbaum and, although she came to the United States in 1926 at the age of twenty-one, she never – to her intense regret – lost her original Russian accent. (The name Rand was derived from the typewriter in which the newly arrived American author wrote her first English language works.) Indeed, it is quite possible that she met my mother, who was also a Russian Jewess, when both their families took refuge on the Black Sea coast during the Russian civil war. They would probably not have got on. For my mother's attitude both to the Bolsheviks and their White Russian opponents was more like 'a plague on both your houses'. This could have had something to do with the fact that, while Rand came from St Petersburg, my mother came from Lithuania, and when her family returned to that bourgeois republic they were greeted by a hostile caretaker with the words 'Who asked you to come back?'

Although she claimed her views were based on pure reason and disliked any attempt to trace them to her own experiences, she maintained a closer link with the Russian-speaking world than she admitted. When she discovered that her favourite younger sister, whom she had not seen for forty-seven years, was alive in the Soviet Union, she arranged for her and her husband, a retired engineer, to visit the USA and hoped that they would settle down in a Russian-speaking circle in New Jersey. To her intense disappointment her sister and brother-in-law did not feel at home in America and decided after six weeks to return to Russia. Even worse: the sister would not read her books and preferred Solzhenitsyn, whom Rand detested for his theocratic views.

Her politics were thus not quite what might be supposed. She had an unhappy flirtation with American conservatives in the mid-1940s but soon decided that they had no principles. She was fiercely opposed to conscription and profoundly disapproved of the intervention in Vietnam and other overseas military interventions. Later she refused to support Ronald Reagan because religion was a minor part of his platform. Imagine what she would have said about George W. Bush. Today's neo-cons would have found her a thorn in their sides.

The second interesting feature was that she made her original impact not by academic or political tracts, but by a series of novels. This was not just a tactic for promoting her views. She declared that for her fiction came first. Like many other authors, she started writing stories as a child and declared she wanted to be a novelist at the age of nine. She wanted to present ideal human beings. But before she could do so she felt she needed to work out a personal philosophy. It was only in the last twenty-five years of her life, after she had finished her novel *Atlas Shrugged*, that she turned most of her attention to essays on philosophy, politics and economics – although not in a way that would be suggested by the degree course at Oxford covered by these headings. She once said that if all philosophers had to embody their ideas in novels there would be fewer but better philosophers.

To the irritation of the mainstream American intelligentsia, her novels were extremely successful, having sold over thirty million copies. This is far more than has been achieved by Friedman, Hayek and all other academic defenders of capitalism put together. Rand even had her face on a US postage stamp, an honour bestowed while Clinton was president. An example of her continuing presence in American, as distinct from English, literary life can be seen in the well-received novel *Old School* by Tobias Wolff. She appears there as one of three writers who are invited annually to meet prize pupils at a posh American school. The other two in her year are Robert Frost and Ernest Hemingway. I cannot say she comes well out of the encounter, but she appears as a force to be reckoned with. If minority views achieve a mass readership and students insist on discussing them, at least a few in the academic world will eventually be forced to take them seriously, as happened in her case.

Rand established a cult still very much alive in the United States. Book after book, not to speak of several websites, have been published there promoting, attacking or qualifying her ideas. She reaches levels to which more staid authors cannot hope to penetrate. My colleague Ed Crooks, economics editor of the *Financial Times*, is extremely well read. But he had heard of Rand mainly because she was idolized by the pop group Rush and especially its drummer and lyricist, Neal Peart. Indeed I discovered a network of websites devoted to the philosophical implications of 'progressive rock', but at this point I realized I was well out of my depth.

The inspiration for Rand's final novel, *Atlas Shrugged*, came from a conversation she had in 1943 when somebody suggested that she should write a non-fiction work outlining her philosophy. 'Why should I? I am not an altruist,' she replied. She then suggested that she might go on strike and proposed an imaginative investigation into what would happen if all the creative people went absent and left the world to the mediocre masses and the 'looters' who were their leaders.

Some friends advised me that I would enjoy more her earlier novel, *The Fountainhead*; and I would indeed have been tempted by the still earlier *We the Living*, based on her Russian period. But as her books are long and she declared *Atlas Shrugged* to be her definitive statement, I persevered with the latter. Viewed as a work of fiction, the quality is decidedly mixed. Her characters are archetypes rather than credible human beings; there is much repetition in the many ideological speeches; and around about page 400 I felt tempted to abandon it. But I was glad I persevered. For she writes with verve and a real gift for storytelling and contrives unexpected twists to the plot. By the time I got to page 800 I decided to devote a weekend to finishing it off (page 1069!).

The third, and most serious reason for coming to terms with Rand is the fundamental challenge she poses to collectivism in all its varieties. As she quite rightly points out, the supporters of competitive capitalism have been on the defensive for hundreds of years, despite the successes of the system, and will continue to do so as long as they leave the moral high ground to their opponents. She stood in opposition to what she regarded as many centuries of religious preaching devoted to the subjugation of self in the interests of altruism. She threw down the gauntlet by exalting 'selfishness', but she did herself no favours thereby. Her own essay on selfishness shows that what she meant was not giving in to the whims of the moment but pursuing a self-chosen heroic purpose in life. Her models were people like Brunel and Henry Ford and in our own day might well have been Bill Gates. The hero of *Atlas Shrugged* spent most of his time in the most menial of jobs in protest against the creeping collectivization of his country.

Rand was at first attracted by the German philosopher Friedrich Nietzsche, who worshipped the rational, purposeful, independent and courageous hero who lived by his own efforts and for his own happiness. But she soon abandoned him as a spiritual ally because, unlike Nietzsche, she believed that the superior man could not be bothered enslaving others and she was totally opposed to physical force other than for self-defence.

In fact both altruism and selfishness become absurdly self-contradictory if taken to such extreme lengths. The heroine of *Atlas Shrugged*, Dagny, only agrees to accept a bracelet from her lover when the latter insists that he enjoys seeing her wearing it. She would not have accepted if the object had been to give her pleasure. This is too tortuous by half. Suppose that her lover derived pleasure from giving her a trinket that he knew she wanted, even though he did not particularly care for it himself. Who is to rule it out as unacceptably altruistic? Rand's true ideal was not happiness in the mundane Benthamite sense but something more like self-regard. It is akin to the Victorian ideal of 'self-realization' which was much debated between John Stuart Mill and his critics.

You do not have to hunt for far-out American authors to see the contradictions in universal altruism either. John Macmurray, the little-known Scottish philosopher whom the young Tony Blair chose as his spiritual guide, wrote: 'If we say that goodness consists of serving the community then everybody must serve. If I want to serve other people, I can't do it unless they're willing to be served. If everybody is to serve, then there is nobody to accept the service. We can't be unselfish if nobody is prepared to be selfish.' Then again: 'The goodness of a man's life is its own quality, its integrity, not in any service that he does to other people or to the state or the church or the future.' These are not passages much cited by the present Prime Minister.

Tucked away at the very end of later editions of *Atlas Shrugged* you can find six principles of objectivism, presumably formulated by Peikoff. Abbreviated and with slight changes in terminology they come to the following:

1. The external world exists independently of human consciousness and is what it seems to be. This is what Bertrand Russell called 'naive realism'.
2. Contrary to the sceptical doubter, full knowledge of the world is possible.
3. Free will is embraced to the fullest extent and any belief that man is a victim of upbringing, genes, economic conditions or any other forces beyond his control indignantly rejected.
4a. Ethical values can be determined rationally and do not reflect subjective preferences.
4b. Rationality rejects any form of altruism. Every man must live for his own sake, neither sacrificing himself to others nor others to himself.
5a. No one has the right to seek his ends by physical force which should only be used in self-defence.

5b. The only social system that bars physical force from human relations is laissez-faire capitalism in which people give value for value as traders.

6. The true form of art is romantic realism. Men are presented in her novels as they ought to be, but realistically in that they are placed on this earth together with the looters and second-hand merchants that surround them.

The earlier principles do not entail the later ones. Contrary to what Rand thought, it is logically possible to accept some of them without accepting others. There is no reason, for instance, for a naive realist in philosophy to be a thoroughgoing capitalist or vice versa. One has to pick, choose and modify among them. What I want to persuade readers is that the effort to do so is worth making.

The doctrine of Rand, which differentiates her from most political economists otherwise on her side, is that she believes that income derived from a person's own efforts rightfully belongs to him and any attempt to tax it away or regulate its use is immoral. The argument reminded me of the clash in the 1970s between the two foremost American political philosophers, John Rawls and Robert Nozick. While Rawls regarded all the resources of a community as a common pool to be distributed according to just principles, Nozick (in his earlier years) believed that the individual had the right to anything he had justly earned or justly acquired or inherited.

The debate between the two schools is perennial. It is based on a mixture of value judgements and factual economic assertions which are almost impossible to unravel. But as a value judgement I would be prepared to take the Rand-Nozick stance that people are entitled to what they earn or legitimately possess. But that does not imply that all non-voluntary transfers to help the less well-off are immoral. Citizens are surely entitled to decide to make these transfers; and from here it is but a short step to advocating compulsion to tackle the free rider problem posed by those who say 'Why should I make voluntary transfers when I know that others will cheat and pay nothing or very little?'

But there is still a chasm several leagues wide between those who think of resources as belonging to individuals who might arrange transfers through political means, and make a modicum of regulation to deal with spillover effects that the market cannot take into account, and those who believe that the state is the ultimate owner and that every individual holding needs to be justified. The tortuous attempt of present-day Conservatives to champion the taxpayer without reducing the role of the state shows how much Rand's teachings are still needed, if with a pinch of Lithuanian salt.

Norman Angell

Entry in *Biographical Dictionary of British Economists,* 2004

Career

Ralph Norman Angell Lane was born on 26 December 1872 in Holbeach, Lincolnshire. He died on 7 October 1967 in Croydon, Surrey.

He was brought up in a well-to-do but unpretentious middle-class household. His father, Thomas Angell Lane, had established a chain of local shops before retiring to become a gentleman magistrate with a taste for French classics. He quietly encouraged Ralph Norman in his precocious reading of political texts. The young Angell attended elementary schools in England, but had the good fortune to be sent to a French *lycée* at St Omer. Having escaped the confining influences of the conventional English public (that is private) boarding school, he found himself at the age of seventeen editing a bi-weekly English language newspaper in Geneva, catering mainly for tourists. Simultaneously he was taking courses at Geneva University. He was, however, essentially self-taught. He happened to read John Stuart Mill's *On Liberty* during an illness at the age of twelve and this was for a long time his guiding light. But he also devoured the work of other 'public intellectuals', such as Voltaire, Huxley, Spencer and Carlyle.

His family would gladly have financed a British university course, probably in Cambridge. But by the age of seventeen Angell was so appalled by the lack of interest of so many of his family and friends in his ideas, and so despaired of the rulers of Europe adopting rational policies that he decided to immerse himself in manual labour in California. Despite being only five foot tall and of frail appearance, he was physically very resilient. For seven years he worked as a vine planter, irrigation ditch digger, cow puncher, and smallholder in the new Western state. But eventually he concluded that life in the wilderness posed quite as many problems as life in a city, and he accepted offers to be a reporter, first for the St Louis *Globe Democrat* and later the *San Francisco Chronicle*. It was not the physical hardships that made for unhappiness. 'This came from the anxieties and uncertainties, the fear of debt, the presence of creditors whenever I should go to town.'

He returned to England for family reasons in 1898 and then earned his living working for small journals, both in French and in English, in Paris. He was in that city during the Dreyfus case, where French anti-Semitism made a deep impression on him, as had American aggressiveness in the Spanish American War and British jingoism in the Boer War. This led to the publication of his first book, *Patriotism under Three Flags: A Plea for Rationalism in Politics* (1903). This fell stillborn from the press; but in the course of occasional contacts he impressed Northcliffe, who appointed him as the first editor and manager of the Paris edition of the *Daily Mail*, a post he occupied from 1905 to 1912. It was during this period that he wrote in his spare time the book for which he achieved lasting fame, and in some quarters notoriety.

The Great Illusion

It originated in 1909 as a short essay, issued at his own expense, under the title 'Europe's Optical Illusion' by 'Norman Angell', a style he later legalized as his own name. Gradually news of it spread by word of mouth. In his autobiography he described the book as 'a publishing success but political failure'.

From 1912 onwards he supported himself as a freelance writer, lecturer and journalist. In all he wrote forty-one books – 'too many' he afterwards wrote. It is for *The Great Illusion* that he will be remembered. He obviously had practical managerial and journalistic abilities. Otherwise Northcliffe would hardly have tolerated someone with opinions almost diametrically opposed to his own aggressive anti-Germanism as a collaborator. Indeed, Northcliffe continued to see Angell after 1912 and offered him the hospitality of the *Daily Mail* for articles which took issue with his own positions.

Angell never seemed to have ambitions for an academic position and wrote mainly for the educated general public. He laboured at telling home truths which academic economists acknowledged but were too ready to take for granted. He was warmly praised for his efforts by Keynes. His chief sorrow was that the wider public, such as the mass readers of the *Daily Mail*, would not abandon their prejudices and perform a little rational analysis. It is perhaps as well that he did not live into the age of late twentieth-century tabloid journalism, television and spin doctors. He was not a conventional pacifist but he advocated British neutrality during the period leading up to the First World War. This brought him into the company of Labour leaders such as Ramsay MacDonald, who opposed participation in the First World War and also of course intellectuals such as Bertrand Russell. The fact that most of his political supporters came from one wing of the Labour party propelled him into that party and from 1929 to 1931 he was a Labour MP.

Doctrinally he was from the beginning a classical liberal and a strong opponent of Marxist theories that war was the product of capitalism – theories that were influential even among Labour Members who disavowed Marx. Although his primary interest was international affairs, he was equally infuriated when such MPs took the view that nothing could be done about the gathering economic depression unless capitalism was abolished. He did not stand for re-election in 1931 because he felt 'better fitted to present the case for internationalism to the public direct, freed from party ties'. He was knighted in 1931; and a dinner in his honour was presided over by the very same man, Lord (Robert) Cecil, who had refused him a passport in 1916. He was far more pleased with the Nobel Peace Prize awarded in 1933.

In the interwar years, he was concerned to promote collective security against the dictators and he devoted some years of his life, before, during and after the Second World War to trying to convince the Americans to come to Britain's side in defence of civilization. He found himself having to fight on two fronts, against the right-wing isolationists and against the American left who, with some sympathizers in the Roosevelt household, wanted to back Stalin in his confrontations with Churchill. Not surprisingly he was later a strong supporter of western defence efforts in the Cold War period. The urge to bury himself in physical activity never deserted him, even though from his sixties onwards he developed severe migraines which prevented him from getting more than four or five hours' sleep a night. He was a keen sailor all his life and bought Northey Island, a small island on the Blackwater Estuary. As far as is known, he showed no interest in partners of either sex, and as he put it, craved his 'daily bath of solitude', but was delighted to entertain his nephew and niece on boating holidays. Despite his health problems, he continued lecturing in the USA until the age of ninety. He was too rational to believe that he could defeat mortality and he died in a Surrey nursing home at the age of ninety-four.

Assessment

His lifelong sorrow was the frequent misrepresentation of *The Great Illusion*. He was alleged to have said that war was impossible because of its great expense, a misrepresentation still current in the twenty-first century. As he so often remarked, he would hardly have gone to the trouble to write and promote this book if he believed that war could not happen or would fizzle out very quickly. On the contrary, the illusion which he tackled was that wars could be economically advantageous. He was writing against a background of the German drive to build battleships and acquire colonies. In a curious way these German beliefs were supported by British jingoists who believed that the Germans were bound to break out in search of *Lebensraum* and that a coming clash was therefore inevitable.

The Great Illusion did not, of course, contain equations and was quite sparse in statistics. But it gave illustration after illustration to show the fallacy of treating nations as if they were individual people. He cited for instance the 'German' acquisition of Alsace-Lorraine after the Franco-Prussian war. Did it give the German people access to steel and coal? No. They had to buy the products of former French provinces just as they did before. Another example was the British conquest of South Africa. The gold and diamond mines remained with their original owners and the British had to purchase their products as before. He also cited the case of small countries such as Norway and Switzerland, which attained high standards of living without colonies or conquests, simply by trading in the open market. War was a waste of resources – or as later economists would put it – a negative sum game.

The basic Angell thesis stands the test of time pretty well. An opponent might cite the success of cartels in forcing up the prices of key commodities for periods of years. But such cartels have never been a main feature of the world economy. The period when the oil producers' cartel (OPEC) did most harm – after the Yom Kippur war of 1973 – was also a period when inflationary overheating in all the main industrial countries was in any case pushing up the market price of fuel and gave OPEC its opportunity. Given the role of Middle Eastern wars in acting as a trigger for such cartel action, it would have been ludicrous to suggest that western economies would have benefited from a punitive expedition to Saudi Arabia, which was the lynchpin of OPEC.

Victors in war have sometimes inadvertently demonstrated the validity of the Angell thesis by trying to force the defeated governments to cover the wartime losses of the winning side. An indemnity was imposed on France after the Franco-Prussian war of 1870–71 and a reparations burden was imposed on Germany after the First World War. The French indemnity was never more than a tiny fraction of the imperial German national income; and it was notorious that German reparations were never paid, as Keynes, along with Angell, had warned they could not be. A more telling criticism might be that Angell assumed too readily the moral standards of nineteenth-century capitalism under which a victorious government continued to buy on world markets and did not just seize the assets of the defeated country. He took for granted, for instance, that the British government would not have wished to destroy its international credit rating by seizing the South African mines after the Boer War. The Soviet Union did not of course always accept the rules of capitalist trade – notoriously so when the Red Army simply seized machinery and industrial plant from the eastern part of Germany which it occupied after the Second World War. But again the benefit, if any, of this captured material to the USSR was far less than the horrendous economic damage inflicted by the German invasion.

The Angell argument is more vulnerable when the enemy is not a conventional state but international groupings of, say, religious fundamentalists who purport to despise the materialism of the West and regard death in terrorist action against the US and its allies as the most honourable fate that can befall a young man. This was not of course a new phenomenon. There had been the kamikaze Japanese pilots in the Second World War; and for centuries in Europe the feudal code treated honour as infinitely superior to worldly riches. Shakespeare's plays contain numerous speeches on these lines, as well as, on the other side, the famous dismissal of honour put into the mouth of Sir John Falstaff.

Neither Angell or any other political economist can 'refute' such codes of honour. Indeed Angell was careful to point out that he did not regard economic rivalries as the only cause of war, but wanted to dispel them as a contributory factor. Nor was he worried by the assertion 'you can't change human nature'. He did not dispute this, but argued that human behaviour could be changed by the equivalent of a Hobbesian sovereign in international affairs. He gave numerous instances where barbaric practices such as duelling, judicial torture or burning religious nonconformists had been eliminated or forced to the margin inside individual countries. He did live long enough to see how easily this moral progress could be put into reverse even in domestic politics and was thus – to the pain of some of his earlier friends on the left – one of the first to argue for rearmament against Nazi Germany and for an alert western defence against the Soviet threat. Indeed the limited part that reason plays in human affairs makes it all the more important that this should be true reason rather than the false arguments of the geopoliticians against whom Angell fought all his life.

The fallacies he fought continued well into the twenty-firstst century. One example was the frequent belief that the US desired or needed to dominate the Middle East for the sake of oil, without realizing that Middle Eastern countries needed to sell the oil as much as the West needed to buy it.

A card game

Angell made one venture into economics, more narrowly understood, when he invented a card game, described in *The Money Game* (1928). This was an attempt to explain matters such as deflation and inflation in visual terms which the ordinary person could understand. It could be regarded as the precursor to the National Income Machine which A. W. Phillips invented at the London School of Economics after the Second World War, in which the flow of spending through the economy was shown by means of coloured water with taps that could be turned on and off.

Such devices went out of fashion with the increasing mathematical complexity of economic models which were more difficult to illustrate by visual devices. Opponents also said that such teaching devices ignored the subtle complexities introduced by the vagaries of human nature into the workings of the economy. But the more sophisticated mathematical models were even more mechanistic and the governing principles were more difficult even for their inventors to discern. If there were ever a serious attempt at mass economic education there would be a case for returning to the Angell-Phillips tradition, so long as it was made clear that these devices can only illustrate guiding principles and cannot encompass the institutional variety of actual economies.

Bibliography

Norman Angell, *The Great Illusion*, William Heinemann, London, 1909.

Norman Angell, *The Great Illusion Now*, Penguin, London, 1910.

Norman Angell, *After All: The Autobiography of Norman Angell*, Hamish Hamilton, London, 1951.

J. D. B. Miller, *Norman Angell and the Futility of War*, Macmillan, London, 1986.

In Defence of the Late Bertrand Russell

Review of Ray Monk, *Bertrand Russell*, vol. II, *1921–1970: The Ghost of Madness*, Jonathan Cape (incorporating passages from my introduction to new Routledge edition of *Russell's Power*, 2004) *The Spectator*, 14 April 2001

The second volume of the biography of Bertrand Russell by Ray Monk seems to have brought out the worst in both author and most reviewers. The typical response has been 'Silly old man. He was lost when he left the rarefied world of mathematical logic and proceeded to make a mess of both his family life and his intrusions into politics.'

To which my riposte would be 'Silly old reviewers'. I brought myself up on the later Bertrand Russell and found much of what he had to say on ethics and politics eminently sensible. He only went to pieces between the ages of ninety and ninety-eight when his pronouncements were taken over by the American radical Ralph Schoenman. It was in that period that he gave up all pretence at even-handedness between the Soviet Union and the USA. Pronouncements of the 'Bertrand Russell Foundation' started describing American and British leaders as war criminals, entirely responsible for the threat to humanity. But the few people who managed to see him in his North Wales home did not find his perfectly coherent conversations at all resembling those of the 'Foundation'; and most of us would be delighted if we could do as well if we lived to that age. In the end Russell did repudiate Schoenman, even if the lead in so doing was taken by his fourth and final wife, Edith.

There is no need to deny that he made a mess of relations in his marriages and with his children. Even here a more charitable interpretation is possible than Monk's. He was undoubtedly – and with good reason – haunted by the fear of madness which had afflicted so many in his family. It is also possible that, like some other intellectuals of his generation, he felt it necessary to demonstrate his rejection of Victorian Christian ethics by an aggressive promiscuity. But his personal behaviour does not invalidate his reflections on the ethics of war or other political pronouncements.

Russell continued to produce philosophy in the second half of his life; and I wish that Monk had said more about his later works and given less, ultimately boring, detail about the day-to-day vicissitudes of his marriages. And although Russell's educational pronouncements are dutifully mocked, his biographer tells us little about the actual methods of the progressive school, Telegraph Hill, which he helped his wife to run in the 1920s, except that his children were unhappy with the impartiality with which their parents felt they had to treat them! But if I had to choose between the occasional dottiness of progressive educational circles of that time and the moralistic sadism of so many of the public and convent schools I have no doubt which side I would have been on.

Although Russell wrote nothing of the complexity of *Principia Mathematica* in his later philosophical writing, this does not make it worthless. On the contrary, according to the general consensus Russell failed in his earlier period to demonstrate either that mathematics could be derived from logic or that either of the two disciplines could be established on a cast-iron foundation. His adolescent desire to put the mathematical proofs of the textbooks on a completely rigorous basis was destined to remain unfulfilled.

Russell's less formal later work may indeed stand the test of time better. Monk mocks his final view that all our knowledge is of percepts which are quite literally 'in our heads'. But this seems to me quite convincing, and controversial mainly because it goes against both postwar English common sense philosophy and the insistence of traditionalists on more elevated explanations.

The later Russell also came to believe that logical and mathematical propositions were useful tautologies which by themselves told us nothing about the world. Indeed I had not realized until I saw his autobiographical reminiscences that in his earlier period he had hoped to find in mathematics some absolute truth, safe from the hurly burly of human existence. He said that his conversion to a more conventionalist standpoint was due to the writings of the early Wittgenstein. I leave to others the task of extracting what Wittgenstein 'really meant'. As in the case of Keynes, this will remain a forever elusive quest. Rather more unfortunate was the lost opportunity of exchanging views with the logician Kurt Gödel, who formulated a theorem saying that in any mathematical or logical system there was at least one proposition that could not be refuted or demonstrated in terms of that system itself. Sadly, a contribution by Gödel to a 1944 symposium on Russell's philosophy arrived too late for Russell to consider in his published response.

The academic world resented the fact that Russell's influence on the public was at its height following the publication in 1945 of his best-seller, *A History of Western Philosophy*, just when his reputation among fellow philosophers was plummeting. But this is all too pious. Russell's *History* is a witty bird's eye view of the main figures in western thought from the pre-Socratics onwards, enlivened by references both to the historical background and to the personalities and quirks of the thinkers themselves. Of course it was not the last word on any of the philosophers covered. But it was a good first word that often scored. I wish somebody would write anything as irreverent, but as informed, on political economy. Monk is right that he was in an obvious hurry to finish the last few chapters; but anyone who has written such a wide-ranging book, which does not contain weaknesses, should cast the first stone.

Monk believes that Russell's books on topics such as the conquest of happiness or 'in praise of idleness' were simply pot-boilers written out of a need for ready cash. Like many other writers, Russell's attitude to his own works varied. He was quite capable of mocking the view that a philosopher has some special expertise in how to cope with the problems of daily life, even while he profited from it. This is most true of the 1920s when he was at his most disillusioned with academic philosophy and had left the university world.

Even so, his interwar essays contained germs of foresight and wit. In *Power*, published in 1938, Russell was able to say that the classic example of power through fanaticism was the rise of Islam. When his followers were reluctant to march against the Byzantine empire, complaining among other things of the intolerable heat of the summer, Mohammed responded 'Hell is much hotter'. Russell also manages a good dig at German philosophical idealism. He states that Fichte was the first of the modern philosophers who veiled their own love of power beneath a garment of metaphysics. Fichte believed that the ego was the sole existing phenomenon in the world. But he also managed to argue that it was the duty of Germans to fight Napoleon. 'Both the Germans, and the French of course, are only emanations of Fichte, but the Germans are a higher emanation, that is to say that they are nearer to the one ultimate reality, which is Fichte's own.'

Russell's sense of humour is always on tap. For example, 'the archetypical American executive impresses others as a man of rapid decision, quick insight into character and an iron will. He must have a firm jaw, tightly closed lips, and a habit of brief and incisive speech.' Today, someone more touchy-feely, spouting management consultant jargon would meet the bill. There are also some bitter-sweet remarks such as 'The more I thought a book of mine was worth, the less I was paid for it.' The contemporary role of spin doctors would not have surprised Russell, who wrote eloquently about power behind the scenes: courtiers, intriguers, spies and wire pullers. The system in which they reign supreme, he observes, is unlikely to promote the general welfare.

Some readers may be shocked about how cynical some of the remarks in his interwar essays seem to be. But it is the kind of cynicism which often marks the frustrated idealist. Russell needs to show that his hopes for a better future take into account the wickedness and hypocrisy of the world and the knocks that he himself suffered in his campaign for peace. Of course those who looked in Russell's pronouncement for genuinely dotty opinions were always able to find a few; for instance, instead of different partisan newspapers he advocated 'a single newspaper in which all parties are represented'. Then we really would see the abuse of power.

In any case, his later general books, especially after the Second World War, give all the appearance of complete sincerity. The one which happened to influence me most was the 1954 *Human Society in Ethics and Politics*. The first part of it had originally been intended for his 1948 volume, *Human Knowledge: Its Scope and Limits*, but was omitted there because of his doubts about how far there was such a thing as ethical knowledge.

The 1954 version is undoubtedly an old man's book. The first section moves uneasily between struggles to work out the epistemological basis of ethics and specific remarks on substantive ethical problems. But for all that it contains more wisdom than many more portentous volumes.

One of my favourite chapters debunks the notion of sin as a muddled concept 'calculated to promote needless cruelty and vindictiveness when it is others who are thought to sin, and a morbid self-abasement when it is ourselves whom we condemn'. Punishment is always an evil; and if it were possible to persuade the public that burglars go to prison, while in fact they were made happy in some remote South Sea island, this would be to the general good. The British philosopher did not claim that there was anything original in this non-doctrinaire utilitarianism, but he put it to good use in exposing morbid beliefs that linger with us to this day. I have always treasured *Human Society* for a particular quotation which I have often inserted into my own works:

If men were activated by self-interest, which they are not – except in the case of a few saints – the whole human race would co-operate. There would be no more wars, no more armies, no more navies, no more atom bombs... I do not deny that there are better things than selfishness, and that some people achieve these things. I maintain however, on the one hand that there are few occasions upon which large bodies of men, such as politics is concerned with, can rise above selfishness, while on the other hand there are a very great many circumstances in which populations will fall below selfishness, if selfishness is interpreted as enlightened self-interest. And among those occasions on which people fall below self-interest, are most of the occasions on which they are convinced they are acting from idealistic motives. Much that passes as idealism is disguised hatred or disguised love of power.

This passage comes from a section dealing with national and political rivalries, where he argues that if human beings really did consult their self-interest they would not blow each other to pieces or inflict horrible injuries for the sake of extending state frontiers or a vain quest for ethnic purity or ideological truth. But can it also be applied to economics? Readers of Adam Smith will understand the apparently paradoxical view that more misery results from people attempting to curb their own or others' earnings in the interests of fairness and equality than from a frank attempt to enrich themselves, at least in societies based on the rule of law. Whether Russell would have accepted the economic inference is difficult to say. He once said that he thought of studying economics, but abandoned the subject as too difficult.

His bedrock view, which transcended the various economic fashions he followed, also occurs in *Power*. 'The really valuable things of human life are individual, not such things that happen in a battlefield, or in a clash of politics or in the regimented march of masses of men towards an externally imposed goal. The organized life of a community is necessary, as a mechanism, not something to be valued on its own account.'

His own economic pronouncements, such as they were, varied. He became a member of the Labour party in the First World War as a result of his disillusionment with the Liberal government which took Britain into the war. He said at the time that he would put up with socialism for the sake of peace. How I sympathize! He later seemed to subscribe to standard left-wing notions that warmongering was inspired by the quest for profits of monopoly capitalists. But by the time of his 1954 volume he came round to the more sober, if boring, view that men and women could be induced to observe the law and the moral conventions of their societies by a mixture of three different motivations: fear of punishment, desire to receive praise and to avoid blame. In any case, the quoted passage is the bridge between my own neo-liberal economic views and a non-Christian neo-pacifism in foreign affairs. The combination is paradoxical only to those who insist on seeing the world in terms of left and right.

Russell's increasing preoccupation with the control of nuclear weapons may be difficult to understand on the part of those who only remember the long stalemate of the last few decades of the Cold War and the period since. Yet the fear of mutual annihilation in horrifying circumstances was a dominating concern between the Hiroshima bomb in 1945 and the detonation of the first H-bomb in 1954. This was vividly captured in *On the Beach*, the 1957 novel by Nevil Shute in which Australia was spared a nuclear holocaust for a brief period, before it too became contaminated with radiation. During this interval a ship was sent to New York searching out an apparent sign of life, only to find that this was due to the swinging of a pendulum against a wall with no living creature in sight. Unfortunately these perils are by no means behind us in a world of nuclear proliferation. The least that British governments could do to contribute to reducing it would be to give up the so-called British nuclear deterrent and the post-imperial illusions that go with it. To say this is quite compatible with relying for the time being on the US nuclear shield as Europe's best defence against aggressors big or small.

Russell's detractors have had macabre fun with what has appeared to them his vacillations between advocating a preventive war and his later preoccupation with nuclear disarmament. It is true that Russell did advocate a preventive war against Russia at least once at a meeting in Westminster School in 1948. He had earlier been very impressed by American readiness to share its control of nuclear materials with the Soviet Union under the postwar Baruch Plan. But the USSR refused and it was clear to Russell that the Russians were determined to get the atomic bomb. He was convinced that there would then be an atomic war between the two great nuclear powers which would be the ultimate horror that would spell the end of civilization. To avoid this, he believed it was urgent for the US to drop the bomb on the Soviet Union and obliterate it as a great power. But once the Soviet Union – and eventually China – had the bomb it was in any case too late; and Russell came to regard mutual nuclear disarmament as the only way of avoiding the ultimate horror.

Russell underestimated the role of the balance of terror in maintaining peace. But this is not something that could have been relied upon indefinitely. There was nothing at all senile in his most famous 1954 radio utterance 'Remember your humanity and forget the rest.' Nor did one have to be a fellow traveller to praise the wisdom of Nikita Khrushchev in pulling his nuclear warheads out of Cuba in 1962 to avoid a confrontation with the USA. Interestingly enough, his climbdown was announced in a letter to Russell himself. Doubtless Khrushchev would have found some alternative face-saving form of retreat had the British philosopher not existed.

Russell was frequently chided with overestimating the role of reason in human affairs. He replied by a much-needed reiteration of David Hume's famous statement: 'Reason is, and ought only to be, the slave of the passions.' Russell added: 'Reason signifies the choice of the right means to an end that you wish to achieve.' What is gained by rejecting that in favour of the wrong means? His lifelong disappointment was that he could not find any logical justification for his hatred of cruelty. He could not reconcile himself to the view that a dislike for torture was similar to a dislike for strawberry ice-cream. But here he really tried too hard. There is no way in which ethical judgements can either be empirically established by scientific methods or logically deduced. They are not that type of thing.There is a difference between disliking cruelty and disliking strawberry ice-cream. But it is not that one judgement is more objective than the other. It is that a person who dislikes one kind of ice-cream will not need to care whether others share his tastes and aversions; but someone who abhors cruelty would want these judgements acted upon by as many people as possible. Richard Hare's theory of moral judgements as universal prescriptive utterances does show that there is a limited sense in which one can argue logically about ethics; but only, in my view, if some non-demonstrable value judgements are taken as given.

On a personal level Russell always believed that the best way to counter the fear of old age and death was to merge one's concerns more and more with that of the human species in general. This is a course of wisdom which few are able to follow. Many of us respond with the quip 'What has prosperity done for me?' Most people achieve a halfway house by identifying their interests with their families and close friends – and more dubiously with those of the nations and other collective groups to which they belong.

Russell was rightly very concerned with the contrast between the conscientious feelings that people sometimes have towards members of their own herd, and their often very hostile attitudes to individuals or groups outside that herd. He concluded that the best long-term hope for the human race lay in the development of a truly scientific psychology which would enable us to understand and master these pathologies. This still rings true; but unfortunately he wrote before either the present developments of evolutionary psychology or its more physical counterpart in molecular genetics. He therefore had to rely on a smattering of Freud together with Pavlovian behaviourism. Maybe we can move on to a fuller understanding if religious fundamentalists or environmental fanatics can be stopped from preventing all further progress?

PART EIGHT

Some Thoughts on Economics

In the study of this subject we must be content if we attain as high a degree of certainty as the matter of it permits. The same accuracy or finish is not to be looked for in all discussions any more than in all the productions of the studios and the workshops.

Aristotle, *Ethics*

A Subject Not in Equilibrium

Review of *The Ordinary Business of Life: The History of Economics from the Ancient World to the 21st century* by Roger E. Backhouse, Princeton University Press, 2002. Published in the UK as *The Penguin History of Economics,* Penguin Books, 2002. *Journal of Economic Literature,* March 2003

There is no need to justify a study of the history of economic ideas. It is a branch of history and will always be necessary so long as human beings are interested in their own past. But there are peculiarities about the subject which create special problems. An author who regards economics as a well-developed science, albeit with an ongoing research agenda, will approach it in a different way from someone who regards it as still inherently contestable.

The first kind of author might be tempted to treat it much like the history of physics or biochemistry. Viewed in this light the history of economics is a specialist field in the history of science, and perhaps also a personal hobby or retirement job for economists.

An author who regards the subject as still far removed from most of the natural sciences in the solidity of its doctrines will adopt a different approach. He might for instance look at the ways in which certain ideas keep cropping up and then dropping out. He will also be inclined to draw links with general history and the political and ideological climate of the time and place when a particular economist was writing. And he will legitimately pay special attention to the theories which have influenced policy.

Roger Backhouse's book is a blend of the above approaches. Its arrangement suggests a history of science method, especially for the modern period. But some of the author's own remarks, especially towards the end, indicate that he has his doubts. The merit of the book is its comprehensiveness. The demerit is that it is sometimes difficult to see the wood for the trees.

The Ordinary Business of Life will be most useful to those who have already a smattering of economic ideas but want to fill in the historical gaps. It might also be an eye-opener to specialist economists who are well trained in the modern mainstream or in their own speciality, but who suspect, like Shakespeare's Coriolanus, that there is a world elsewhere.

There is an underlying story. This tells how economics began as a branch of statecraft and commercial regulation which did not have a name of its own – the Greek word *oikonomicos*, which first appeared as the title of a book by Xenophon, merely meant 'estate management'. With the post-medieval commercial expansion, political economy developed in the form of writings specifically devoted to the subject, although the authors were often philosophers, statesmen or merchants who also engaged in many other activities. From around the late eighteenth century political economy became a fully fledged subject of its own, although still accessible to the interested citizen prepared to take some trouble. High-minded British prime ministers such as Robert Peel and William Gladstone almost certainly knew the works of Smith and some of his successors. More self-consciously worldly prime ministers such as Melbourne or Disraeli did not.

By the late nineteenth century, political economy had become economics with a growing army of professors and faculties, yet it was still penetrable to those who had done an undergraduate course touching on the subject or otherwise made an equivalent effort. But by the last third of the twentieth century it had become a highly technical subject, accessible only to those with an appropriate mathematical background. Backhouse does not deny the technical achievements, but clearly believes that there was loss as well as gain from the self-generated internal development of the subject at the expense of stimulus from real world policy problems.

The flavour of the book can only be given by samples skipping over the centuries. In contrast to the many authors who appear to think that economic thinking began with Adam Smith, Backhouse does begin with two chapters on the Ancient World and the Middle Ages. He dutifully excavates the proto-economic ideas to be found in Plato and Aristotle. But he says all too little about Rome, which was one of the great world empires with a flourishing trade and commerce. No one should expect an economic *Decline and Fall*; yet it would have been interesting to delve a bit further into the ideas which governed commerce and activity within the Roman world, even if they were not the subject of specifically economic treatises.

The author does, refreshingly, say a little about the Old Testament and in particular the institution of the sabbatical year every seven years, during which all debts were to be cancelled, and the Jubilee every fifty years during which all land was to revert to its original owner. Backhouse records that there is no evidence of the Jubilee Year ever being enforced. He does not say whether the sabbatical year fared better. But he does offer a more general assessment: the Old Testament is not about withdrawing from the world. Money corrupts only when it becomes people's sole motive, as in the worship of the Golden Calf. Here surely is the *via media* between Gordon

Gekko's 'Greed is good' and the anti-materialist sermons of so many bishops.

Jumping two millennia, Backhouse gives a fairly full account of David Ricardo, who was a theorist in the modern sense, even though he used arithmetic rather than algebra. One might have liked, however, a clearer underlining of the revolutionary aspect of his law of comparative advantage, which implies that two countries can profitably trade with each other, even if one is much more efficient than the other in every product, provided that the differential varies. This is one of the few well-established economic doctrines which cannot be met with 'I did not need an economist to tell me that.' Yet it would not command the majority in almost any legislature of the world and is equally opposed by the American or European farmer fighting for state protection and the Seattle anti-globalization demonstrator. Some of the arguments on the subject between economists and others are hardy perennials. In 1903, fourteen leading British economists signed a letter to *The Times* in favour of retaining free trade; they were opposed by most contemporary economic historians. For all the refinements of modern trade theory the argument still goes on in the old way.

It would have been good, if before leaving the classical period, Backhouse had analysed in more depth the English New Poor Law of 1834, which was supported by some contemporary political economists and gave all of them a bad name. It is difficult to read any nineteenth-century English novelist without realizing how the horror of being sent to the poorhouse affected several generations.

The prevailing doctrine of less eligibility said that state support for a person without means should not make him better off than the least well-off person in a job. Welfare programmes which provide a better standard of living than is available to low wage-earners are indeed a disincentive to work. It is today possible to tackle the problem from the other end by topping up the pay of unskilled workers by means such as the US Earned Income Tax Credit or the British Working Families Tax Credit. The early nineteenth-century British economy could not afford to do this. But there was still no need to insist that all welfare should be delivered indoors, still less to separate husbands, wives and children. And surely for those who were too old to work the question of disincentives did not apply. Too many perfectly humane modern market economists praise the work of classical economists and also enjoy in their leisure the writings of Charles Dickens, but without bringing together the two sections of their brains.

Coming to the first half of the twentieth century the author notes the domination of Alfred Marshall's 1890 principles over British economics. Marshall did indeed provide a handy set of tools for analysing specific markets; and his division between short and long period remains useful. But the great disservice of his partial equilibrium analysis was the lack of a scheme for explaining the interrelations of different markets and thus of the whole economy. Neo-classical economists had to turn to the much more abstract general equilibrium analysis of Leon Walras and his modern successors, which have been highly praised for their rigour, but which give us little feeling for how real world economies function.

It is almost comic to see how imperfect competition has recently been presented to the world as a revelation. Imperfect and monopolistic competition were in fact extremely familiar to mid-twentieth-century students who had read the works of Edward Chamberlin or Joan Robinson; and there was a good deal of interwar discussion of their policy implications. But they re-emerged as sudden discoveries in the late twentieth century when radical critics found to their delight that mainstream general equilibrium theorists had assumed perfect competition, more for reasons of mathematical convenience than for any insight that this was how the world works. As a result they played into the hands of many interventionist economists, especially in Oxford and Cambridge, England, who encouraged their pupils to believe that the slightest departure from perfect competition or the existence of externalities enabled them to advocate any political measure that caught their fancy.

It was this dialogue of the deaf which renewed interest in the teachings of Austrian economists such as Friedrich Hayek, which viewed competition as a discovery process and market prices as a way of utilizing diffused information, and which did not have to work perfectly or be in equilibrium to be superior to centrally directed systems. The crucial point is that the Austrian school, like Adam Smith before, envisaged competition as an ongoing process rather than as an end-state. More mainstream approaches to information theory and even to the public choice analysis of politics are still predominantly cast as a search for equilibrium conditions. Backhouse gives the Austrians their due. But a surprising omission is the contributions of European sociologists such as Weber and Durkheim, who had much to say about the conduct of economic life even though they did not put their insights into equilibrium equations.

The author is at his happiest in twentieth-century America. Here he emphasizes the continued role of the US institutionalists from Veblen to Galbraith, who provided an ongoing dialogue with the neo-classical mainstream until the conquest of the universities by the mathematical general equilibrium approach in the last third of the twentieth century. Yet he does not mention the rise of a new, much more sophisticated institutionalist school led by the Nobel Prize-winner Douglass North, who have emphasized the importance of institutions and legal rules if markets are to do their job. If North and his followers had received more attention, there would have been less disastrous advice given to the post-Soviet economies by international bodies, and more distinction made between countries such as Poland and the Czech Republic, which had a tradition of property rights and the rule of law, and countries such as Russia, which did not.

Earlier in the twentieth century US economists scored by their much greater emphasis on business cycles and money, in contrast to their relative neglect in Europe. None of this intellectual ferment prevented the disaster of the Great Depression. But at least it provided Milton Friedman and others with the instruments for investigating *ex post* the role of the Federal Reserve in what happened and suggesting some guidelines for avoiding future disaster.

Coming back to his own British side of the Atlantic, Backhouse joins the fashionable denigration of the *General Theory*, which has even affected admirers of Keynes's other works. Of course Keynes did not initiate the concept of public works in a depression; and in some practical ways Roosevelt was a Keynesian before the master. But there remains one truly revolutionary idea in the *General Theory*. In standard neo-classical economics an increase in savings brings about a reduction in the rate of interest and an associated increase in investment. Keynes suggested that it might instead lead to a reduction in output and employment. One certainly should not expect in a general history yet another detailed exposition of the still unresolved 'Keynes versus the classics' debate that dominated macroeconomic writing for about thirty years after 1936. An impartial assessment today would be a boring 'it all depends'. But at least it is worth underlining the contribution that Keynes made to the debate.

The author emphasizes the mathematization of economics in recent decades. The use of complex mathematics is indeed *de rigueur* nowadays in any economic analysis which wants to be taken seriously. A low-level explanation is that it is used as a filter to limit the number of discussants, rather like the footnotes and references which are almost equally *de rigueur*. Every economics editor hears from all too many people who believe they have fathomed for themselves the working of the economic system (or for that matter the key to world history) on their kitchen tables. Debate on all these homemade insights could take more time than there are man hours in the world – my own shameful technique is to suggest that such authors send their ideas to prime ministers or presidents who have large staffs to write polite stonewalling replies.

Mathematics is of course just a language or set of techniques, to be employed when useful, and should not be a central issue. Backhouse's valid criticism is of the way in which mathematics has been introduced, which has loosened the links, strong in earlier centuries, between economic research and the economic problems facing society. Much research has been driven by an agenda internal to the discipline even where this has not helped solve any real world problems.

Economics is what economists do and there is no point in saying it should be something else. The Nobel Prize is the one great accolade which the academic mainstream can still confer. But one only has to look at the correspondence columns of the *Financial Times*, or the books that leaders such as Bill Clinton are occasionally photographed reading as they board aircraft, to see that contributors from other areas such as business schools, modern history, departments of politics and government – not to speak of media-appointed experts from no discipline at all – are serious rivals for public attention. Not all of what they say can be dismissed as nonsense; but unfortunately many of these outsiders have lost sight of – if they ever knew – some of the long-established concepts common to most economic schools, such as comparative advantage and the circular flow of income. Backhouse ends his narrative by reminding us that academic promotion and salary depend on regular publication, and reputations are made by claiming much, not by being modest – in other words by product differentiation. Karl Popper once said that in the physical sciences too much money was chasing too few ideas. This could also be true of fundamental economic research.

Another issue left hanging is whether economics is best viewed as applied logic. Is the domination of rational choice models right and proper? Or should it be the study of how economies actually behave? Backhouse cites some of the ample experimental evidence that in small-scale experiments, even when sizeable sums of money are at stake, human beings are not rational. The orthodox reply is that businesses that do not approximate in their behaviour to profit maximization will dwindle and disappear to the benefit of those that do. On some readings the fundamental theorem of economics might be stated – in contrast for instance to Freud – that people are rational despite appearances to the contrary in big decisions. It would have helped if the author had tackled Friedman's early and still controversial methodological paper, arguing that the realism of economic assumptions does not matter so long as they provide testable hypotheses.

Economics can be regarded either as a set of tools for analysing problems; or it can be regarded as an explanation of how economic systems work, their virtues, defects and possibilities of reform. Keynes in his time embraced both views. In his general introduction to the interwar Cambridge Economic Handbooks he originally wrote: 'The theory of economics does not furnish a body of settled conclusions immediately applicable to policy. It is a method rather than a doctrine, an apparatus of the mind, a technique for thinking, which helps its possessor to draw correct conclusions.' In the late 1930s he wrote a new concluding paragraph, where he spoke about 'an outbreak of controversy and doubt' – largely stirred up by his own *General Theory* – which had temporarily destroyed all hope of certainty and lucidity. The controversies to which he referred were about how the economy worked and what its main tendencies were, and not just about the tools of analysis.

One way of studying the history of economic thought would be to list the questions which have troubled human beings for centuries and examine how they have been tackled by different writers at different times. Why there is unemployment. What to do about famines. How to finance wars. Must technological progress put people out of work? Why have some nations grown much richer than others? A study along these lines would not need to take a dogmatic stance on the scientific standing of the subject, or the progress made, but could still make interesting observations. Backhouse's book is not quite that; but at least it provides much of the material for anyone brave enough to tackle the big issues.

Some Useful Economic Ideas

Speech to the British Association for the Advancement of Science, 11 September 2000

One cannot help noticing that economics is not seen even by the educated public as a particularly exciting growth area. You only have to go into any half-serious bookshop to see the boom in books on popular science, some of them meretricious, but some of them at a very high level. Nothing of this kind exists in economics where you only see textbooks, business guides and the occasional polemic against capitalism and all its works. The public could even be right. Despite numerous technical advances and the enlistment of computer technology, it may well be that there has been no great development in fundamental economic ideas comparable to that in evolutionary biology or the mushrooming of rival cosmological ideas about the age of the universe or the nature of time. But not everything can be exciting. The common law or the principles of hydrostatics matter even though they are not at the cutting edge of intellectual development.

A lot of time is spent in discussing whether economics is, can be or should be a science. It is also wasted in arguing about the role of mathematics, which is simply a useful language, but not an end in itself. A worthwhile field of investigation might be not the philosophy of economics or its logic, but the economics of economics. In other words, to treat economists as they treat other economic agents, as people trying to gain as much as they can from operating in the market place. The rewards of this market, as in other markets, will be some mixture of cash, prestige and congenial conditions; but you have to start out by asking where the demand is. As I have already made my own attempt at this kind of analysis, I will not repeat it today.[1] Instead I shall list a few of the main economic ideas which might be of value to people with no particular interest in mastering techniques or passing exams in the subject.

It is a matter of temperament whether one attaches more

importance to key principles or to detailed applications or to research at the frontiers. There is also a political subtext. Those who emphasize principles are suspected of having what Professor Solow calls a 'right-wing libertarian' agenda and are afraid that research results are all too likely to be used as an excuse for government intervention. There is something in this. But politics is not everything. As someone who has to present economic ideas to a partly non-specialist public, I have had to make a deliberate choice between publicizing and backing ephemeral pieces of research – liable to be overthrown by the next document from another university with a different ideological prior – and sticking to basic ideas which change more slowly and which readers are less likely to have to unlearn.

To give an analogy. Some popular science writers like to go to town on numerous contradictory stories: for instance saying that Professor X 'has shown' that certain kinds of fat diet can, suprisingly, help you to lose weight, only to be followed by another story, soon after, that Professor Y has overthrown the idea. Still, this is much more exciting than emphasizing basic physiological or nutritional principles. But it is likely to leave the reader confused, and either totally sceptical of experts of all kinds or believing only those experts who agree with his preconceptions.

At any rate, here, for what it is worth, is my list of basic ideas. They have very different logical status.

1. (At the risk of boring you.) Demand curves slope downwards. If the price of a product becomes higher less of it is bought. If it becomes lower more of it is bought.

    At first sight this is so trivial as to elicit the response: 'It did not take an economist to tell me that.' The proposition only becomes interesting because of the numerous cases in which it is denied. The controversial example is of course wages. Any number of public figures have a vested interest in denying that if you pay a group of people more, less of their services will be demanded. A very different example is congestion taxes. If people have to pay more to take their cars into town centres at busy periods more people will either stay at home or use public transport. Yet another example are the numerous and erroneous assertions that the demand for a country's products has nothing to do with the exchange rate.

2. If a higher price is offered, more of a product will be supplied, and less if a lower price is offered. This is not quite as general as the law of demand. The narrower, or more specific, the product or service in question the more likely it is to apply. I am as sure as I am of anything that if nurses' pay were doubled, without a corresponding increase in other kinds of pay, more nurses would

be forthcoming and the problems of the Health Service would be much alleviated.

3. A much more interesting principle is that of comparative advantage in international trade. Most people can see that if one country is more efficient at producing steel and another at producing bananas it pays to specialize and exchange. But what not one person in a hundred appreciates is that it still pays to trade even if one country is more efficient at making both bananas and steel, say because it has a highly developed hothouse industry.

    The comparison that matters is the ratio of costs within the same country. If the United States can produce 10 bananas for every ton of steel while Brazil can produce 100 bananas, it pays for the two countries to trade with each other, even if the USA can make both products more cheaply. There is no need for Brazil to protect itself against superior US efficiency by restricting imports of either bananas or steel. The conclusion that countries of very different levels of development and efficiency – in the modern jargon, countries that are a long way from convergence – can still trade profitably is important even if the content of the trade has to be observed by the market and is not easily predicted by academics.

4. The circular flow of income. I am not quite sure what the logical status of this concept is; and the absence of a verb is deliberate. But it is important none the less. Most perverse pieces of neo-protection spring from ignoring it. The point is that there is a continuing flow between purchasers who desire to buy, the incomes received from supplying their needs and still further purchases.

    The ignorance of this flow is probably the most important single source of perverse economic policies today. For instance, it is assumed that if Britain loses arms orders in pursuit of an ethical foreign policy the workers in the arms industries will simply waste away in idleness. It is not asked whether there will not be other purchases at home or abroad to make up the difference. To take another example: many alarmist writers worry about what will happen once China or India is able to produce cheaply vast quantities of products which are now made in the West. But few people go on to ask what the Chinese and Indians will do with their export earnings. Presumably they are selling these cheap goods to make a living and not to line their bank vaults with sterling, dollar or euro notes.

    The circular flow of income can be helped by sensible policies, such as efforts to maintain an adequate but not excessive flow of total spending; and here is where the contribution of Keynes is relevant. The interested citizen needs to know mainly that there is, or can be, such a circular flow and that there need be no fear of one country being undercut in everything by another.

5. If total spending ('aggregate demand') rises sufficiently quickly the result will be inflation. It may seem question-begging to say 'sufficiently quickly'. But we are much more sure of the principle than we are of the exact speed limits. A few orders of magnitude can be given. There are very few economies where spending can rise at above 5 per cent per annum without inflation; and at above 10 per cent, inflation is almost certain.

    A sudden or unexpected drop in total spending – or even in its rate of increase – is likely to produce not merely lower inflation or lower prices, but recession and unemployment. This is normally expressed by saying that wages, and possibly prices, are 'sticky downwards'.

    These two assertions taken together seem to me to embody the element of truth in both monetarism and the Keynesian Revolution, without being dogmatic about highly controversial, more specific relationships. But I have to admit that I have been unsuccessful in persuading economists that this is the case. They prefer, even when talking to the general public, to assert more detailed dogmatic propositions, ones, for instance, about the role of money or about the rate of capacity utilization at which inflation takes off, which can only confuse the interested spectator.

6. Opportunity costs. This is not any kind of even vaguely scientific law. It is simply a useful idea. Most people when they talk about the cost of something mean how much money they have to spend on it. The idea of opportunity costs is to look behind this and ask what we have to give up in order to acquire certain products. In many instances the money cost is as good an approximation as we can hope to get. But there are instances when it is wide of the mark. Take a museum on a weekday morning with very few people in it. The extra resources we have to sacrifice to admit a few more people are infinitesimal. Take the same museum with a popular exhibition on a Sunday afternoon. The cost of every extra visitor is, in the short-term, the inconvenience of queuing and lesser enjoyment for those who are already in it. In the longer term it is seen in a greater expenditure on museum staff, maintenance and perhaps in the end an enlarged building. I leave the implications for the debate on charging for you to think about.

7. This leads one to another useful concept. This is to look at the impact of marginal changes. In other words, instead of looking at the impact of using peak hour electricity on total cost, look at the extra cost involved.

8. When private market institutions are working badly, look at the

structure of property rights. This is not a magic wand. It is very difficult for instance to establish a property right to fresh air; and if it were, there might be a horrendous amount of litigation. The principle is simply a hint to examine something which would not occur to those innocent of economics. One obvious contemporary example is that of fishing rights. The plain man will not see much alternative to arguments about fishing quotas and territorial disputes. But the economically literate will not be surprised that the absence of property rights to the sea bed should lead to over-fishing.

9. Another maxim is to look for price mechanism remedies. Too much argument at the moment is between environmentalists who want an ever-growing list of activities to be prohibited and red-faced businessmen who protest that the country's prosperity is being strangled. Why not, however, ask whether by putting an appropriate tax on activities with undesirable overspills we could not reduce their extent without having to stop them altogether? Or, if there have to be quotas, does it not help to make them tradable so that they will be purchased by those who can make best use of them? As far as I know, Iceland is the only country that has so far established a system of individual transferable share quotas for fishermen in its territorial waters.

These principles of looking at price mechanism remedies and property rights are often the most promising approaches to tackling the market failures which obsess so many economists of interventionist bent.

10. The saying of Adam Smith: the sole purpose of production is consumption. People may make things for a hobby and they may take legitimate pride in the products they make for lawful gain. But in the end you have to ask why they make x rather than y. And you do then reach the needs or desires of the consumer. It has been fashionable to call for more investment. But the only rational ground for more investment is to increase our capacity to produce; and the only rational ground for that is to satisfy the consumer even more.

11. Another Adam Smith assertion: that people will benefit their fellow creatures more if they follow their self-interest than if they consciously strive to serve other people. The basic reason for following Smith arises from a critical inspection of human history, which can never be a hard science but which can lead to such plausible inferences. The test is to compare the success of societies which have allowed a good deal of scope for self-interest or profit-seeking with those which have tried to regulate everything in the supposed public interest.

The self-interest doctrine depends, of course, on many

background conditions, such as the rule of law, an accepted system of property rights and some limits on criminal activity. Again the assumptions cannot all be stated *a priori*. We discover what they are in conditions when they are absent, such as in many post-communist countries today. There is thus government failure as well as market failure.

12. Economics as a subject has an individualist basis. The effects of policies are assessed by looking at their impact on individuals. This has nothing to do with selfishness. One can reasonably take into account feelings of altruism which may exist. The difference is that they are examined in terms of the well-being and interest of those who feel altruistic. Economists adopt these procedures mainly because they cannot think of any others. But I am very happy with them for philosophical reasons which I have explained elsewhere.[2]

13. The following assertion is more speculative and, as far as I know, not to be found in any textbook. It has often been noticed that some people, especially leaders in business or fashion, want to amass far more wealth than they can possibly use, even on the most self-indulgent and sybaritic basis. The ultimate explanations here probably reach back into evolutionary psychology and the competition of the male animal to fertilize as many females as possible. We benefit from this seemingly irrational fetish. If Henry Ford had stopped developing the motor industry when his own personal wants had been satisfied, the cheap mass-produced car would have been long delayed. If the Medici rulers of Florence had stopped acquiring wealth when their personal needs were satisfied, we would not have had most of the art and architecture of the Renaissance. The desire to pile up endless treasures beyond rhyme or reason would not be a healthy basis for the great mass of human activity. But we all benefit from the fact that some people are made that way.

14. Income differentials. Why do people in comfortable and congenial occupations sometimes earn more than those doing difficult and dangerous work? Economic ideas can give at least a handle on this problem. The question is: why do not people move from the less attractively rewarded to the more attractive jobs until the differentials are evened out? The obvious answer is that many people cannot make such a move. But why? They may not be eligible for the more comfortable jobs, for instance, through lack of qualifications. Here the fashionable emphasis on education and training may help; but not all differences between people can be eradicated.

15. More important from a policy point of view are the barriers that the more favoured groups erect against entry. Apart from obvious

cartel restrictions, such groups may insist on unnecessarily high or irrelevant entry qualifications. Or they may try to use the governments to limit entry by hook or by crook. Highly respectable professionals such as lawyers and doctors are well versed in such techniques. The hottest such issue now concerns immigration where entrenched domestic lobbies will go to any lengths to stop immigration that threatens their positions. Another reason for differentials in net rewards, not only to labour but also to capital, is mistaken expectations. Such disappointments are inevitable in any market economy and all that policy can do is to provide a safety net for the losers.

Finally, a major area of ignorance. We do know that market economies are subject to cycles of boom and bust. We are a long way from being able to explain why, although the list of hypotheses is a mile long. Governmental authorities might still be able to moderate them even without understanding completely their causes. At present the fashionable approach is to hope that if inflation targets are successfully pursued and the regulation, national and international, of banking and other financial activities is improved, we will moderate these cycles. But the jury is still out on this approach and I would not attempt to sell it to the public as any kind of established principle.

Some of you will have noticed that I have said nothing about Pareto optimality, chaos theory, Nash equilibrium, the NAIRU, the so-called fundamental theorem of welfare economics, multiple equilibria, and a good many other concepts – not even maximization. This is not because they are unimportant or uninteresting; nor because interested observers should be debarred from following the debate. It is simply that they are much more items of professional discussion and investigation than ones which politicians, permanent secretaries and business leaders would be better off if they understood.

The main reason for favouring a formal approach is not the rather pious reasons put forward by the academic industry but a rather practical one. It may well be true that insight, intuition and common sense are more important than either mathematical reasoning or formal forecasts. But one cannot rely on there being a sage like Keynes or Friedman on the spot. Most policy decisions most of the time will have to be taken by highly fallible human beings operating, as they have been brought up, in a conventional mode. The main virtue of formal training is to limit the scope for disastrous error by people of this kind. A similar justification may apply to policy frameworks such as inflation targets, or medium-term budgetary rules. It is all too easy to pick holes in them from a perfectionist standpoint; but the economic rule-book needs to be judged by the prevention-of-disaster criterion rather than by how well it conforms to some idealized notion of what theoretical physicists are supposed to offer. We cannot rely on having sages.

Notes

1. Refers to Chapter 21 of *The Economic Consequences of Democracy*, Gower, 1977, 1988.
2. 'In Defence of Individualism', p, 209 et seq. above.

What They Did Not Teach You in the Economics Course

An undelivered lecture, December 2000

There was a famous book entitled *What They Did Not Teach you at Harvard Business School*. I was inclined to call my talk *What They Did Not Teach You in the Economics Course*. But I cannot claim to know exactly what is taught in your course. And of course I realize that you are not taught all the same things, as you go to different courses with different tutors and read different textbooks.

It is, however, amazing how few books there are on how economic systems actually work. On the one hand, there are strictly academic books which concentrate on quantitative techniques and mathematical relationships on which students can be examined, but which do not answer very directly the questions that practitioners of history or government have about the economy. On the other, there are numerous voices from other disciplines, or no discipline at all, which make strident assertions such as 'the rich are getting richer and the poor getting poorer', picked up from a few media headlines.

I find it striking that so many of the people who come to talk to me about recent economic events or government policy come from the faculties of politics and modern history. At the end of the day it does not really matter from which faculty studies come, so long as their work is enlightening. But in my experience professors of politics, international relations or sociology do not – with a few distinguished exceptions – deal well with economic issues, irrespective of their political views.

The content of textbooks is often called in highbrow circles 'The neo-classical–Keynesian synthesis'. But I have been warned by academic friends that many students regard this as simply 'economics' and I would have to explain that it is only one variety of the subject. My own view is that this synthesis is fine as far as it goes and needs to be taught, even if different authors put a different emphasis on the neo-classical and the Keynesian parts of the synthesis. But most varieties leave out important matters.

More years ago than I like to think of, I made a list of what were then new developments in economics, which were hardly known to many British practitioners (*Participation Without Politics*, Institute of Economic Affairs, first edition 1975, last published 1979). Some textbooks now mention them, but they still receive far too little emphasis.

1. The application of the theory of competition to the political market and to the struggle for votes and power. This is now known as public choice and some mainstream textbooks pay it a little bit of lip service but hardly more. As I then wrote, 'Much British thinking on economic policy is rendered worse than useless by a sharp contrast between the faults of real world markets and the actions of some non-existing and improbable, ideal, benevolent and omniscient government.'

2. The analysis of property rights and the effects of alternative allocations on the use of resources. We all have our own views on whether the distribution of property rights can be improved. But it is not property rights, but their absence, which is anti-social. It is because no one owns pleasant vistas, or the ocean bed, that market disciplines do not apply and that governments have to go in for clumsy attempts at direct regulation such as the EU Common Fisheries policy.

3. The economics of benevolence and charity. This is a worthwhile branch of mainstream economics in its own right, made specially topical by Gordon Brown's big extension of tax relief and other incentives to private benevolence. An incidental benefit of this subject is that it brings home to people, in a way that no abstract argument can, the difference between privately chosen and selfish aims.

4. The most interesting trend in my opinion has been the development of political and moral philosophy with the conscious aim of throwing light on questions such as the just distribution of property rights, the legitimacy of coercion by a democratically elected government, the appropriate extent of state power and much else. Those of you interested in political and moral philosophy will still probably find these matters discussed under the heading of 'Rawls and Nozick', although there are many other contributors. You cannot make a thoughtful contribution to economic policy without at least a nodding acquaintance with this kind of discussion.

5. The analysis of markets as a discovery procedure in a world where tastes and techniques are changing and relevant information scarce and expensive. You cannot overcome this criticism just by adding a few differential equations to the neo-classical system so

that the analysis can be called 'dynamic' and the mathematics made more complicated.

The point of this criticism is somewhat different. It is about the need to study the operation of markets as a system for tackling, however imperfectly, the interactions between human beings. Again this has been made much more concrete with the fall of the Iron Curtain and the disappointing experience that many former communist countries have had in rebuilding their economies. This applies especially, but not only, to Russia itself. The point that many western advisers missed was that it was not enough to remove controls on prices and wages, to privatize a few state industries or even to balance the budget and introduce currency convertibility. None of these things will work properly without a whole lot of other institutional changes, such as an effective legal system, the rule of law and a state which can police it, clear and secure property rights and a social safety net. Not to speak of the introduction of standard western accounting and banking techniques, which are less and less known the further you move from the German/Polish frontier towards Moscow and the former Soviet Far East.

So far as these 'new' types of thinking are known at all, it is as imports from the United States. But in fact at least one of these approaches (markets as a discovery procedure) was originally made by Austrian economists and imported via the USA. It is about time to remind people that Adolf Hitler was not Austria's only contribution to the modern world.

The two main alternatives or supplements to the neo-classical mainstream might be called the 'Austrian approach' and the anti-globalization left. The Austrian school is ultra free market, while the anti-globalization left is very sceptical about the liberalization of capital markets or even free trade negotiations and would be quite sympathetic to those who demonstrated in Seattle and Prague. They nevertheless have a surprising amount in common. They both emphasize market capitalism as a process and distrust the idea that it is a solution to a set of equations. Both emphasize political and legal institutions and the exercise of power. The left-wing critics have at last got beyond the Marxism dismissal of institutions as mere superstructures and now regard them as an influence in their own right.

In my remaining few minutes I would like to switch tack completely. When talking to business or political audiences, a favourite technique of mine is to expose what I regard as economic humbug. That is to demolish beliefs which are popularly regarded as common sense economics, which are really self-serving beliefs by business spokesmen or out-of-date sermonizing by politicians. Indeed, I sometimes call the fallacies I try to demolish 'business economics'. There have been two notable recent attempts to do this. One was by David Henderson, formerly head of economics at the OECD, entitled *Innocence and Design* (Basil Blackwell, 1986), based on his 1985 Reith lectures. The other is *Economic Fallacies* by Geoffrey Wood (Institute of Economic Affairs, 1999).

One problem about such attempts is that many of them are not strictly logical fallacies but can seem to be true on the basis of certain occasionally plausible assumptions. For that reason I prefer to call them Lumpeneconomics after the German word used by Karl Marx to describe the *Lumpenproletariat*, that is, ill-educated workers who did not understand their own interests and took to casual rioting, ultra-nationalist demonstrations or criminal acts instead of attending discussion classes on the dictatorship of the proletariat.

Favourite examples include structure snobbery – in other words, the belief that certain sectors of the economy, such as manufacturing, are inherently superior and that other sectors, such as hamburger stands or Chinese laundries, are inherently inferior. Another example is the cult of competitiveness in ministerial speeches and exhortation. But competitiveness is a comparative term. Not every country can be more competitive against every other. Against whom should the world be more competitive? The moon? or Mars? Yet a further slogan is convergence, especially in relation to European Monetary Union. Many of the great and good want convergence not merely in matters relating to inflation but in terms of real performance in output, employment and productivity. The worst example of this is the British espousal of the level playing field. This may be a natural cliché for spokesmen with a public school background, but is in danger of ruling out all the conditions under which international, or even inter-regional trade can take place.

In my experience, no amount of economic training can prevent people from uttering these fallacies if it pays them to do so. One problem about driving them out is that there is no fallacy or piece of special pleading which some distinguished economist has not advanced at some time. There is a more important reason. Suppose, for instance, you are an economist at the Department of Trade and Industry. Ministers from all the main political parties insist that the UK must be 'more competitive' (at the very same time as the Bank of England has to follow an interest rate policy which makes us less competitive in one of the few meaningful senses). Such an economist may nevertheless think that the UK, like any other country, can improve its economic performance and tries to massage the word competitiveness into meaning better performance. This undoubtedly leads to less bad policy than if they followed the immediate instincts of the politicians. The harm arises if they gradually begin to believe their own phraseology or if it misleads the readers of their own White Papers.

I shall nevertheless assume that I do not need to labour why these ideas are fallacies to an audience such as this and instead concentrate on one of the most deep-seated fallacies of all – and one where even this audience may need some persuasion.

I refer to the whole concept of national export drives: the Export Credits Guarantee Department (ECGD), the exhibitions to promote British goods in embassies abroad, royal visits to dubious regimes, receptions for unpleasant dictators at Buckingham Palace, the Queen's Award for Exports. The lot. The reason for my emphasis is my recent interest in the contradiction between the British government's claim that it is pursuing a foreign policy with an ethical dimension and the very strong official involvement, especially on the part of the DTI, in promoting arms sales. A very popular view is that such arms sales may be undesirable, but that they help promote jobs, growth and employment. I have come to the conclusion that we will never really stop dubious arms sales until the myth of the export drive is nailed once and for all.

Inside the Crystal Ball

Financial Times, 3 January 2003

New Year is the time for crystal-gazing and for spoilsports to have fun in exposing the abject failure of past prophecies. I should like to do something more modest, which is to examine, in all its nakedness, the basis of the short- to medium-term forecasts of the whole economy that – whether we like it or not – lie at the heart of economic policymaking. Such forecasts are neither mumbo-jumbo nor science but have a simple core that is disguised by all the mathematics.

There are three essential elements. The first is an estimate of the trend rate of sustainable output growth. The second is an estimate of the 'output gap', indicating how far from trend the economy is. Third, there is the estimate of how fast we are moving towards or away from the trend path.

There are, correspondingly, three ways in which forecasts can go wrong – quite apart from the effects of international catastrophes such as oil price explosions. They can overestimate or underestimate the extent and speed to which the economy is moving towards or away from trend. They can make a false estimate of the trend rate itself. Or they can make a mistake about the sustainable level of economic activity, looked at in terms of physical capacity or the unemployment rate and related labour market indicators.

Most vulgar attention is devoted to the immediate movement away from or towards trend. This can be affected not only by underlying forces but also by all kinds of temporary forces, such as changes in indirect tax or in the prices of imported commodities. The Bank of England rightly believes that it would be both difficult and harmful to try to offset such temporary shocks and that, if the economy can be steered towards trend growth, these short-term factors will come out in the wash. The further ahead you look, the more the fundamentals dominate the picture. That is why it uses a two-year horizon. Short-term mistakes in predicting the immediate prospect for demand are in my view the least important source of error. If the central bank gets this wrong, it can remedy matters next time round by easing or tightening policy. It probably would not greatly matter if it mainly looked at what is happening now, which is no easy matter to discover.

The second, and more serious, source of error is to underestimate – or, more usually, overestimate – the trend rate of growth. The latter is determined by the growth of productivity plus the change in the working population. In the UK, productivity growth has been astonishingly stable for many decades despite all government efforts to improve it. The big source of error has been in estimating changes in the active labour force, whether caused by immigration or changes in participation rates. Another source has been wishful thinking by governments that believe that they have fundamentally improved productivity. Owing to the wonders of compound interest arithmetic, modest errors of a fraction of a per cent per annum in estimating the trend growth rate can add billions to government deficits, even on a cyclically adjusted basis.

The third, most important and least discussed source of error is in estimating the sustainable level of economic activity. Without such a view it is impossible to estimate the output gap. Over-optimism here can lead to accelerating inflation, and excess pessimism to errors of a deflationary kind, although because of labour market rigidities there is not the neat symmetry that some economic theorists like to posit.

Lord Burns, who was a distinguished academic forecaster before he became a Chief Economic Adviser to the government, has remarked that the forecasts have not become any better over the thirty or more years he has been watching them, despite improved techniques and much larger personnel. The world is an uncertain place and no amount of effort or cleverness on the part of the forecasters will prevent significant mistakes. Business people who criticize inaccurate forecasts are oblivious of the fact that they are paid – pretty generously – to deal with uncertainty; and while good policy can reduce unnecessary uncertainty there remains an irreducible amount – which, incidentally, is also found in hard sciences such as physics.

Many official economists would be delighted if they could dispense with conventional forecasting. But unfortunately attempts to use short-cut methods such as money supply targets have come to grief. Monetarism was never intended for short-term steering. The basic contention was merely that sticking to a modest and stable growth of the money supply would achieve low average rates of inflation over a period and help to reduce booms and slumps in real output. Unfortunately there has never been enough confidence in the behaviour of any particular measure of the money supply for it to be used in this long-term way.

My own view is that the core model of trend and output gaps is too useful an aid to thinking to be dispensed with altogether. But the detailed forecasting process needs to be relegated to a minor role. The chief enemy of reform, however, is the insistence of so many people on a crystal ball for viewing the future. They might as well use tea-leaves or consult a pet astrologer.

Economics Should Not Be Seen as Religion

Financial Times, 15 August 2002

Is economics a form of religion? Alas, it depends on what you mean by religion. According to the 1990 edition of *The Dictionary of Christianity in America*: 'If belief in a god is necessary to define a religion, secular humanism does not qualify. If on the other hand religion, or god, is defined as one's ultimate value, then secular humanism is a religion.'

The US Supreme Court has tended to follow the second definition. Mainstream economics is undoubtedly a form of secular humanism. I should prefer to call it an ideology. But it is foolish to argue over definitions and the best recent study of the subject by Professor Robert H. Nelson is entitled *Economics as Religion: From Samuelson to Chicago and Beyond* (Pennsylvania State University Press, 2002).

I was myself brought to see that economic teaching involves an overarching stance, more than it does hard scientific results, when some years ago I conducted a questionnaire study based on multiple choice questions given to students. Nearly all the correct answers involved a policy stance and very few a simple prediction akin to that in elementary physics. Nelson came to this realization when he worked as an economist for the US Department of the Interior and he found much of his time taken up by a 'theological' battle between economists and environmentalists. The economists were certainly prepared to give some weight to environmental effects, but nevertheless espoused economic growth. The ultra-environmentalists, such as Bruce Babbit, Secretary of the Interior under Clinton, saw the world as an ecosystem in which every single species had to be preserved, as an instance of God's creation.

When I mentioned this subject to some of my colleagues, they had no doubt that economics was a form of theology. By this they had in mind the heresy-hunting, fierce insistence on doctrinal purity and anathematizing of dissenters so characteristic of religious argument.

Nelson, however, takes theology seriously and does not use it as a term of abuse. His main point is that the overriding beliefs that have guided economic thinking in the second half of the twentieth century are losing their potency. But a new foundation has still to be found.

He starts off with a paradox. Economists of varying stripes assume that individuals will pursue their self-interest in the market and that this can be made to work to the general good. But there is a problem. 'The pursuit of self-interest should not extend to the various forms of opportunism, such as cheating, lying and other types of deception, misrepresentation and corruption within the market place.' Nor should it extend to political opportunism, that is, attempts to use government to extract benefits from others, to protect a particular firm or groups of workers. Moreover property rights, contracts and other legal arrangements need to be fairly and consistently enforced. We hardly need reminding of these caveats after recent corporate scandals, let alone the disappointing attempts to introduce a market economy into the former Soviet Union. But how can we produce a faith which will accept self-interest, yet observe all the surrounding conditions and qualifications?

Nelson takes the surprisingly fruitful approach of looking at the doctrines of the leading American textbook that appeared after the Second World War, namely Paul Samuelson's, *Economic Analysis*. Nelson has no difficulty in showing that Samuelson's text was founded in the American progressive tradition. He believed that the market, subject to suitable correctives, could be used as an instrument for social progress. Unfortunately, it was difficult to persuade non-economists, even of the same political persuasion, to see it that way; and there was some resistance among some economists themselves, more in Europe than in the US.

Samuelson, especially in his early editions, was not free from political bias. He was eloquent on the evils of private enterprise monopoly, but low key on the effect of unions and minimum wages. For such reasons my own Cambridge tutor was not keen on the book. But, like so many other students, I was attracted to it because – unlike texts with titles such as *The Theory of Price* – it gave prominence to the policy problems which made the headlines. It was like starting physics with atomic theory rather than with Newton's laws of motion.

Even though the majority of students probably regarded the book as a pleasant, if long-winded, way of preparing for examinations, nevertheless the message seeped through. It had probably a greater effect on mindsets among American than European readers. Although few business or professional people harangued their friends with the doctrines of Samuelson, they probably had a more lasting influence on the sort of people who become Federal Reserve or IMF economists, or who advise presidents.

By the mid-1970s, the Samuelson approach was under challenge from the Chicago School. One problem about assessing Chicago is that it never produced a single text equivalent to Samuelson's. The advocacy of its best-known member, Milton Friedman, of certain monetary policies, gave a misleading impression. The main effort of Chicago academics, on whom Friedman drew in his popular writings, was devoted to analysing sector by sector the effects of government attempts to improve matters. They always managed to convince themselves that such efforts made matters worse. Regulators are all too easily captured by the industries they are supposed to regulate; and in any case in a slow and subtle way the market often develops its own correctives.

They were helped by the dogma that their subject had nothing to say about value judgements: if private negotiations to compensate those who had been injured by some polluting development led to an efficient solution, then economics had nothing to say about the resulting effects on the distribution of income. A further strand to the Chicago analysis arose from the theoretical analysis of the effects of politicians who were guided by their own self-interest, and who were more likely to provide support for particular interest groups than to promote the general welfare.

In the last decade or two, both the progressive and the libertarian versions of market economics have been challenged – not just by traditional socialists or conservatives who dislike change, but by a school of 'new institutionalists', of whom the most prominent member is the Nobel Prize-winner Douglass North. They pay a lot of attention to history and institutions: to questions such as why China has been more successful in moving towards a market economy than Russia, despite greater Russian willingness to remove controls. The new institutionalists remind us that there is no shortage of markets or self-seeking behaviour in areas which have failed to achieve an economic take-off, whether in West Africa or in southern Italy. What they lack in such places is the basis of trust and institutions which would enable them to make long-term contracts and refrain from Mafia-type raiding on each other.

This new institutionalism covers a great variety of approaches and has yet to coalesce into a school. It ranges all the way from inserting some extra variables into mainstream economic equations to calls for a return to the traditional study of political and cultural history. What has yet to be established is how people can come to see the value of self-interest in its limited market role while developing the institutions and constraints that make it a force for good.

Nelson does not claim to have found a new faith which will resolve the paradox of self-interest. His own avowed inspiration comes from Frank Knight, an interwar economist little known in Europe apart from one technical book early in his career, but who was the true founder of the Chicago School and to whom its members still pay lip service. Unlike his postwar successors he was highly sceptical of the effects of economic growth in improving the human condition and also of the use of scientific method in any of the so-called social sciences. His core belief was in human freedom. A student once succeeded in getting his money back because he had devoted a large part of his classes to an anti-Catholic harangue instead of his official subject.

At this point one needs to go slowly. Nelson summarizes the prevailing economic religion of the second half of the twentieth century as the pursuit of economic efficiency. By this he seems to mean two rather different things. First, he means rationality in the sense of choosing the least costly way of achieving any human objective, whether pursuing a jihad or building a mosque or cathedral. The second of his meanings is the pursuit of economic growth, where his strictures may indeed apply. It is vital to hang on to rationality – and I would add, to respect for evidence – if we are not to retreat to the dark ages. But economic growth could well, in the more affluent countries, recede as an objective in the way envisaged by Keynes.

Index